AF262563

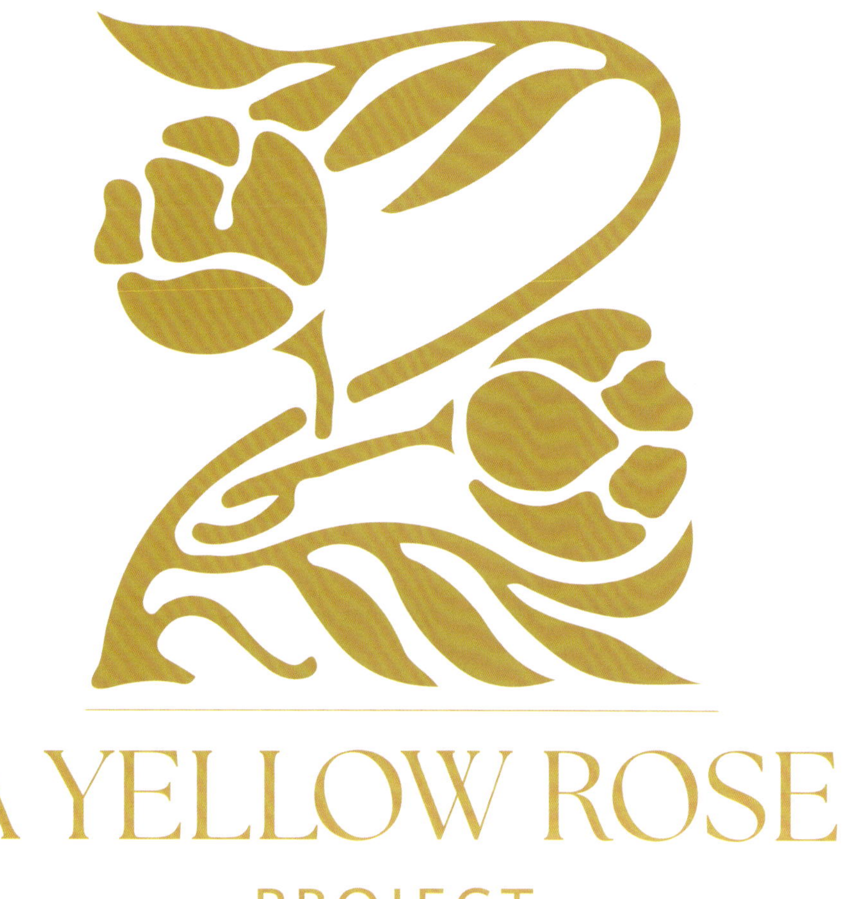

A YELLOW ROSE

PROJECT

PIONEERING WOMEN: LEADERS AND TRAILBLAZERS

TEXAS WOMAN'S UNIVERSITY

AnaLouise Keating, General Editor

With assistance from Kimberly C. Merenda

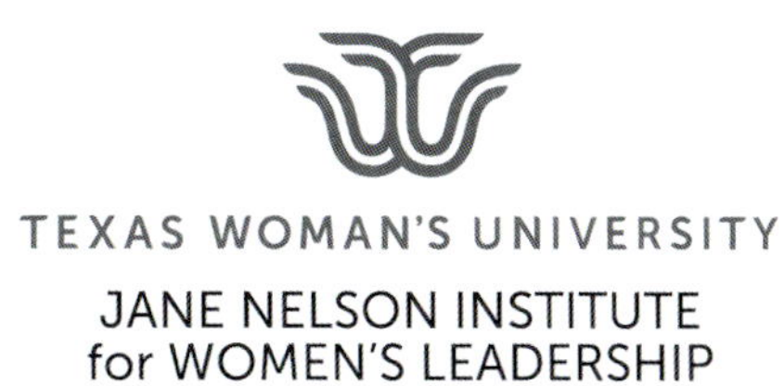

TEXAS WOMAN'S UNIVERSITY

JANE NELSON INSTITUTE
for WOMEN'S LEADERSHIP

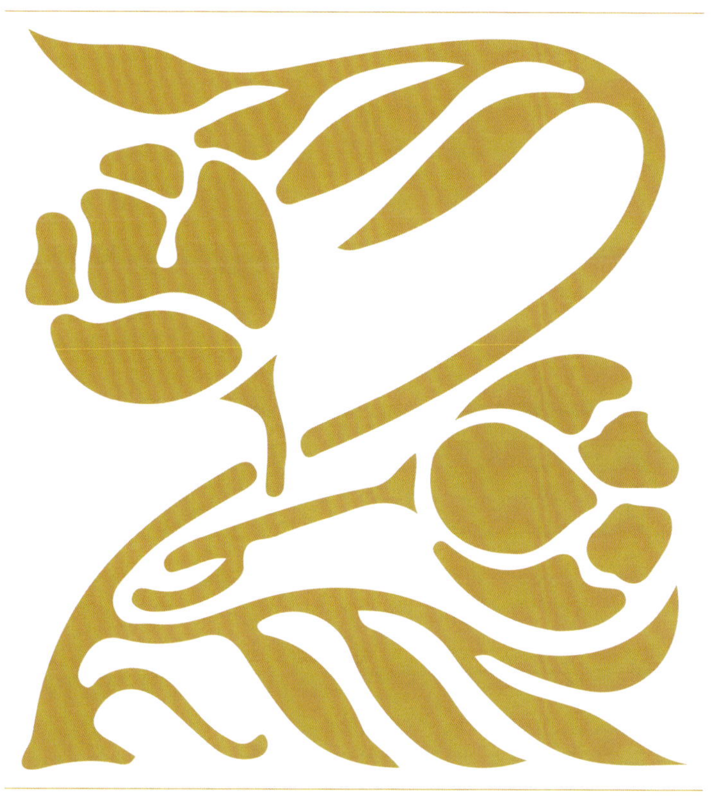

A YELLOW ROSE

PROJECT

RESPONSES, REFLECTIONS, AND **REACTIONS** TO THE NINETEENTH AMENDMENT

Meg Griffiths *and* Frances Jakubek

TEXAS A&M UNIVERSITY PRESS | COLLEGE STATION

♾ This paper meets the requirements of ANSI/NISO Z39.48-1992
(Permanence of Paper).
Binding materials have been chosen for durability.
Manufactured in China through Martin Book Management

Library of Congress Cataloging-in-Publication Data

Names: Griffiths, Meg (Photographer), editor. | Jakubek, Frances, 1988–
editor.
Title: A yellow rose project / Meg Griffiths, Frances Jakubek.
Other titles: Pioneering women, leaders and trailblazers.
Description: First edition. | College Station : Texas A&M University Press,
[2025] | Series: Pioneering women: leaders and trailblazers | Includes
bibliographical references.
Identifiers: LCCN 2024047556 (print) | LCCN 2024047557 (ebook) | ISBN
9781648433139 (cloth) | ISBN 9781648433146 (ebook)
Subjects: LCSH: United States. Constitution. 19th Amendment—Centennial
celebrations, etc. | Women—Suffrage—United States—Pictorial works. |
Women—Political activity—United States—Pictorial works. | Women's
rights in art. | Suffrage in art. | Photography—Political
aspects—United States. | Women—Suffrage—United States—History.
Classification: LCC TR681.W6 Y46 2025 (print) | LCC TR681.W6 (ebook) |
DDC 324.6/230222—dc23/eng/20250210
LC record available at https://lccn.loc.gov/2024047556
LC ebook record available at https://lccn.loc.gov/2024047557

Unless otherwise stated, all photos appear courtesy of the artist.

Front cover: Toni Pepe, *Mrs. Nixon*
Back cover: Lisa McCarty, *Votes for Women 1920–2020*

FOR ALL THE MOTHERS OF MOVEMENTS
AND FOR
Paula Riff

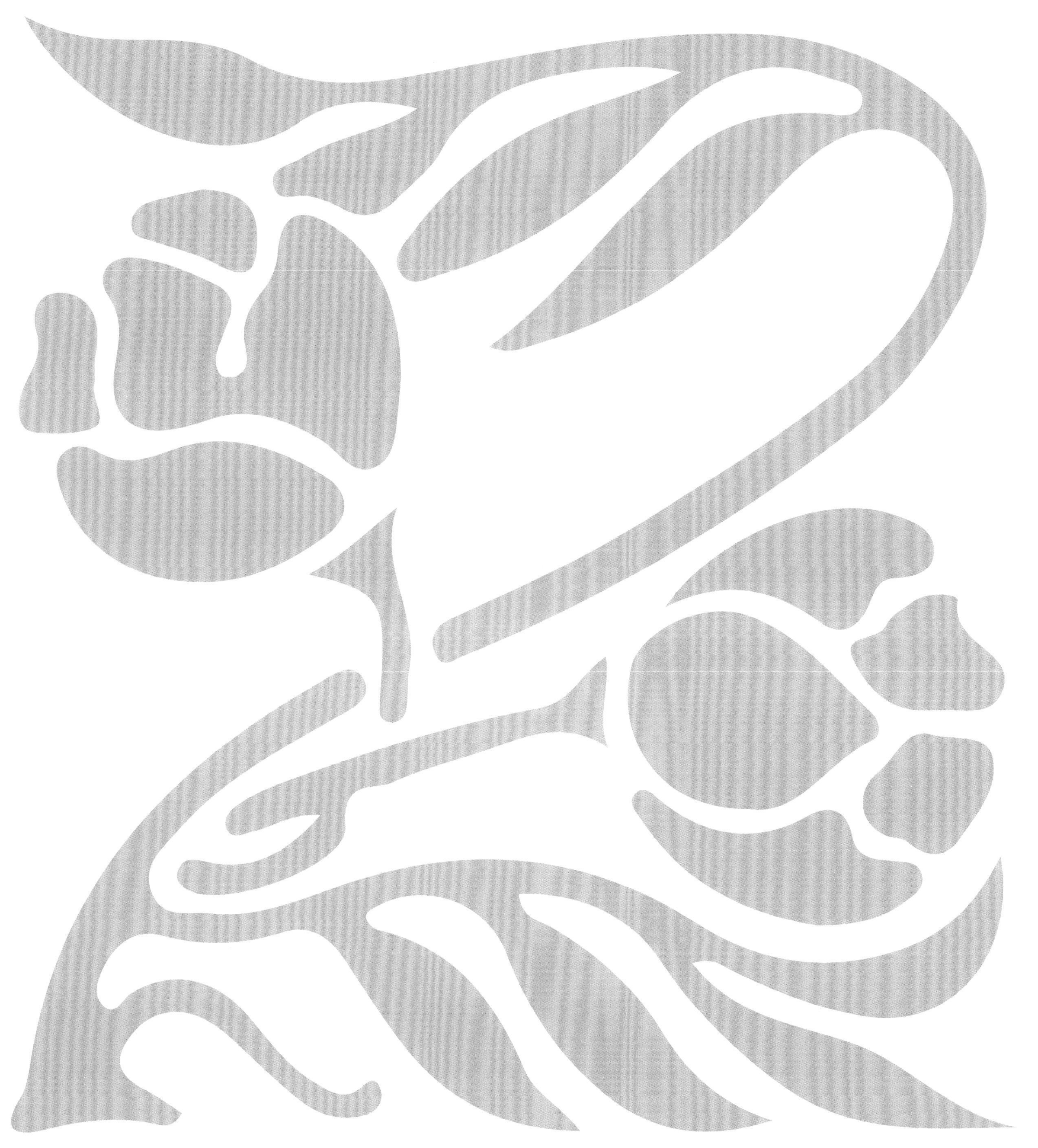

CONTENTS

PREFACE
Imprint of History

A photograph is an expression in material form. It is a conduit. It is a vehicle of time, in time, and for all time. The photograph, the most ubiquitous of art forms, is familiar. People in the United States make pictures, read them, share them, and now, like them. They are in our pockets and purses, forever sitting on our computer screens, adorning our walls in frames, in markets, on billboards, in newspapers, and books. They are everywhere. Daily 5.3 billion photos are taken and fourteen billion are shared through social media (Matic Broz, 2024). We use images to reach out, meet people where they are, to communicate and share topics both tough and banal. It is the one given medium that feels natural, accessible, and universal and of the moment. But photography is also the medium that connects us most immediately to key points in history. The iconic 1864 *carte de visite* portrait of Sojourner Truth, "I sell the shadow to support the substance." Inez Milholland atop a horse on her 1913 cross country campaign by Harris and Ewings. Dorothea Lange's 1936 *Migrant Mother* cradling her children. Marc

Riboud's young woman protesting the Vietnam War with a flower. Photographs imprint history, channeling light through a box of air. It is the photograph that we use to reflect, respond, and react to culture in time, over time, perhaps all time. Such images stay with us. We believe these will, too.

WHERE DO WE BEGIN?

In gratitude, with grace. Those are the two words that come to mind when I think back over the experience that has unfolded and continues to unfold through *A Yellow Rose Project*, from inception to the printing of the book you hold.

Frances and I met in person for the first time in New York in April 2019. We were seated in a red-bricked atrium of an intimate little restaurant named Bea huddled up at a small table in the corner of the room. On the opposite wall, there was an old 1940s, black-and-white film projected up high on a screen, just past a delicate little tree lined with twinkle lights. There was some sort of lull in the conversation, and I remember mustering up my mind to ask Frances something along the lines of, "I was thinking about doing some sort of large-scale collaboration with women . . . would you be interested in doing that with me?" I was thrilled Frances said yes, and we are both in awe of all the women who have made this project possible.

What started as a simple idea grew into a dear friendship and an inspiring collaboration with women from across the United States. It gave us a deep connection to something larger than ourselves. It led us to a new kinship, a shared understanding of what it means to be a woman at this moment in time—refracted through distinct perspectives and backgrounds. It became a celebration, acknowledgment, reckoning, and protest. And it would draw us to confront our own positions, as two white women with certain privileges and power. We came to carry a real sense of responsibility to all those that have entrusted us with their images and words and we feel the profound responsibility of caring for this project. All of this was made possible by our shared love for photography.

Trust is no small feat. I have said this many times. Frances and I are humbled so many women have put their faith in us. And for a long time, I asked myself: Why? Who are we? Why did so many women volunteer to help? I've settled into the fact that, as artists, we are collectively in the service of others—enmeshed in making, conversing, and sharing an art form we both truly love, the photograph. We are two incredibly distinct individuals, women at varying stages of our own professional careers and lives. Frances is an image maker, independent curator, a consultant for artists, and someone who has had over sixteen years of gallery and museum experience. I am a mother, artist, and have been working in higher education for over thirteen years with the last eight at Texas Woman's University, the largest state-supported public university predominantly for women. Our collective experiences span community, non-profit spaces, and educational institutions from private, to large public R1 universities, and to smaller state institutions. We see ourselves as stewards of this medium and supporters of women in our field.

Back in 2019, we sent out over 200 emails to women across the country asking them to participate in a large-scale photographic collaboration. They were invited to make work in response, reflection, or reaction to the ratification of the Nineteenth Amendment. The goal of the project was to provide a focal point and platform for image makers to share contemporary viewpoints as we approached the centennial. Our mission was to gain a deeper understanding of United States history and culture from this point in time to build a bridge from the past to the present and on to the future.

I now see how the energy for this project was born out of the 2016 US election. Seeing women of all ages and racial and ethnic backgrounds take to the streets, donning pink hats and holding protest signs arm in arm, was one of the most moving things I will see in my lifetime. I had just given birth to my son, Oliver. I'd brought a precious, perfect human into the world at a time where a man could get elected to office who had perpetrated unthinkable crimes against women. Elected to the highest station of service in our country, that human should have been a role model for all our children, however they would choose to identify. It was unconscionable. Yet, despite this overwhelming knowledge people marched—women stood up and marched as they have been doing for over one hundred years now. We found a well of inspiration in the power of women to shape public perception, and the perseverance to continue this arduous fight to obtain equal rights far beyond ratification. Frances and I set out to gather women with distinct visions and voices to nurture this conversation through the image.

There really was so much we did not know when we set out to do this project. We have learned a great deal. We originally thought the project would be a celebration. But we realized that the ongoing fight for women's rights was just that, ongoing, fragile, and hard-fought. The struggle has not ended. Despite the passage of the suffrage act on August 18, 1920. It took many more years for *all* women in the United States, regardless of race, to be given the same privilege. Due to state laws and prohibitive policies, many women are still unable to fully exercise their rights. To help explore that truth, we asked women to look upon our history from various perspectives, inviting both a critical eye and one that sees how far we have come.

It was during this period of learning that I came across a beautiful essay written by Martha S. Jones called "The Politics of Black Womanhood, 1848–2008." Jones shares a quote from Sojourner Truth, "women's fates were linked, but not because they were the same" (2019). This statement rings as true today as it did then. Women walk distinct paths to womanhood, and they are not the same, but they intersect and affect one another. It is in the movement toward one another, toward supporting and lifting us all, that we move toward real equality.

We wanted varied visions of women of all ages and at all stages of their careers to be a part of this project. To have a rich and thoughtful response to this anniversary, we wanted to invite a diverse group of women whose perspectives would not be the same. Keep in mind, just because we made a request for women to participate does not mean everyone could or would want to. There are any number of reasons for this. We were essentially commissioning women to make work for this project, and the only thing we could offer in return was our time, labor, and energy to work for them. This was something we offered in exchange for creative content. At the time, it was just a hope and a promise to try and make good on what we set out to create together.

Frances and I also understand the full weight of the centennial. We acknowledge and know that the history we were both taught growing up was not the full story. Many women have been written out and their contributions in the fight for civil and women's rights have only recently been uncovered. We, too, understand why choosing to make work about this complicated history and the current issues at stake was not something everyone would want to partake in. Asking women to step away from other important art making practices and give us something on a timeline about this topic, well that is a woman's choice. It is a woman's right to choose how they want to spend their time, labor and energy; what they want to do with their bodies—their lives. Right now in our country, we have a lot of important work to do and projects to make. Frances and I respect that more than anything.

As much as we could, we wanted women to feel some grace—to give women space and show support. When we began this journey, we could not have foretold that less than a year later human lives would be turned upside down in various and inequitable ways due to the global pandemic in 2020. This would greatly affect women and minorities disproportionately. Amidst health concerns and protocols, rising death tolls, work, food shortages, caregiving, political disorganization, and extreme fatigue, we would be asking women to make photographic work for us. There was also nothing that could have prepared our country for the protests that were ignited—the momentum and support the Black Lives Matter movement would garner, and the subsequent reckoning that the United States would face as a result of the death of George Floyd. Frances and I knew that having a 2020 deadline for our project was just one more thing on top of all the many things affecting everyone to varying degrees.

Frances and I carefully considered the one hundred and five images included here, representing each woman in the project. This book presents a contemporary collection of expressions prompted by this remarkable and historical event from this current moment in time. The images speak to the movement leading up to ratification, the legacy we have inherited because of it, and the work we will continue to do because of it. Some images draw upon personal histories and share a glimpse into the present lived experience. This can be seen through intimate portraits of others or the self, domestic spaces, protest scenes, and documentation of the here and now. Other visuals use archival images, news clippings, and writing to speak about erasure, time, and memory. Themes surrounding the body and gesture come into play in various ways, alluding to issues of power, sexuality, choice, vulnerability, and endurance. We see generations of women represented and connected, whether that be within the images or by those who authored them. The resulting body of work imbues the power, responsibility, and unique complication of being a woman in the United States from a kaleidoscope of viewpoints. This art project aims to show the undeniable strength and resiliency we possess as a whole when we are united for a higher purpose.

Since the launch of the project in 2020 and now onto production, it has been a continual surprise how relevant and timely this call and work remains. With each passing year, new laws and policies are being generated and struck down that further unravel the complicated tapestry that weaves our experience together in this country. In a short time, we have been stripped of the right to choose and family plan with the overturning of *Roe v. Wade*. A parent's right to care for and protect their own children, threatened and criminalized through LGBTQIA+ discriminatory laws. An educator's ability to teach the truth about our imperfect history using works of literature censored. How could we have known a few years later the pendulum of progress and hope would swing so far in the opposite direction? In many ways this project has become a means to educate, inspire, and empower people of all ages. To remind us that rights once hard-fought are not to be taken for granted. It is through this process of showing up and standing up, in that long tradition of women before us, that we must participate, have the tough conversations, and make the choice to voice our truths, whether through the photograph or through the ballot box.

Brene Brown said "Language shows us that naming an experience doesn't give the experience more power, it gives us the power of understanding and meaning" (2021). If a picture is worth a thousand words, what do our over one hundred voices say here? It is our hope that it gives you, dear reader, the power of understanding and with it a road map to find your own meanings and make your own history.

Meg Griffiths

ACKNOWLEDGMENTS

There are no words to encompass the gratitude we feel to all our artists. We thank you from our hearts for your time, labor, creativity, and dedication to *A Yellow Rose Project*. You are the soul of this piece of history we have made together. Thank you for trusting us to be the stewards of this portion of your life's work.

We are immensely thankful to the estate of Elizabeth T. Dew. A special heart-filled thank you to Therese Griffiths, the biggest champion of our dream and this project from the beginning.

For their brilliant historical and contemporary insights, we are indebted to Shannon Perich, Lisa Volpe, Rachel Michelle Gunter, PhD, and Christina Bejarano. The unique context you provide to situate these works of art in time were integral pieces of writing to provide a fuller understanding of this project.

We are incredibly grateful to Mary Kathryn Paynter for crafting an iconic logo that embodies history, celebrates the contemporary, and transcends trends. Gabrielle Sanchez, your research and dedication established *A Yellow Rose Project*'s digital presence and produced an archive and a resource— we are forever thankful.

The encouragement of friends and colleagues, including Jeanna Muñoz, Roula Seikaly, Natalie Zelt, Odette England, Aline Smithson, Mary Virginia Swanson, J. Sybylla Smith, and Robin Deary, helped to shape and communicate our vision. Thank you to Eliot Dudik for connecting us at that cozy dinner in 2019. A special thank you to Susan kae Grant, who empowers women to always think larger than the self. Thank you to Joan Brookbank for your time and meticulous attention to detail in service of the mission of this project.

Patricia Bernstein and Marie Piazza, thank you for sharing our voices and visions. Your tireless press and public relations work was invaluable in attaining opportunities for these photographs to engage in accessible ways across the United States. Gail Finley, thank you for connecting us to Patricia and Marie. You are a powerhouse, and we appreciate all the brainstorming sessions and check-in phone calls.

Our heartfelt appreciation goes to Samantha Johnston, Desanka Beslic, the Colorado Photographic Arts Center, Reed Art and Imaging, Lissa Cramer, Boston University, Toni Pepe, Pitch Black Editions, and Atelier 4 for their generosity and care in producing and transporting the exhibition. Thank you to Lisa McCarty, whose handmade pins accompany each exhibition and brought this project into the physical realm.

Thank you to Dr. Gullion for sharing *A Yellow Rose Project* with Dr. Sahlin, and their combined encouragement to submit a book proposal for the TWU Book Series. Dr. Kimberly Marenda and Dr. Ana Louise Keating, thank you for all the behind-the-scenes assistance.

We express our gratitude to Texas Woman's University, the Pioneering Women: Leaders and Trailblazers TWU book series committee, Texas A&M University Press advisory committee, blind reviewers, and Texas A&M University Press for transforming this project into a lasting resource for future generations. Special thanks to Thomas Grant Lemmons for his patience, guidance, and enthusiasm and to Marguerite Avery, Abagail M. Chartier, Amanda Werts, and Christine Brown for the support

in bringing the book to fruition. Thank you to Nancy and Ted Paup for championing the arts and for supporting the creation of this historic book. We are grateful beyond measure.

To our outside editors, Dr. Susan Harper and Devin Griffiths, thank you for your wordsmithing!

Our deepest appreciation goes to the individuals and institutions that envisioned and hosted exhibitions and programs of this project, including Marcus DeSieno, Lily Brooks, Kalee Appleton, Kathya Landeros, Rafael Soldi, Kyra Schmidt, Clover Archer, Greta Pratt, Stirling Goulart, Megan Jacobs, Elizabeth M. Claffey, Arthur Fields, Rana Young, Rebecca Drolen, Colby Parsons, Blake Weld, Deanna W. Titzler, Cynthia Pollard, Matthew Flores, Monique Bird, Thalassa Raasch, Rachel Cox, Riel Sturchio, Christa Bowden, Priya Kambli, Aaron Fine, Natália Marques da Silva, PhD, David Johnson, James Arendt, Logan Woodle and Easton Selby. Thank you for welcoming *A Yellow Rose Project* into your academic spaces and for creating a platform to engage with its message.

None of this would be possible without the support of our families, partners, and friends, who were there for us every step of the way. The biggest gift one can receive is the gift of time and care. Thank you for listening and your unwavering encouragement through this entire process.

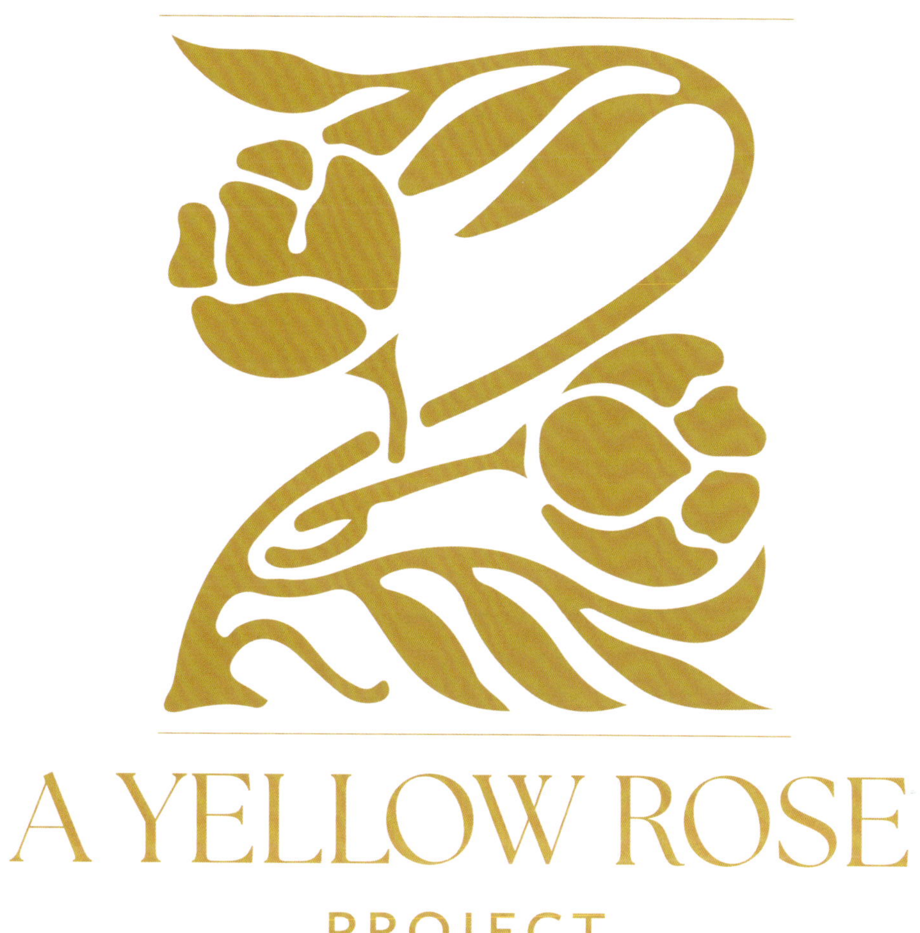

A YELLOW ROSE

PROJECT

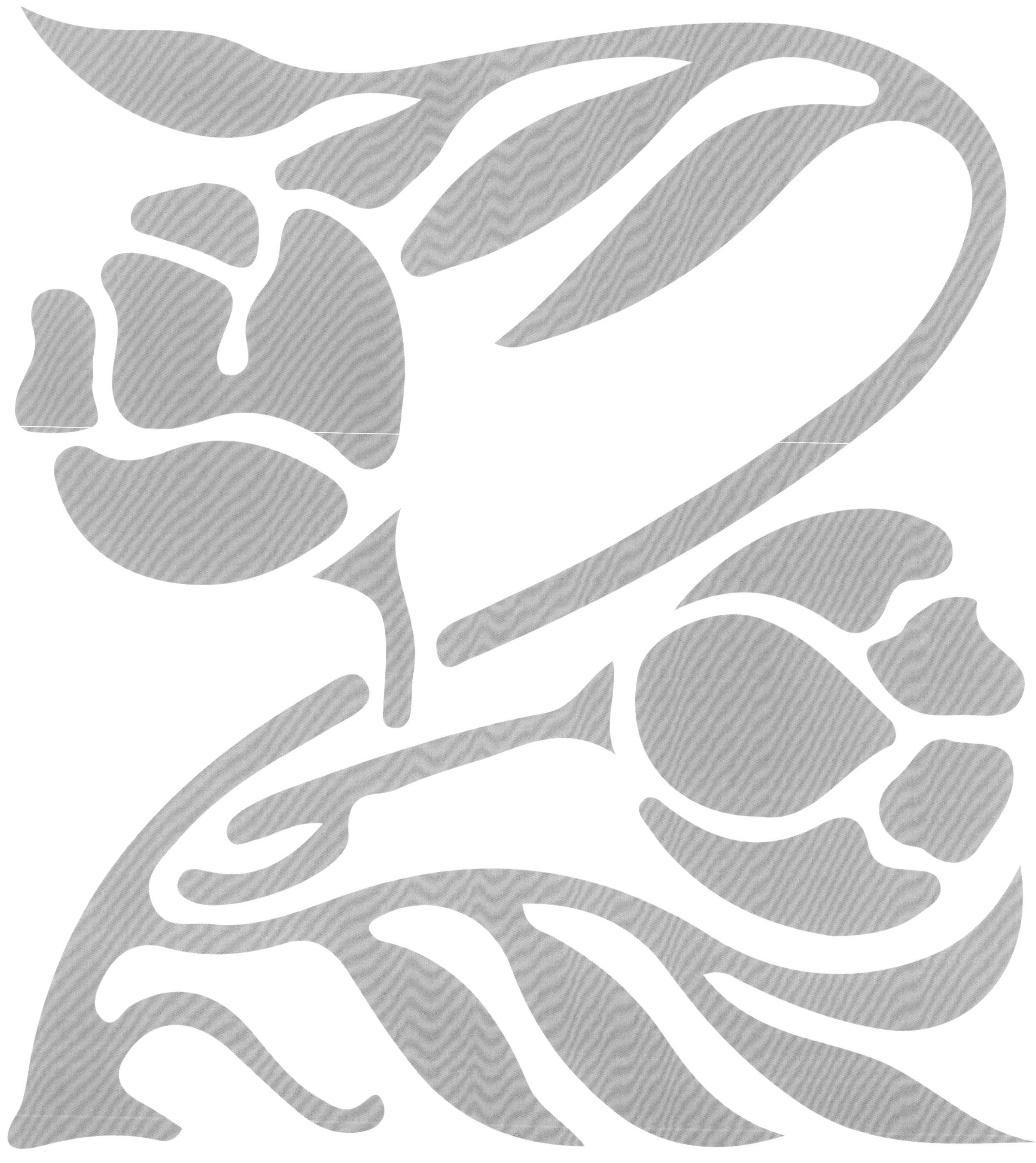

Introduction

How Far Have We Come in One Hundred Years?

LISA VOLPE

It was a hot August in Nashville, Tennessee, in 1920, and social tensions had reached a boiling point too. Hailing from all around the country, men and women descended on the Tennessee statehouse to lobby for or against the ratification of the Nineteenth Amendment. The one-block area between the Hermitage Hotel and the state Capitol had become the epicenter of the national, decades-long struggle for women's suffrage. Months before, in June 1919, Congress declared it unconstitutional for states to discriminate based on sex to deny voting rights, but thirty-six states needed to vote in favor of the amendment for it to become law. With thirty-five states voting in approval, Tennessee was next to decide. A special session of Tennessee's House of Representatives was called to decide the fate not only of the amendment but also of the rights of women across the country. When legislators from across the state arrived in Nashville for the critical vote, they were greeted by two competing lobbies. Those against women's suffrage could be identified by the red roses they wore, while those promoting the movement wore yellow roses. On August 18, 1920, a crowd decorated in red and yellow filled the one-block plaza and spilled out of the packed galleries of the Capitol. As the vote was being called, no one knew what the outcome might be. Sitting in her hotel room a block away at the Hermitage, suffrage leader Carrie Chapman Catt heard the shouts of joy outside her window and saw yellow roses waving. The amendment had passed.

In 2020, temperatures in Portland, Oregon, in August, were high and social tensions were burning. The May 25, 2020, killing of George Floyd by Minneapolis police sparked ongoing, nationwide protests against police brutality, led to calls to "Defund the Police," and renewed the proclamation that "Black Lives Matter." In Portland, protestors facing off with local and federal law enforcement were met with excessive force night after night. Over several weeks, clashes grew more violent as tear gas, rubber bullets, and the forced removals of protestors in unmarked vans became commonplace. Portland became the focal point and symbol of the ongoing struggle for racial equality. Then on July 18, Bev Barnum and her Wall of Moms appeared. Thirty women linked arms and created a barrier between law enforcement and protestors in an effort to "protect others from being injured." By the night of the nineteenth, the wall was composed of 150 women, and the number swelled to 500 by the end of the week. Every night in August 2020, the Wall of Moms appeared in Portland dressed in their signature color: yellow.

How far have we come in one hundred years? From women waiting outside the Tennessee statehouse wearing yellow roses to women wearing yellow T-shirts linking arms on Portland's streets, the need for social change and social activism remains. While the suffrage movement of 1920 granted voting rights for some women, it notably did not remove barriers for women of color from the democratic process. In 2020, the Wall of Moms protecting Black Lives Matter protestors used their bodies to shield those racialized people who had previously been excluded. One hundred years after the ratification of the Nineteenth Amendment, the struggle for justice, humanity, and the American promise of true equality continues. And women continue to lead the way.

Linked by the color yellow—utilized throughout history to signify a common cause—comparison between the suffrage movement and our current time reveals the messiness, frustrating sluggishness, personal cost, and complexity of change. Change does not occur with the ratification of a law or with the formation of an activist group. It is a longer, difficult process that requires work from us all. "Freedom is not a state, but an act," noted Congressman John Lewis, an act that requires not only political process but also art and poetry (Lewis, 2012). This book uses the weapons of art, wielded by women, to reflect on, fight for, and promote freedoms.

A Yellow Rose Project takes the centennial of the ratification of the Nineteenth Amendment as a moment of reflection. Aligning the historic with the present—the yellow rose with the yellow shirts—these included works of art expose the complexities of our collective past and our social present. How far have we come? Each photographer whose work appears in this project have utilized their talents to create photographs that examine the history of the Nineteenth Amendment, along with their own personal history and current place. The wide variety of viewpoints speaks to the long and varied path for change. Combined, these artworks survey the long movement, celebrate the victories, and point toward future, imperative struggles. Symbolically, each stand as a yellow rose.

Lisa Volpe is the curator of photography at The Museum of Fine Arts in Houston. She wrote this August, 2020.

Women's Suffrage to Now
(1920–2020)

CHRISTINA BEJARANO

Landmark anniversaries encourage us to stop and take stock of what has been accomplished or yet needs to be overcome in the time that has passed. One landmark anniversary that the United States recently celebrated was in August 2020, with the one hundredth anniversary of the formal adoption of the Nineteenth Amendment into the US Constitution. The Nineteenth Amendment stated that the "right of citizens of the United States to vote shall not be denied or abridged by the United States or by any state on account of sex," which we all assume provided a sweeping granting of the right to vote for all women in the United States (US Const. amend. XIX). However, the centennial anniversary was an opportune time for us to reassess what had truly been accomplished with the passage of the Nineteenth Amendment and how much has yet to be accomplished. The centennial anniversary of the Nineteenth Amendment was commemorated by many, including scholars, activists, politicians, and journalists. The commemorations highlighted the unsung "sheros" of the women's suffrage movement, as well as the ongoing struggles for equality.

A Yellow Rose Project provides an artistic remembrance of the ideals of democracy and equality, which we all strive for in our American democracy. In this piece, we remember the women who were not included in the Nineteenth Amendment's granting the right to vote and reassessing how far we have come in women's fight for political equality.

ONGOING FIGHT FOR VOTING RIGHTS

First, we can acknowledge that we need to tell a fuller story of women's voting rights. Those who identified as women joined forces across various organizations to challenge the opponents of women's participation in politics. The opponents challenged that women may have lacked the qualities necessary for equal citizenship and thus needed to restrict their activity to the home. There was a mass movement of women and their coalition partners who fought for women's political equality around the world. Before the passage of the Nineteenth Amendment, women were excluded from the vote in most of the territories and states in the United States. Wyoming was the first territory (and later state) to provide women with suffrage in 1869 and 1890. Women were fighting for formal representation in US politics provided by the legal right to participate in politics with the vote. Even after the Nineteenth Amendment was ratified, women continued to fight for their political rights, including the right to hold political office. The suffragists also introduced the Equal Rights Amendment in 1923, which would add the constitutional amendment to ensure equal rights for men and women. The battle for the passage of the ERA has continued, and in 2020 it received the pivotal ratification of the required thirty-eight state legislatures. However, we are still waiting on the remaining steps of the ratification process, which requires that Congress reintroduce and officially pass the constitutional amendment.

We can also acknowledge that suffrage was not provided to all women at the same time. Many women from racial and ethnic minority populations in the United States still had to fight for their right to vote, as well as a host of other civil rights that they continue to fight for today. The civil rights movement brought diverse groups together in the fight for civil rights in the United States. The federal government was pressured to pass the Civil Rights Act and the Voting Rights Act, which would begin to provide rights of social and political equality for racial and ethnic minority populations in the United States. Even after the passage of the Nineteenth Amendment (as well as the Fourteenth Amendment, Fifteenth Amendment, and the Indian Citizenship Act of 1924), there were hard-fought struggles to

invalidate additional formal and informal restrictions on the vote for racial/ethnic minorities including literacy tests, property requirements, both informal and formal white primary laws, and poll taxes. With the passage of the 1965 Voting Rights Act (VRA) and the ratification of the Twenty-fourth Amendment (which outlawed poll taxes), the federal government started to address and eliminate restrictions to the vote for racial/ethnic minorities. The VRA of 1975 addressed the ability of Black people to vote and introduced the requirement of preclearance from the federal government for any changes to voting over an expanded geographic area of the country. The Voting Rights Act was extended several times, including the pivotal extensions in 1970 and 1975, which broadened the coverage of the act to protect more racial/ethnic minorities in the United States, including language minorities.

However, the 2013 Supreme Court decision of *Shelby County v. Holder* weakened key VRA protections, which has resulted in the current climate of increased voter suppression efforts against racial and ethnic minority communities across the country. The voting restrictions and obstacles include strict voter identification requirements, strict voter registration restrictions, limited early voting, and limited absentee voting. In terms of the strict voter identification laws, in some states women are "still significantly more likely to change their name when they marry or divorce," which can create additional challenges to attaining the required forms of identification (Montoya, 2020). There are additional intersectional considerations to consider, since women who are young, low-income, elderly, disabled, women of color, and/or transgender are disproportionately impacted by most of the voter identification laws. In addition, women with disabilities, those who are transgender, and those who are incarcerated or formerly incarcerated continue to face additional struggles to exercise their voting rights.

WOMEN'S POLITICAL PARTICIPATION

Since the passage of the Nineteenth Amendment, women's political participation in the US has grown and evolved. Soon after the passage of the Nineteenth Amendment, women did not dramatically increase their participation in politics. In fact, only one-third of eligible women voted in the 1920 election and "among those women, party affiliation, class, religion, and ethnicity, rather than sex, influenced their voting decisions" (Dolan et al, 2019). Since the 1980s, women have registered to vote and turned out to vote at higher rates than men in every presidential election in the United States. In addition, since 2004 women from every racial and ethnic group have also voted at higher rates than men.

As a result of this gender gap, there is now more attention paid to the importance of the women's vote by both political parties and the media. There are also gender differences in the support for the political parties and candidates in elections. With the difference between men and women in the choice for the winning candidate, the gender gap in vote choice, has historically had the majority of women preferring the Democratic candidate in every presidential election since 1996.

In the 2020 presidential election, there was record high voter turnout even amid the pandemic and increased voter suppression. In addition, women registered to vote and voted in higher numbers than men in that election. In fact, women cast "nearly ten million more votes than men" with "68.4 percent of eligible adult women casting a ballot" according to the Center for American Women and Politics. Women of color (WOC), those from racial/ethnic minority populations, also had a record high voter turnout in the 2020 presidential election, with Black women participating at the highest rates among women of color. As a result, increasing attention is on the growing impact of the WOC vote, especially with the two largest and fastest growing populations of WOC voters, Black women and Latinas. In addition, the gender gap in vote choice in recent presidential elections can be further broken down to demonstrate that the majority of white women have supported the Republican candidate and the majority of women of color have supported the Democratic candidate. In the 2020 election, this gender gap trend continued with a majority of women supporting the winning Democratic candidate, Joe Biden. However, the majority of white women supported Republican candidate, Donald Trump, and the majority of women of color supported Joe Biden.

Women have made significant progress since the passage of the Nineteenth Amendment and now represent an important political force in US elections. We can recognize that even though women received formal representation and the right to vote with the Nineteenth Amendment and subsequent Voting Rights Act, we are still fighting for greater political equality. There is still the argument that women are not well-represented in US politics, both in terms of the number of women elected to political office and the responsiveness of the representatives in office to women. In 1920, there were no women elected to the US Congress, the national legislature, and we have since progressed with more women elected to political office. In fact, the 2020 election had a record number of 126 women elected to the US Congress. However, even with the 2020 election records, women still represent less than thirty percent of the 535 seats of the US Congress. *A Yellow Rose Project* provides an artistic assessment of women's view of their political equality since the passage of the Nineteenth Amendment.

We can consider the ramifications of women, who make up a majority of the US population, not trusting that they have access to political equality.

Christina Bejarano is a professor of political science at Texas Woman's University.

A Yellow Rose Project

A Photography and History Journey

SHANNON PERICH

A Yellow Rose Project is among the most exciting photography collaborations to be seen in a long while. Each work in this book stands on its own as a meaningful artistic and political assertion in relation to a reflection on the one hundredth anniversary of the Nineteenth Amendment. Taken together, this collection becomes a heady swirl of histories, ideas, politics, and photography while valuing each woman's style, expression, and medium.

The Nineteenth Amendment guaranteed women the right to vote. As the visual responses and reflections on the anniversary of that seminal Constitutional change demonstrate, the impact was, and continues to be, an uneven experience among women. To make that clear but not overtly didactic, the selection of works by project directors Meg Griffiths and Frances Jakubek from the larger pool of choices is extremely thoughtful. The works could have been organized by a series of themes, instead they are laid out in a visual rhythm taking the reader on an aesthetic journey that prevents emotional and intellectual exhaustion. This smart design affords time and space for each photograph to be seen and noted on its own with only a few images on the pages before and after to provide for comparison or context. One does not succumb to the weight of the theme—reflecting on the Nineteenth Amendment— and makes it to the end of the viewing journey with a heart that is lifted by the equal respect given to each contribution, a brain that is tickled with ideas, and a soul that is nudged to action and self-examination.

The inherent nature of a book is to suppress the materiality of the photographic works—what we see are photographs of photographs presented in some regular way. In doing so, primacy is given to the image content. In the accompanying exhibition, for those lucky enough to see it, visitors would see the dimensionality of threads and fabrics, differently sized papers (or metal, in one case), a range of paper substrates to support a variety of photographic processes, and maybe Heidi Kirkpatrick's wooden blocks with photographs of lips, *Let Our Voices Be Heard* (Fig. 54). The visitor would move in or back away from each work to get a better look, creating a physical relationship with individually framed objects. The materiality and physical study of works offer a set of cues to better understand each photographic work. Those physical traits are visible to some degree on the pages here, but we must work a little harder and remind ourselves we are looking at reproductions of actual objects designed to fit the dimensions of the book we are holding. Your relationship with each object is more or less even. I invite you to carefully contemplate the various processes of image making and materials as you assess the works in tandem with titles and dates.

As a photography project, the medium itself must be discussed at the outset. *A Yellow Rose Project* brings forward the varied ways we understand the meaning of *photography.* The broadest understanding is the use of a light-based mechanism to record a realistic image, either in color or black and white—snapshots, studio portraits, news, documentary photography, still lifes, and other set-up scenes. We know it's a photograph because actual things (real or contrived) existed and were mediated by an apparatus, or a light-sensitive medium (such as cyanotype, tintype, and anthotype), and are presented in an analog or digital format (print or digital photograph) for the viewer to see it.

The maker's relationship to the light-based, image-making product varies widely. For each maker, the weight of the content versus the weight of the process and format varies. For example, on the farthest end of the spectrum Ellen Carey's *Crush & Pull* (Fig. 36), about the Polaroid process and materiality, is the image—inseparable and intertwined—speaking directly to photographic production. Some may suggest that the content is all that matters in the end, but to fully understand a photograph's overt message and the subtle inflections, one must consider where the maker placed emphasis before, during, and after production, dancing among technology, artistic constructions, and expressions.

In a way, Emily Sheffer's *The Ideal Scrap Book, 1905–1906* (Fig. 104) points inward to the scope of content seen in this book and outward as a construction of loosely related yet disparate, mostly flat objects. It is a contemporary print that reinterprets a historic object from the Library of Congress giving us a chance to reevaluate how we understand that particular item across time. As such, *A Yellow Rose Project* invites reflection on what the Nineteenth Amendment might stand for today. For some, it is about achievement of a political ideal, an abstraction, of what it means for women to vote. Along the spectrum of interpretation, some works sit squarely to face the act of voting. Other works exist in parallel, rubbing shoulders with ideas and issues related to women's suffrage. The intermingling of the types and functions of photography employed to generate content to explore an array of themes associated with the Nineteenth Amendment is exciting!

The makers of the works included in this book (not all identify strictly as photographers) demonstrate that photography is multi-functional. Sometimes it is conventional and familiar; other times it mixes and twists processes, genres, and conventions. Everything here is contemporary photography. It is a useful term to help understand that we are looking at works produced, with a couple of exceptions, around 2019–20. *A Yellow Rose Project* invited participants to reflect on a one-hundred-year-old political and legislative event, so we understand the maker's feet are planted on a particular spot on the timeline of history. Already, some of the current events that resonated so deeply just a few years ago are moving into history. How *contemporary* various works may be is relative. This is not a critique by any means, only to say that this project in and of itself is a historical event that marks a particular moment in time. It will hopefully be useful to researchers on the 200th anniversary of the Nineteenth Amendment when they are looking to understand how we used photography to mark and reflect on the past century of American women's suffrage.

Many of the artworks incorporate photographic images, processes, or strategies that point to other ideas resonating within the maker's current notions and aesthetics. Family photography, for example, is seen and employed both subtly and directly. In the west, we are culturally trained to regard these photographs with graciousness, to understand that a particular photograph may mean more to someone else than to us. Yet, we appreciate the sentimental value and function of the family photograph (snapshot or professional) to hold someone dear as we generally have our own, and we can imagine standing in for the one the maker incorporates into their work. Aline Smithson's color photograph of a woman holding a 1920s or 1930s sepia-toned portrait of a middle-aged woman on the ground covered with tulip magnolia leaves from the series, *Women I Don't Know* (Fig. 30), is such an example.

Whether using casual or formal family photographs, it often embeds a sense of nostalgia and can tell a specific person's story while resonating with a wider narrative. Tsar Fedorsky's colored studio portrait sitting in a poorly sized frame on a dusty wooden bureau (Fig. 59), for example, is likely a scene we've experienced somewhere. We don't know these women, but we have relatives somewhere down the line that might have been like them and we know of unnamed women in old frames on dusty surfaces. Carol Erb's *Did She Vote? Lynn Turner Worden* (Fig.

101) begs the question of not *who* or *which party* her maternal grandmother voted for, but whether she actually cast a ballot. This is startling for those of us who want to presume that most women would participate in the election process as soon as given the chance. Christa Bowden is painfully able to respond to the question. Her poignant text embedded in *I'll Never Know* (Fig. 16), about her grandmother and how she voted, points to a personal and sometimes difficult subject about which candidate or party one voted. Voting is not theoretical, academic, or unemotional. So much is at stake personally, locally, and nationally.

Toni Pepe's *Mrs. Nixon* (Fig. 44), re-photography of a 1970s press print of open-mouthed, fist-shaking, placard-carrying women outside of the White House, imparts the passion of their protest. Kristine Thompson's *Suffrage in Washington D.C. 1918–2017* (Fig. 11) is three photographs in one bringing together early protestors with today's activists. The image itself is a photograph of a news reference file card, a 1918 Harris and Ewing photograph in the upper right corner of three women with a protest banner at the White House calling out President Wilson, and an embedded digital photograph in the opposite corner of a hand holding another negative of a tightly packed scene of women wearing pink knitted pussy hats.

Photography, as a tool, can bring the past and present together through re-photography, collage, and digital manipulation closing the gap between then and now. Ileana Doble Hernandez's lone contemporary counter-protestor bearing a round blue sign, "Keep Abortion Legal," standing next to a lone black and white 1920s protestor lifted from a different time and place (Fig. 32). Anne J Berry's *1920 to 2020* (Fig. 19), Ann Marye George's *Age and Antiq-*

uity (Fig. 99), and Claudia Ruiz Gustafson's *Forward* (Fig. 20) all find creative ways to bring multiple photographs together to evaluate the past, present, and future. A single photograph incorporating hand-written text, Karen Zusman's subject seems to address the abolitionist Sojourner Truth in *Dear Sojourner* (Fig. 51), updating her on today's struggle for Black women and asking through her prayers to invoke change through votes. Keeping with the strategy of blending the past and present, but shifting from combination photography to still life, Meg Griffiths pays homage to previous women activists in *Subtle Fusion of Time* (Fig. 84), an elegant color photograph of a display on a table. A Susan B. Anthony silver dollar, birth control pills scattered in a nod to Margaret Sanger, and a snapshot of the US Capitol point to national issues, while a cryptic note, graphic snake, and other personal symbols bridge a historical past with a lived experience.

Attention to the act of voting is drawn by Kat Kiernan's strip of photo booth pictures to comprise *The Voting Booth* (Fig. 18). The monochromatic set of four photographs presents a woman folding a piece of paper in an old-fashioned style of voting. Amy Thompson Avishai's slick American flag covered in water drops in *Voting Day, Easthampton, Massachusetts* (Fig. 14) might be about how the weather can impact voter turnout or a metaphor about what rhetoric sticks depending on how we *paint* the symbolic meaning of the flag. Carla Jay Harris's tryptic (Fig. 61) begins with a grade school class photograph of a Black girl in pigtails with "Our American Constitution 1787–1987" printed under her primly folded hands and is followed by a cropped portrait of a woman with her hand over her heart above an "I voted today" pin. The final image is an exterior scene of an American flag hanging on a wrought iron gate. Individually and together, these works invite us to think about what we vote for, where we place our allegiance, and how we define patriotism.

A couple of documentary projects represented in *A Yellow Rose Project* pay particular attention to voting rights. Carolyn McIntyre Norton and Betty Press photographed the aged Ellie Davis Dahmer (Fig. 8), who is a living connection to the Civil Rights and segregation era of the American South. Dahmer's life history and activist work are summed up by her murdered husband's words, "If you don't vote, you don't count" (Wilson, 2 Sept. 2020). The work of Black women to lift up other Black women is not isolated to the South as Colleen Mullins discovered in her neighbor's collection of achievements. Mullins documented Frankie's desk and awards after her lifetime of contributions in San Francisco and the Black community (Fig. 66). In her portrait project with young women, Rania Matar's subject, *Kayla* (Fig. 65), offers a sense of what is at stake: "Not voting makes it one step closer for a white man I've never met, that particularly doesn't care for my rights, solely because I'm black and also a woman . . . [to] decide what I can and can't do with my reproductive parts" ("Rania Matar," Artists Statements).

Exploring some of the issues that women vote for, Kris Sanford's photograph, *Women's March, Lansing, Michigan* (Fig. 10), foregrounds five points of view set in front of the state capitol building. Nancy Baron's abundant use of the WWII phrase associated with Rosie the Riveter, "We Can Do It," in *To Be Heard* (Fig. 98) *i*mplores that women's voices and experiences be taken seriously as it relates to disability. Megan Jacobs brings the early twentieth-century actress and feminist Julia Marlow to life with her Gen Z feminist doppelgänger, Tilcara Web, to advocate for women's rights, including those of the LGBTQIA+

community (Fig. 58). After *A Yellow Rose Project* began, there have been several election cycles, and the most recent has protected same-sex marriages for those such as Emily and Anne depicted in a photograph by Susan Rosenberg Jones (Fig. 60).

At the same time we celebrate the power of women's votes, we acknowledge not all women have been able to vote with equal ease and access. Frances Jakubek goes right to the heart of registration challenges in *New Jersey Voter Registration Form* (Fig. 7) with a government-issued document that is unreadable, convoluted, and impossible to complete. This work points to systematic, legislative, and literacy prohibitions. Sara Bennett's photograph, *Linda* (Fig. 9), of a purple-haired, green jumpsuit-wearing inmate in an institutional-looking room is from a series that investigates the lives of incarcerated women who have lost the right to vote.

Which women have been able to vote is a theme the makers called out with subtle and not so subtle strategies. Yael Eban and Brea Souders present a pair of photographs (Figs. 28 and 29) of individual, rephotographed, and cropped 1950s or 1960s hands and wrists of two women with different skin tones suggest inequality among those who raised their hands in hope of having their voices heard. Also drawing attention to tamped-down voices, Kyra Schmidt uses an unstable photographic process with a snippet derived from a historical archive. *Chinese Girl Wants to Vote* (Fig. 56) addresses the ways in which archives have the power to highlight and hide some people. Also thinking about historical materials, Keliy Anderson-Staley employs a wet collodion process popular in the late 1850s through the late 1860s. Her tintype *Daniela,* of the self-assured, Native American woman of the same name (Fig. 3), moves us back and forth across time

thinking about who got to photograph whom and for what purposes. Daniela's portrait, with her long dark hair, wide beaded necklace, and patterned fabric, might remind some of Gertrude Kasebier's (American, 1852–1934) portrait of Zitkála-Šá (Dakota, 1876–1938), also known by her government name Gertrude Bonnin, whose story and image circulates periodically on social media. Among other things, Zitkála-Šá was a voting rights activist whose name is included in the series that Cindy Hwang created. In Hwang's series *The Forgotten Suffragist,* she depicts a set of brightly hued, collectible cards in which faces are absent. A yellow card meant to honor Tye Leung (Fig. 2), the first Chinese American woman to vote in 1912 and to enter into civil service for the US government, presents a black rectangle where her portrait should be.

Other makers also incorporated suffrage and voting history by paying homage to particular suffragists, the symbols of the movement, women associated with voting and activism, and marking the lives of lesser-known women. Broad reminders of what it took to advocate for the Nineteenth Amendment are offered by Laura E. Migliorino's memory-like digital collage *Courage* (Fig. 53) and Sandra Klein's *The Banner* (Fig. 43) using a petition with signatures. Bringing in the pre-photography practice of cut paper silhouettes and using contemporary models, Susan kae Grant spotlights Katharine A. Morton (Fig. 23). Noelle McCleaf created and photographed a sacred altar to note sacrifices made by Marie Louise Bottineau Baldwin (Fig. 41). Chehalis Deane Hegner's composition, sharing the name of the subject, asks us what we know of the whole of Mary Ann McClintock's life and history (Fig. 35). In *Alexandria and Shirley* by Sheri Lynn Behr, the colorful sizzling outline of US Representative Ocasio-Cortez is underpinned by the ghost of the first Black woman elected to Congress, US Representative Shirley Chisholm (Fig. 5). Ellen Feldman's *Suffragists Knew— Dare to Act!* (Fig. 92) is a diptych pairing a public viewing of Elizabeth Warren's Presidential candidate debate on a CNN television broadcast and women signing messages of support on a life-sized photograph of Ayanna Pressley US Representative is an actual call to action: Women! Run for elected office!

The symbols and rhetoric of the movement speak to language and visual culture that has propelled itself across the century. Lisa McCarty repurposes images of banners and pennants housed at the Smithsonian National Museum of American History in her cyanotype pins, *Votes for Women 1920/2020* (Fig. 4). Astrid Reischwitz's *Working Woman with "Votes for Women" Plate* (Fig. 40) is a colorized photograph featuring a woman with her hands on her hips standing over two men, hopefully calling them to action on her behalf. Alice Hargrave's *Suffragist Bird, River Tyrannulet (female calls)* (Fig. 69) marks the first suffragists' conference together with the passing of the last passenger pigeon, Martha; an environmental nod to all the birds slaughtered for fashionable hats.

Highlighting purposefully hidden and erased histories, S. Billie Mandle's rectangular frames hold multiple layers of ghostly images of the home built by the dynamic and impactful women's rights activist Esther Lape and her partner, lawyer Elizabeth Read (Fig. 72). The pair donated their 147-acre property to the US Department of Interior in 1972 to become Connecticut's first wildlife refuge, yet the state named it after a male senator and only notes Lape's history as being interested in wildlife. If women who rubbed shoulders with the likes of Eleanor Roosevelt are marginalized, what about the history of ordinary women? The painting centered in Kathya Maria

Landeros's *Latina Girl* (Fig. 67) begs this question as well. Latinas are not a homogenous group. As such, she is a buried and amalgamated representation. The 1920s women with computer punch card faces are counted but individual identities are lost in Sarah Hadley's *On the Steps* (Fig. 27). Odette England's mid-century, color snapshot (Fig. 73) of a woman in shorts and bare legs, whose face is covered by yellow rose petals, echoes this historical note about all the unnamed women who propelled women's rights.

Unsurprisingly, *A Yellow Rose Project* generated several works that incorporated yellow roses and the color yellow. Rachel Loischild specifically referenced the December 6, 1913, issue of *The Suffragist,* responding to "gold, the color of light and life, is as the torch that guides our purpose, pure and unswerving" in her scanned botanical composition *#180* (Fig. 57). Kalee Appleton's *Untitled* (Fig. 63) calls out two feminist authors. It shows the poster titled "The Awakening," referencing Kate Chopin's novel, tacked to yellow wallpaper, a nod to Charlotte Perkins Gilman's story, "The Yellow Wallpaper." Moving from interior constructions of self to the construction of exterior and public space, Leigh Merrill casts a pale-yellow light across her digital combination of street and architecture photographs (Fig. 89) creating an ambiguous fictional space that, in this book context, begs to ask what happens when women aren't present and visible.

Complementing yellow are works in blue. The color, not symbol, derives from the iron salts in the cyanotype process. These works are generally one-of-a-kind prints. Historically, there are just a few cyanotype photo superstars. In particular two women are standouts, Anna Atkins (English, 1799– 1871) and Bertha Jaques (American, 1863–1941). It's hard to see cyanotypes without holding their histories in mind, especially as the process is relatively unchanged. A piece of paper (other materials can be used, too) is coated with the wet formula and dried. Then objects (2D or 3D) are deliberately placed on the paper, effectively blocking portions of the surface from UV light. Priya Kambli uses personal objects traditionally used on altars in *Devhara #1* (Fig. 12). Whereas Lily Brooks's *Henriette DeLille* (Fig. 15) uses negatives contact printed onto paper, which is then exposed to UV light. Washed and dried, et voila, the print is done. Unless like Edie Bresler's *Our Right* (Fig. 96) and Paula Riff's *Because of Sunflowers* (Fig. 64), one adds color or other elements. These particular works, when seen in person, have a body to them offered by the thickness and texture of watercolor paper choices, as well as a directness by seeing the hand of the maker. Rachel Phillips's *Growing Pains* (Fig. 37) is an obscured cyanotype because of the way the Library of Congress made the image available through its scanning method and in the way the artist tinted it yellow. The image, made on the back of an envelope, is of a young woman using an exercise pulley system, and was produced by another significant woman photographer Frances Benjamin Johnston (American, 1864–1952). Among her most well-known photographs is a self-portrait as an independent "new woman."

Blue, used symbolically with the red and white of the American flag, is dotted throughout the project. It is strikingly used to rhetorically represent loud and crushing patriotism in Patty Carroll's *Bedridden* (Fig. 95). Owners of The Congress Inn, shown in the work by Tamara Reynolds (Fig. 93), might hope that wrapping the hotel in red, white, and blue will diminish the double entendre. A more subtle use is found in Jeanine Michna-Bales's distant figure on the hill in *Ready for Battle* (Fig. 62).

The politically symbolic pink of the early twenty-first century is found in the pink pussy hats crocheted and worn with ecstatic empowerment and rage, like Greta Pratt's young activist holding the hand-painted poster and asserting, "Anything you can do I can do Bleeding" (Fig. 91). Katie Benjamin turns the Presidential seal pink in *Study 03* (Fig. 21) to note that this political threshold has yet to be crossed. Lindsey Beal offers a pink, 1960s Library of Congress protest photograph in *Second Wave* (Fig. 102). It is not only a new wave of feminism but also a rise in environmentalism. The pink comes from the use of beets in the eco-friendly photographic process Lindsey uses called anthotype. Alyssa Minahan's *Untitled* (Fig. 71) is pink from unfixed photochemistry and is unstable. Although pale pink and unstable, the decomposing fabric in Gail Samuelson's photograph *Silk Blouse* (Fig. 25) has more to do with photographs that serve in the stead of three-dimensional material objects than the color.

Material culture is an important part of preserving history and commenting on current lives. Contemplating materiality and definitions of femininity with romantic sensibilities are seen in Deedra Baker's cut glass and bubbly liquid shadow in *Manifest* (Fig. 76), Preston Gannaway's ethereal *Untitled* (Fig. 42), Sarah Pollman's warm, monochromatic *Dragonfly* (Fig. 47) of a pin on a fish print, and Molly Lamb's slash of light across a lace cloth and fragile porcelain flower in *My Great-Grandmother's Yellow Rose* (Fig. 50). In a practical vein, Yvette Meltzer's *Advances for Women Celebrating 100 Years* (Fig. 85) is a photograph of her sanitary napkin belt. Its presence under women's wardrobes in the 1950s represented freedom as it allowed her to be physically active during menstruation. A more public wardrobe accouterment and cultural expression is hats. Suffragists often wore extravagant hats, as do some church-going Black women on Sundays. Mary Beth Meehan's photograph of a scalloped white fabric with silver and green threads centered by an embellished pale green straw hat in *Tell the Story* (Fig. 38) brings a powerful conflation of histories together. Likewise, the soiled flats in *Shoes* by Sasha Tivetsky (Fig. 49), tucked under their grandmother's sitting room ottoman, recall the idiom about walking in someone else's shoes. In homage to the many feet that paved the way for the Nineteenth Amendment, Tami Bahat photographed a pair of black button-up boots on a black string with a black background in *Strung Along for Too Long* (Fig. 90).

Textiles, in particular clothing, lace, embroidery, crochet, and other such delicate materials, are often placed squarely within the domain of domestic femininity. The first and last images in this book utilize threadwork. Marina Font's *Equality* (Fig. 1) incorporates stitches to create angel wings, a riot of flame-like loose threads, and a ribbon sash or banner with the word "Equality" over a black and white photograph of a nude woman. The combination of materials, depiction of a woman, sewing, and photographic practices, point to the Suffrage movement, domesticity, photographic ideas, archetypes, and gestures and are all rolled together to point to openness and agency, sacred and profane, real and ideal. It is a fitting opening image. US Representative Maxine Waters gets to have the last word in Diane Meyer's *Maxine* (Fig. 105). Two stacked screenshots of Waters in conversation with conservative, white, male Fox TV commentators, whose faces are pixelated using cross stitch, and her words stitched along the bottom, "I'd like to say to women everywhere don't allow these dishonorable people to intimidate you or scare you. Be who you are. Do what you do."

Speaking back to men and power—they aren't the same thing!—hasn't always been easy. The discomfort of young women overwhelmed by men is suggested by the young woman seated in the center of a row of men in Rana Young's *Untitled (Probe 1)* (Fig. 26). Her tight smile is matched by her slightly drawn-in shoulders. Her hands are folded tightly on her lap with knees together, while the men have their hands on spread knees. Their faces are hidden but their body language speaks volumes. Jordanna Kalman points directly to photography's complicity in perpetuating the dominance of the male gaze in her series *History of Photography,* as seen in the example [Robert] *Frank* (Fig. 77). In her work *Liked* (Fig. 78), Cassandra Zampini presents layered, mirrored, and reversed images to examine definitions of sex appeal accepted and imposed upon women as they photograph themselves in particular poses and stand for before and after cosmetic surgery photographs. Marky Kauffmann's *Eloise in Blue Dress* (Fig. 97), with its fallopian tube and uterus-like bodice, revels in the complexity of joy and toxicity of women's fashion. The elegantly gloved hand and arm of a young woman, so common of a previous era, is used in a series of photographs by Emily Peacock (Fig. 88). She documents a strange performance in which the woman builds a phallic monument.

Definitions of what it means to be a woman are sometimes created in response to what it means to be a man. Perhaps one of the most public examples where this struggle exists is as the wife of an elected official. Serrah Russell appropriated and altered Annie Leibovitz's *Vogue* photographs of First Lady Hillary Clinton (Fig. 46) by fracturing and altering how she is depicted and seen by the external world. Countering that view, Russell pairs the image with a quote from Clinton referring to the morning after the 2016 presidential election, "I could finally let my smile drain away. We were mostly quiet." Greer Muldowney pinpoints a phrase in a letter highlighting where women's lives are defined by men's actions in *Be a Good Boy* (Fig. 45). The words are pulled from the letter to Harry Burns from his mother and presented as an inflection moment for Burns's seminal vote. However, why must a mother tell her adult son to be a good boy and to what behaviors might she refer? Men are presented in this project as ominous and threatening, often drawing attention to how they have suppressed women's choices and harmed them.

The black and white photograph by Elizabeth M. Claffey (Fig. 81) of a discarded sweater dragged between two thresholds is distressing and suggests a crime scene reflecting violence against a young woman. Ashley Kauschinger's photograph of a white dress, the color that many suffragists wore as a sign of unity, is draped in wilted yellow roses, the symbol of the Nineteenth Amendment. However, the homage is tainted by the shadow of the gnarled hand placed to grab and grope between the dress wearer's legs in *After The Vote (US Suffragist 1920)* (Fig. 79). In *Covered in Filth (Epstein Is The Worst Kind of Virus) July 4th, 2020* (Fig. 83), Katelyn Kopenhaver also points to the systemic condoning of sexual abuse by standing by a pool and wrapping her youthful body in a sheet with her declaration about the serial abuser. The protection of the right to vote is not protection from violence, nor does it come with additional justice for women. Claire A. Warden's *No. 15 Genetics* (Fig. 22) is an enigmatic print of a finger with what looks like a piece of dangling tissue

from a torn hand. It is a cross between a marked-up crime or anthropometric study photograph and an inked finger for voting, which calls to mind that voting is even harder in some parts of the world. K.K. DePaul's *Silent No More* (Fig. 52), a tintype with tape over a girl's mouth, implores us to act for those who can't speak. Melanie Walker's *MisJudge* (Fig. 34), with its looming dark man, speaks to injustice for many women that is meted out by men. Farah Janjua's *Afghan Eyes* (Fig. 55) is complex. It serves as a reminder of women who have fewer freedoms by Western standards. It is a real woman who has permitted herself to be photographed, which might counter the well-known exoticized eyes of Steve McCurry's photograph with the same title. Rebecca Drolen's abstraction, *Balloon Study No. 1* (Fig. 87), which might be seen as a mess of tangled penises, offers some humorous relief.

Gender, women in particular, is perhaps an obvious theme addressed in *A Yellow Rose Project* as it is closely associated with the Nineteenth Amendment. Gender is evident in every photograph included in this project by how makers define themselves, who is depicted, and the topics explored. Collectively, gender (in broad and loose definitions) is approached in this project with a satisfying matter-of-factness like being with a combination of close girlfriends and a few new folks who are happily familiar and enticingly dynamic.

Women look closely to see each other, express themselves, and exert power. Marie Triller photographs women who embody physical power. Her photograph, *Portrait of an Athlete* (Fig. 82), of her sister Maureen competing in a fitness competition is a rendering of muscular, mental, and emotional power to climb an actual and metaphorical rope.

Sharing in the power of community, Sarah Hoskins's photograph of a Kentucky organization of Black women, *The Benevolent Sisters, Their 99th Year* (Fig. 103), is from a series that reflects their role and support of the women around them. Larissa Ramey's *Dirty Hands* (Fig. 86), with strategic editing of text, shows us that we can shape what we read by dismissing most of it and building a powerful personal narrative.

Joni Sternbach's *Premature* (Fig. 74), depicting herself pumping milk, points directly at motherhood. Other photographers present children honoring their individuality and contemplating the world they will grow to inhabit. Jennifer McClure's white child at a window looking at a mural of an only slightly older Black girl with her fist in the air in *Untitled* (Fig. 70) prompts one to think about how to face race and economics as a challenge toward equity. Ashleigh Coleman's *Power(ful)* (Fig. 94) depicts an awestruck girl in an oversized red t-shirt holding a Princess Power sword, shooting out a terrific array of sparks. Let's hope she can harness and embrace that power. *Ishy's Haircut* (Fig. 48) portrays a passive, beautifully lit girl watching two men handle a dog by Maude Schuyler Clay, and Hye-Ryoung Min's photograph, *Untitled from the series Yeonsoo* (Fig. 68), from a series featuring her seven-year old Korean niece Yeonsoo hiding behind a plant, are meditations on those who find themselves in quiet places and offer their actions in less overt ways. Letitia Huckaby's photograph, *Sugar and Spice* (Fig. 24), wraps past, present, and future into a call to action. The photograph is printed on a vintage cotton-picking sack with a small Black girl and her innocently untied shoelace, rendering her even more vulnerable, hold-

ing a sign that reads, "Enough." It should not be on her shoulders to bear so many challenges that have been noted throughout this project. Adults should act on her behalf.

Thalassa Raasch's *Blooming roses with wind* (Fig. 75) is a black and white photograph in which yellow roses are stripped of their color and hover over a mess of light and darkness from which they grow. Julia Bennett's yellow and purple flowers in *Five Wounds* (Fig. 39) is meant to reference suffering and joy. Both photographs are fitting metaphors for the challenges of being a young woman in the 2020s, fighting to find and create one's identity while wrestling with the whispers and hurricanes of external voices. Manjari Sharma's *Uncertainty* (Fig. 33) launches a conversation about identity and to whom we attach ourselves. The distressed-looking young woman in Frances F. Denny's *Anna (Red Hook Tavern)* (Fig. 31) suggests young adulthood is not all joy. Tara Cronin's *Entry* (Fig. 100), an image of a blurry young woman in a corner of a room lined with hospital bracelets, comes from a series related to self-harm and hospitalization. The lovely and graceful photograph, *Hada 2* (Fig. 13) by Ina Jang, of a visible but faceless young woman, seen but not seen, is also disconcerting and worrisome. Sara Macel's photograph, *Dana at Fifteen* (Fig. 80), captures the tension in which Dana seems about to launch from the family car and looks at the viewer with distrust. Have we served our teens well enough? Not all photographs of young women express a range of angst and anxiety of young adulthood and personal challenge. Bootsy Holler places herself in nature to connect with the world around her in *Tybee Island* (Fig. 17). Tracy L. Chandler's *Elize and Lenee* (Fig. 6) offers us two young women who seem to be comfortable with who they are and support each other.

A Yellow Rose Project takes us on a visual journey across time through photography to reflect on the history and impact of the Nineteenth Amendment. The project worked to build a website, share the photographs through exhibitions, and now as a book. This chapter has attempted to offer points of conversation among the various works, but only starts to scratch the surface of each maker's oeuvre for which there are multiple interpretations and ways to see it in contexts of the art world, the history of photography, and the history of the impact of women's suffrage. There is so much more to be said. Hopefully, you are excited to find your own words about what the Nineteenth Amendment means to you and those you care about. And of course, that you employ your power by voting.

Shannon Perich is the curator of the photographic history collection at the National Museum of American History. Her chapter was written February 5, 2023.

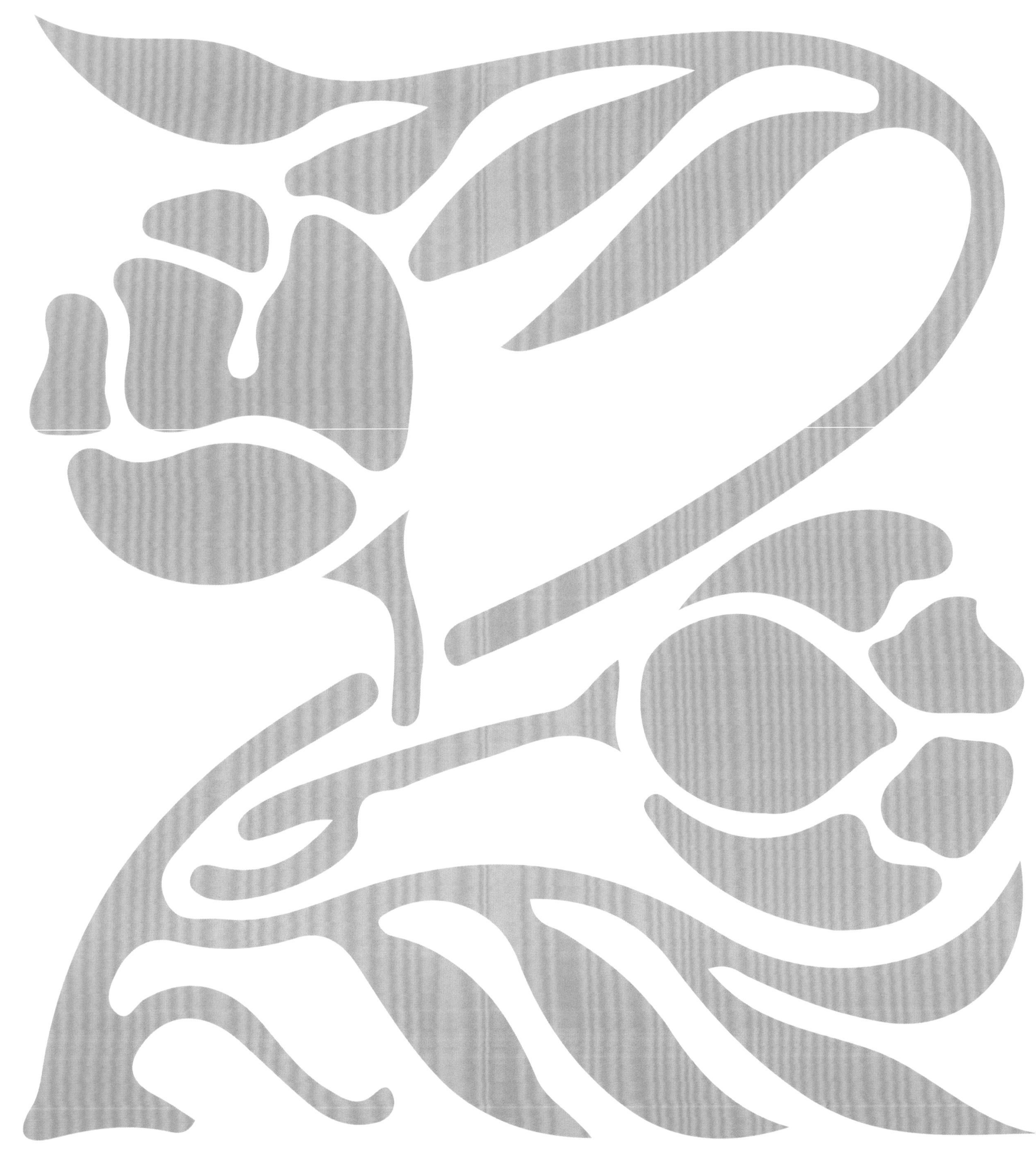

A Yellow Rose Project and the History of Woman Suffrage

RACHEL MICHELLE GUNTER

A Yellow Rose Project consists of more than a hundred artists' responses to the centennial of the Nineteenth Amendment. The artists reflected on the history of the suffrage movement, its symbols, and women's rights and voting rights since 1920. Those familiar with the suffrage movement will recognize the white dresses and yellow roses that appear in several pieces, as well as many of the more famous suffragists referenced. However, other names and images may be less recognizable. This chapter seeks to contextualize the incredible artwork of *A Yellow Rose Project* within a brief history of the suffrage movement from its early nineteenth century origins through the present day. Included in this section are the last names of artists whose pieces connect with particular moments discussed, in the hope that as you read the history, you can turn to the specific art pieces referenced.

The American women's suffrage movement grew out of the small but powerful abolitionist movement to end slavery in the United States. As women, both Black and white, spoke out against slavery, they faced criticism for speaking publicly as women and for speaking about the sexual violence so common in American slavery. In the early nineteenth century, the Cult of True Womanhood was a set of standards by which society judged American women: they were to be pious, pure, domestic, and submissive. Speaking in public violated these norms. Baker's (Fig. 76) piece contemplates the suffrage movement as pushing back against the Cult of True Womanhood. The concept of women's suffrage was incredibly radical to a society in which women speaking in public was shocking in its own right.

White abolitionists Lucretia Mott and Elizabeth Cady Stanton first met at the World Anti-Slavery Convention in London in 1840. After expending the energy and expense to get to London, the women arrived at a convention of men who promptly barred women from participating. Several abolitionists left in protest. Mott and Stanton reunited at the Waterloo Tea Party in July 1848, where they met with Mott's sister Martha Wright, Jane Hunt, and Mary Ann McClintock, who is pictured in Hegner (Fig. 35).

The women decided to hold a convention for women's rights at Seneca Falls that same month. The Seneca Falls meeting became the origin myth of the suffrage movement. There participants drafted and voted on the Declaration of Sentiments. Using the basic outline of the Declaration of Independence, the Declaration of Sentiments began with a series of injuries women suffered at the hands of men, including denial of education, professions, and rights to their children. Then the attendees voted on eleven rights that would remedy these injuries. Most controversial on the list was woman suffrage—the only right that wasn't unanimously supported by those in attendance. However, after the formerly enslaved Frederick Douglass argued that woman suffrage was the best way to secure all the other agreed upon rights, the meeting passed the suffrage resolution.

Sojourner Truth spoke out against slavery and for women's rights. She was born into slavery in New York State around 1797. She gained her freedom and successfully sued to have her child returned to her as part of the northern states' gradual elimination of slavery over several decades after American independence. Truth supported herself through lecturing and by selling carefully crafted *carte de visite* photographs captioned, "I Sell the Shadow to Support the Substance." In each portrait, Truth posed with objects like knitting, books, and flowers, which historian Allison Lange argues portrayed "mainstream notions of femininity, even though her political speeches suggested no such thing" (2020). Truth deliberately chose to display these objects for her intended audience. Suffragists from Truth in the mid-nineteenth century to those leading national suffrage organizations in the 1910s carefully constructed their images as feminine or domestic, hoping to advance the cause. Anti-suffrage cartoons routinely depicted suffragists as masculine and unsexed by their political goals. Acknowledging both the incredible barriers Truth faced and the continuing fight for equality today, Zusman (Fig. 51) shares her hopes for 2020 and the future for women in her poem addressed to Truth atop her own carefully constructed portrait.

During the Civil War, suffragists supported the American war effort and hoped that both Black people of all genders and white women would be enfranchised after the conflict. Shortly after the war in 1867, both Cady Stanton and Susan B. Anthony joined the campaign for a state suffrage amendment in Kansas using the state flower—the sunflower. As Loischild (Fig. 57) notes, the color yellow was adopted by the suffrage movement and would be displayed prominently at the final state ratification in 1920. Black suffrage and woman suffrage were on the ballot separately in Kansas in 1867, and both amendments failed. Politicians and activists decided that the two measures needed to be separated for either one to have a chance at success. Congressional Republicans argued that the nation could only manage one great reform at a time.

Suffragists were leery of the Fourteenth Amendment, which established birthright citizenship, equal protection before the law, and due process. They feared the implications of inserting the word *male* in the Constitution for the first time. But it was the Fifteenth Amendment, which enfranchised Black men only, that divided suffrage ranks into two separate organizations. In 1869, Lucy Stone and her husband, Henry Blackwell, founded the American Woman Suffrage Association (AWSA), which supported the Fifteenth Amendment. Stanton and Anthony founded the rival National Woman Suffrage Association (NWSA), which opposed the Fifteenth

Amendment for prioritizing Black male voting before white woman suffrage. While the AWSA focused exclusively on voting rights, the NWSA also supported married women having property rights in their own name, legalizing divorce (especially for abandoned wives), and opening colleges and trade schools to women. Congress passed and the states ratified the Fifteenth Amendment in 1870, barring states from preventing a person from voting based on "race, color, or previous condition of servitude" (US Const. amend. XV). Women, both Black and white, would have to wait.

In 1872, hundreds of suffragists, including Susan B. Anthony. attempted to vote in an act of civil disobedience. They hoped they could convince the courts that under the Fourteenth Amendment American women were birthright citizens and therefore deserving of voting rights. While Anthony was arrested and convicted, the judge in her case used technicalities to bar her from appealing to a higher court. Virginia Minor's case made it to the Supreme Court, which ruled in *Minor v. Happersett* (1875) that voting was not a right guaranteed to citizens nor restricted to citizens (as many states allowed immigrant residents to vote in the nineteenth and early twentieth centuries). The decision solidified the need for a federal women's suffrage amendment.

While beginning the long slog for a federal amendment, suffragists pushed for local and state victories when and where they could. Some western territories added women's suffrage to their territorial constitutions in the two decades after the Civil War. Several more then included suffrage in their state constitutions after achieving statehood: Wyoming in 1890, Colorado in 1893, and Utah and Idaho in 1896. Following these states' passages, the movement hit what is sometimes referred to as the doldrums. No

state passed a state suffrage amendment from 1896 until 1910. Meanwhile, Black voting rights were curtailed by new state constitutions in the South and by Jim Crow voter laws, including the all-white primary, literacy tests, and poll taxes.

In 1890, the two rival suffrage associations merged to form the National American Woman Suffrage Association (NAWSA). They began a renewed push for suffrage that began to bear fruits in 1910, when Washington state granted woman suffrage, followed in 1911 by California and in 1912 by Arizona, Kansas, and Oregon. That same year Democrat Woodrow Wilson was elected president, and suffragists sought to use the inaugural festivities to draw attention to their cause. Leading NAWSA's Congressional Committee, Alice Paul organized a suffrage parade. The day before the presidential inauguration, Inez Milholland led the procession on her white horse, Grey Dawn. On the float behind her, suffragists displayed a banner demanding a federal suffrage amendment. Behind the twenty floats, suffragists marched in delegations by states, professions, or the universities they attended. Paul had extended an invitation to Black students at Howard University, but white southerners wanted the parade to remain all-white. Parade organizers suggested Black women march in segregated delegations at the back of the parade. Despite the controversy, Black women marched in the parade, mostly as groups of Black college, sorority, or career women. But three Black suffragists marched with their state delegations, including Ida B. Wells of Illinois. Indigenous women marched as well. Marie Louise Bottineau Baldwin (Fig. 41) marched with her fellow lawyers and law students. When a crowd of nearly a quarter million people spilled into the streets blocking their parade route and the marchers were met with violence, local police refused to clear the path or protect them. Finally, a group of Black police officers offered the suffragists protection.

As suffragists continued working for a federal amendment, Milholland was sent to the West in 1916 by the National Woman's Party (NWP), which had broken away from the more moderate NAWSA earlier that year. The NWP encouraged women in the West who already had the vote to use it against the incumbent Wilson as punishment for not getting a women's suffrage amendment through Congress. Milholland kept up a strenuous schedule until she collapsed during a speech and passed away a few weeks later of pernicious anemia at the age of thirty. Her final words were: "President Wilson, how long must this go on? No liberty" (Bernard, 7 Aug. 2020). Both Michna-Bales (Fig. 62) and Ruiz Gustafson (Fig. 20) pay tribute to Milholland's sacrifice.

The NWP protested for suffrage outside the White House as Silent Sentinels with signs holding President Wilson responsible for their continued disenfranchisement and controversially comparing him to the German Kaiser in the midst of World War I. Thompson's piece (Fig. 11) compares this protest with the 2017 Women's March, also in the nation's capital. Eventually the suffragists were arrested for obstructing the sidewalk. The imprisoned Alice Paul began a hunger strike to protest the suffragists' incarceration and treatment. Frustrated, Superintendent Raymond Whittaker and forty male guards attempted to end the suffragists' protests during the Night of Terror. They dragged, choked, clubbed, and kicked the thirty-three imprisoned suffragists. Lucy Burns was shackled all night with her hands above her head; Alice Cosu suffered a heart attack and was denied medical care until morning. The guards began force-feeding those who refused to eat, includ-

ing Paul. When the Night of Terror was publicized, the suffragists got a hearing before a judge, who released them after deciding their arrest, conviction, and imprisonment had been illegal.

In states where a full suffrage amendment seemed like a long shot, suffragists sought partial suffrage—the ability to vote in some, but not all, elections or for all offices or amendments. In 1913, women in Illinois received presidential suffrage by exploiting a loophole in the state constitution that didn't apply the same general voting requirements to those voting for electoral college representatives. These women helped choose the president before they could help choose their own mayors or governors. In some municipalities, women received school board suffrage long before full women's suffrage. Kiernan's piece (Fig. 18) points us to the separate ballot boxes used in some states where forms of partial suffrage required it. In Arkansas and Texas in 1917 and 1918 respectively, women received primary suffrage—the ability to vote in the primaries in their state but not in the general election. Primary suffrage could be enacted by a state law with a simple majority in the state legislature and the governor's signature, while full suffrage was a more daunting task requiring state constitutional amendments and public referenda. Each hard-fought suffrage victory at the state level—whether for full or partial suffrage—made Congress that much friendlier to women's suffrage.

In January 1918, President Wilson asked for women's suffrage as a war measure. He hoped to lead the peace talks, as well as the formation of the League of Nations. However, to be a leader in international democracy, the United States had to catch up to those nations that had already enfranchised women. Still, it was a full year after Wilson's request that the

House of Representatives passed the Nineteenth Amendment. The Senate followed suit in June 1919. For an amendment to become part of the US Constitution, three quarters of the states must ratify it by a simple majority of their state legislatures. In 1919, this meant thirty-six states were needed to ratify. The press jokingly referred to the number as the "perfect thirty-six," a well-known pop culture reference to the ideal woman's measurements and particularly to silent film actress Mabel Norman's bust size.

By August of 1920, thirty-five states had ratified the amendment, but the remaining states were toss-ups at best or unfriendly to suffrage at worst. Only three southern states had ratified—Texas, Arkansas (Fig. 50), and Kentucky. Most white southern politicians feared that passing a federal women's suffrage amendment could inadvertently lead to federal enforcement of the Fifteenth Amendment, which they were violating with Jim Crow voting laws. All eyes looked to Tennessee to see if the Susan B. Anthony Amendment would become the Nineteenth Amendment or not. Congressmen, suffragists, and anti-suffragists descended on Nashville. Those in support of suffrage wore yellow roses; those opposed wore red roses. It looked like the antis had it by a single vote. And then, in a shock to those watching with suspense (Fig. 33), Representative Harry Burn, thought to be an anti, voted for ratification. Unbeknownst to the onlookers, Representative Burn had received a letter (Figs. 37, 45) from his mother that morning encouraging him to "be a good boy" and vote for suffrage. Tennessee ratified by a margin of 50 to 49. The Nineteenth Amendment became part of the US Constitution.

The Nineteenth Amendment did not give women the right to vote. It simply prevented states from barring a person from voting based on their sex. Black women in the South remained disfranchised by Jim Crow voting laws intended to target Black voters without explicitly mentioning race (Figs. 38, 43, 66). Poor women of all races still were barred by poll taxes that required annual payment to the state to cast a ballot. In those states, women whose husbands controlled the family finances could only vote if their husbands allowed it. Most Native Americans remained disfranchised as well. The Indian Citizenship Act of 1924 declared any Indigenous person a citizen, who didn't already have citizenship by treaty with their Indigenous nation, but states continued to bar Indigenous people from voting despite their citizenship, since the courts previously had established voting was not a right guaranteed to citizens. Women and men in the American territories remained governed by a Congress where they had no formal representation or rights to participate in federal elections. Asian immigrants were not allowed to naturalize due to the Chinese Exclusion Act (Figs. 56, 2), leaving Asian immigrants voteless as well. Bresler's piece (Fig. 96) contemplates the Native Americans, Asian Americans, and Black Americans that remained disfranchised after 1920.

Several artists contemplate the changing roles of women in the nation after the Nineteenth Amendment (Figs. 6, 104) and how women in the artist's ancestry might have responded to it (Fig. 101). After World War I, the United States swung politically conservative during the 1920s, even as much of the nation became more socially liberal. The Great Depression returned liberal Democrats to power through World War II. Due to a national labor shortage, women went to work in industries previously closed to them. After the war however, American society pressured women to return to the home, and while some willingly returned to family life, others chafed at being forced out of jobs and careers they found fulfilling. Carroll (Fig. 95) satirizes expectations of domestic perfection that American women found particularly frustrating during the 1950s and 1960s. Fedorsky (Fig. 59) contemplates the hopes and dreams of her own mother and other young women in mid-twentieth century America, as well as the barriers they faced. These artists make clear that the fight for women's rights and justice did not end with the passage of the Nineteenth Amendment (Figs. 25, 39).

Too often though, people overlook moments in which a movement builds quietly and in the background without much fanfare or major breakthroughs—like the so-called suffrage doldrums. But the work in these moments is vital to the future success of the movement, which to outsiders seem to erupt out of nowhere or even to be disconnected from the movement's earlier iterations. Older histories referred to the suffrage movement as the first wave of women's activism and to the women's liberation movement of the late 1960s and 1970s as the second wave, as if all women's activism receded or ceased between the two movements. Today, women's historians dispute this analogy, focusing on the work that took place in between the great eruptions. As Coleman (Fig. 94) explains in the artist statements section, her piece reminds us of this lesson contemplating "metamorphosis—change that is sometimes slow, sometimes hidden, oftentimes painful, then blazing into the foreground, striking everyone with awe and terror and wonder."

The civil rights movements of the 1960s further altered voting rights. Utah was the last state to drop its ban on Native American voting in 1962. The twenty-fourth Amendment ended the poll tax in 1964. The Voting Rights Act of 1965 returned democracy to the South for the first time since the rise of Jim Crow. It placed much of the South under preclearance, arguing that the region's strong history of racist disfranchisement, they should have to get the federal government's permission to make any substantive changes to their voting laws. To get approval, these states had to show that the laws would not have disparate impacts on racial minorities. The law allowed for federal voting registrars to help Black voters circumnavigate racist registrars in the South.

Women learned strategies from the civil rights movement and pushed further for women's liberation in the 1960s and 1970s. President John F. Kennedy formed the President's Commission on the Status of Women (PCSW) in 1961. In 1966, at the third national conference of the commission, twenty-eight women left to form the National Organization for Women (NOW). Yet when NOW later protested outside the White House in 1971, the press reported that both President Nixon and his wife did not believe American women faced discrimination (Fig. 44). In 1967, Kathrine Switzer registered for the all-male Boston marathon, using her initials to hide her sex. When discovered, the race organizer tried to force her from the course and was stopped only when her fellow (male) runners physically intervened. Triller (Fig. 82) reminds us of the connection between political rights and women's rights in other realms, including sports.

In 1972, Congress passed the Equal Rights Amendment (ERA) originally authored by Alice Paul in 1923 (Fig. 99). It reads: "Equality of rights under the law shall not be denied or abridged by the United States or by any state on account of sex" (86 Stat. 1523). However, they added an expiration date for ratification. If the three-quarters of American states necessary had not ratified by that date, the amendment would die. That date passed in 1979 without the three-quarters required to make the ERA part of the Constitution. However, activists continue to question the legitimacy of the expiration date. Their work led Nevada to ratify the ERA in 2017, Illinois in 2018, and the final necessary state, Virginia, in 2020. The House of Representatives then passed legislation to remove the time limit, but the Senate has not taken up that measure as of this writing.

American history is a cautionary tale. Read it closely enough and you'll see that no victory or loss is complete. There is always another election, another law, another win or loss. In 2013, the Supreme Court gutted large sections of the Voting Rights Act in *Shelby County v. Holder*. No longer restricted under preclearance, every former Confederate state attempted to pass voter ID laws that disenfranchised voters without addressing voter fraud or gerrymandering in any meaningful way. Macel (Fig. 80) reminds us of the disenfranchising efforts of recent years and the current generation of activists fighting for voting rights.

In 2016, American women held their breath. Many wondered if the first female president would be elected as the last of the generation born in 1920 watched. Would a female president be in office during the suffrage centennial of 2020? Hillary Clinton accepted the Democratic Party's presidential nomination wearing suffrage white (Fig. 81). But many women were devastated when the *hardest glass ceiling* remained intact (Fig. 46). Women's rights activists were further disheartened that Clinton lost to a man who had spoken openly of assaulting women on the campaign trail (Fig. 79). However, a majority of white women voted for Donald Trump in 2016, which led Bowden (Fig. 16) and others to

contemplate women's votes and how they used them.

In response to the 2016 election, activists organized the Women's March in January 2017. The main event took place in Washington, DC, but activists organized marches all over the country. Sanford contrasts the NWP Silent Sentinel protest with the Women's March at the Michigan State Capitol (Fig. 10). At these events, women donned pink pussy hats that were usually handknit or crocheted. Kauffmann (Fig. 97) contemplates attire that society sees as feminine, including the dress, and how it can become a symbol of empowerment. Women's rights and voting rights activists organized during the Trump presidency. Meyer (Fig. 105) points us to the words of Representative Maxine Waters encouraging Democratic women: "don't allow these . . . dishonorable people to intimidate you or scare you. Be who you are. Do what you do" (Waters, 2017). Thompson Avishai (Fig. 14) shows us her hope as a voter in the 2018 midterm, noting that despite the political struggles regarding women's rights, "a record number of women [ran] for office" (Alter, 18 Jan. 2018).

Activists organized the 2020 Women's March in October 2020, just weeks before the presidential election and as Republicans in Congress were fast-tracking the confirmation of Judge Amy Coney Barrett to the Supreme Court in defiance of rules they had created for nominees during the Obama administration. Women held signs, one reading "Anything you can do I can do BLEEDING" (Fig. 91), reminiscent of historical women holding signs like "resistance to tyranny is obedience to God" (Fig. 32). The march encouraged women to vote and all people to vote for women's rights. Voter turnout efforts gained traction using the suffrage struggle as inspiration (Fig. 4). Young voters (Fig. 65) turned out in larger than expected numbers in 2020, a fitting tribute to the suffragists who fought for young women's right to do so.

More than a century later, the movements to secure and protect voting rights, women's rights, and civil rights remain unfinished. Jacobs (Fig. 58) links the suffrage generation's struggle to Gen Z's struggle for bodily autonomy. Zampini (Fig. 78) joins the fight for women's rights to their objectified bodies, a problem exacerbated by social media. Huckaby (Fig. 24) connects suffrage, the Civil Rights movement (as shown in Norman Rockwell's work), and the modern movement for gun reform using the words of Dr. Martin Luther King Jr.'s grandchild, Yolanda King, at March for Our Lives in 2018. As explained in their artist statement section, Raasch (Fig. 75) uses the yellow rose in full bloom to show the symbol of woman suffrage "resist[ing] the conflicting sexual, cultural, and political pressures that seek to categorize, identify, and oppress women." While many struggles for women's rights are ongoing, it is also important to acknowledge the victories achieved. Rosenberg (Fig. 60) shows us a couple celebrating the recognition of their own rights after *Obergefell v. Hodges* decision in 2015 legalized gay marriage throughout the nation. Feldman (Fig. 92) wonders if suffragists could have imagined women like Elizabeth Warren and Ayanna Pressley serving in Congress and uses the memory of the suffragists to encourage future activism.

As Truth's portraits once did, many of the pieces in *A Yellow Rose Project* call us to think deeply about the images and stereotypes of American women.

Harris (Fig. 61) situates a young Black girl next to an "I voted" sticker and an American flag, forming a self-portrait that "examines and recontextualizes the relationship between the Black female body and what it means to be an American," an examination that could certainly start with portraits of Phillis Wheatley, Maria Stewart, and Sojourner Truth ("Carla Jay Harris," Artists Statements). Warden (Fig. 22) connects themes of identity and perception with voting practices through the fingerprint. In her piece, Zusman (Fig. 51) dances while holding yellow roses for suffrage next to a poem she wrote called "Dear Sojourner." She couples Truth's fight for abolition and women's rights in the nineteenth century with the continuing fight for voting rights, women's rights, and civil rights. She juxtaposes the hope caused by another crack in the glass ceiling—a female vice president of color—with the despair of disenfranchisement efforts and police brutality. Her photo, showing her own dancing body next to symbols of women's suffrage with a poem of hopes and dreams, calls us back to the careful depictions of Truth's portraits, which sustained her work all those years ago.

Rachel Michelle Gunter is a public historian and professor of history at a community college in North Texas.

GALLERY

OF

WORKS

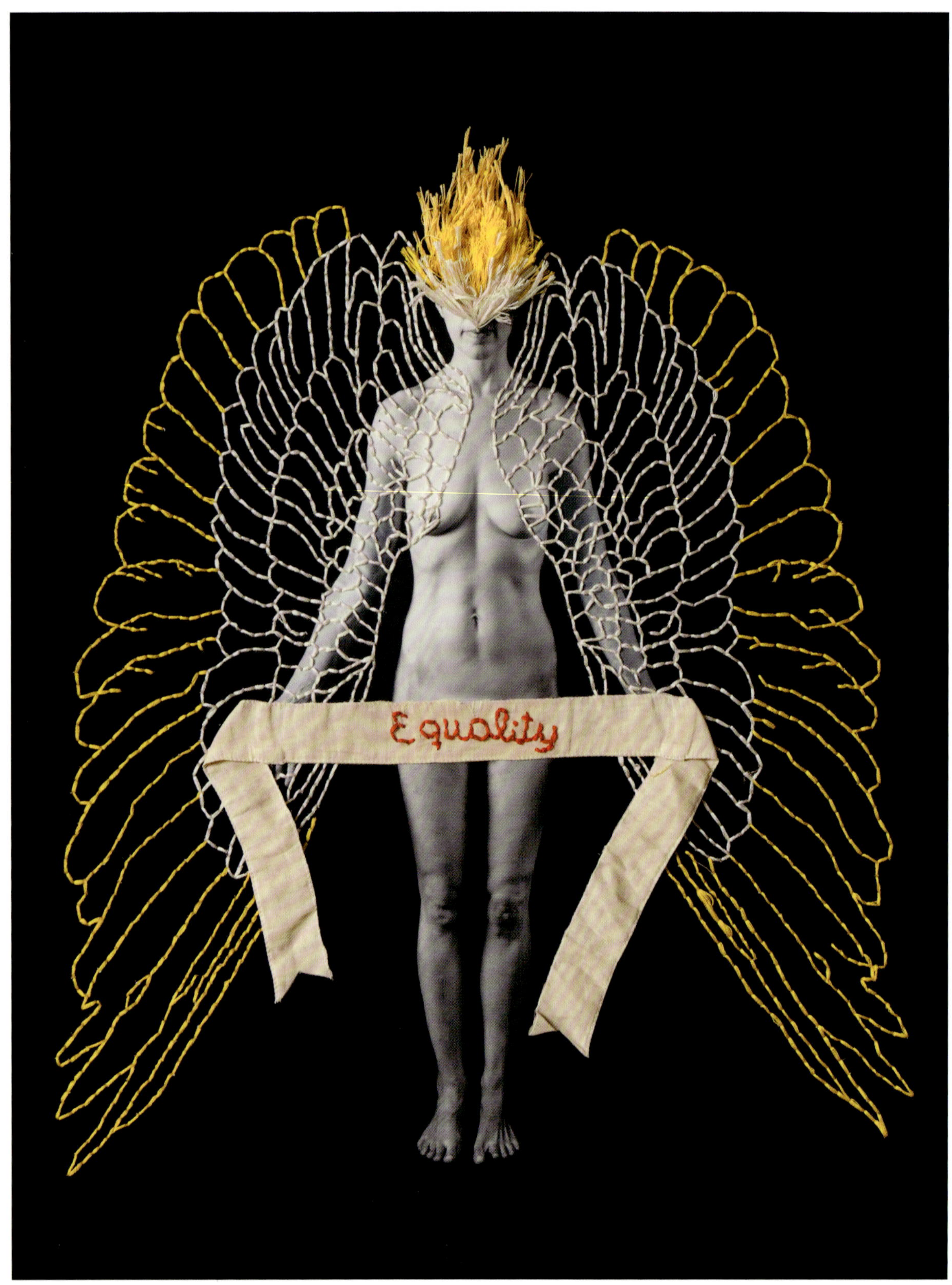

FIGURE 1. Marina Font. *Equality.* Courtesy of Dina Mitrani Gallery

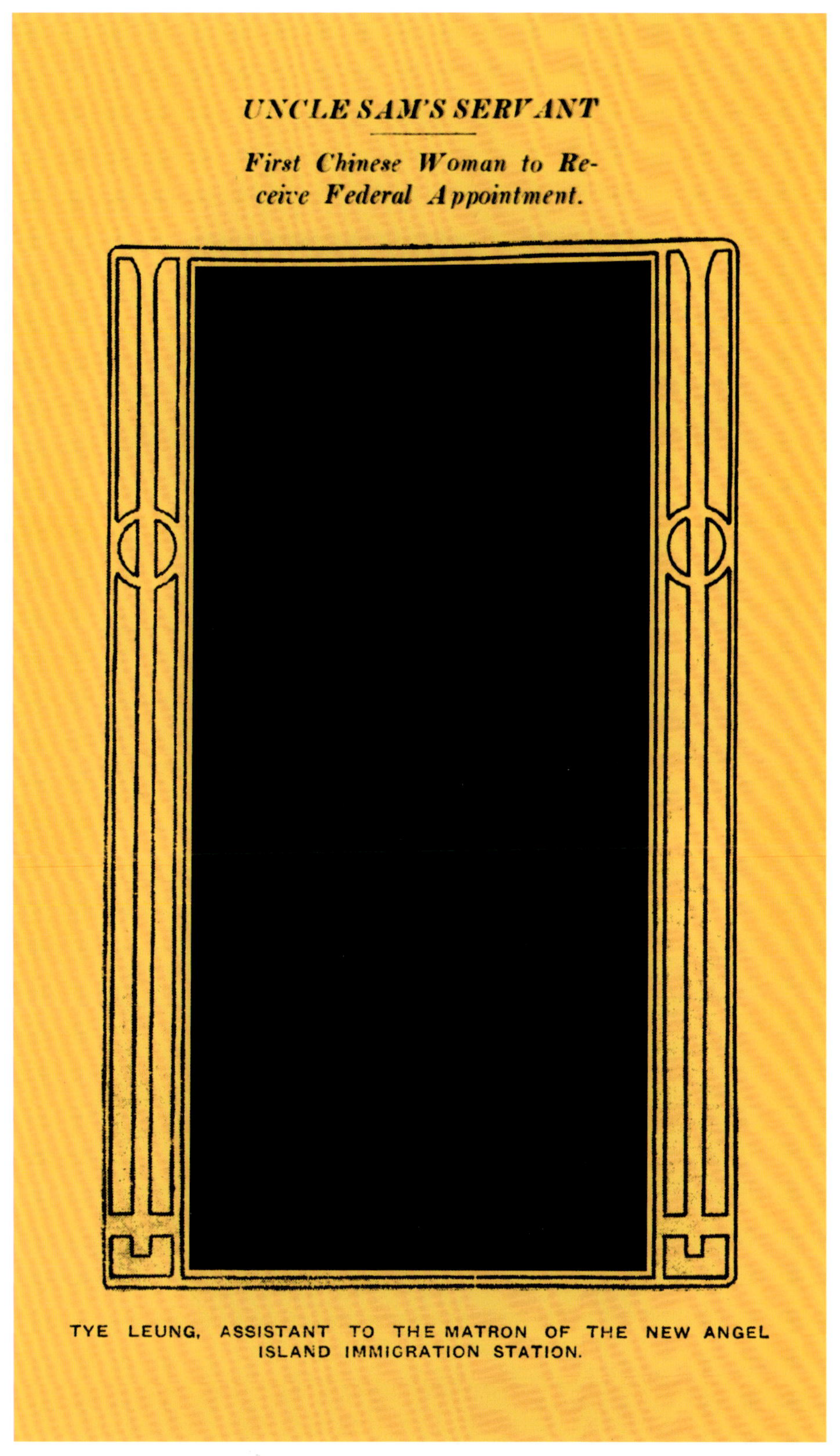

FIGURE 2. Cindy Hwang. *Forgotten Suffragist No. 3 Tye Leung*

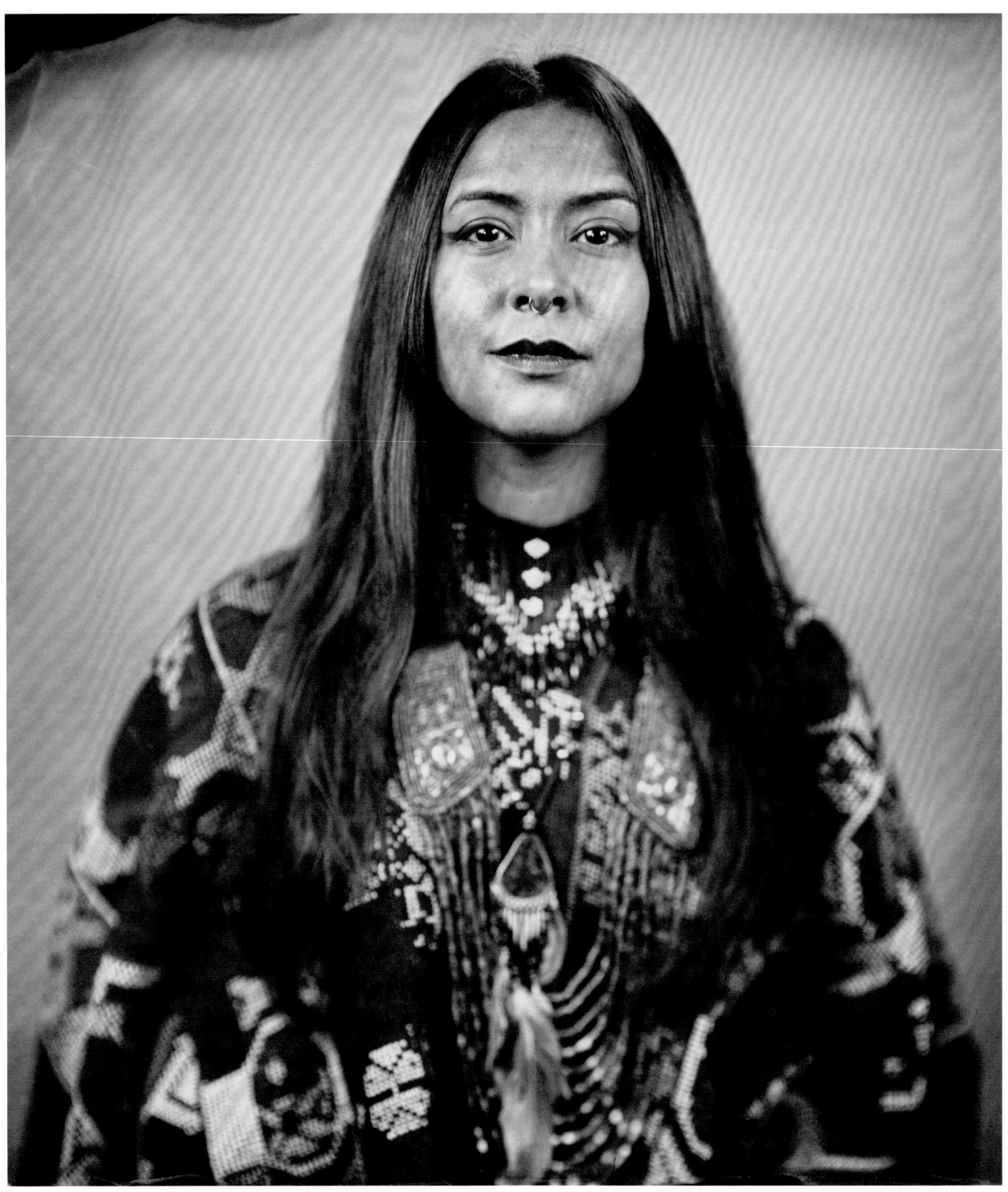

FIGURE 3. Keliy Anderson-Staley. *Daniela*

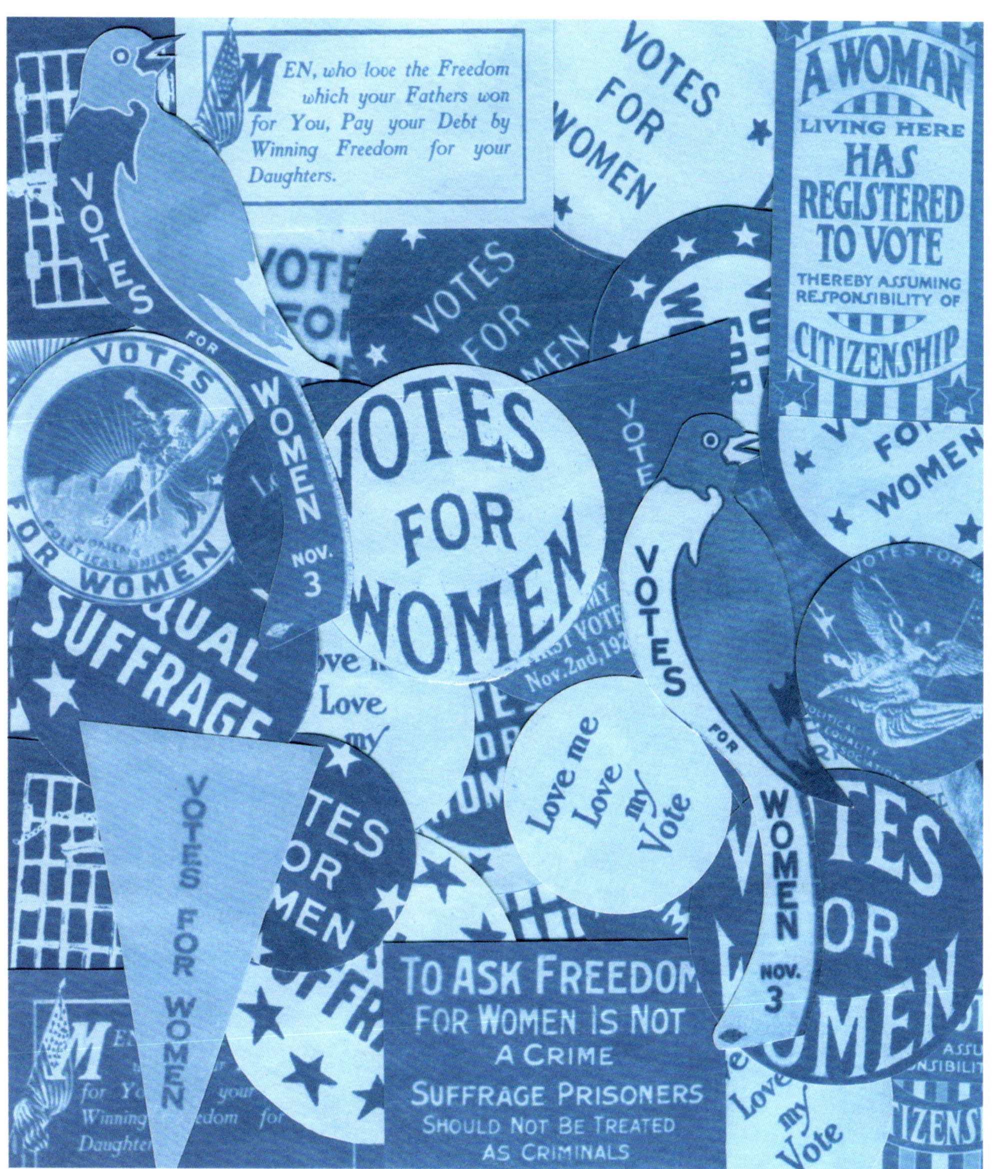

FIGURE 4. Lisa McCarty. *Votes for Women 1920–2020*

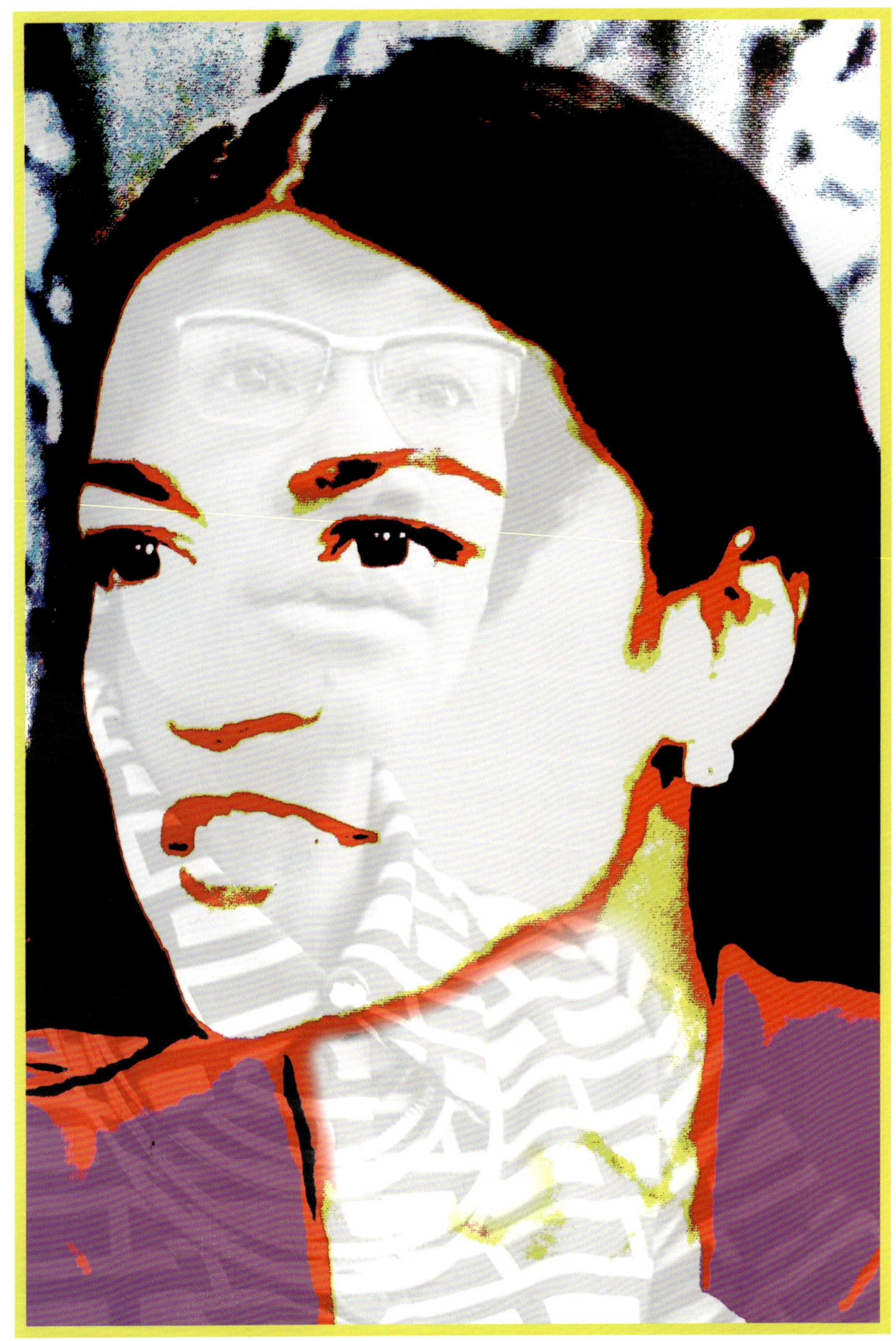

FIGURE 5. Sheri Lynn Behr. *Alexandria and Shirley*

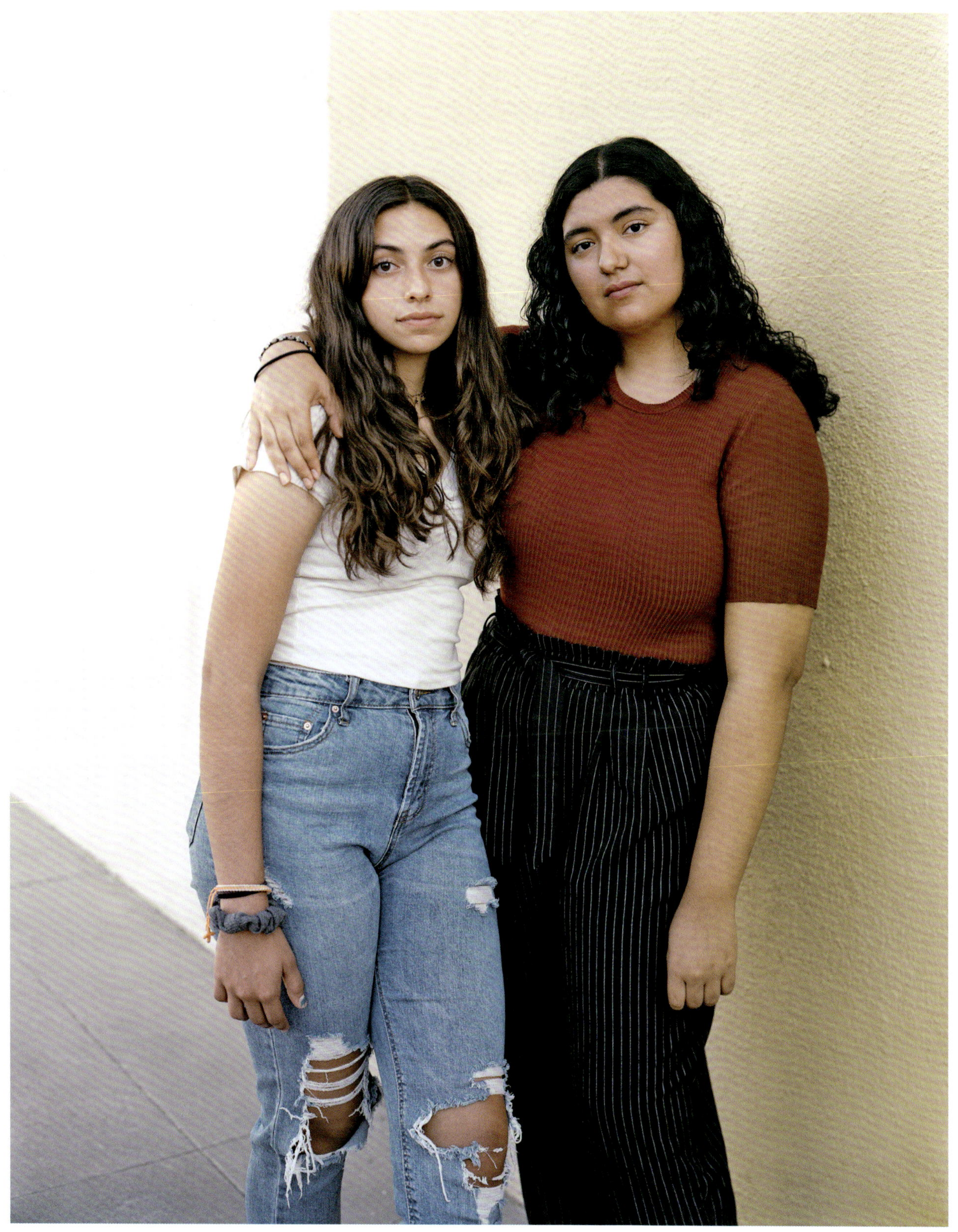

FIGURE 6. Tracy L. Chandler. *Elize and Lenee*

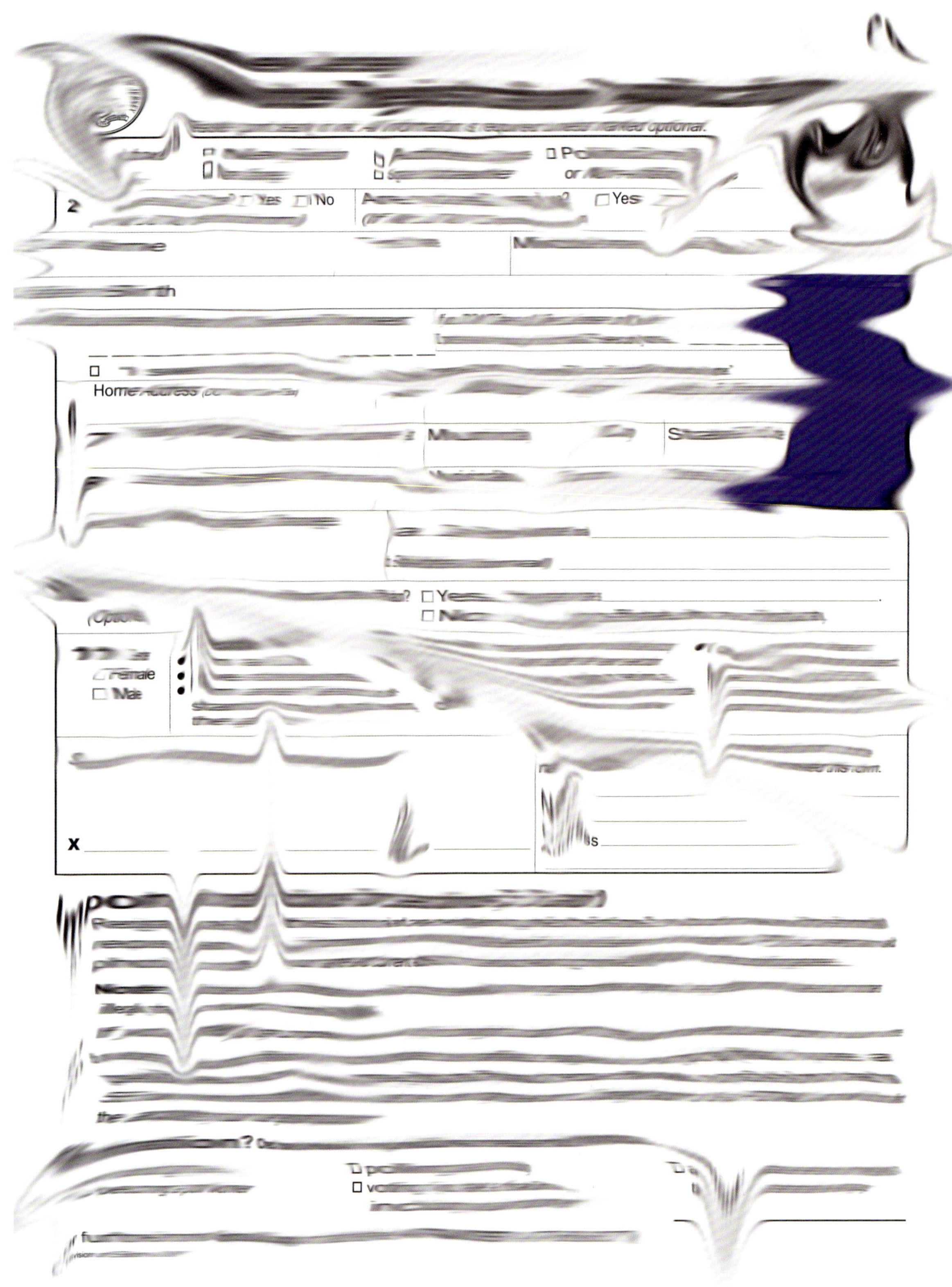

FIGURE 7. Frances Jakubek. *New Jersey Voter Registration Form*

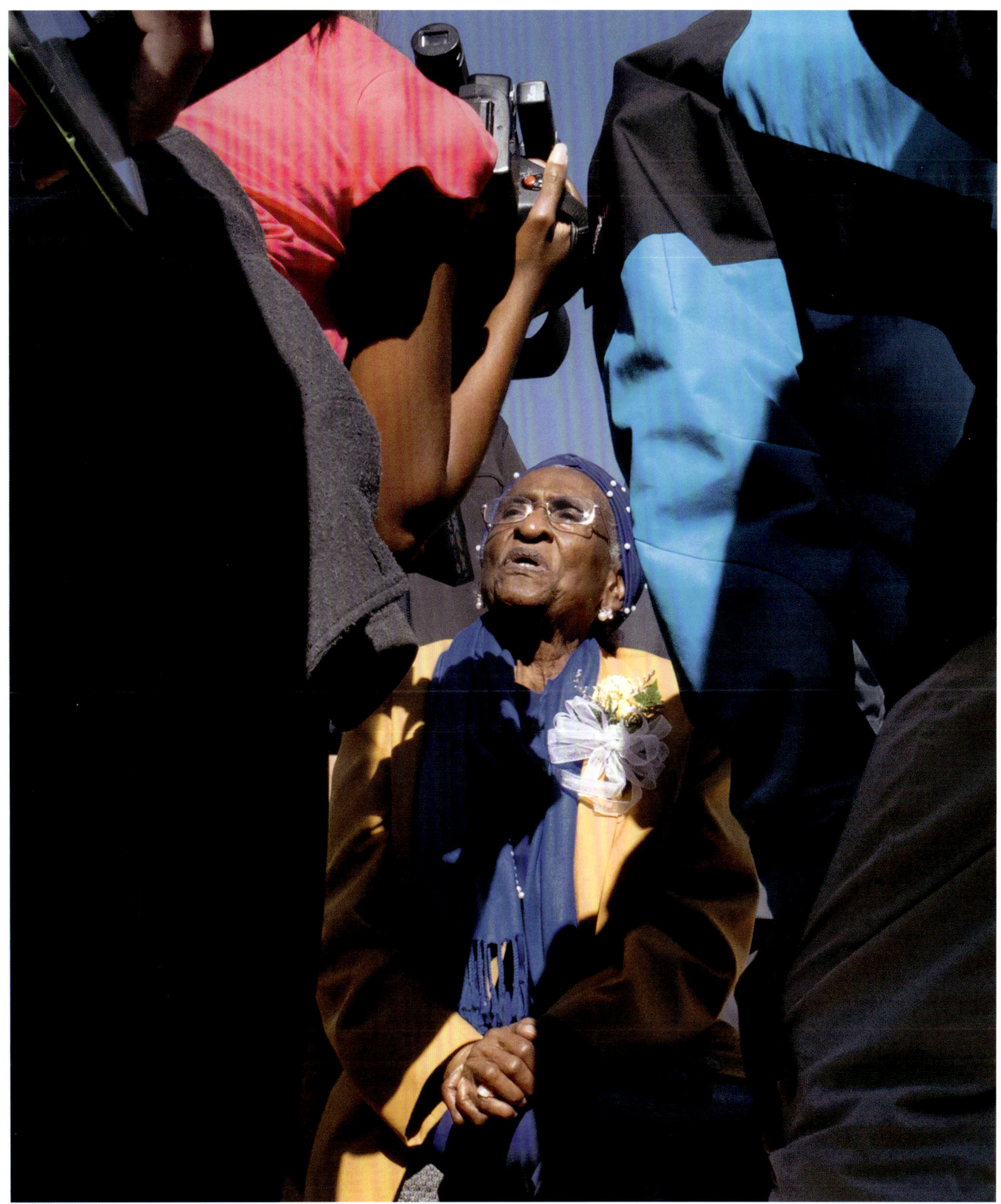

FIGURE 8. Carolyn McIntyre Norton and Betty Press. *Ellie Davis Dahmer*

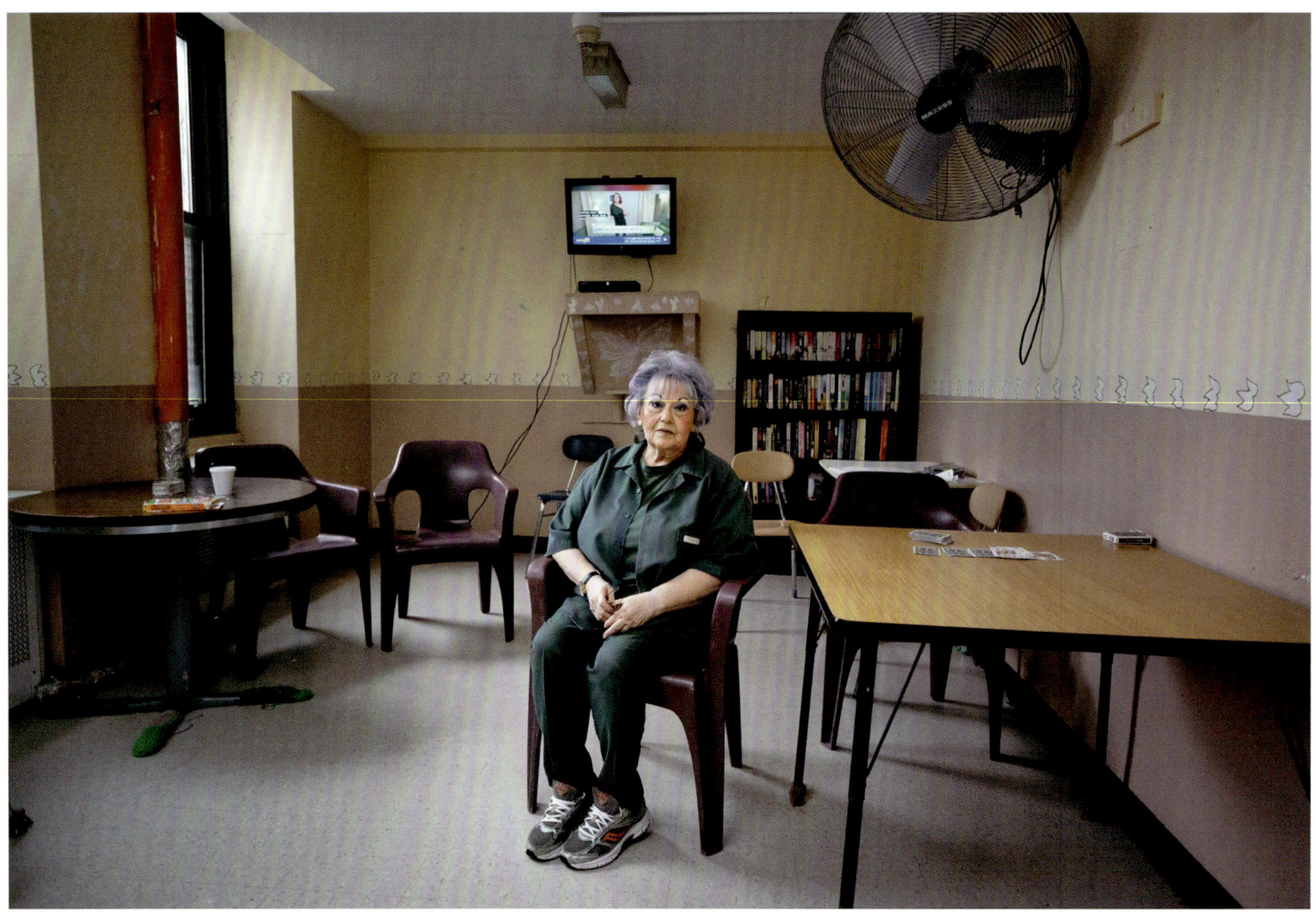

FIGURE 9. Sara Bennett. *Linda*

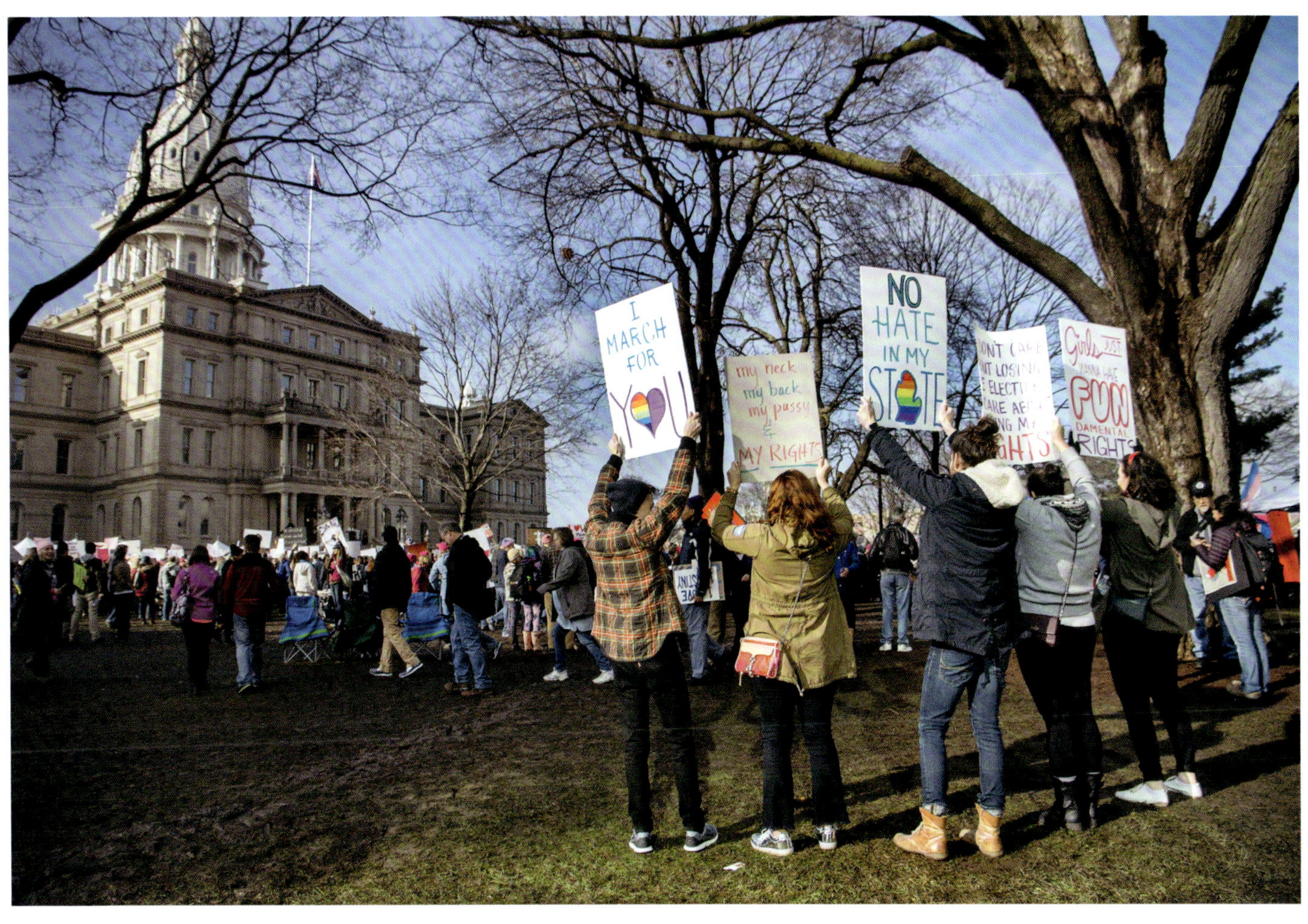

FIGURE 10. Kris Sanford. *Women's March, Lansing, Michigan*

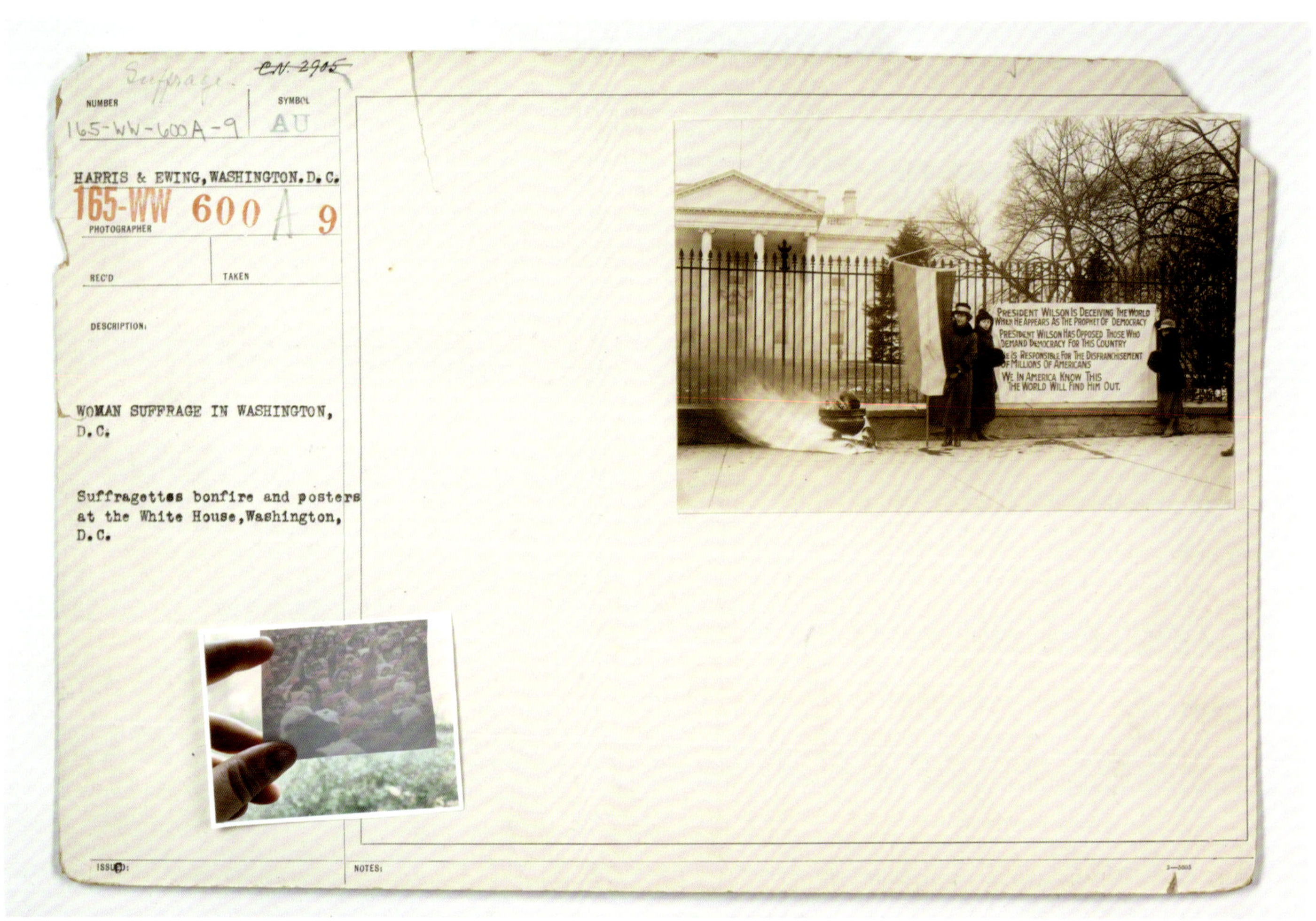

FIGURE 11. Kristine Thompson. *Suffrage in Washington, D.C. 1919–2017*

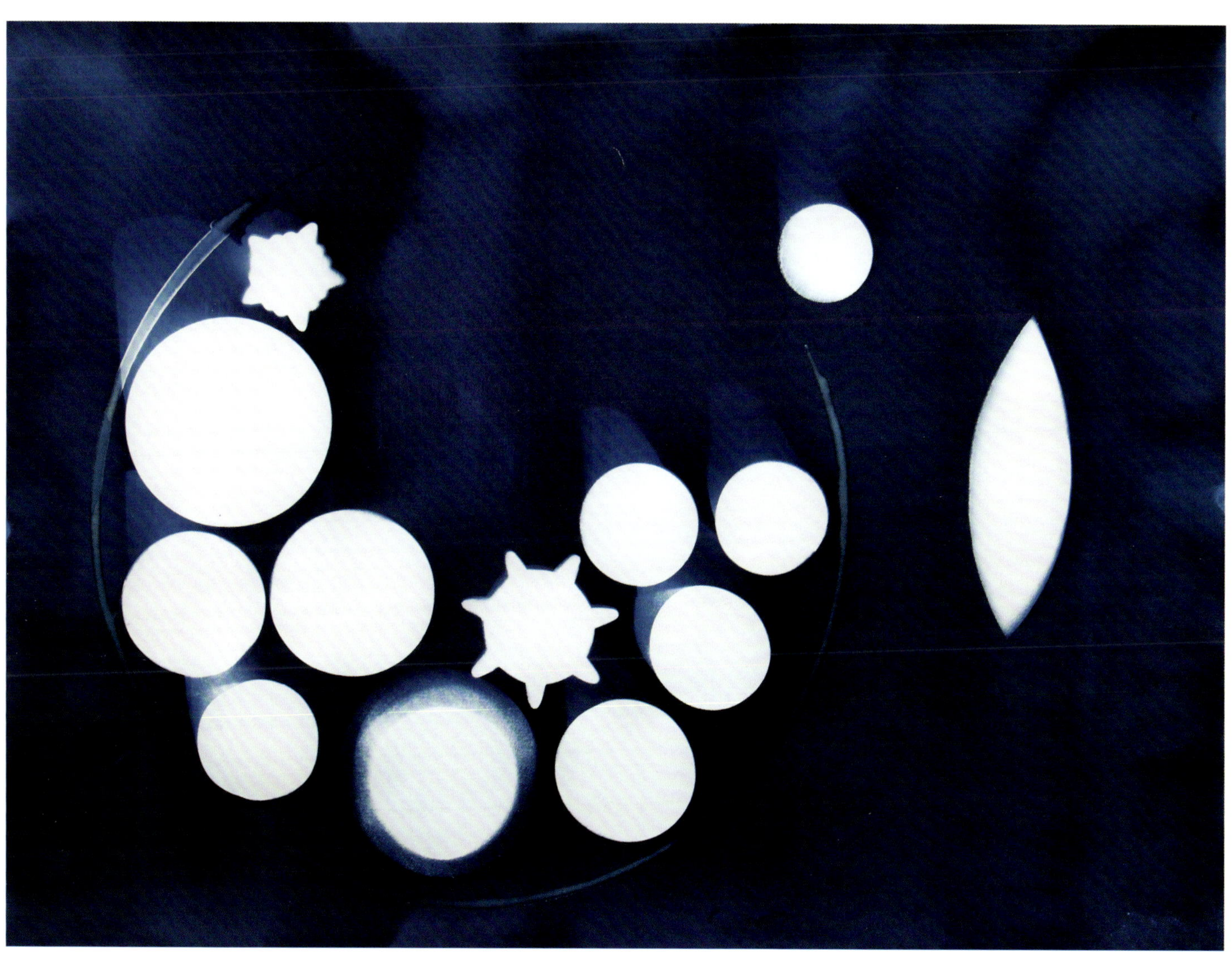

FIGURE 12. Priya Kambli. *Devhara #1*

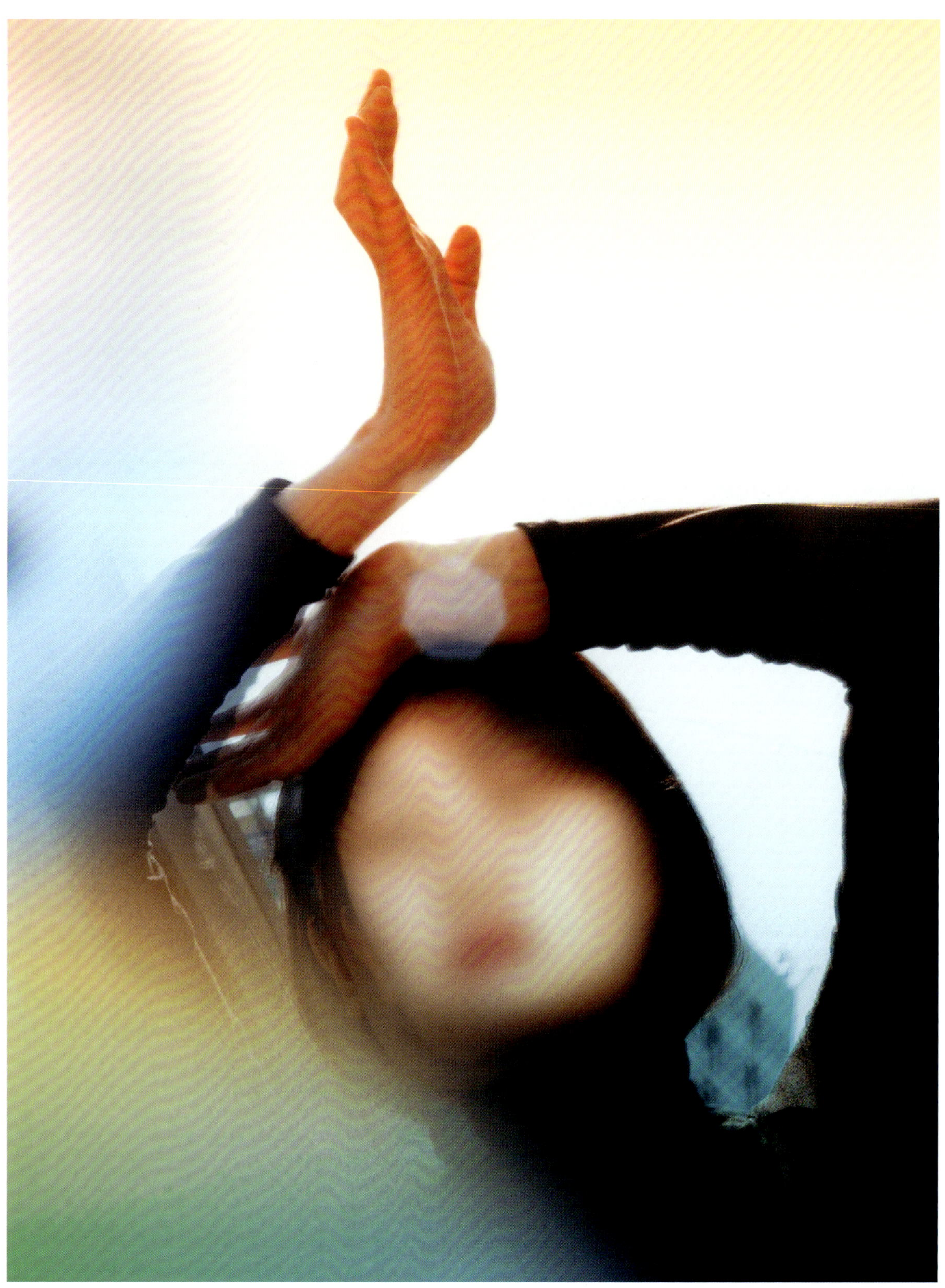

FIGURE 13. Ina Jang. *Hada 2*

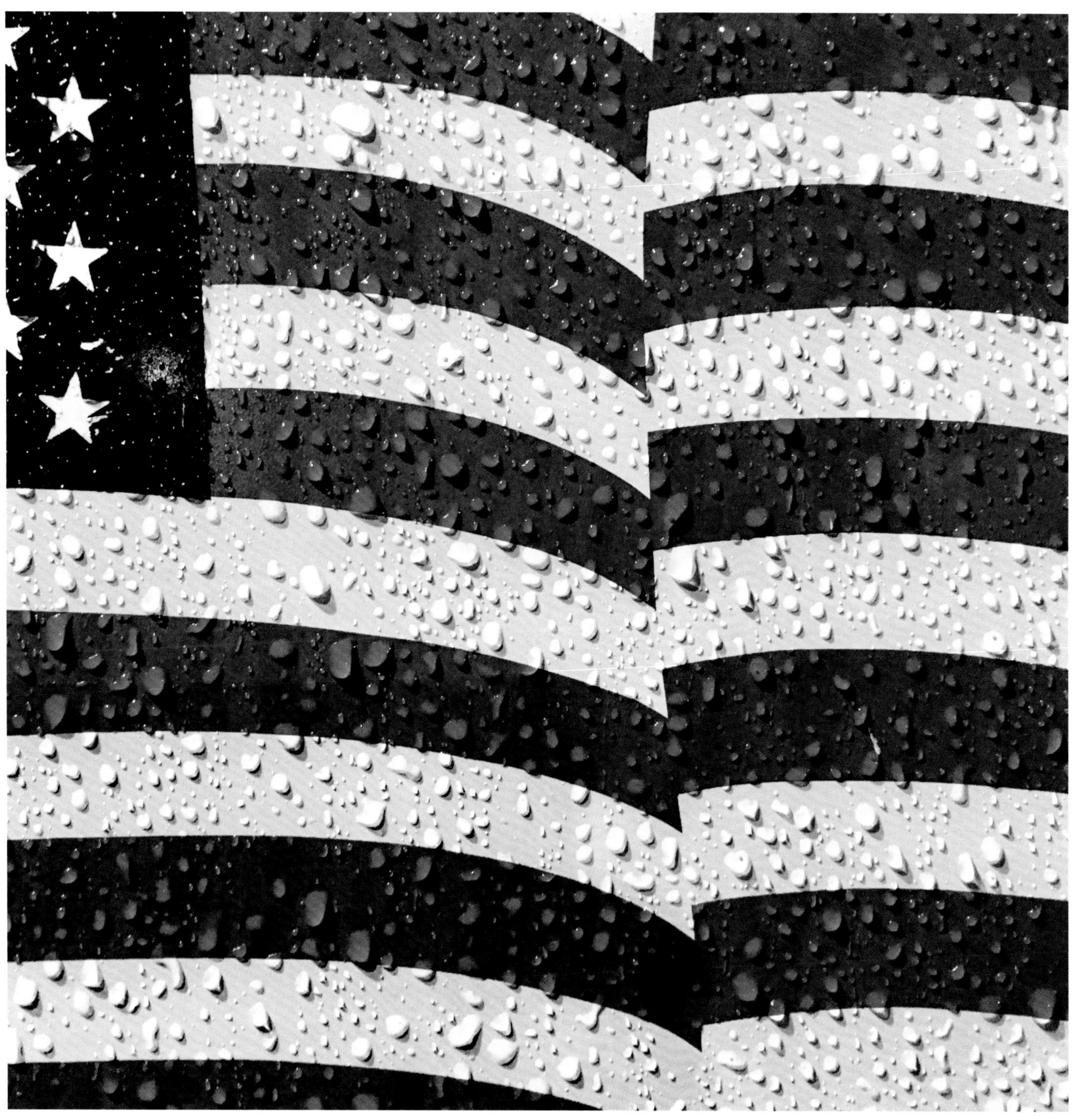

FIGURE 14. Amy Thompson Avishai. *Voting Day, Easthampton, Massachusetts*

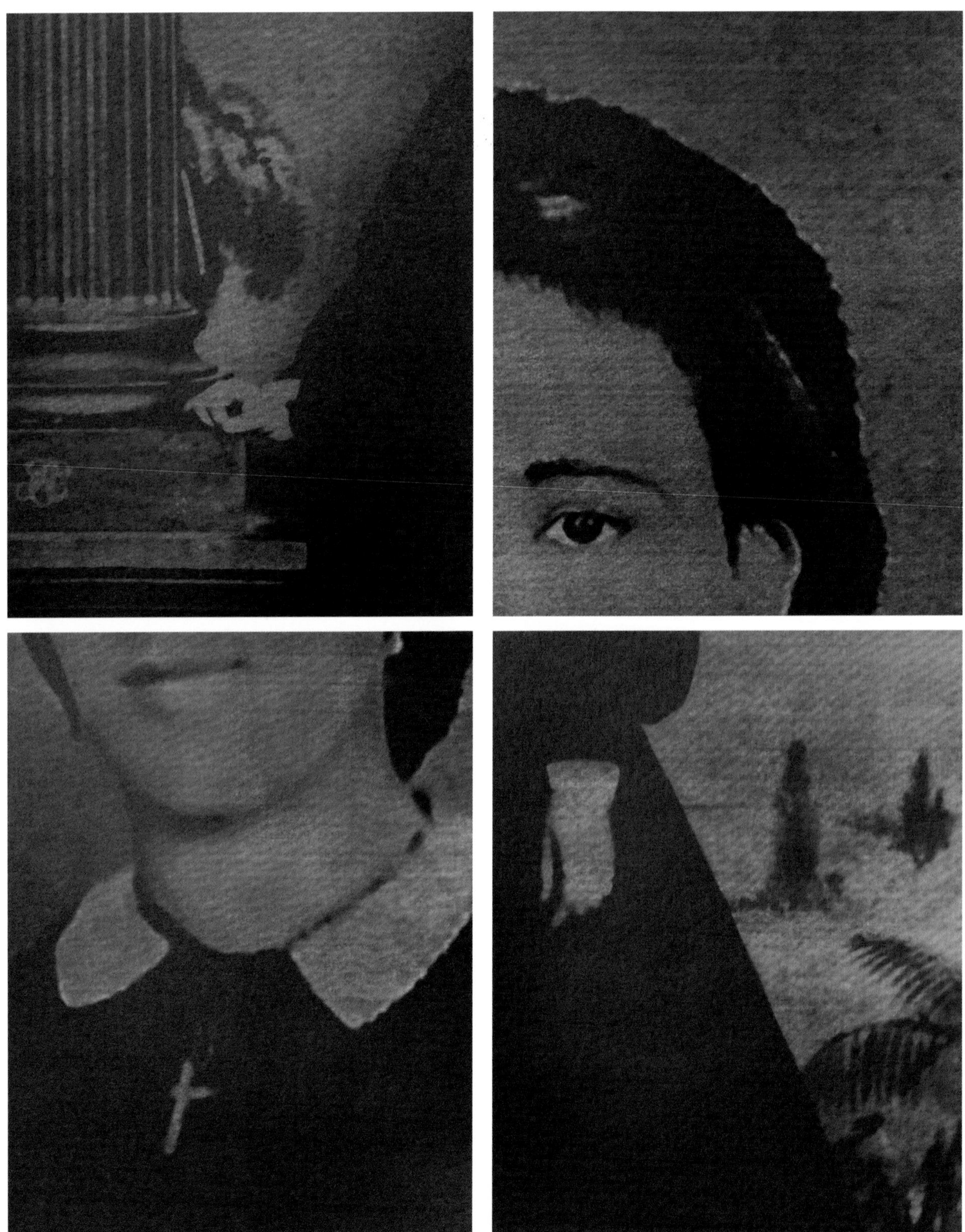

FIGURE 15. Lily Brooks. *Henriette DeLille*

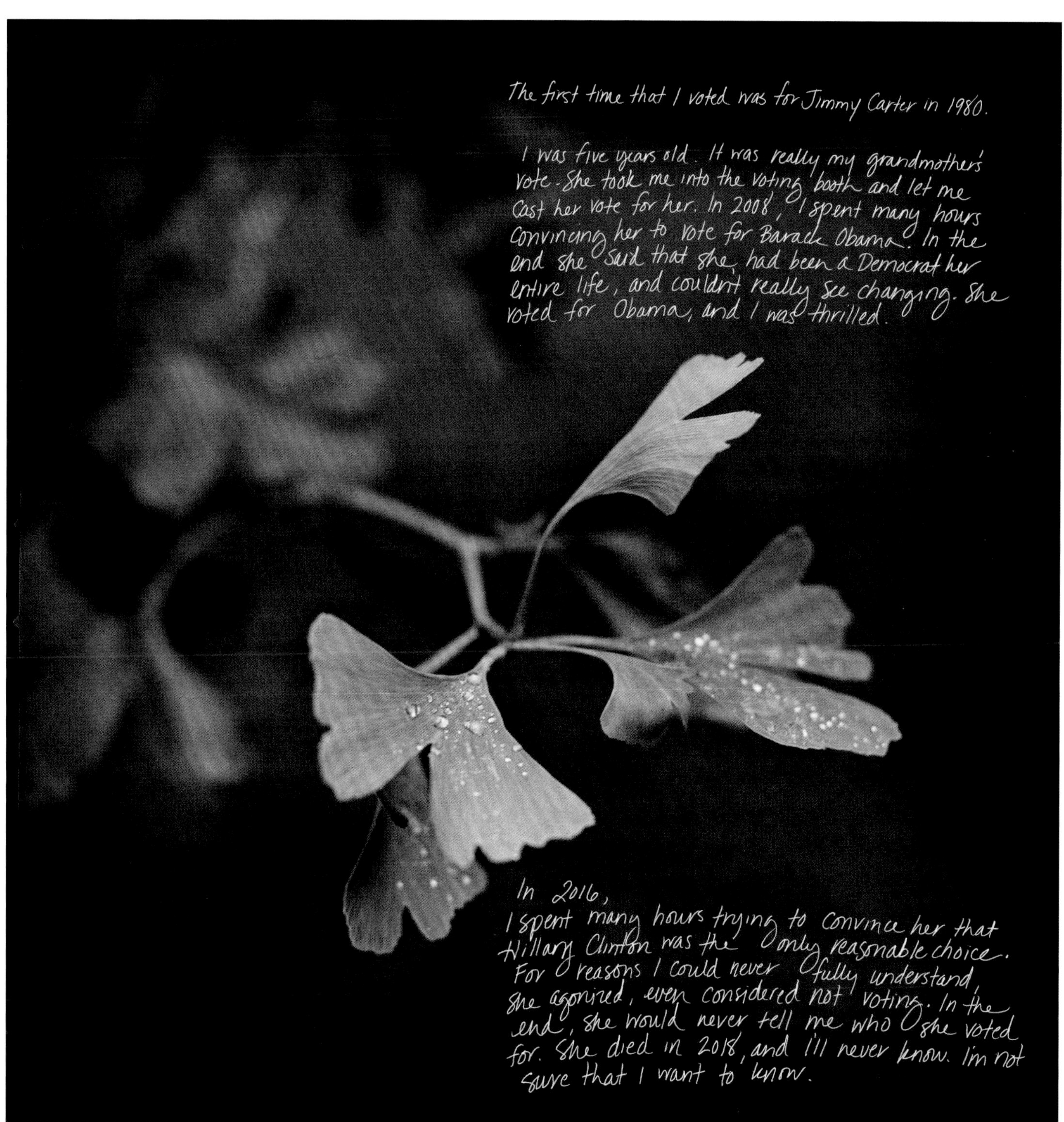

FIGURE 16. Christa Bowden. *I'll Never Know*

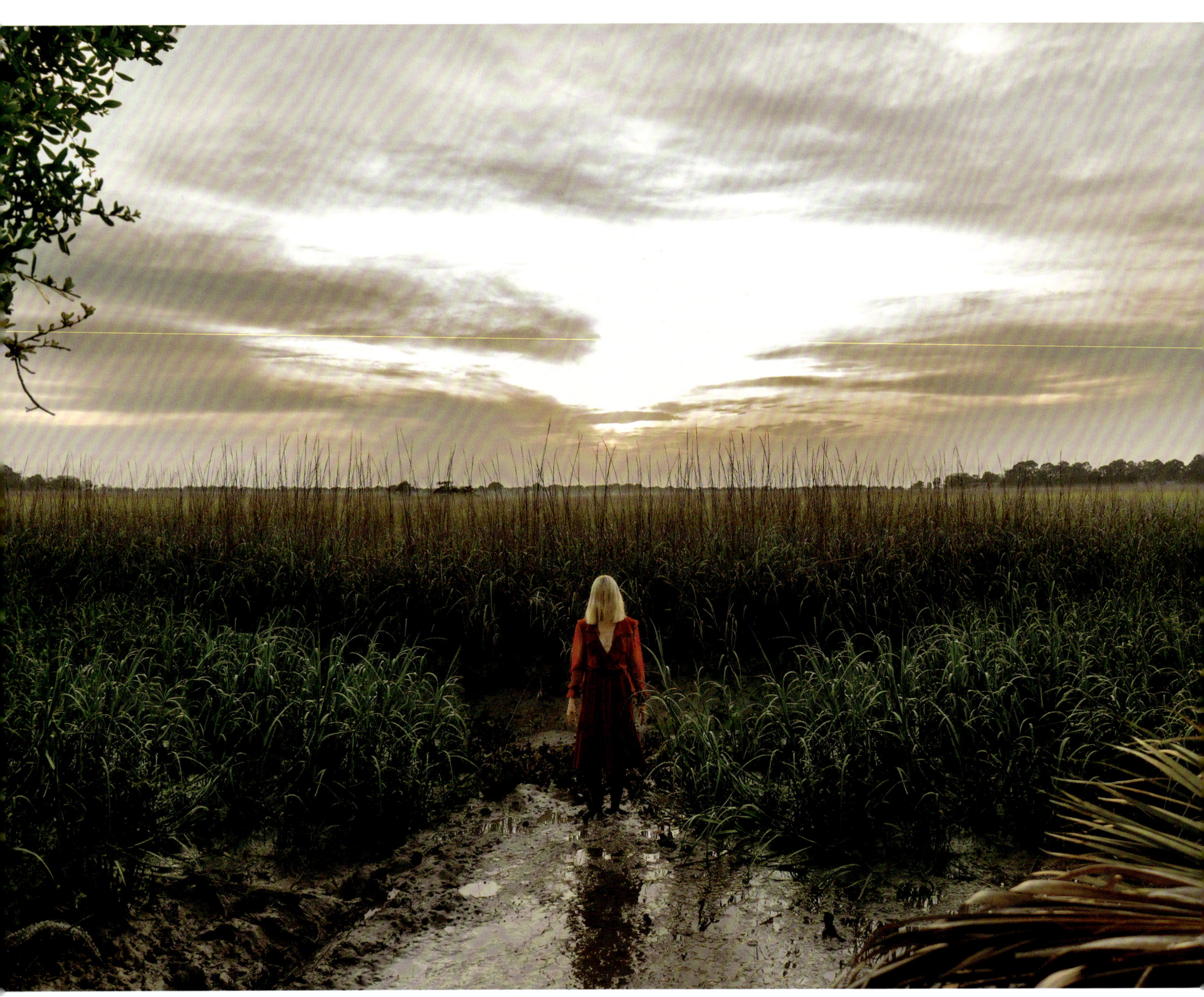

FIGURE 17. Bootsy Holler. *Tybee Island*

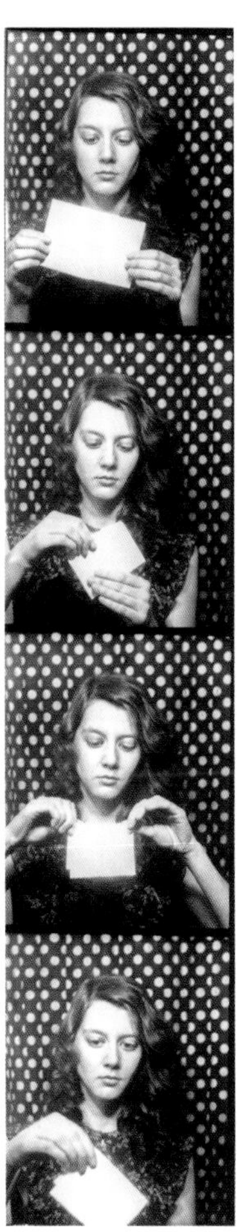

FIGURE 18. Kat Kiernan.

The Voting Booth

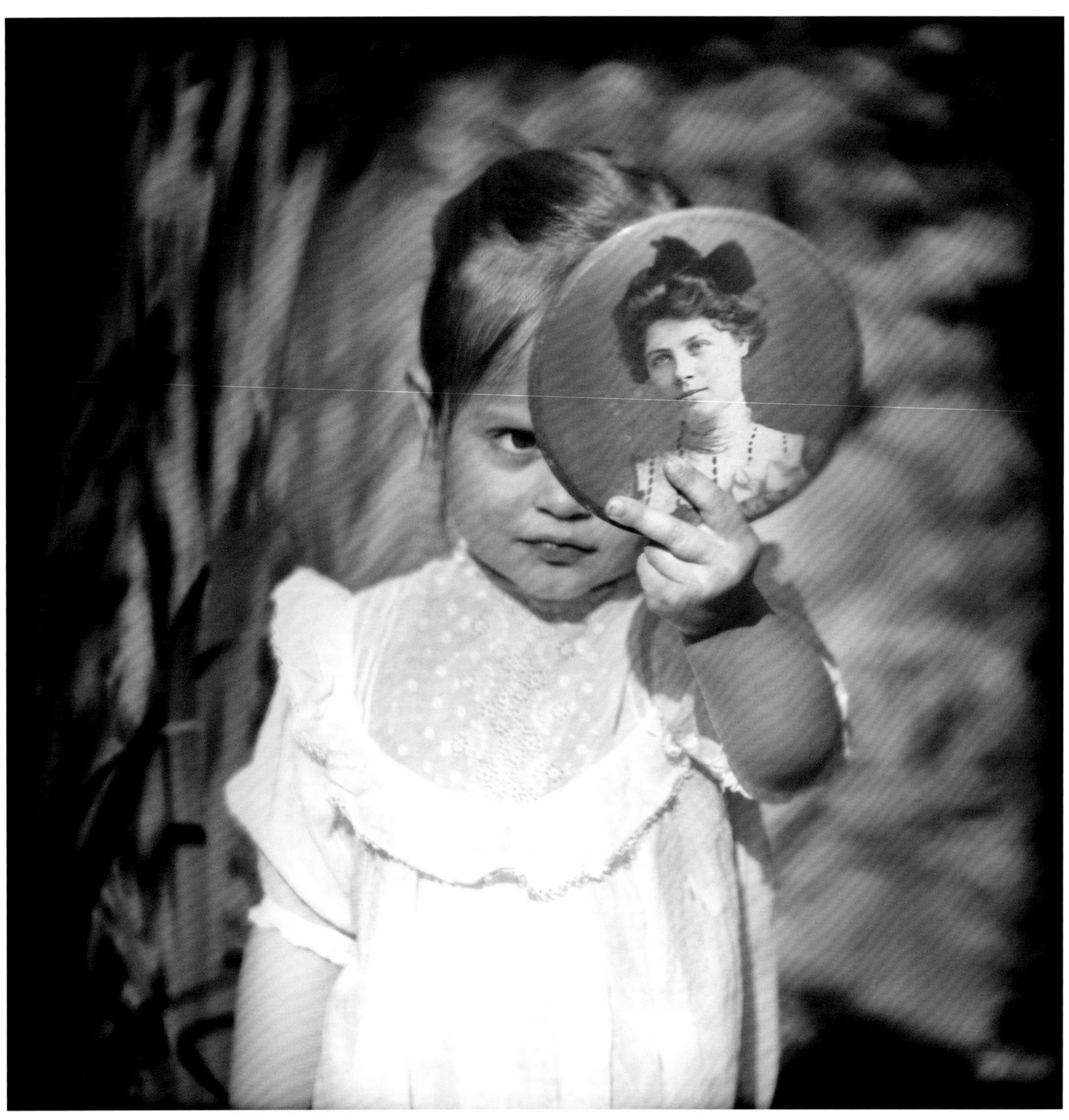

FIGURE 19. Anne Berry. *1920 to 2020*

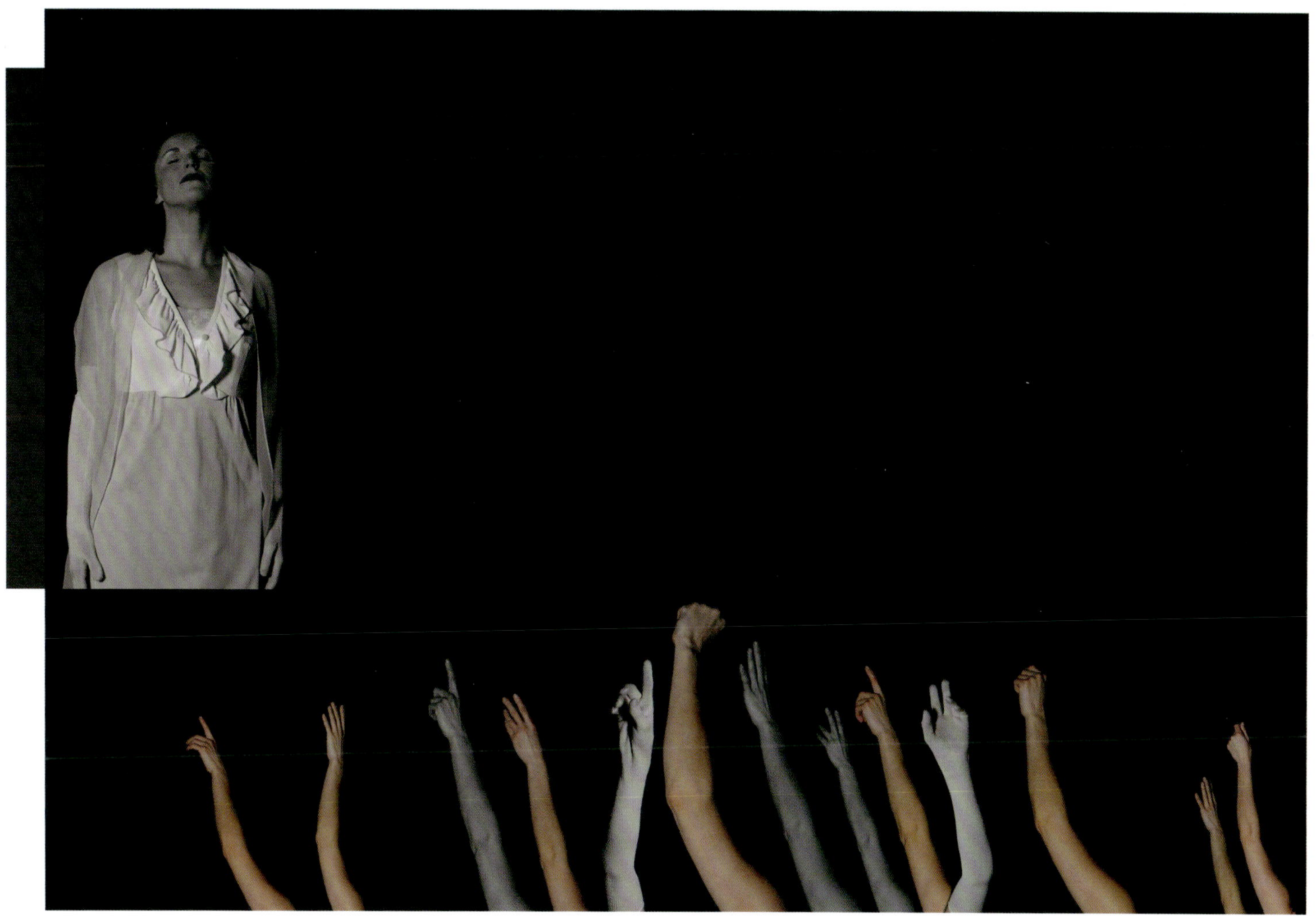

FIGURE 20. Claudia Ruiz Gustafson. *Forward*

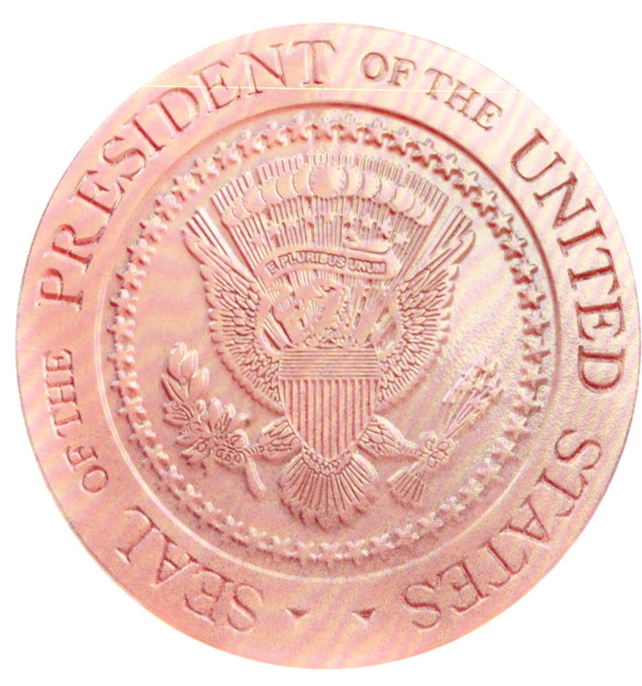

FIGURE 21. Katie Benjamin. *Study 03*

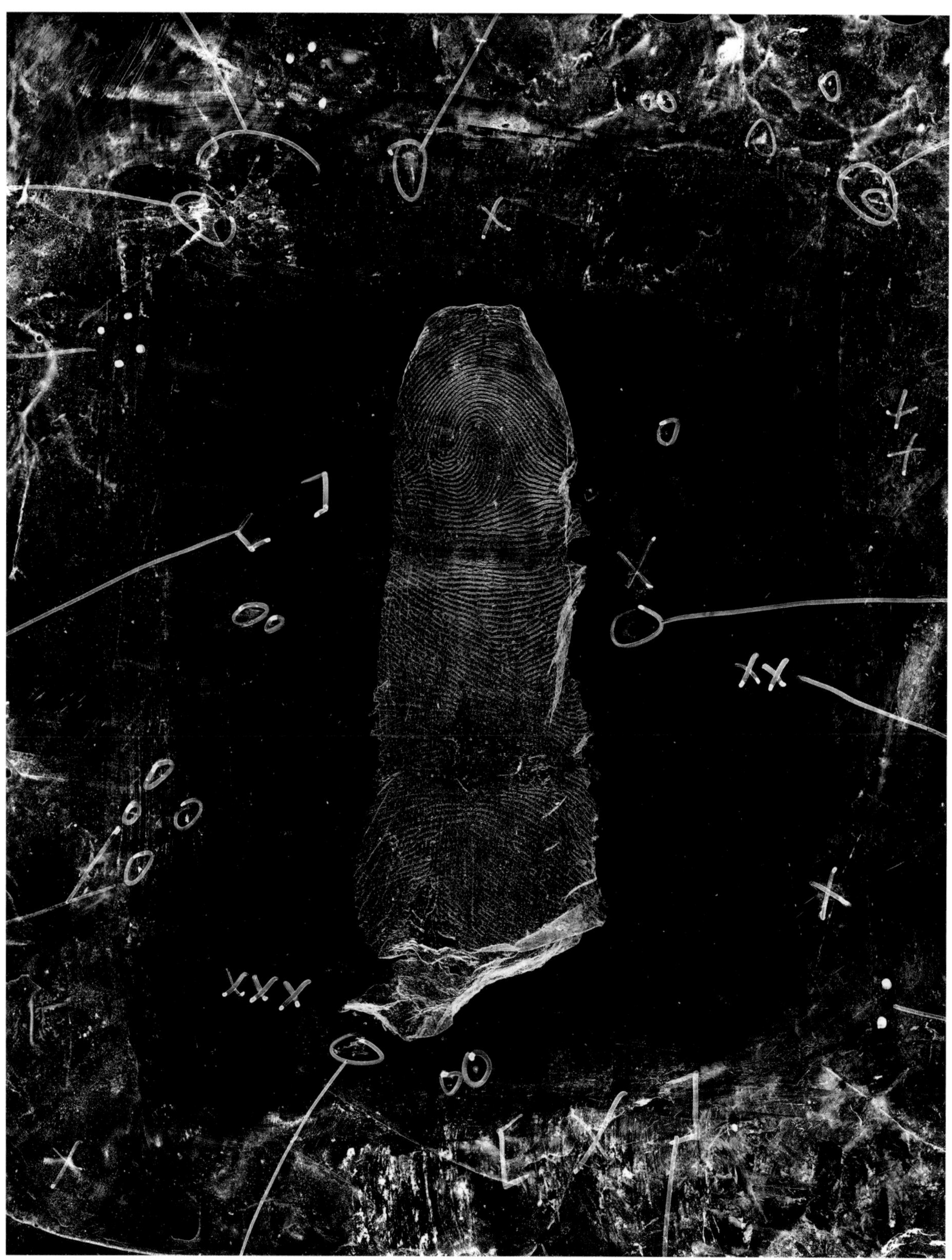

FIGURE 22. Claire A. Warden. *No. 15 Genetics*

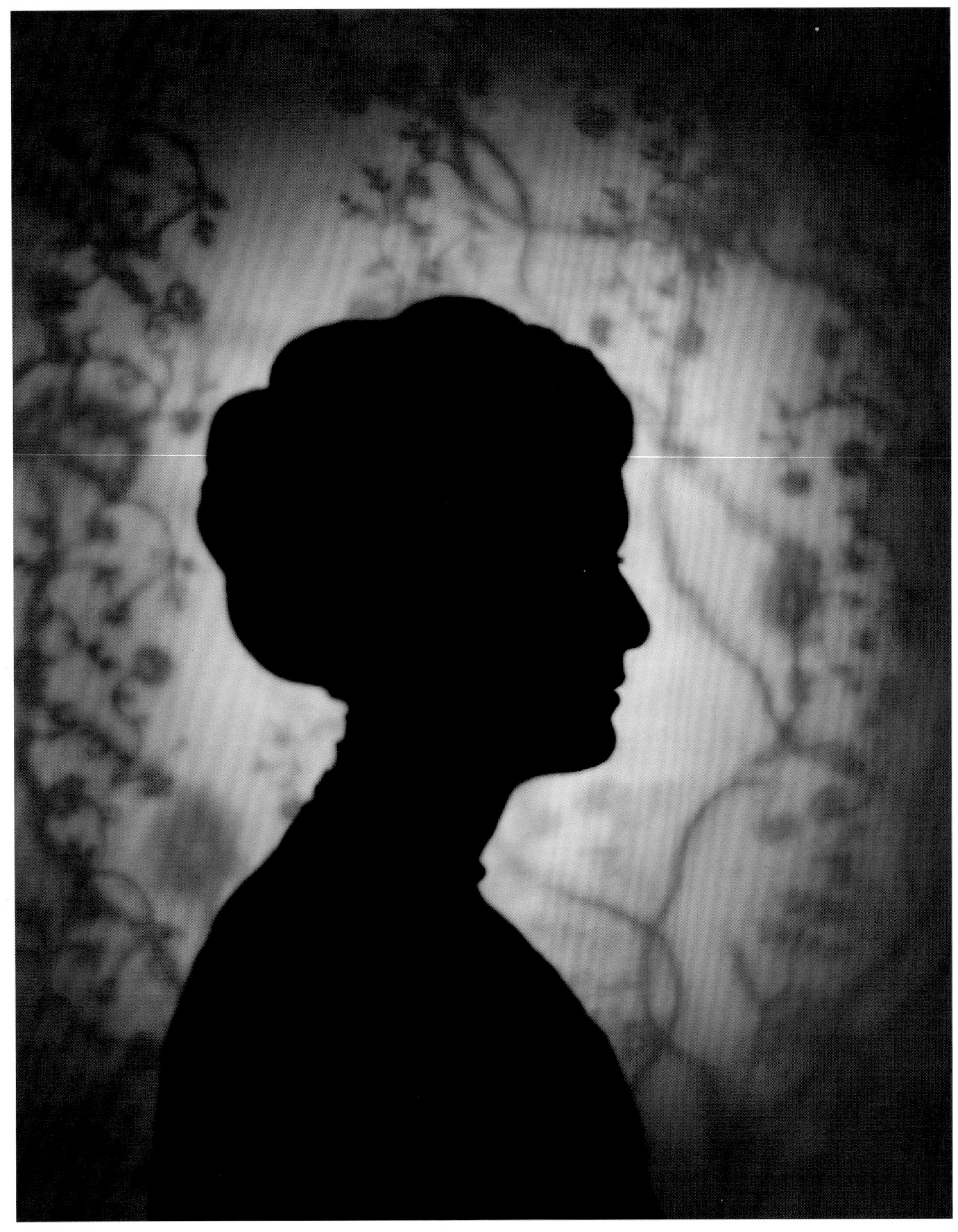

FIGURE 23. Susan kae Grant. *Katharine (Mrs. Robert A.) Morton (1878–1956)*

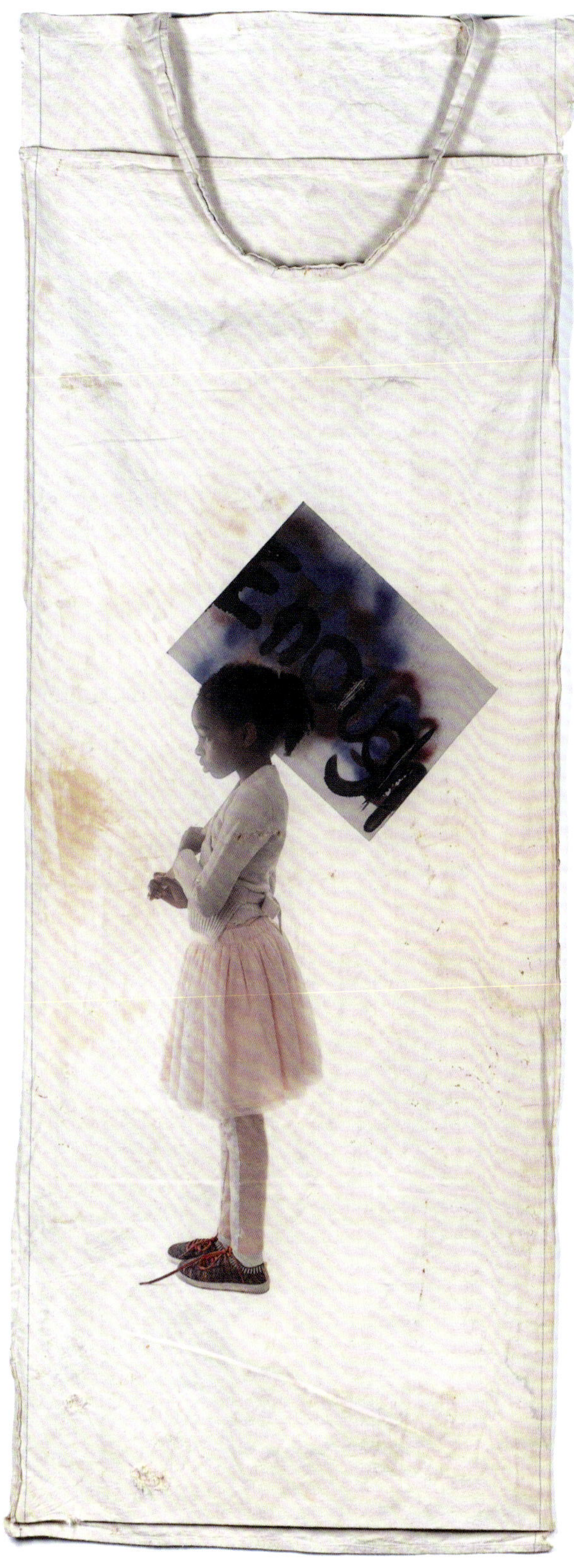

FIGURE 24. Letitia Huckaby. *Sugar and Spice*

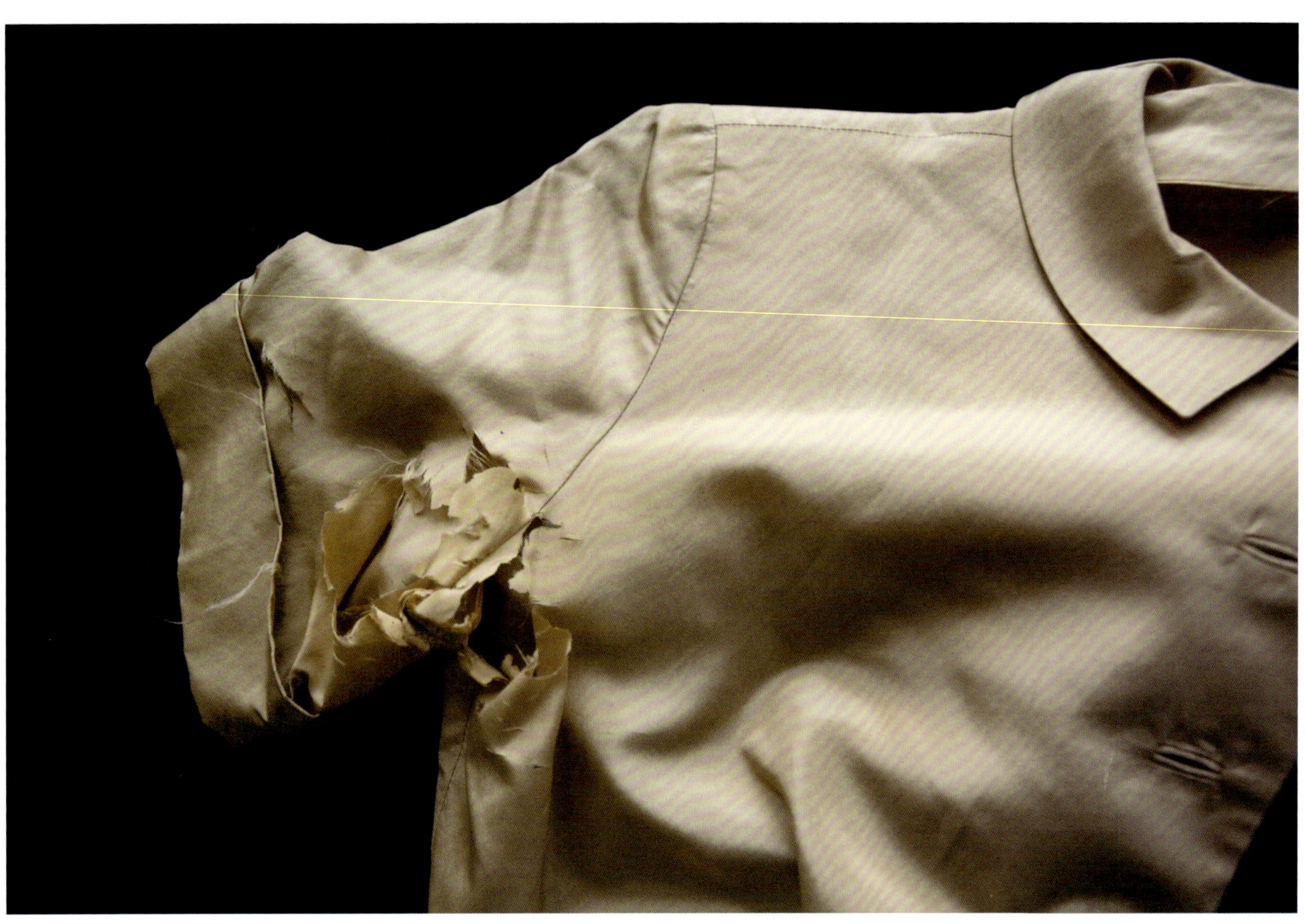

FIGURE 25. Gail Samuelson. *Silk Blouse*

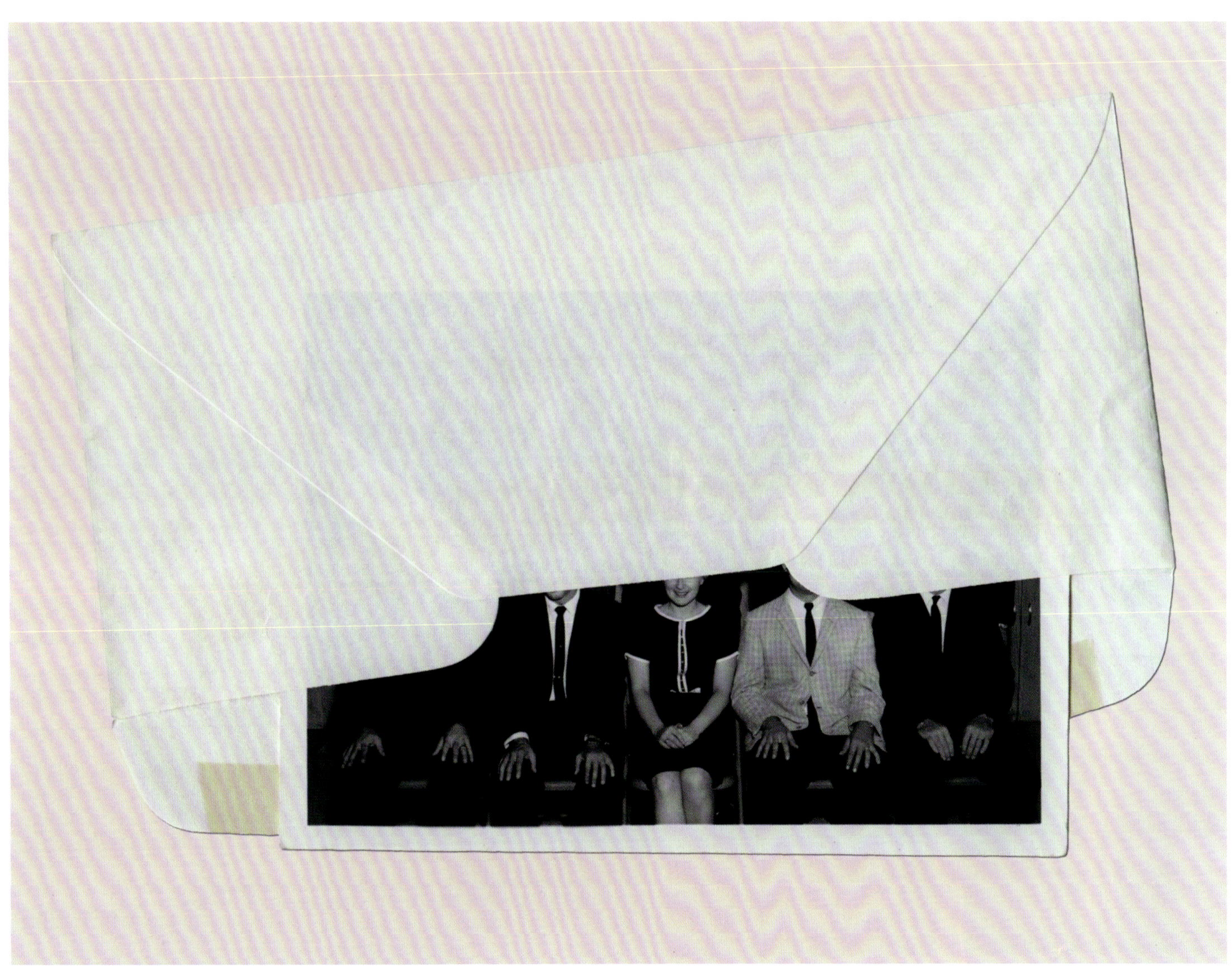

FIGURE 26. Rana Young. *Untitled (Probe 1)*

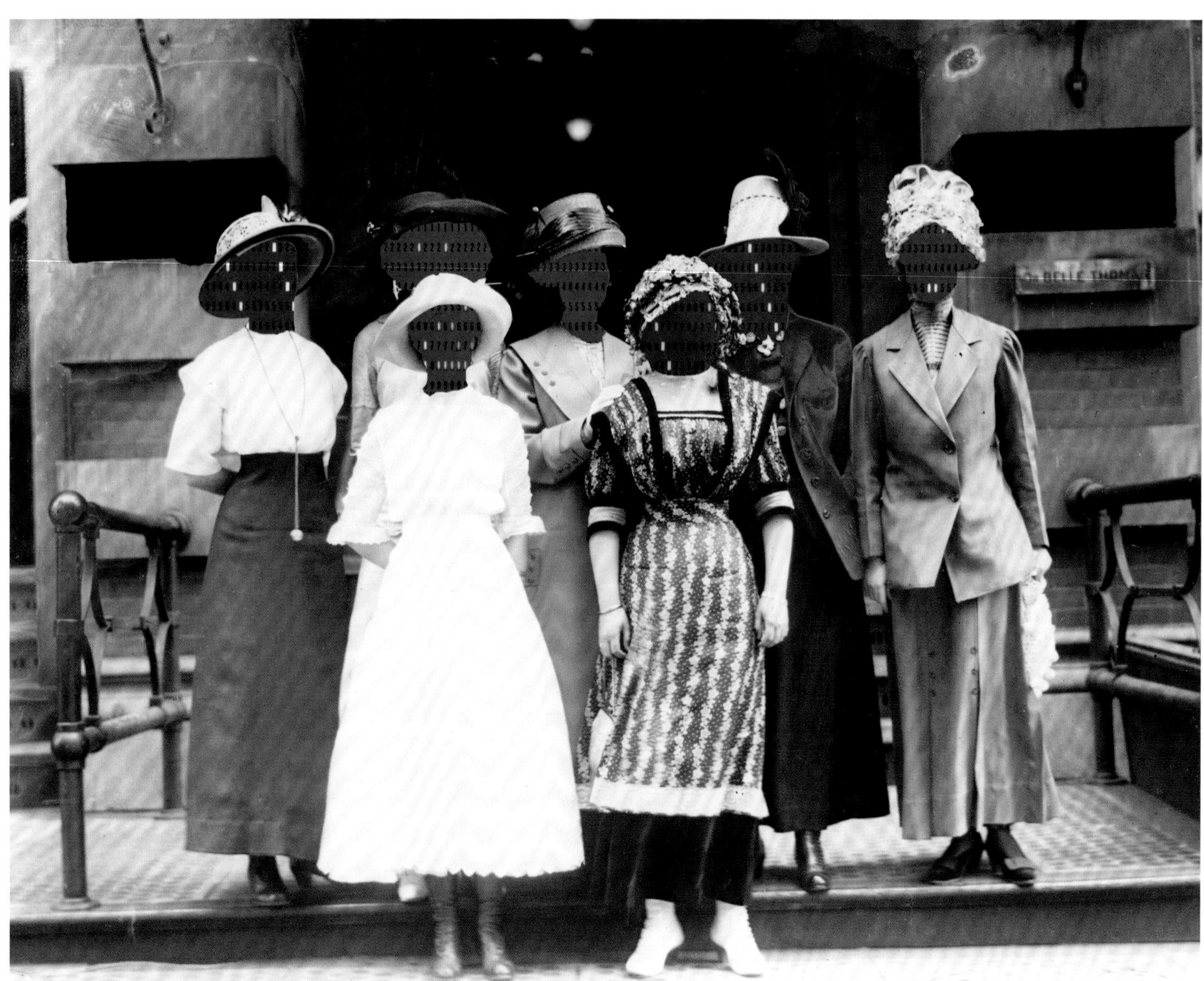

FIGURE 27. Sarah Hadley. *On the Steps*

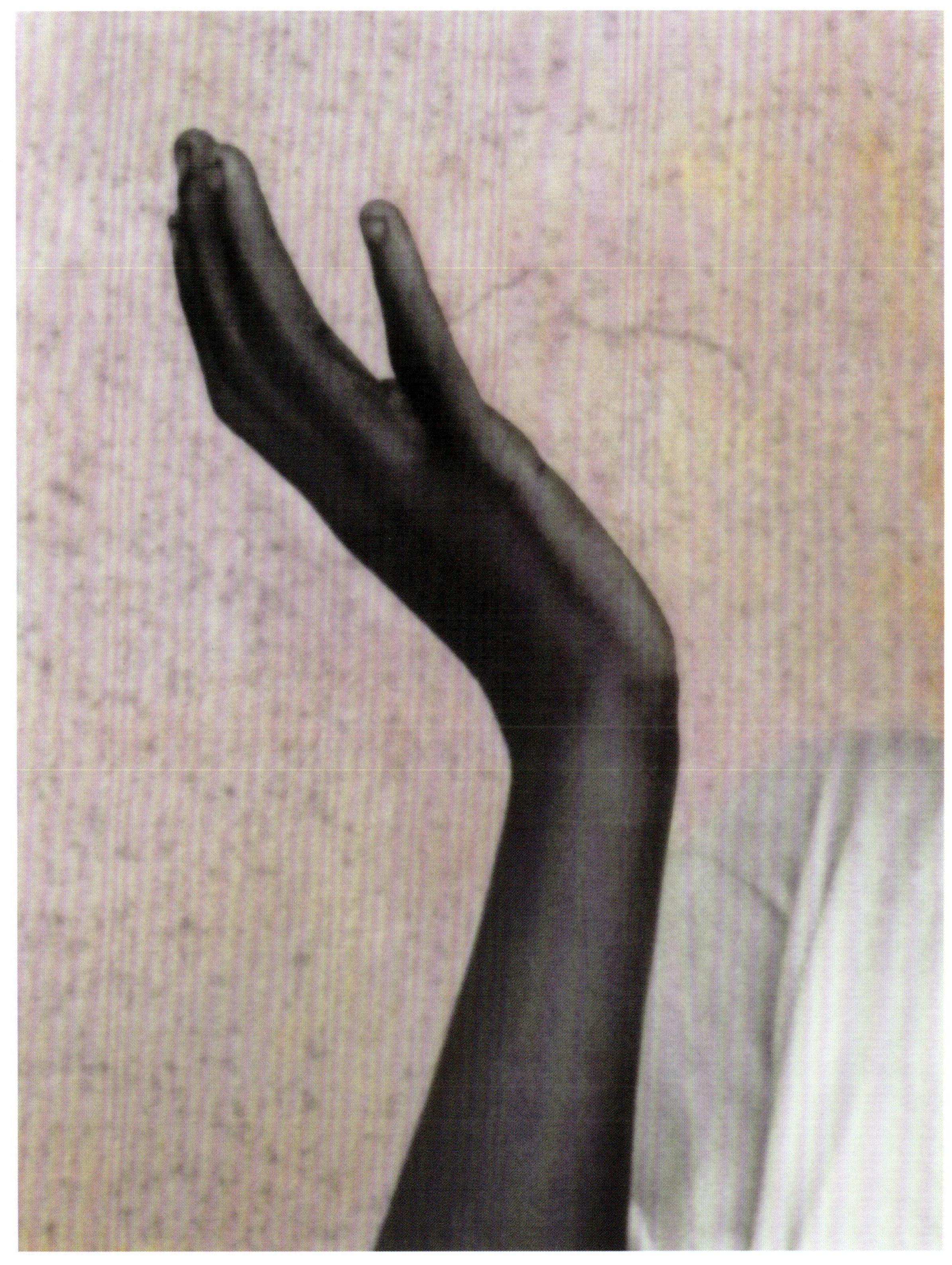

FIGURE 28. Yael Eban and Brea Souders. *Untitled*

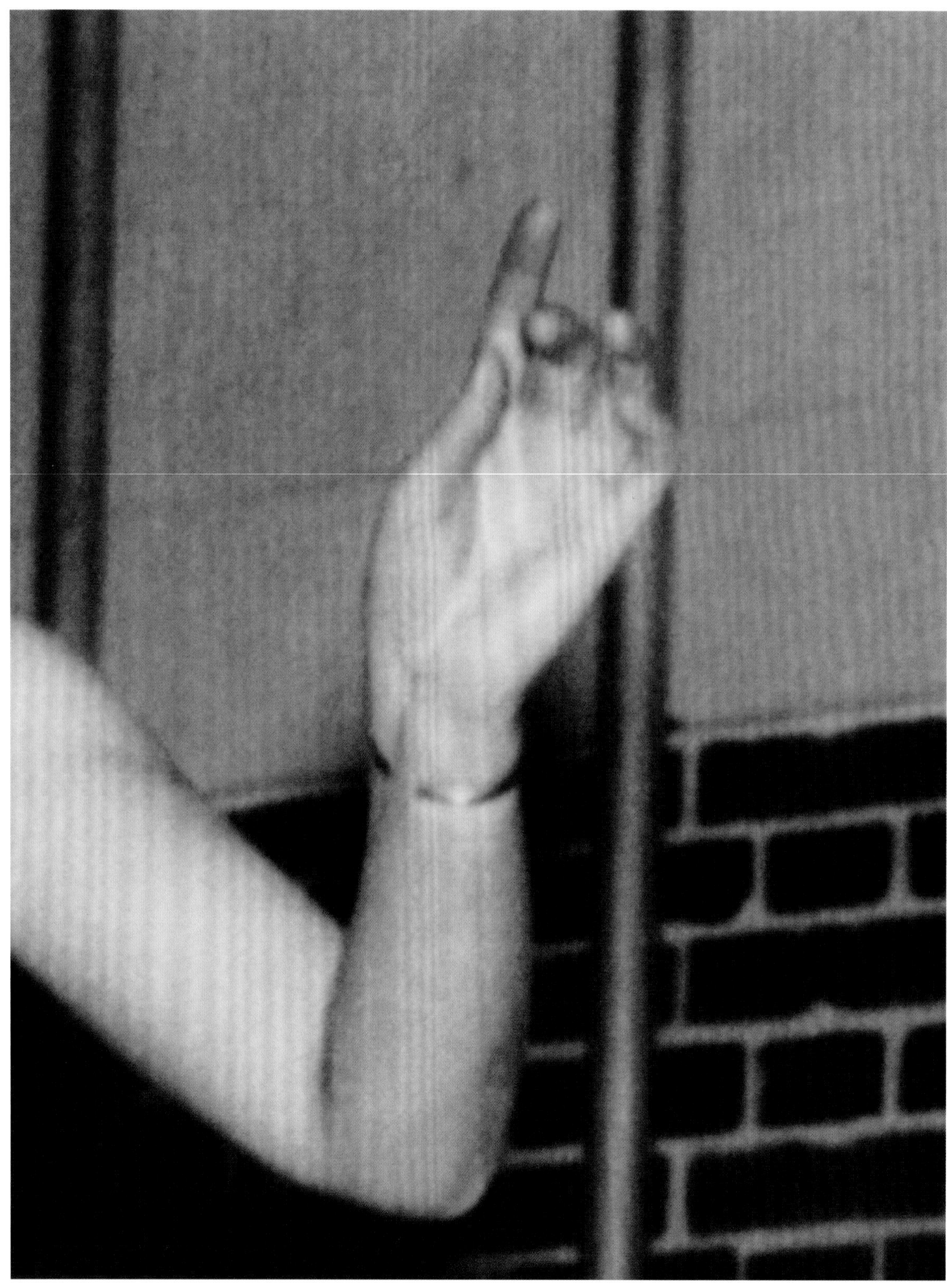

FIGURE 29. Yael Eban and Brea Souders. *Untitled*

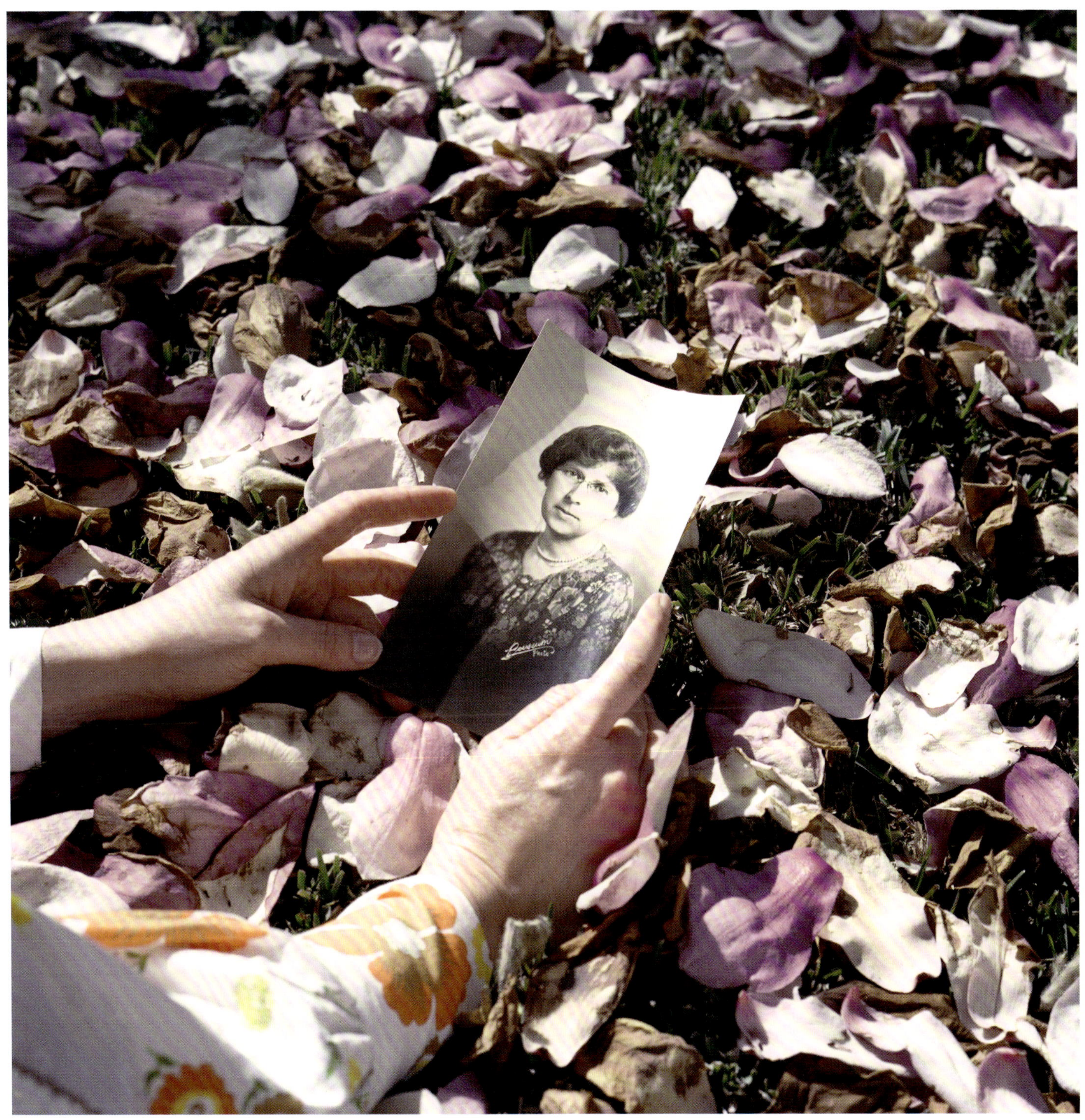

FIGURE 30. Aline Smithson. From *Women I Don't Know*

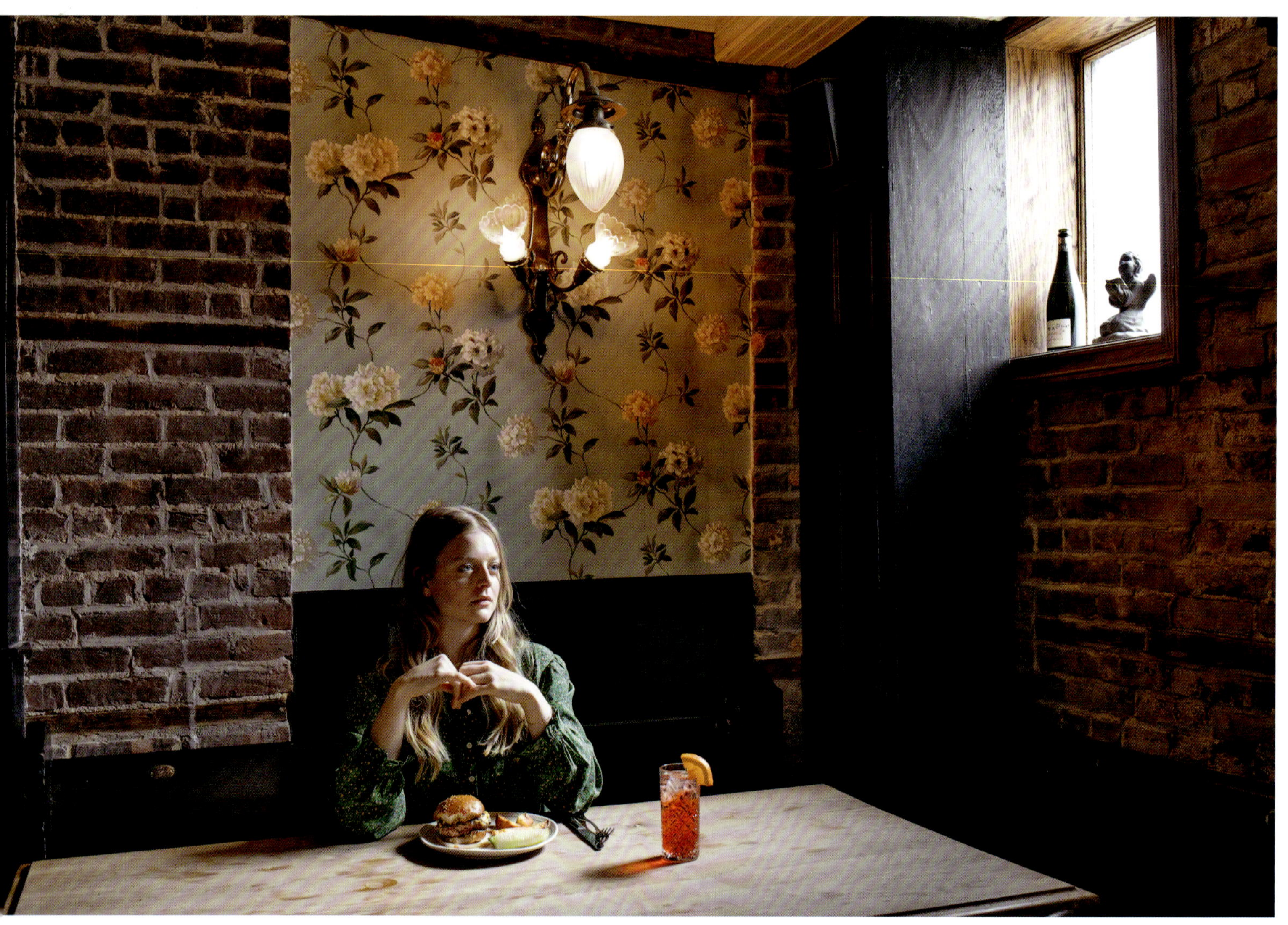

FIGURE 31. Frances F. Denny. *Anna (Red Hook Tavern), 2020*

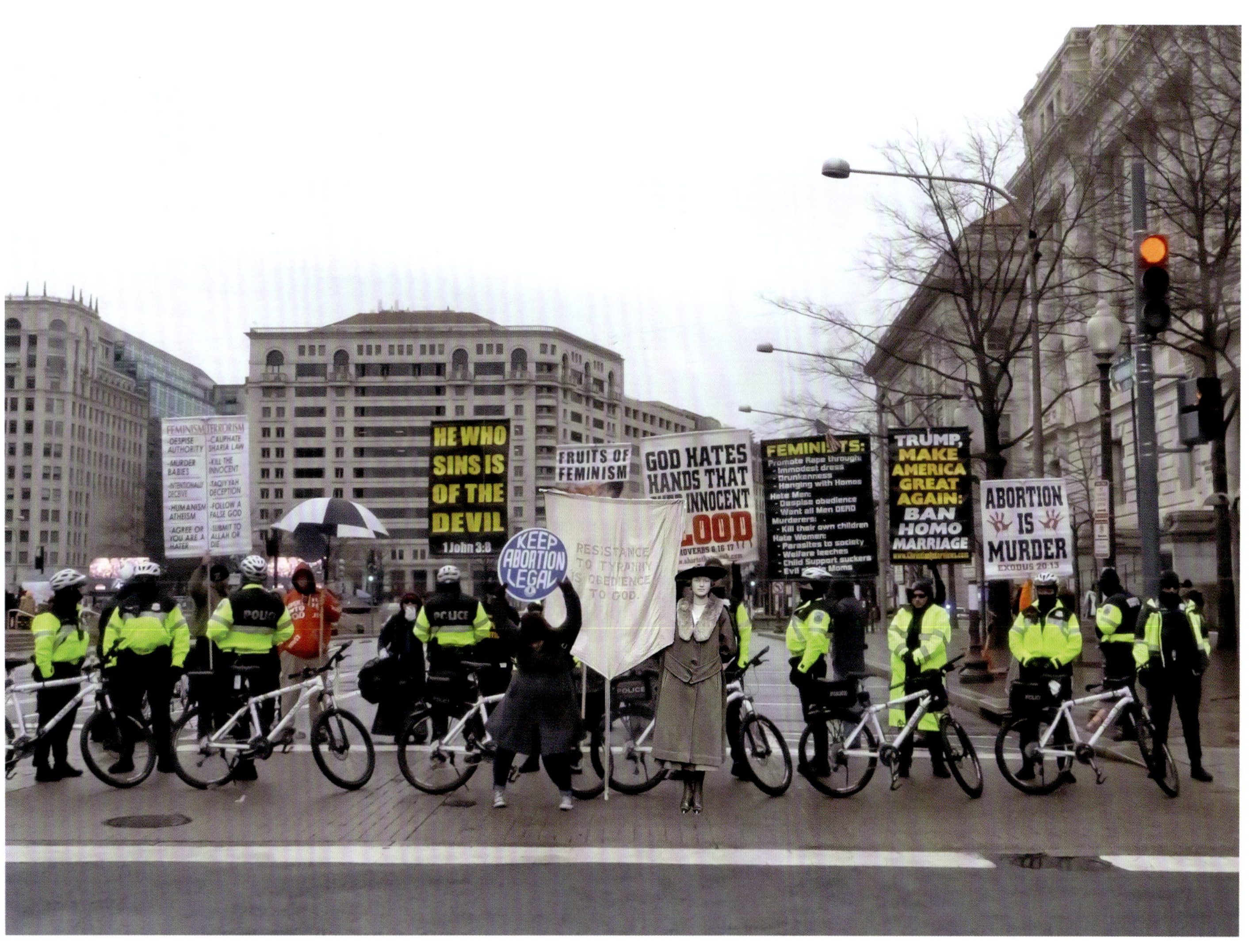

FIGURE 32. Ileana Doble Hernandez. *Resistance*

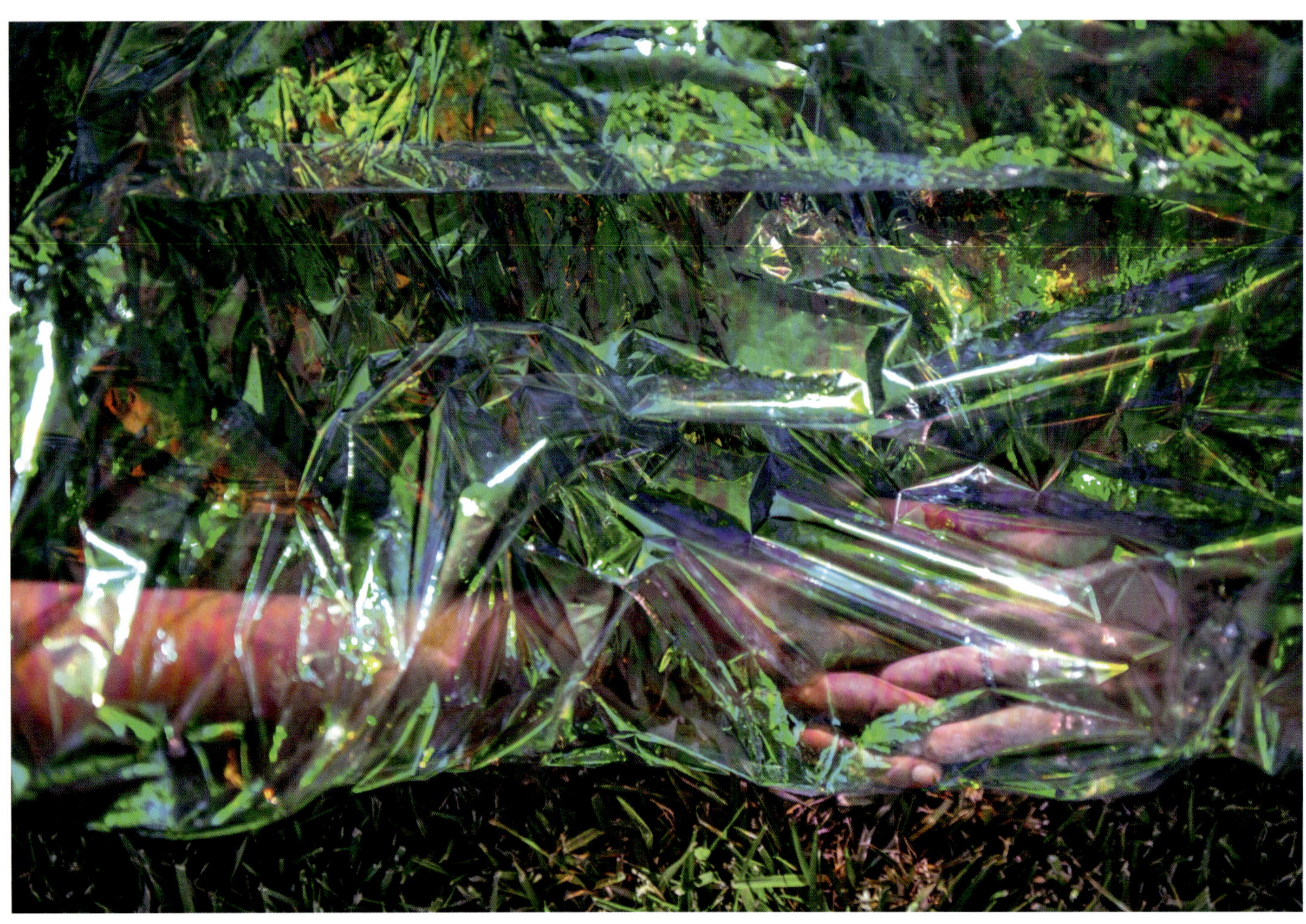

FIGURE 33. Manjari Sharma. *Uncertainty*

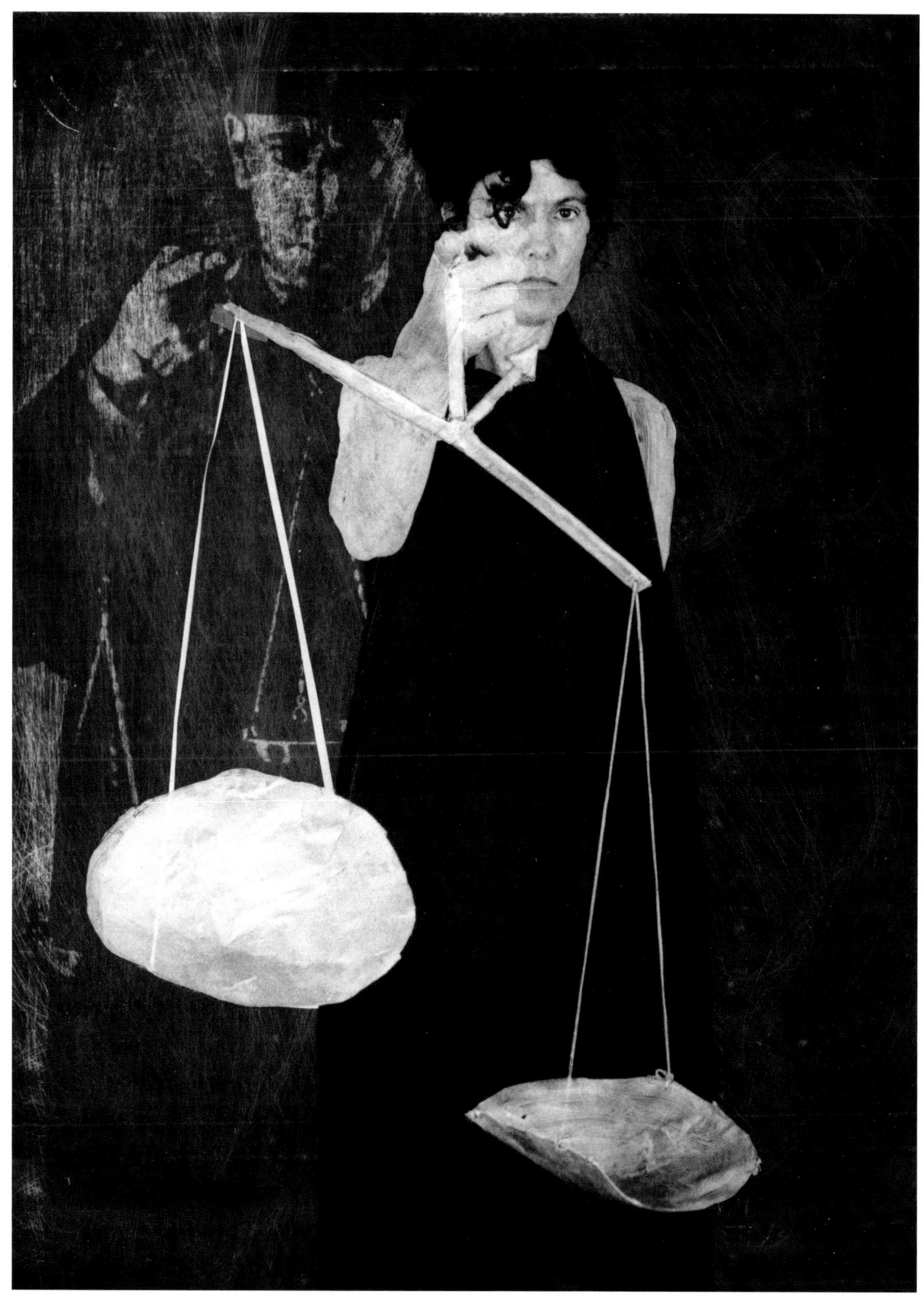

FIGURE 34. Melanie Walker. *MisJudge*

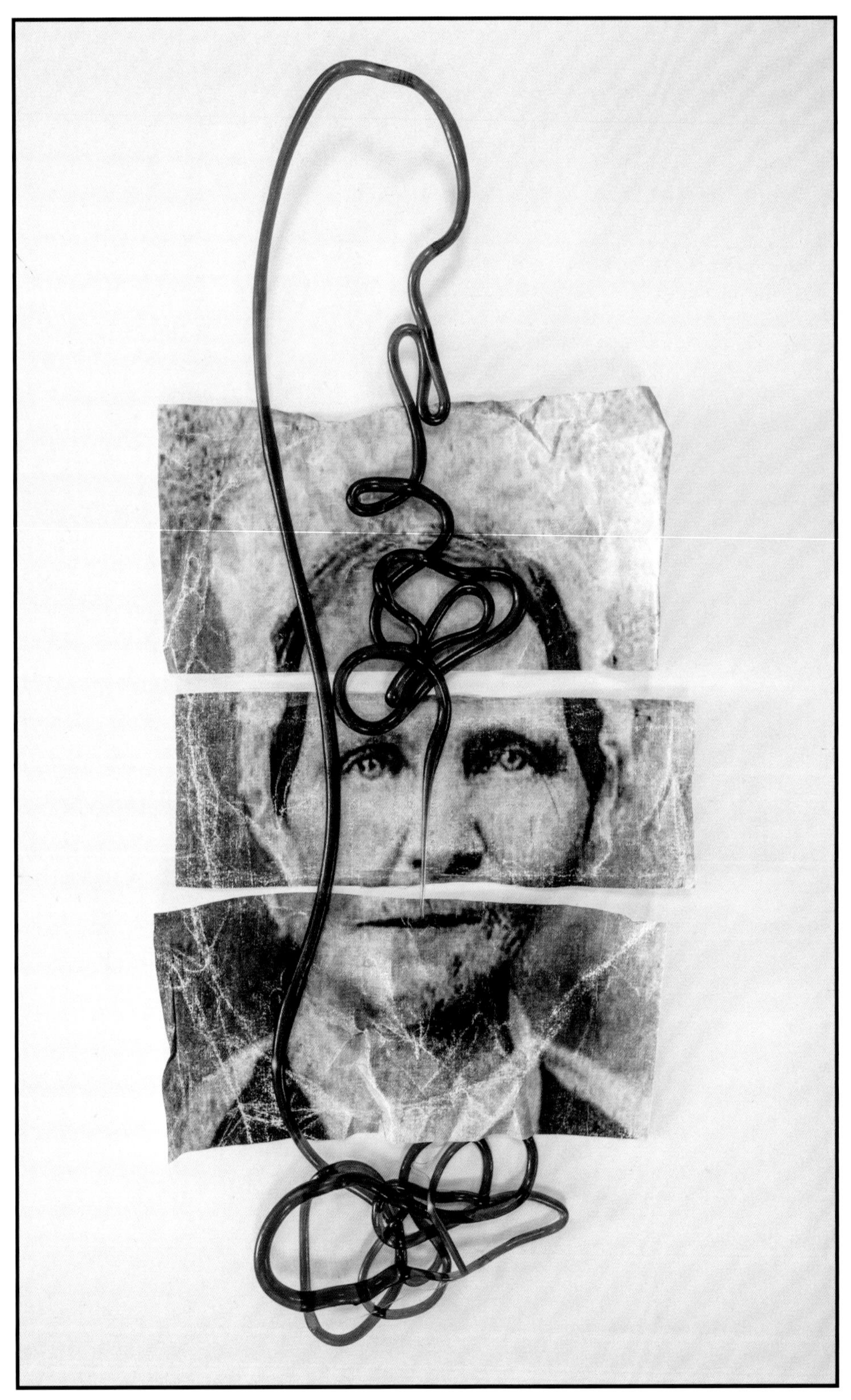

FIGURE 35. Chehalis Deane Hegner. *Mary Ann McClintock*

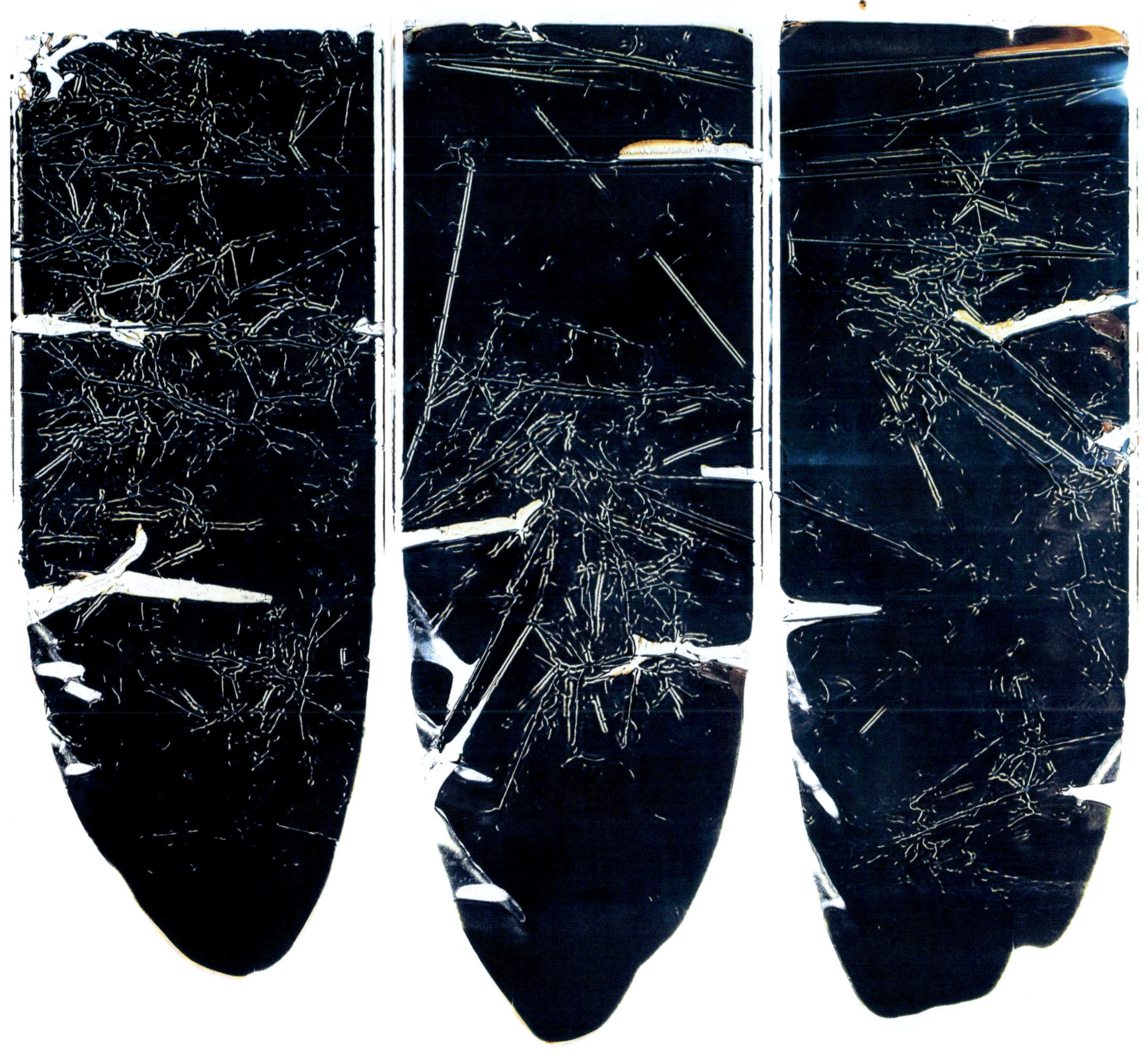

FIGURE 36. Ellen Carey. *Crush & Pull*

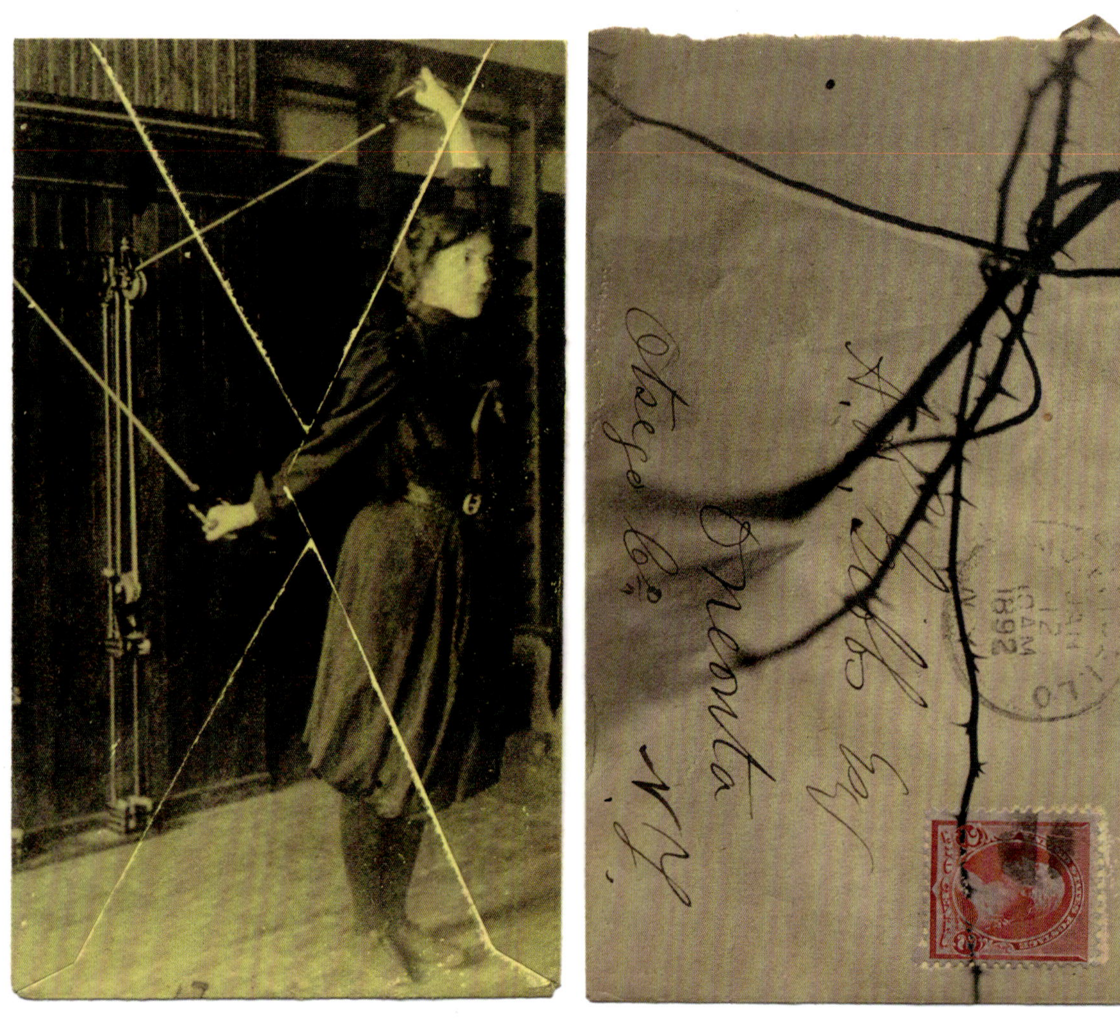

FIGURE 37. Rachel Phillips. *Growing Pains*

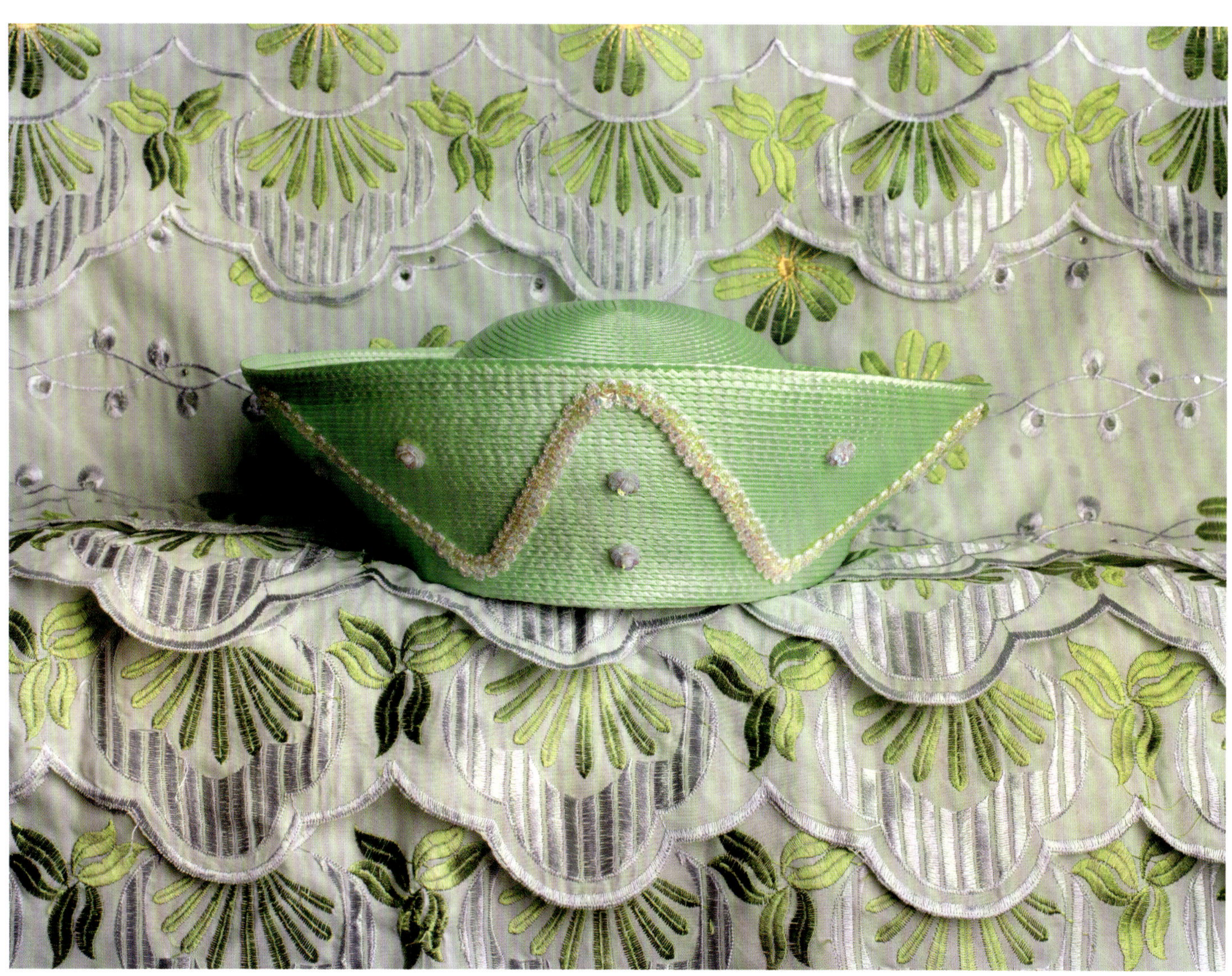

FIGURE 38. Mary Beth Meehan. *Tell the Story*

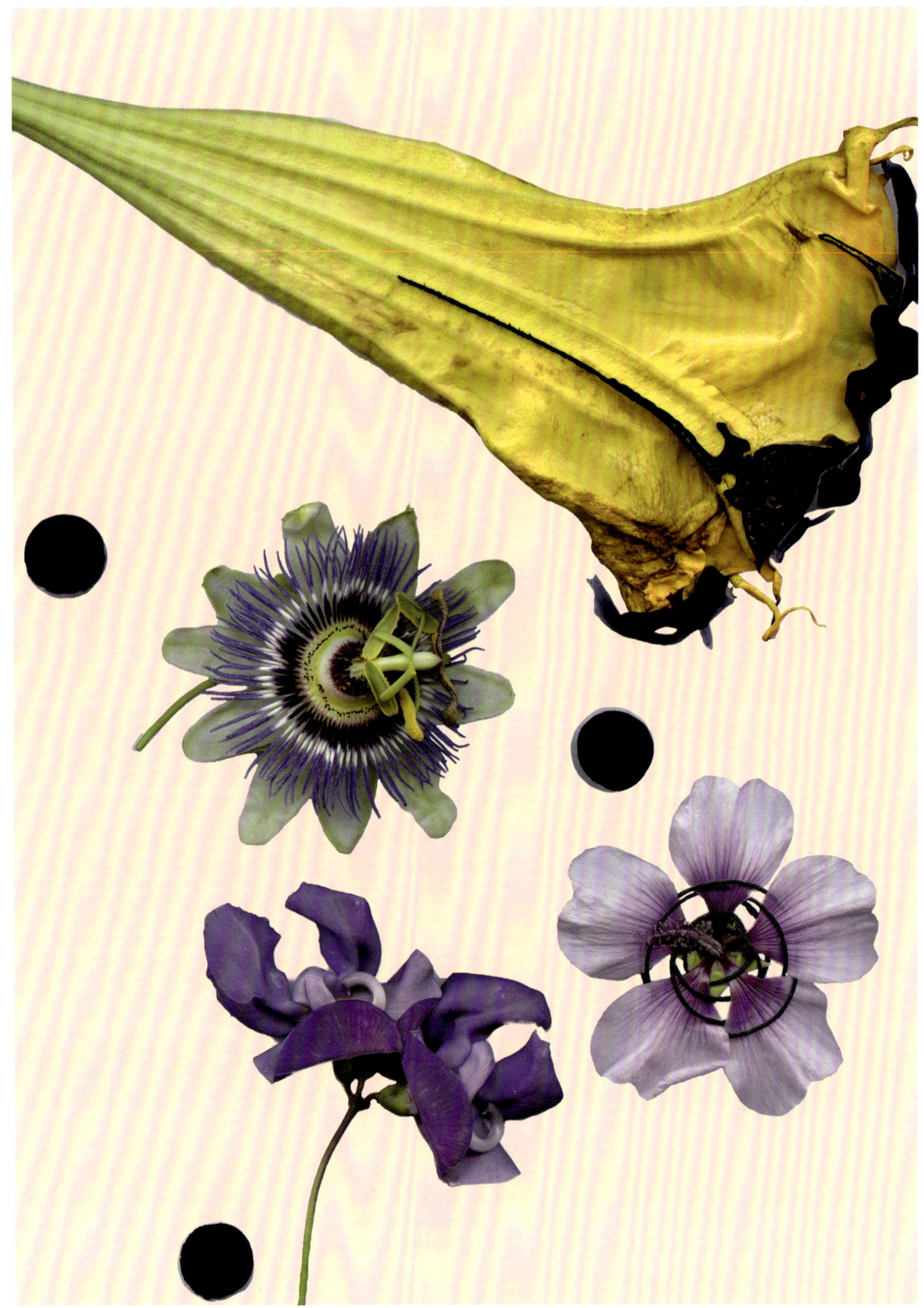

FIGURE 39. Julia Bennett. *Five Wounds*

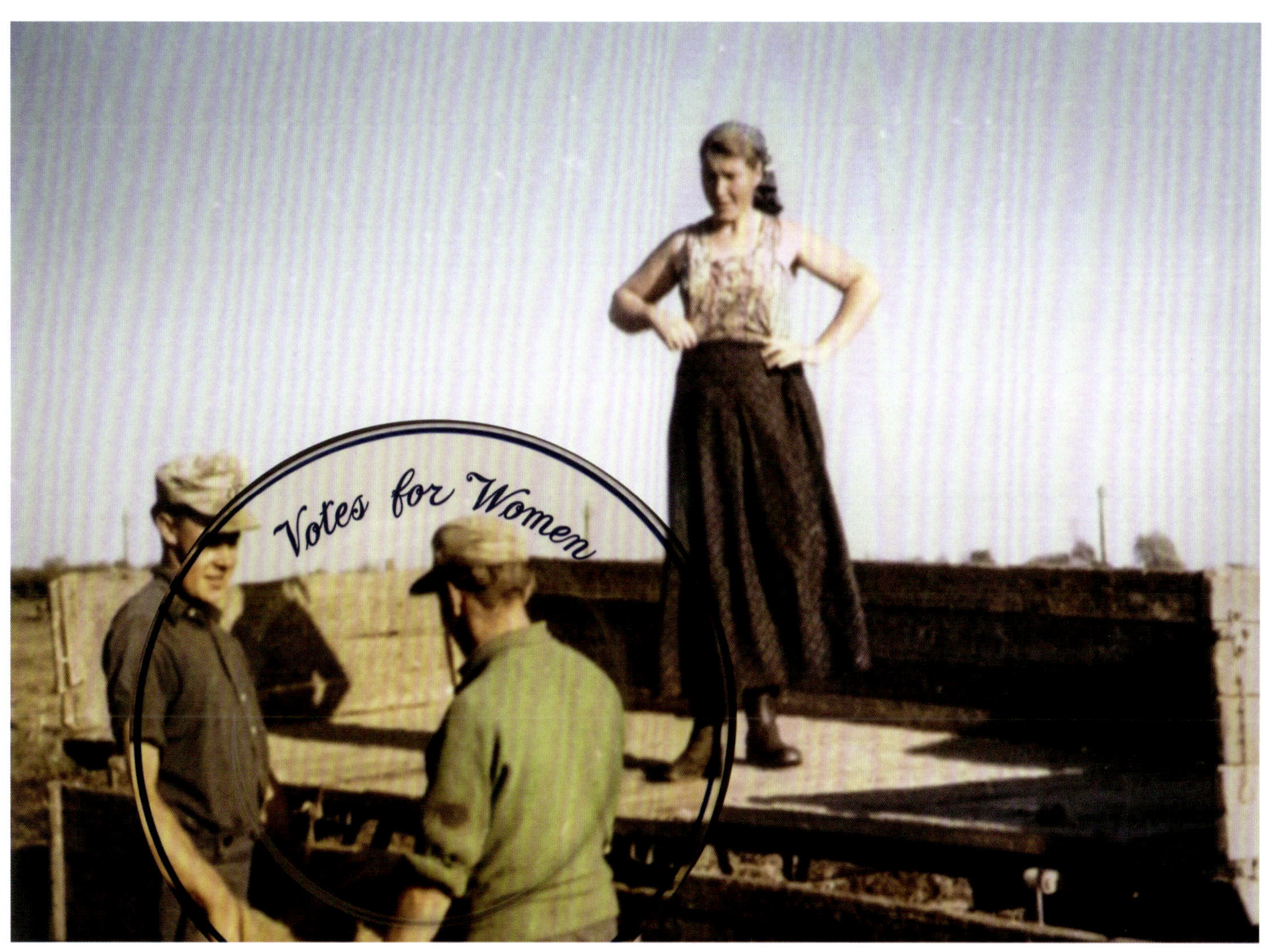

FIGURE 40. Astrid Reischwitz. *Working Woman with "Votes for Women" Plate*

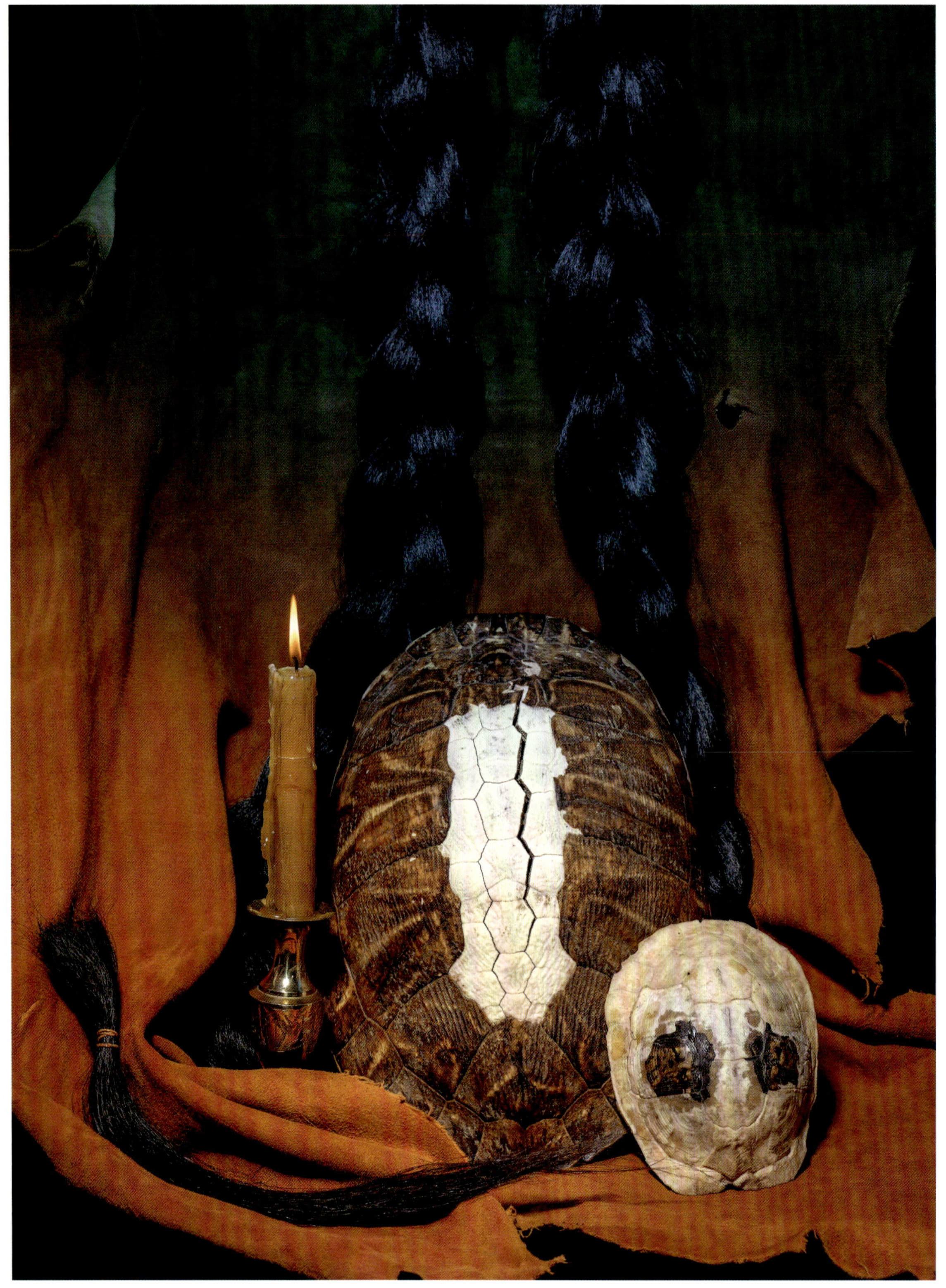

FIGURE 41. Noelle McCleaf. *Altar for Marie Louise Bottineau Baldwin*

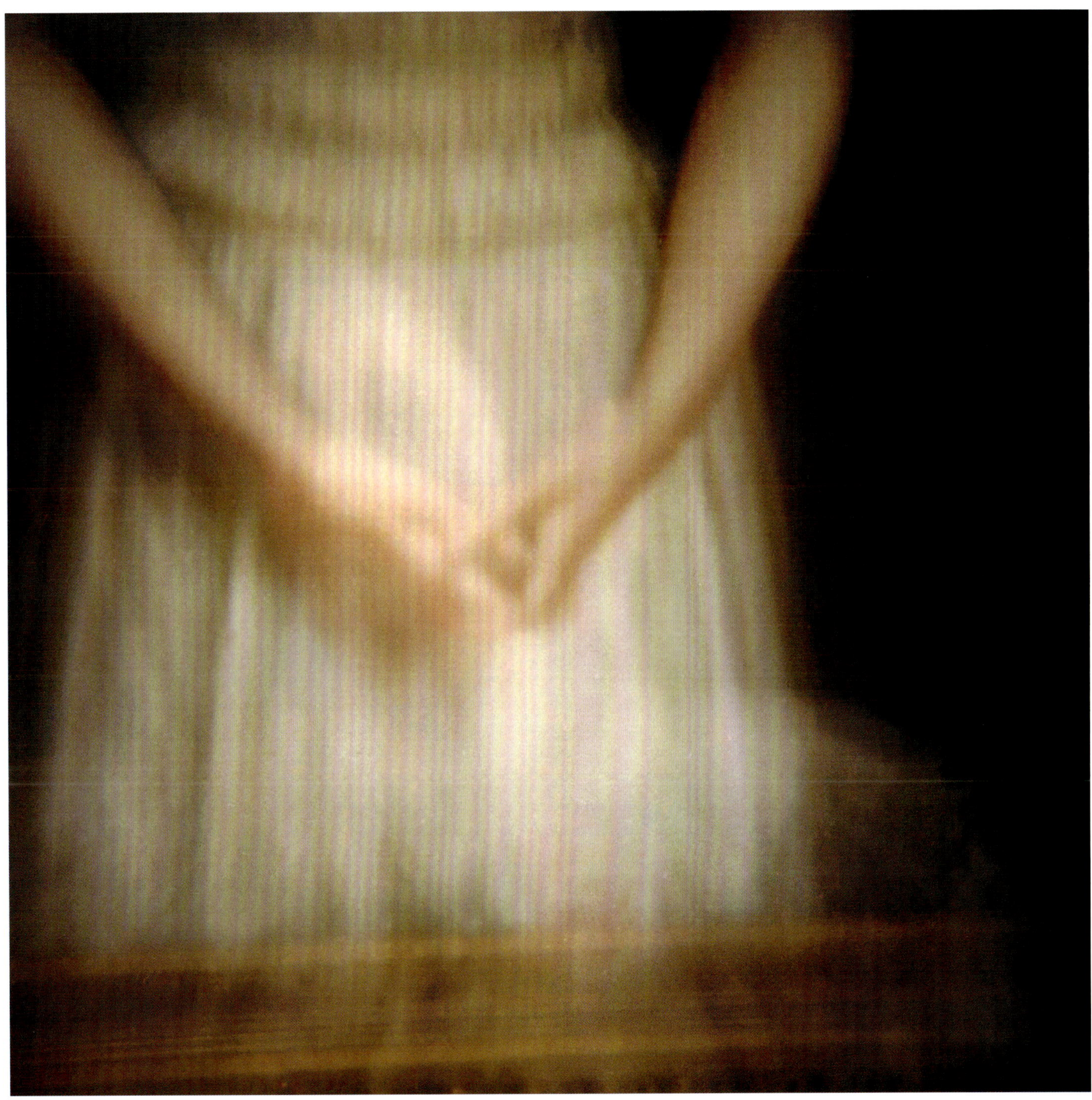

FIGURE 42. Preston Gannaway. *Untitled*

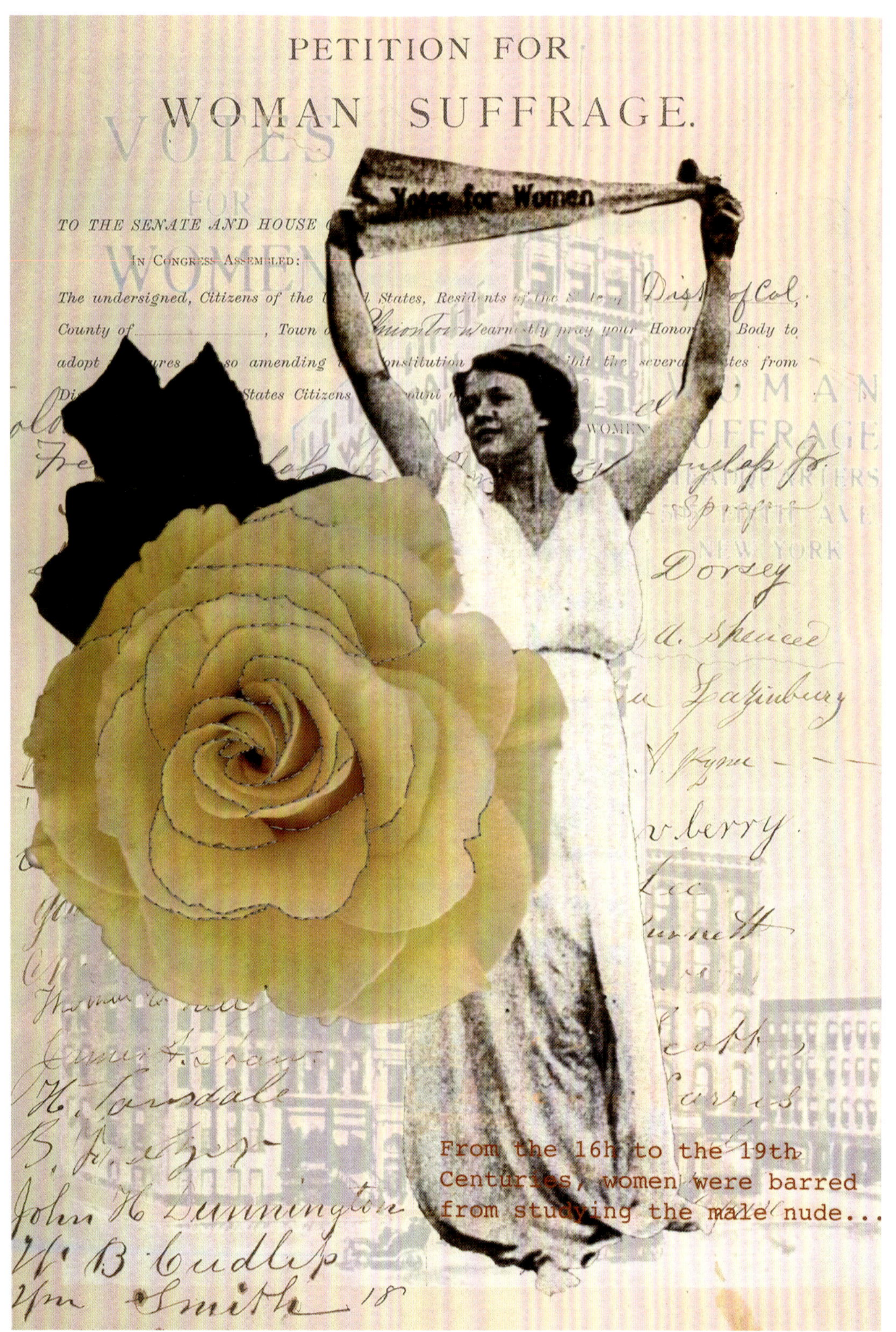

FIGURE 43. Sandra Klein. *The Banner*

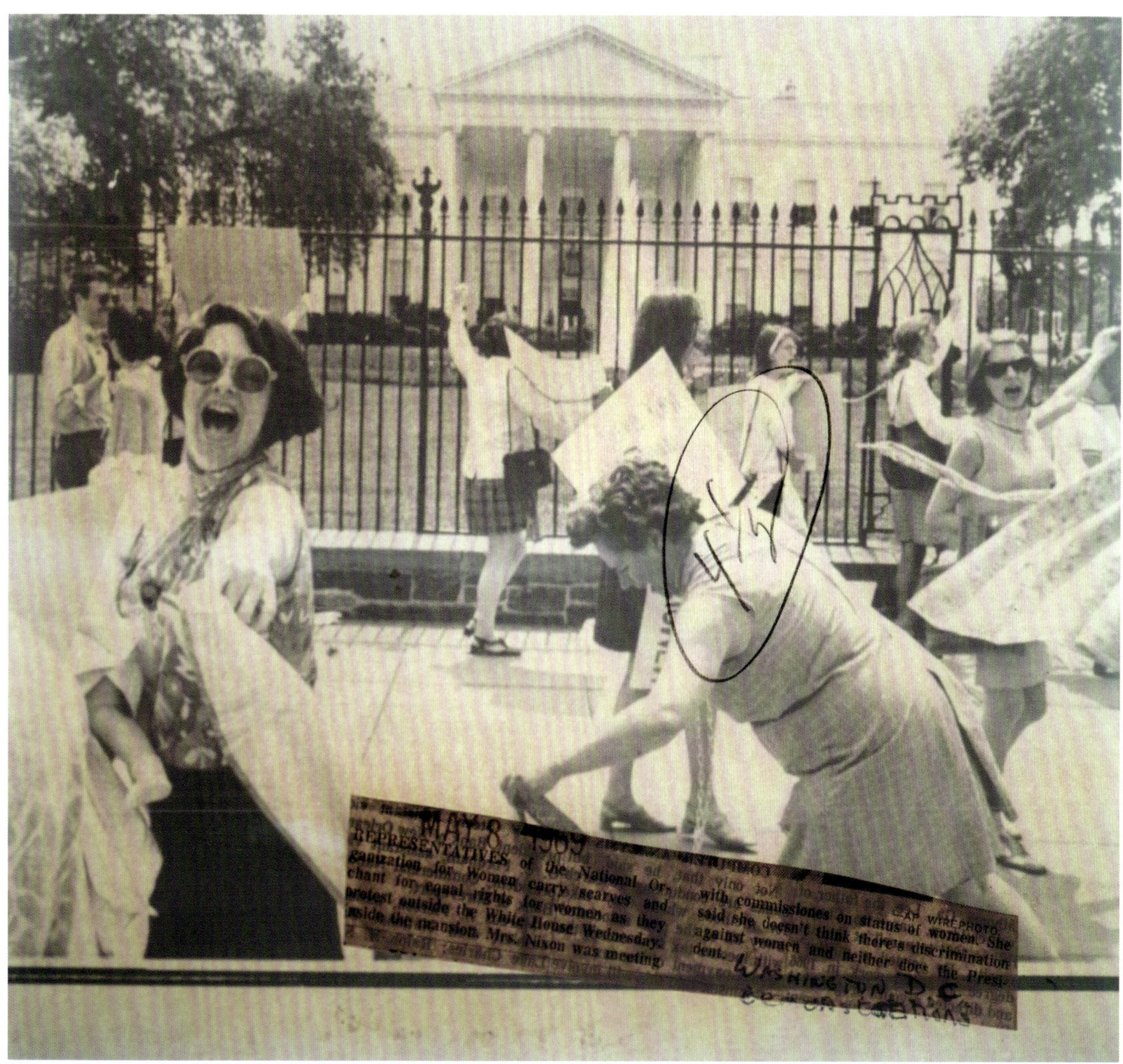

FIGURE 44. Toni Pepe. *Mrs. Nixon*

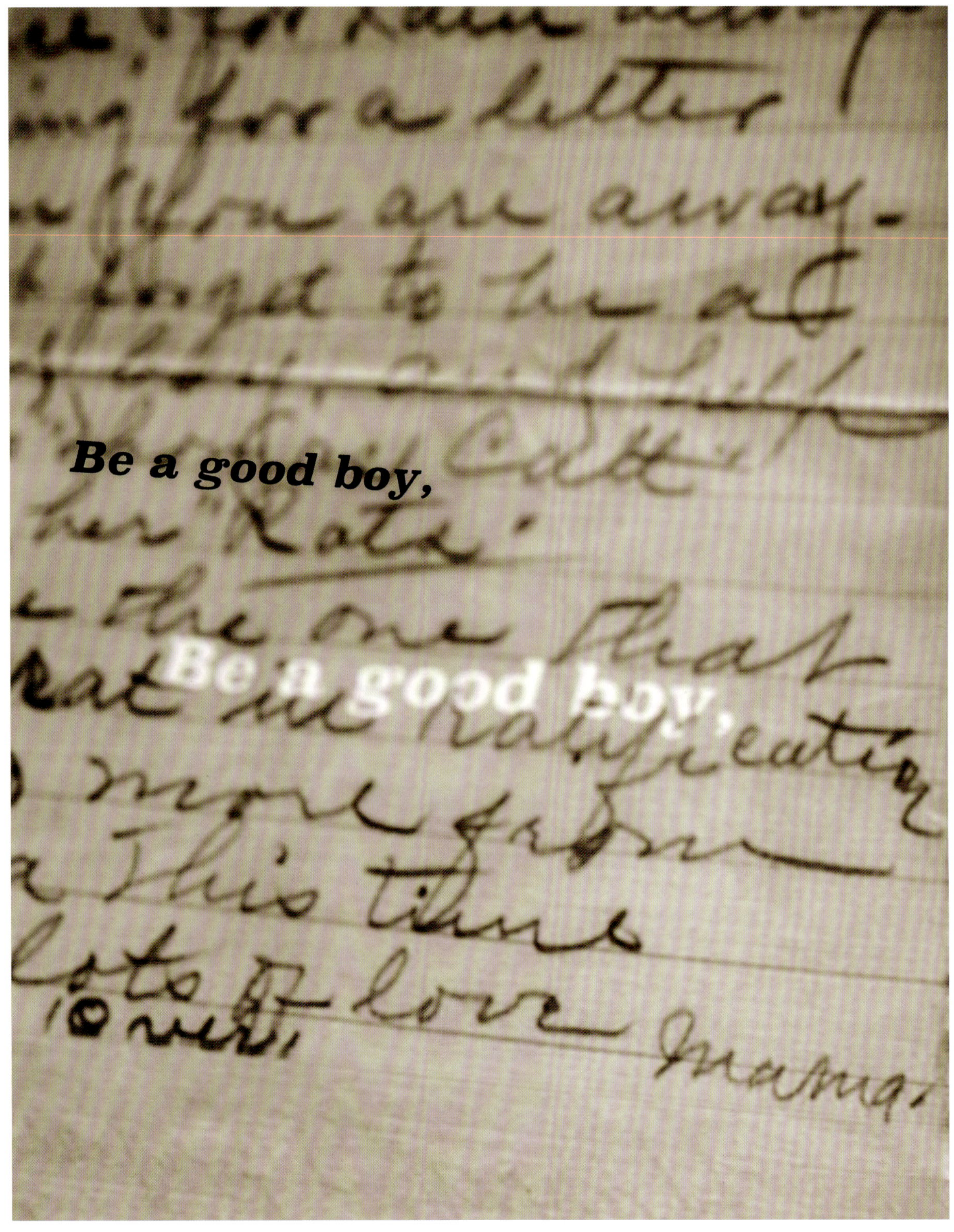

FIGURE 45. Greer Muldowney. *Be a Good Boy* from the series *Rhetorical Image*

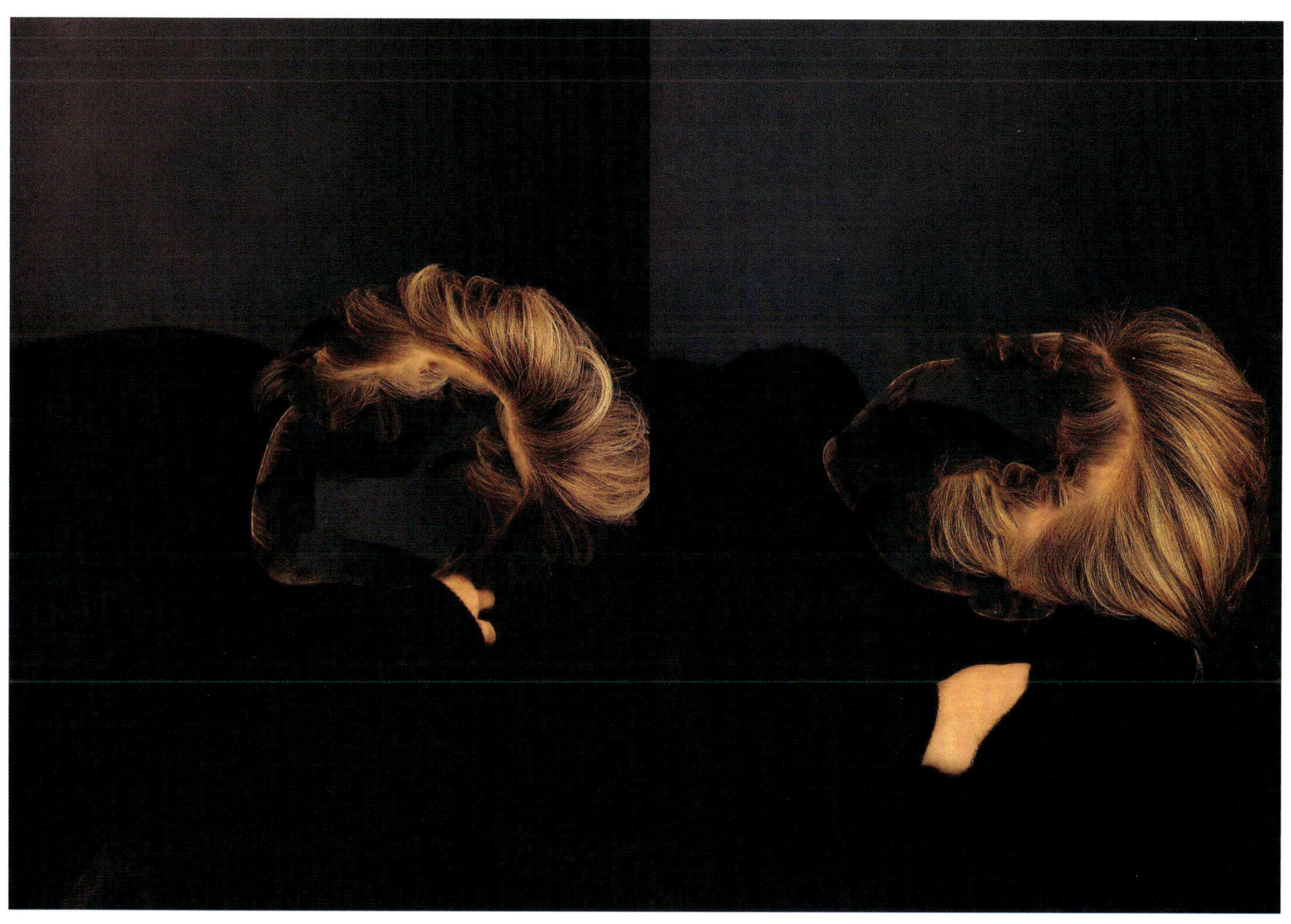

FIGURE 46. Serrah Russell. *I could finally let my smile drain away. We were mostly quiet.* Digital collage using photograph by Annie Leibovitz from Vogue Magazine *archive (1993)*

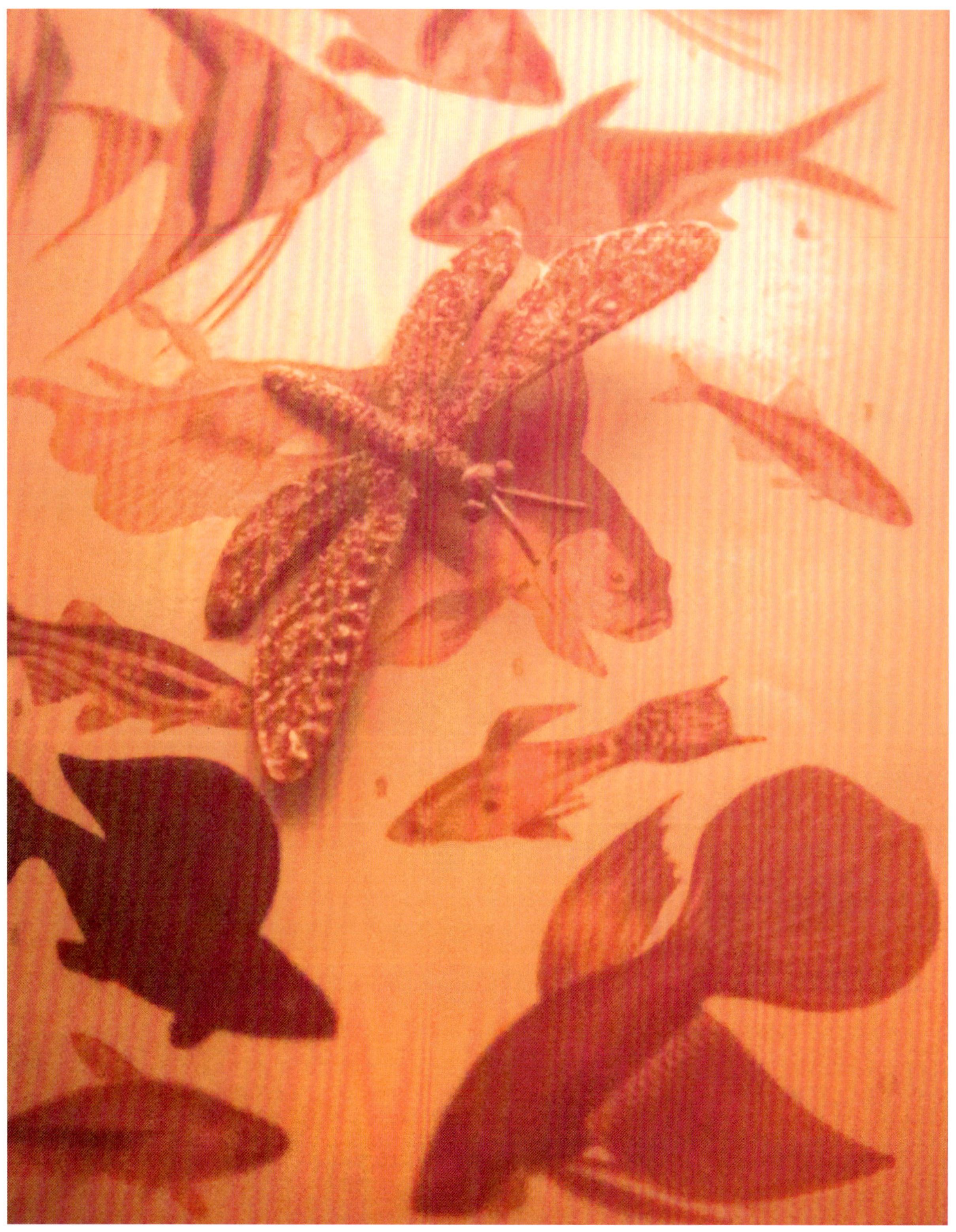

FIGURE 47. Sarah Pollman. *Dragonfly*

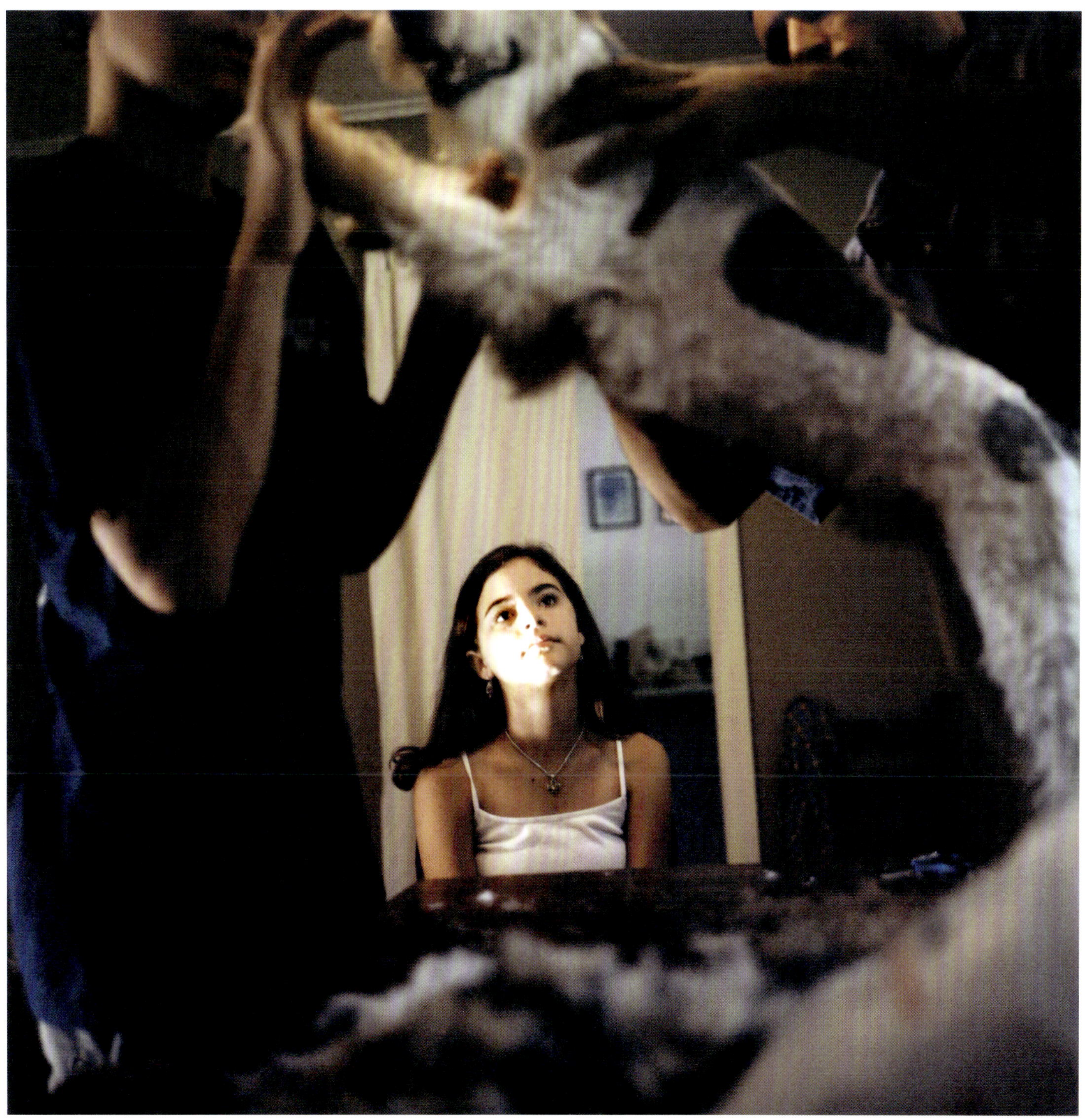

FIGURE 48. Maude Schuyler Clay. *Ishy's Haircut*

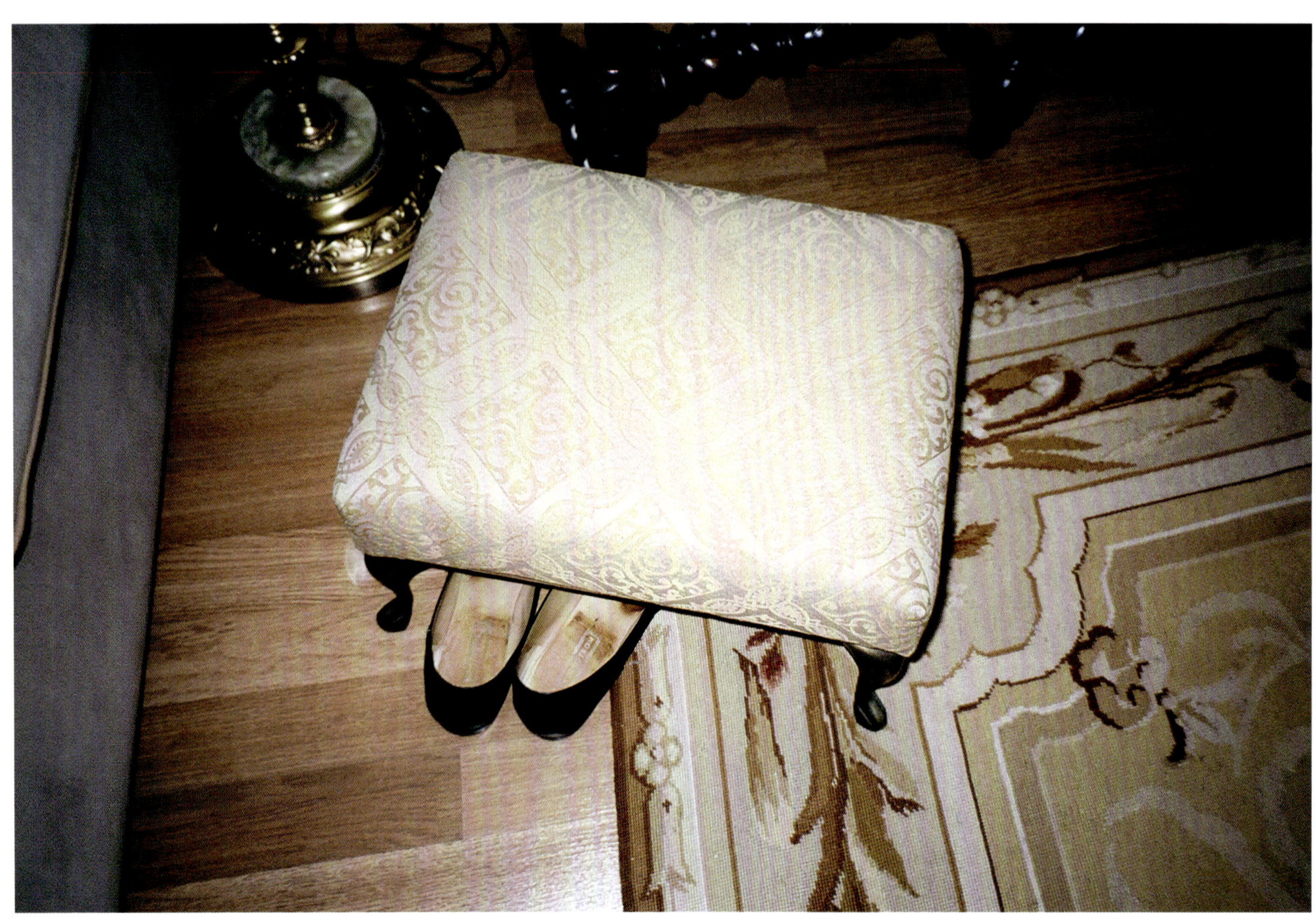

FIGURE 49. Sasha Tivetsky. *Shoes*

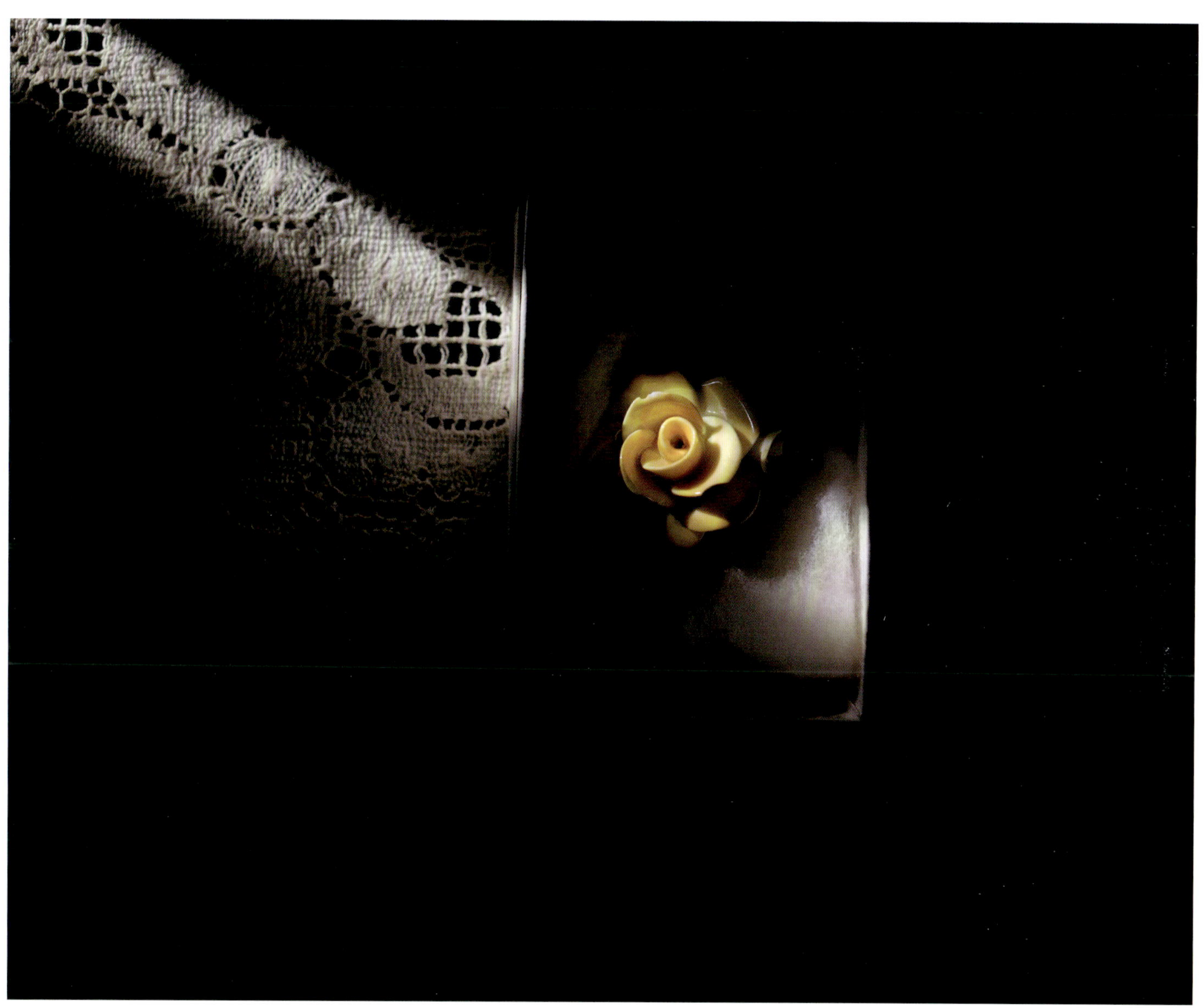

FIGURE 50. Molly Lamb. *My Great-Grandmother's Yellow Rose*

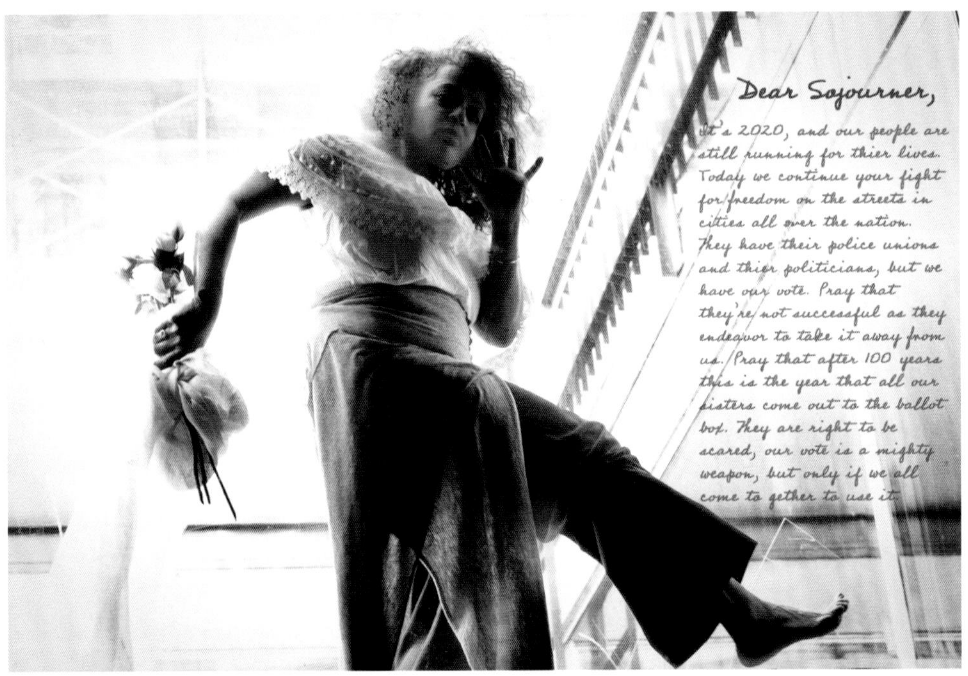

FIGURE 51. Karen Zusman. *Dear Sojourner*

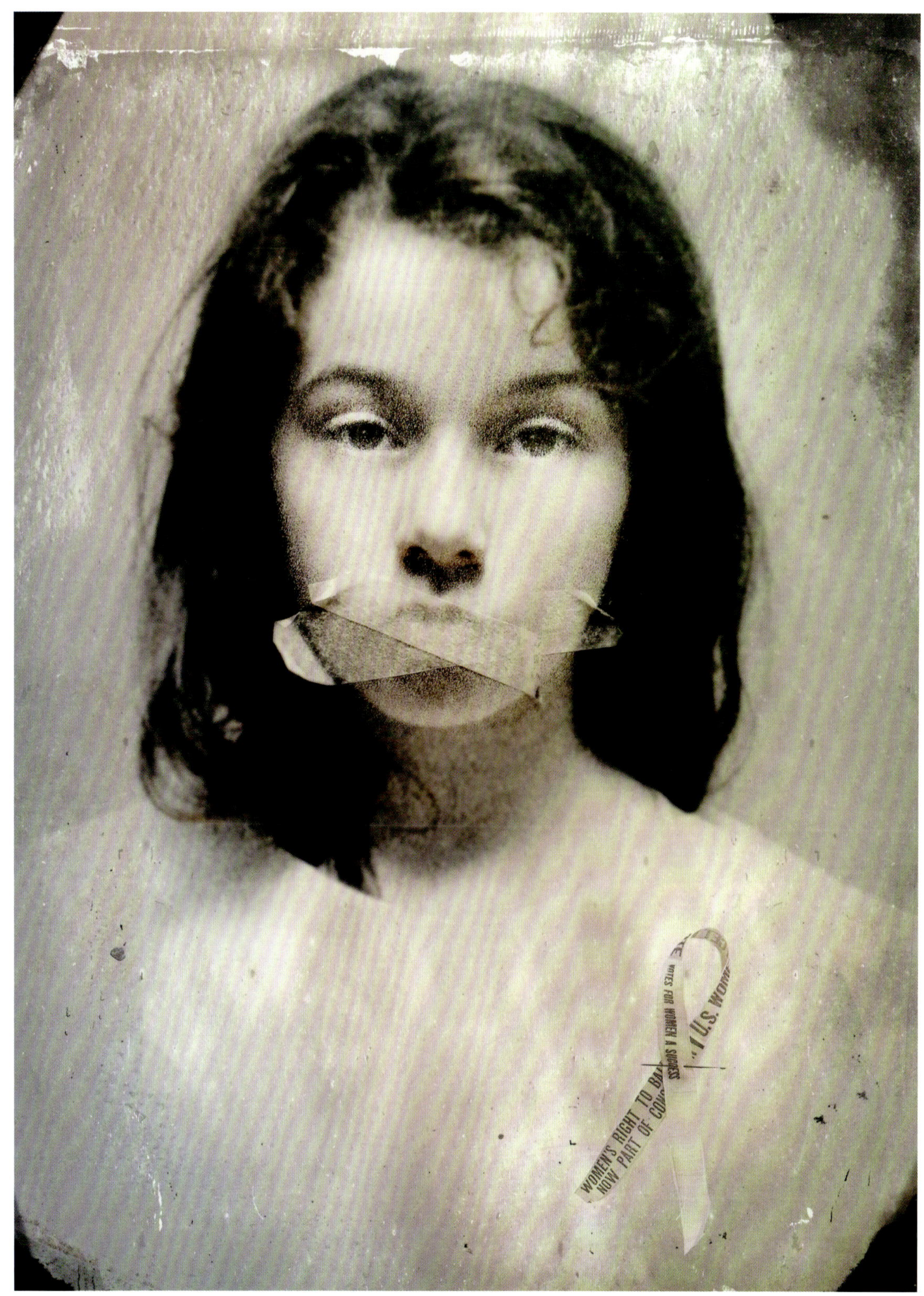

FIGURE 52. K.K. DePaul. *Silent No More*

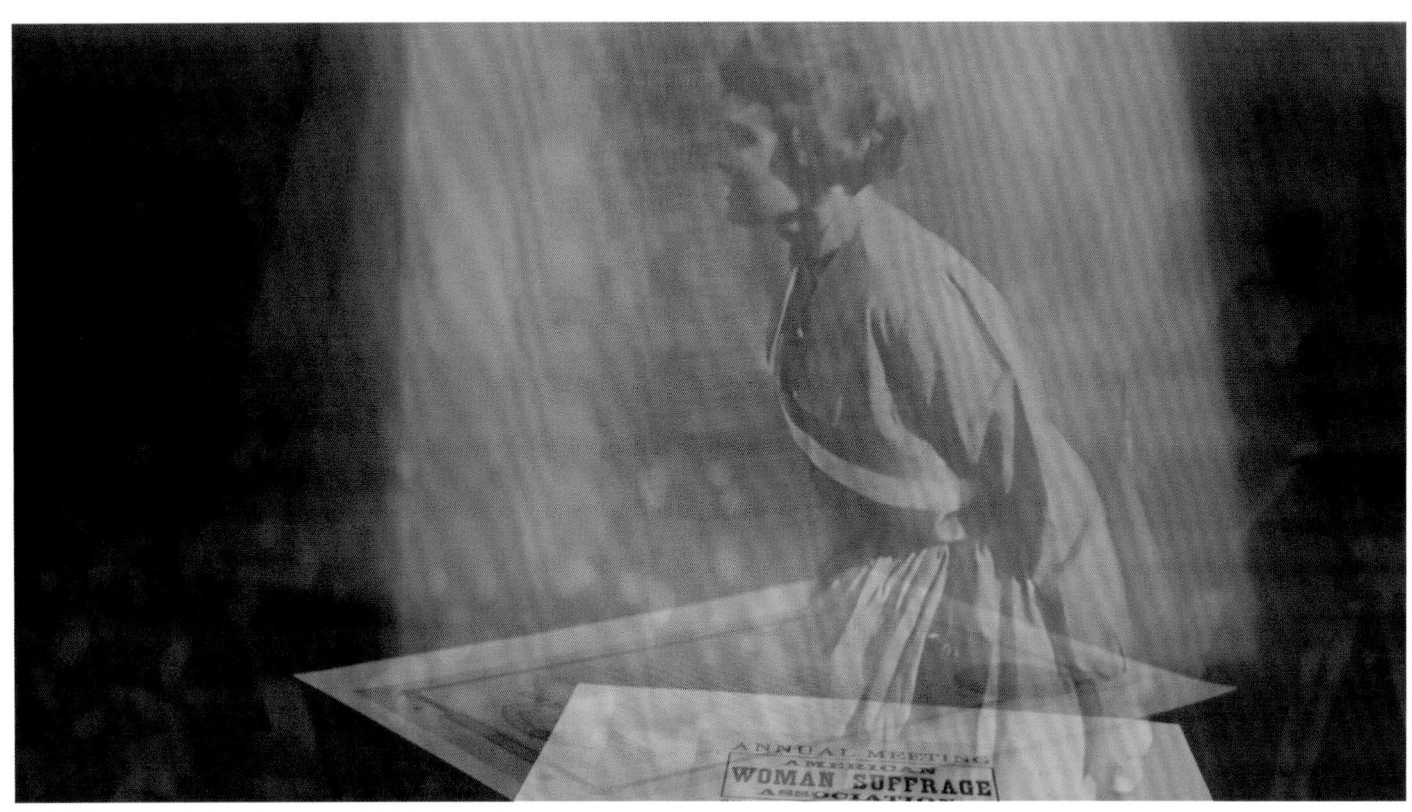

FIGURE 53. Laura Migliorino. *Courage*

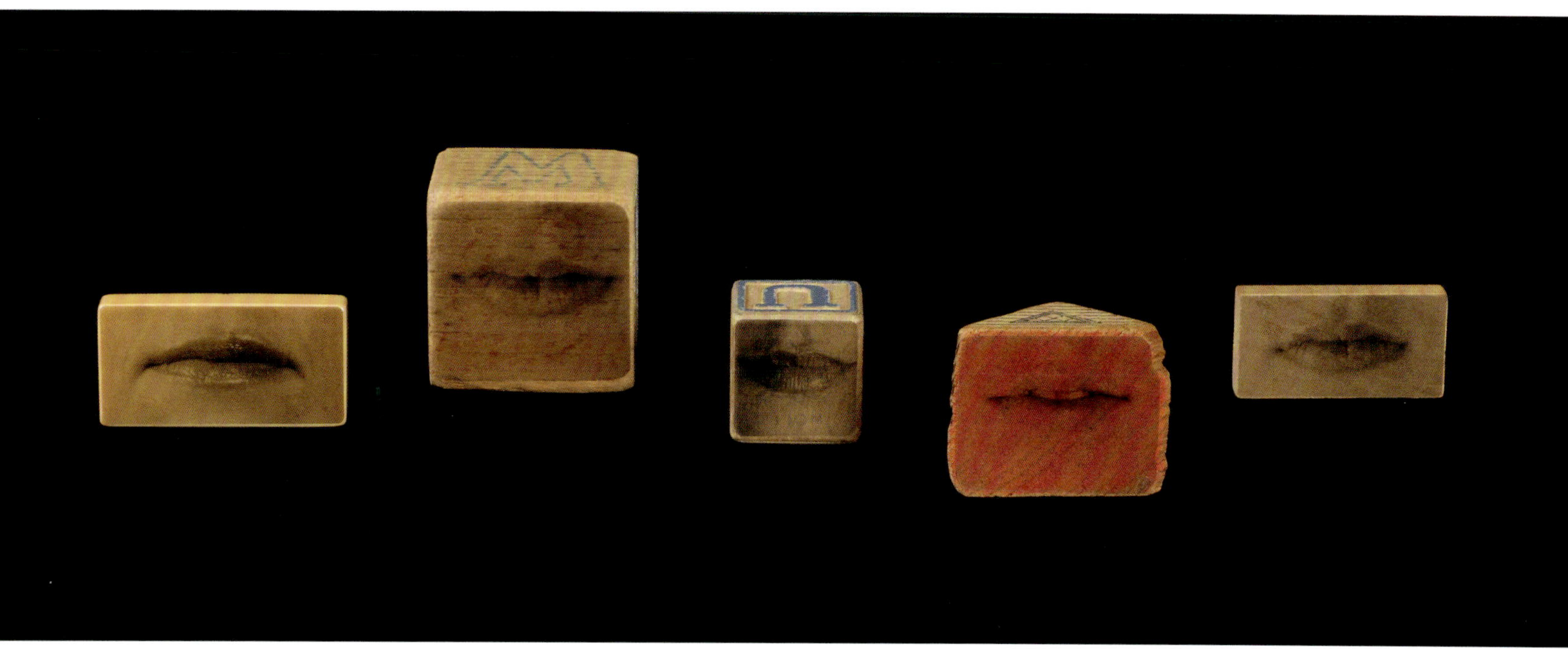

FIGURE 54. Heidi Kirkpatrick. *Let Our Voices Be Heard*

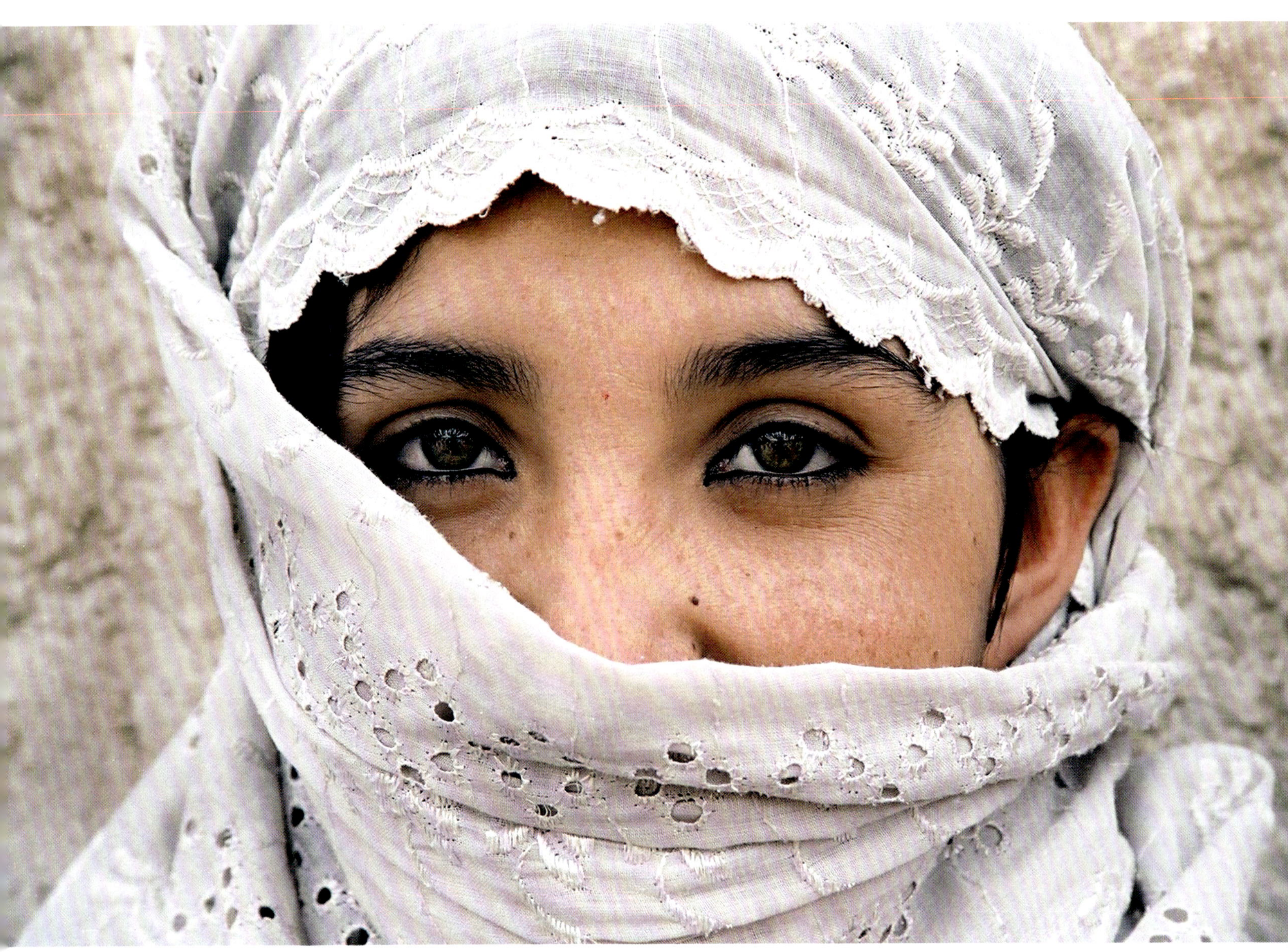

FIGURE 55. Farah Janjua. *Afghan Eyes*

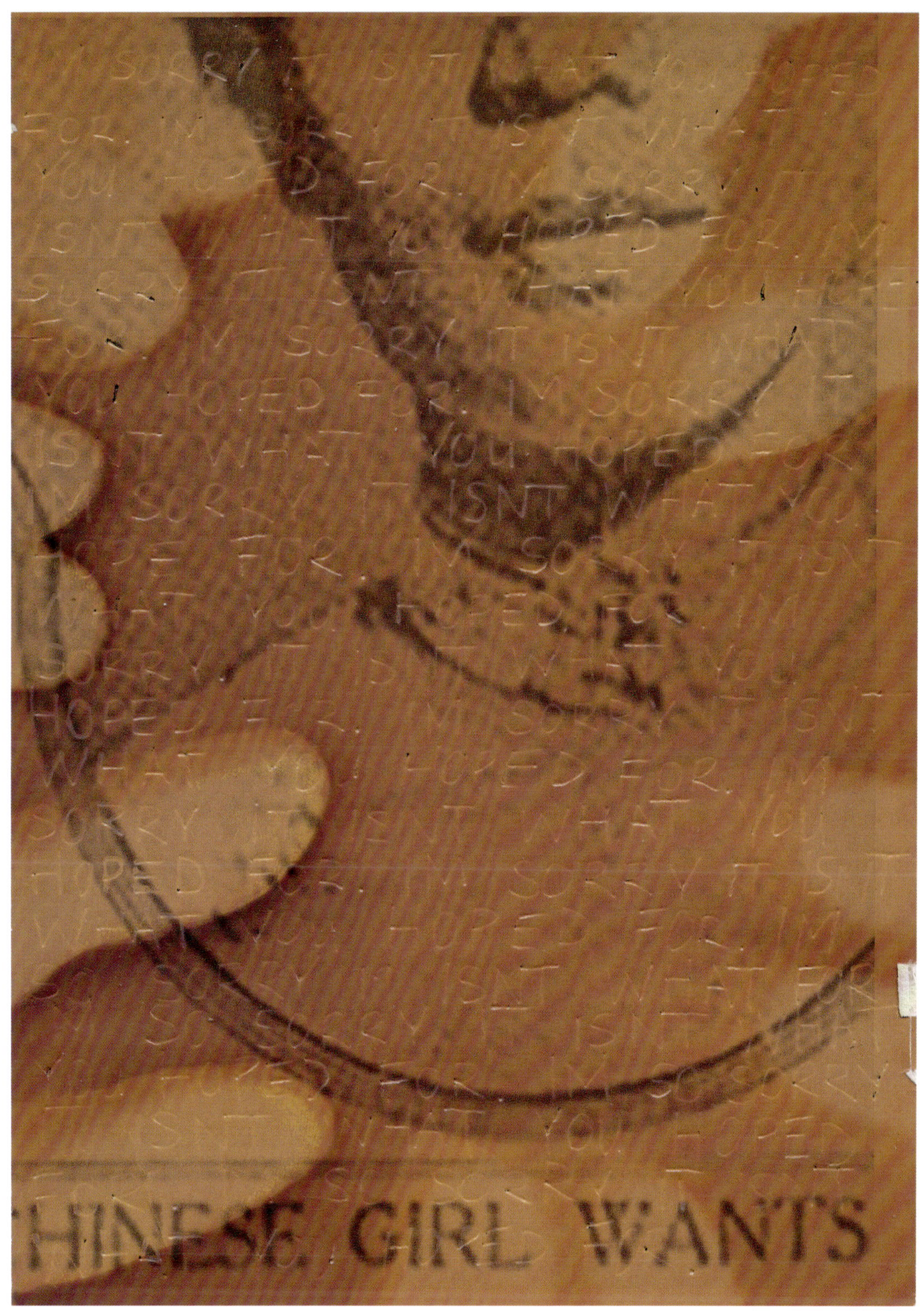

FIGURE 56. Kyra Schmidt. *Chinese Girl Wants to Vote*

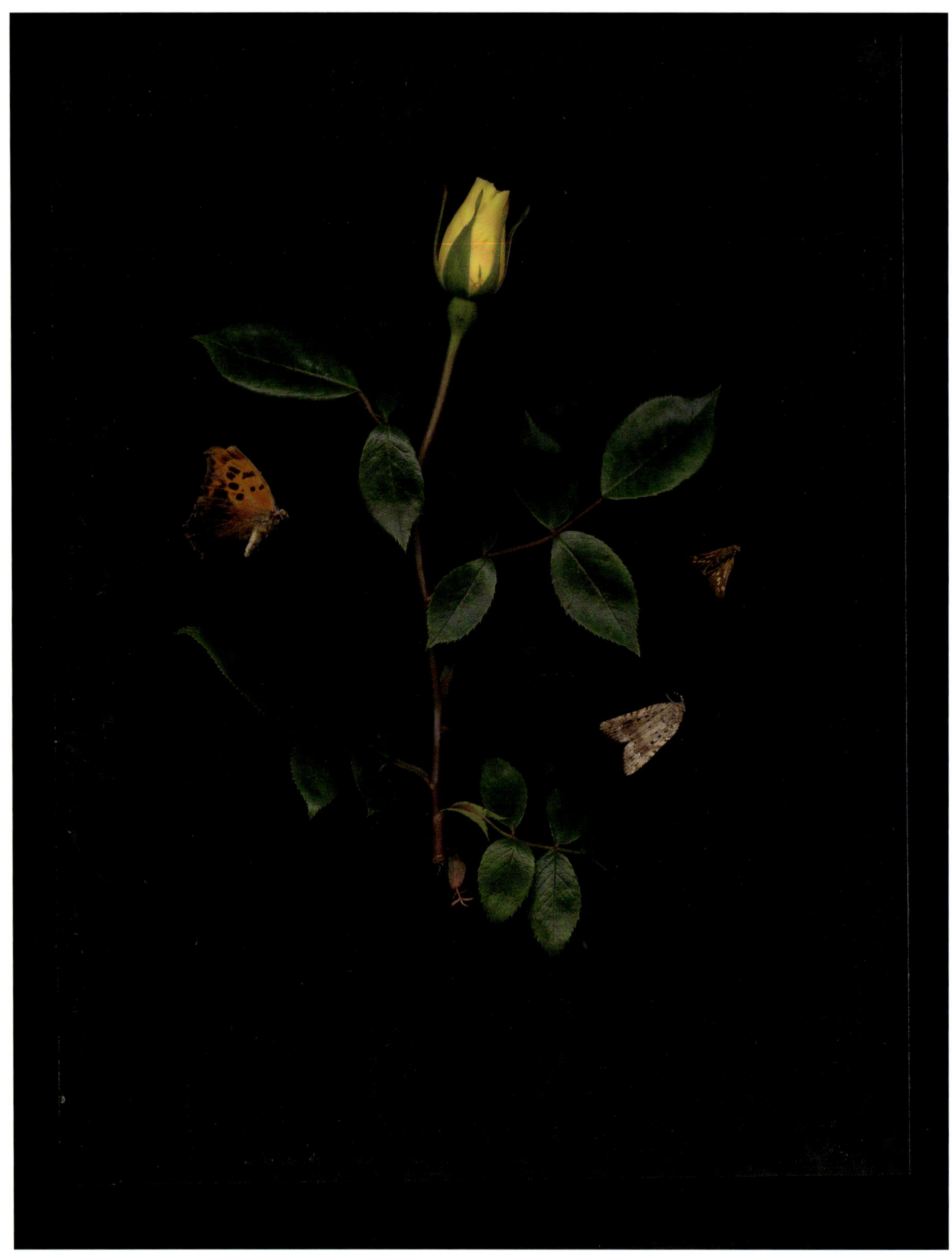

FIGURE 57. Rachel Loischild. *#180*

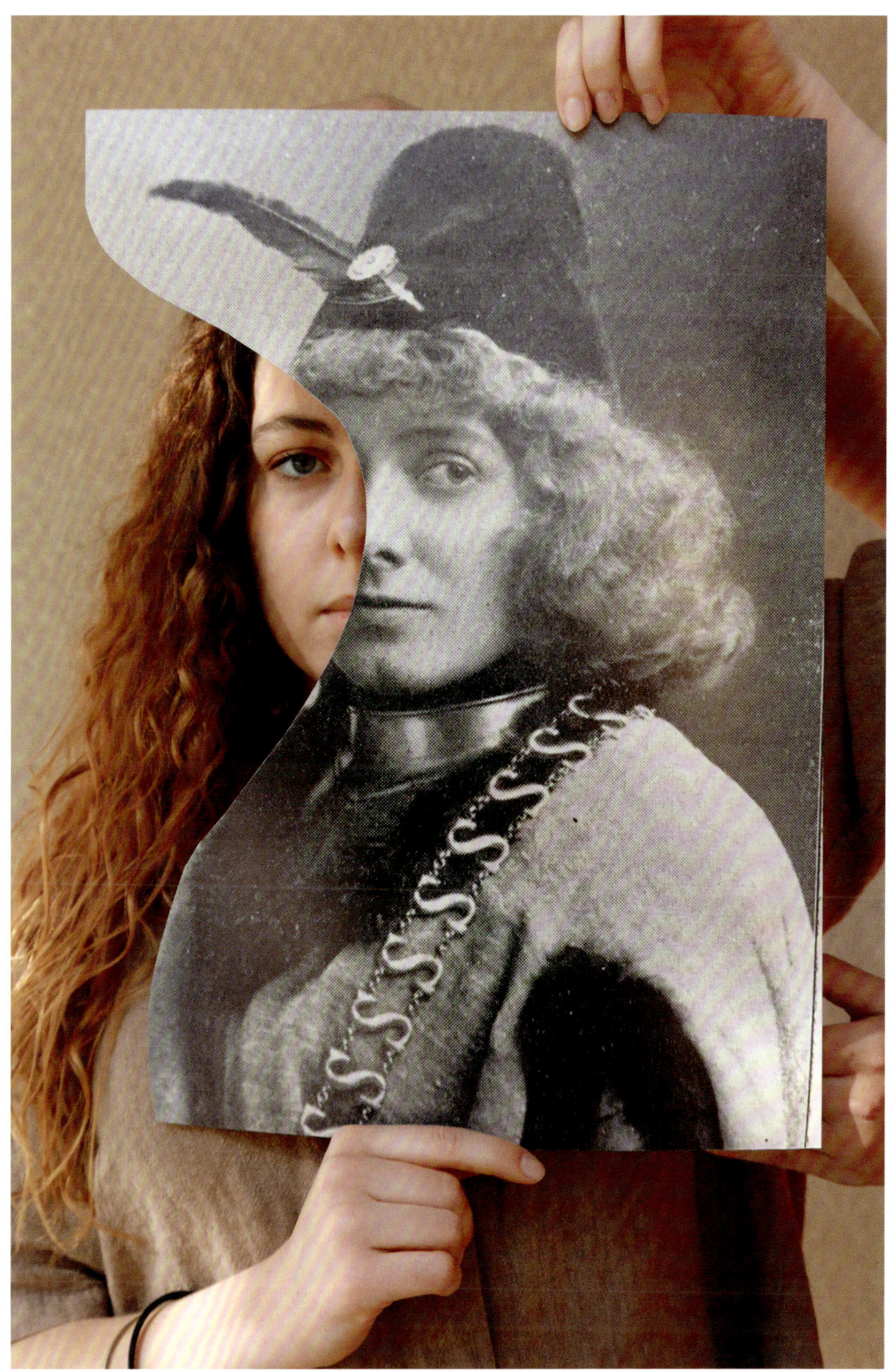

FIGURE 58. Megan Jacobs. *Equality Then & Now*

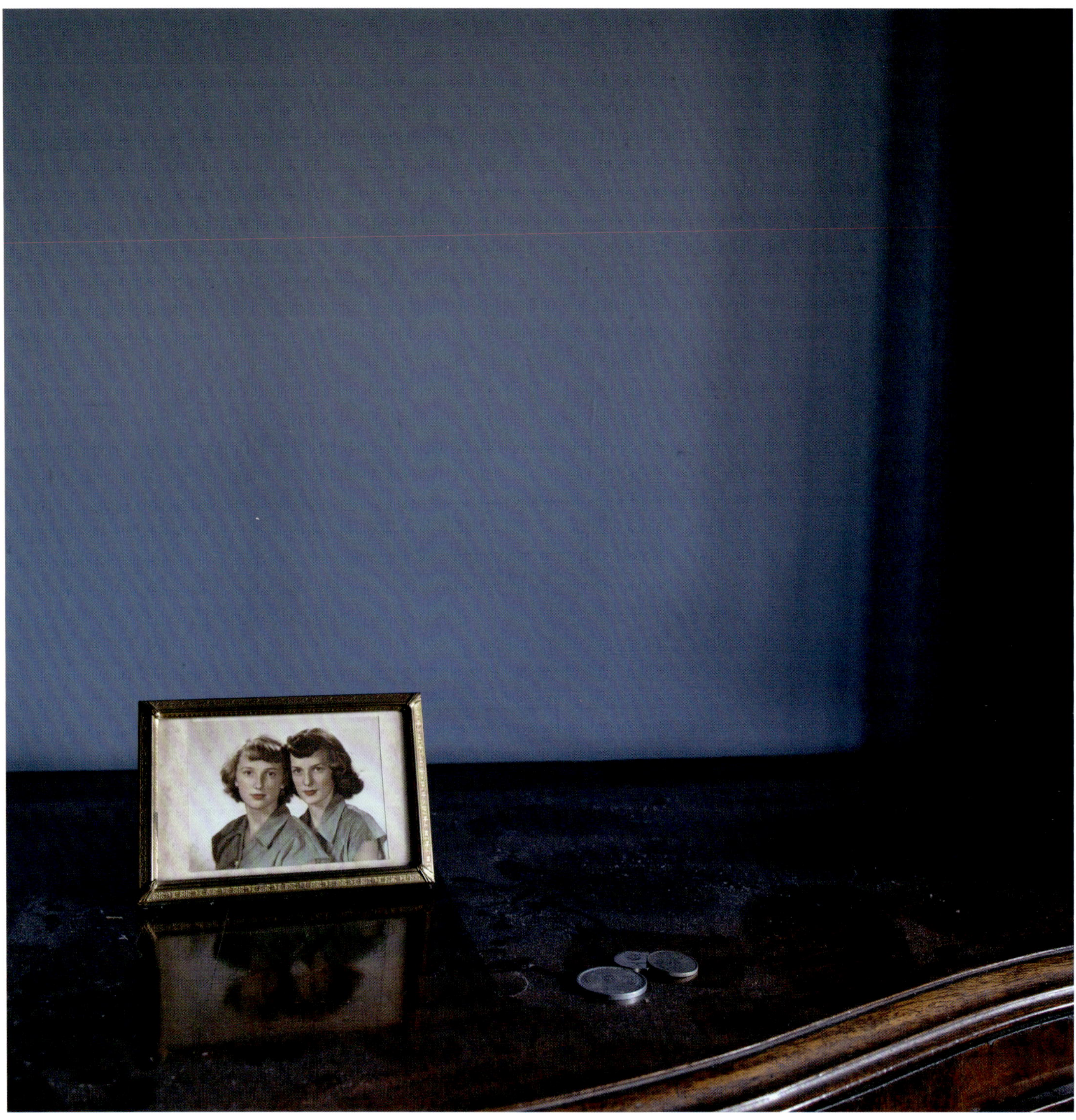

FIGURE 59. Tsar Fedorsky. *A Yellow Rose*

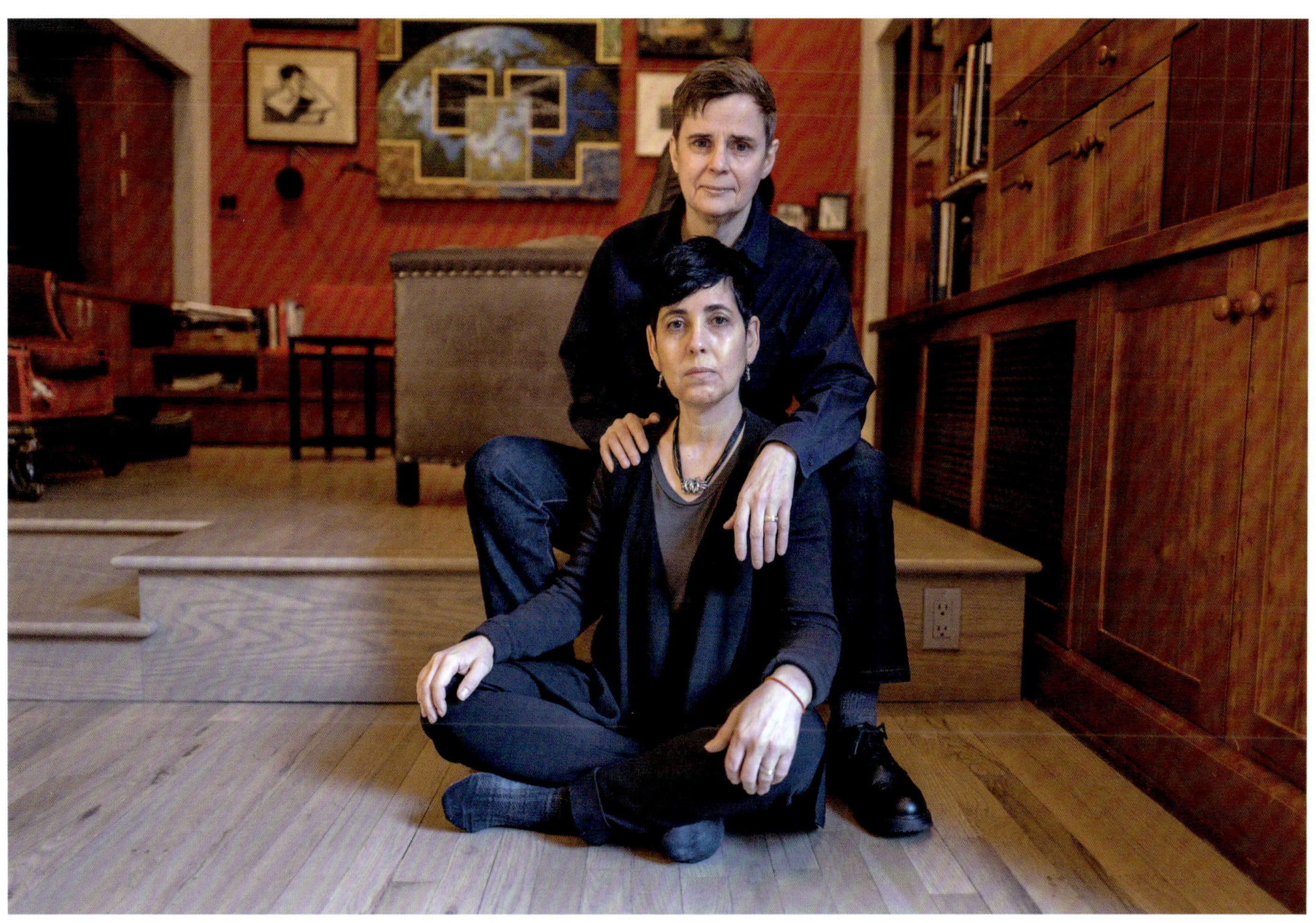

FIGURE 60. Susan Rosenberg Jones. *Emily and Anne*

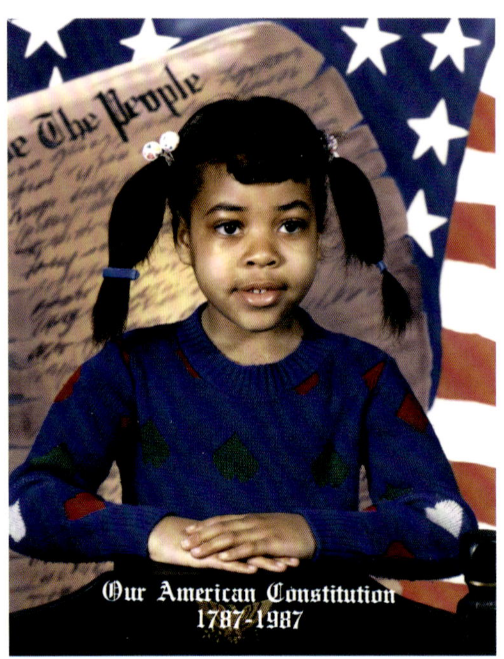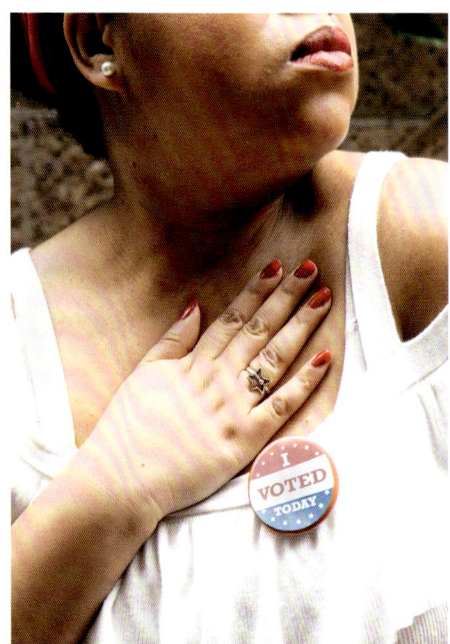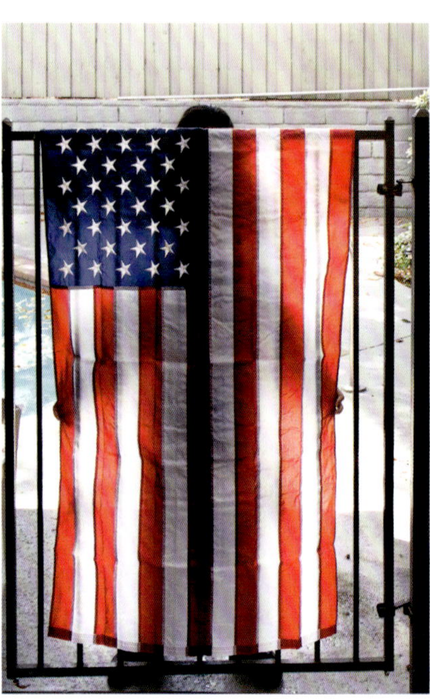

FIGURE 61. Carla Jay Harris. *aTriptych*

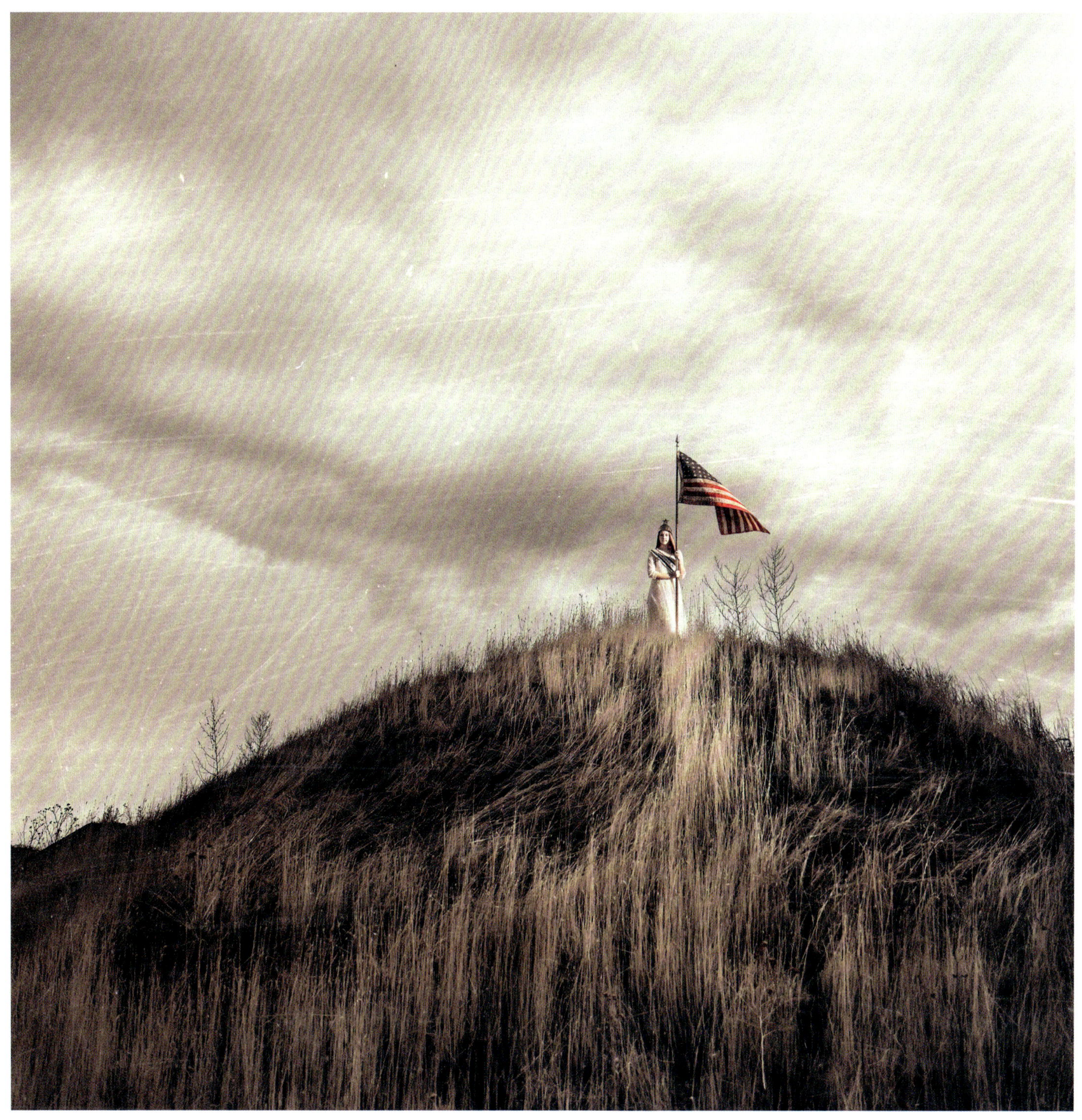

FIGURE 62. Jeanine Michna-Bales. *Ready for Battle, 2019*.
Courtesy of PDNB Gallery & Arnika Dawkins Gallery

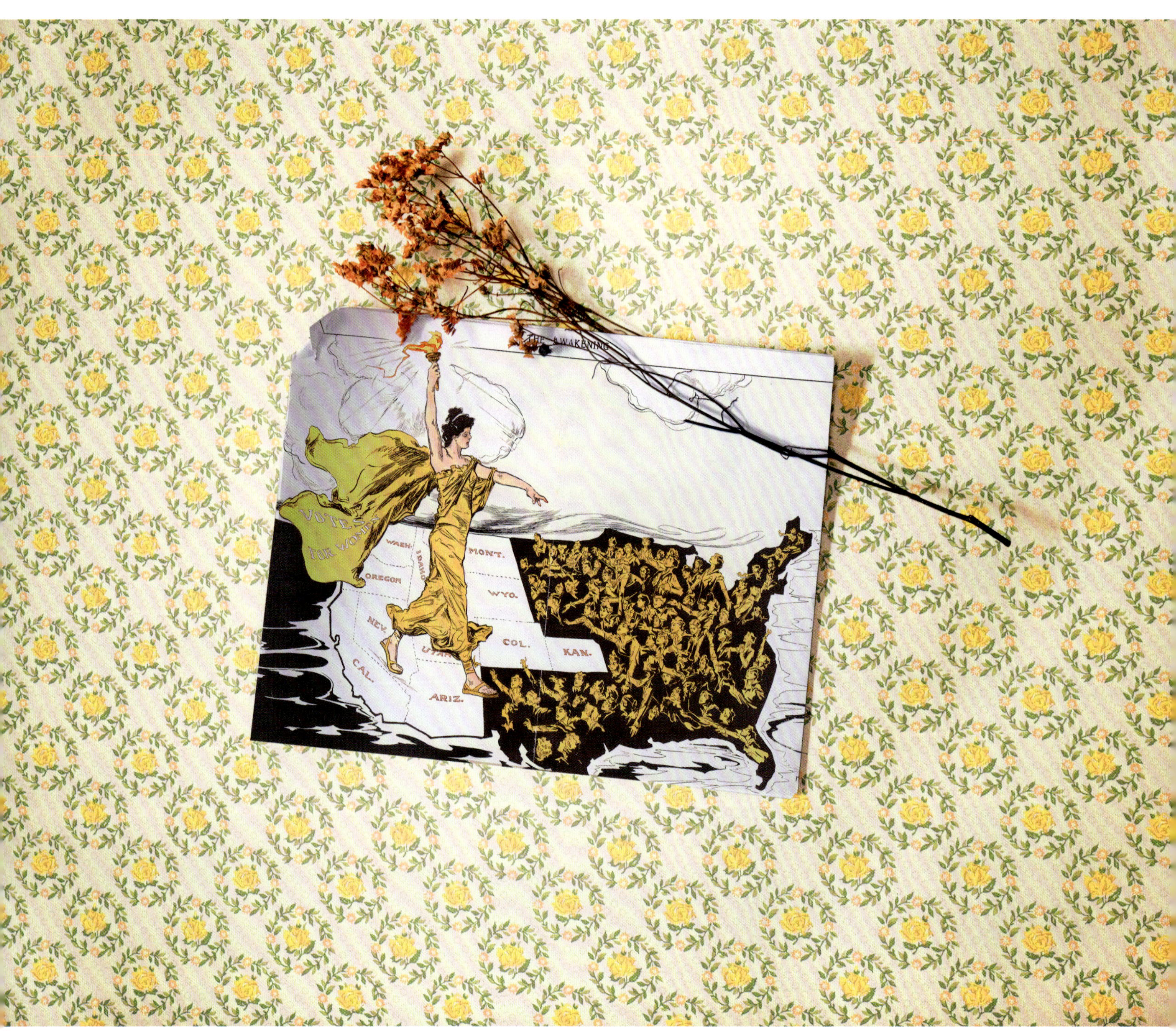

FIGURE 63. Kalee Appleton. *Untitled*

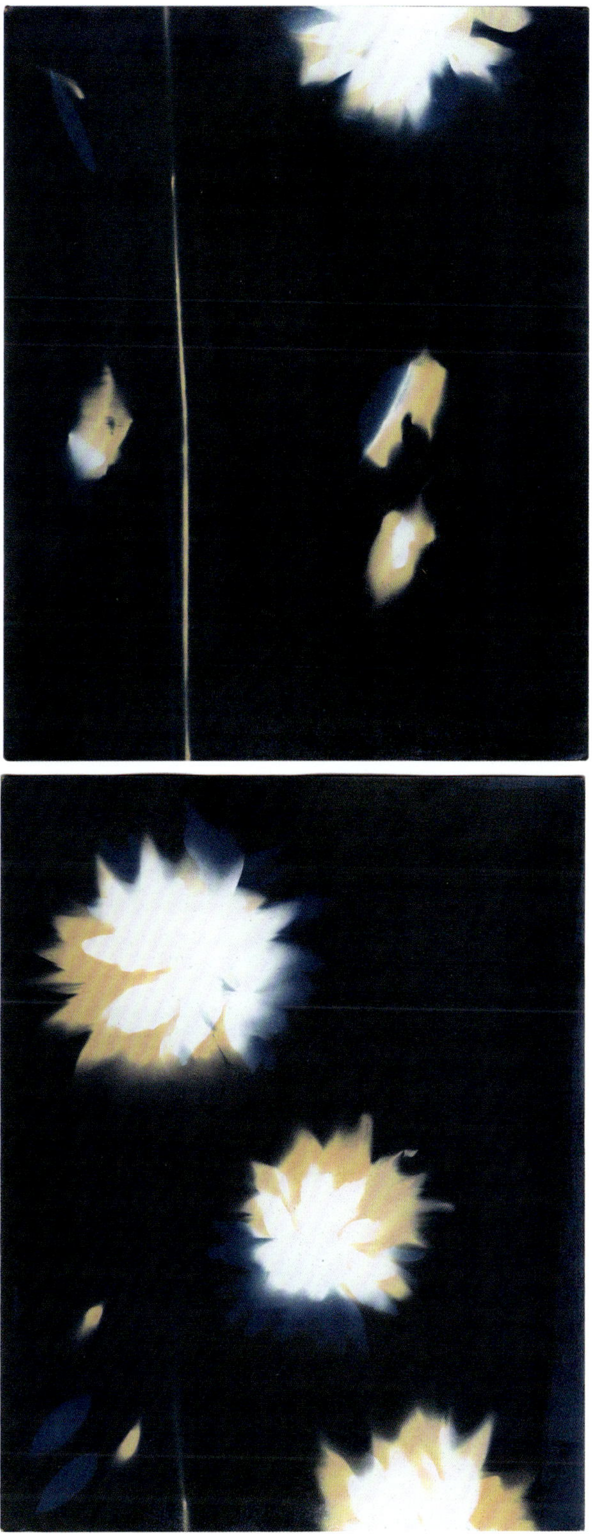

FIGURE 64. Paula Riff. *Because of Sunflowers*

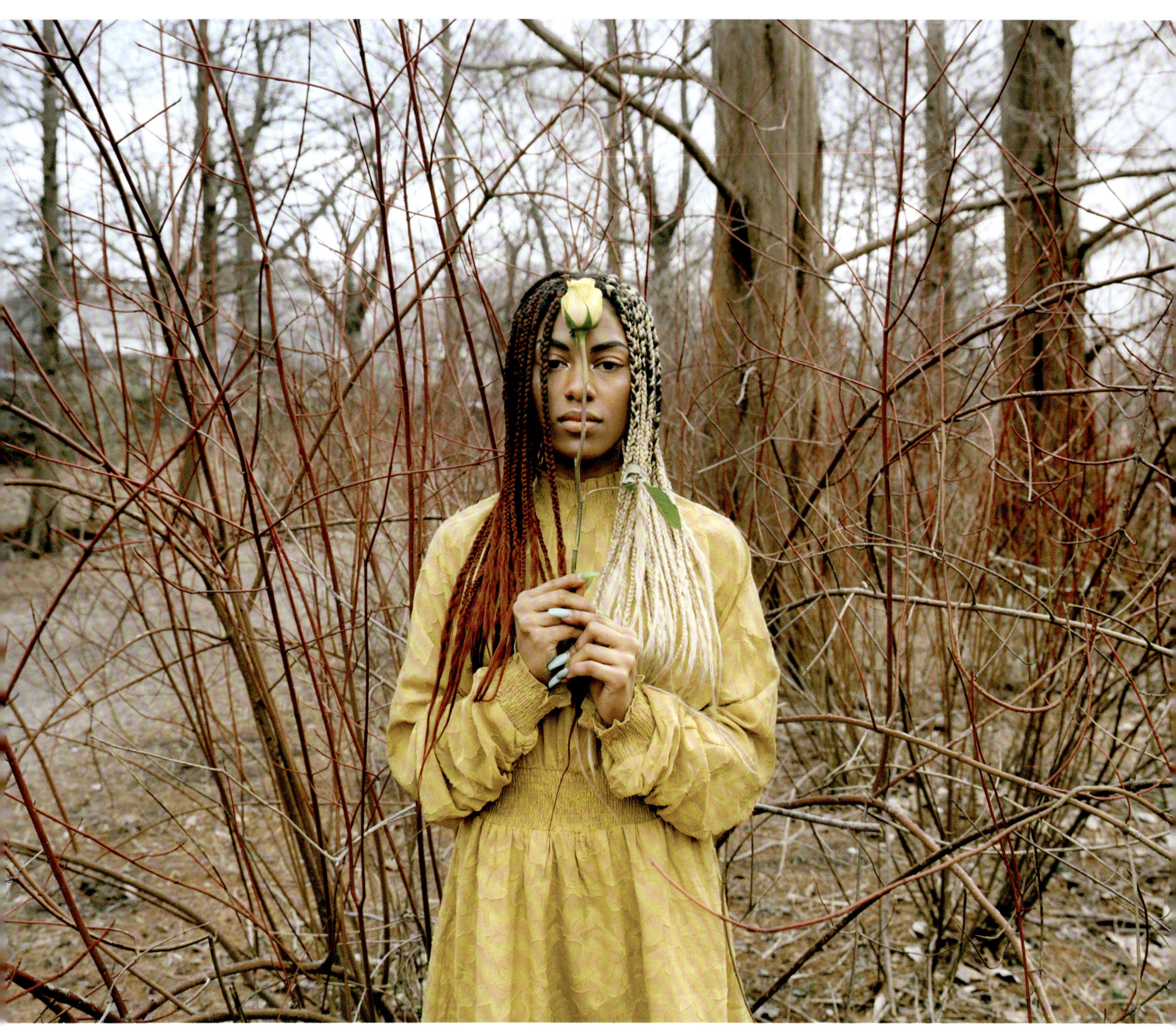

FIGURE 65. Rania Matar. *Kayla*. Courtesy of Robert Klein Gallery (Boston)

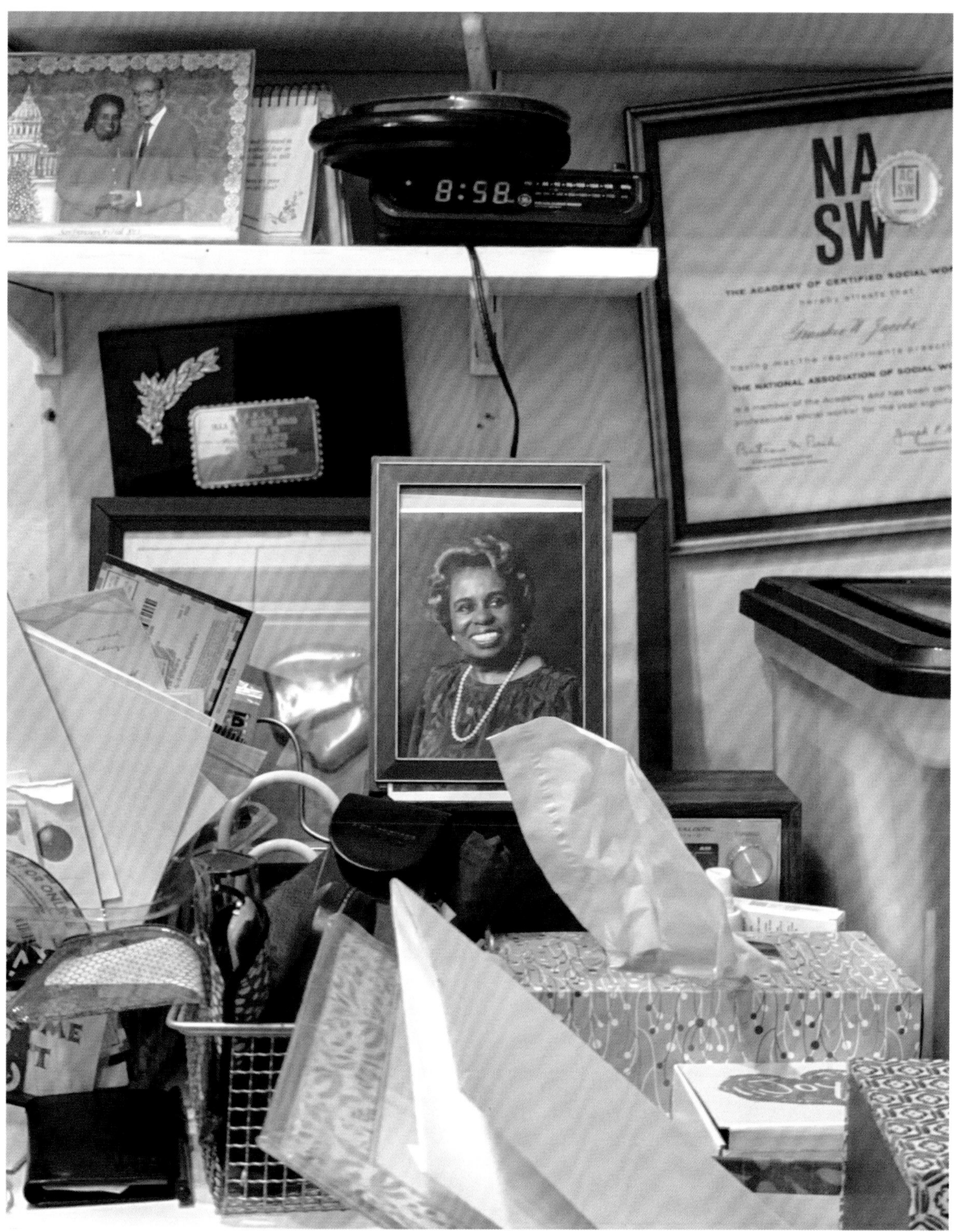

FIGURE 66. Colleen Mullins. *8:58 AM*

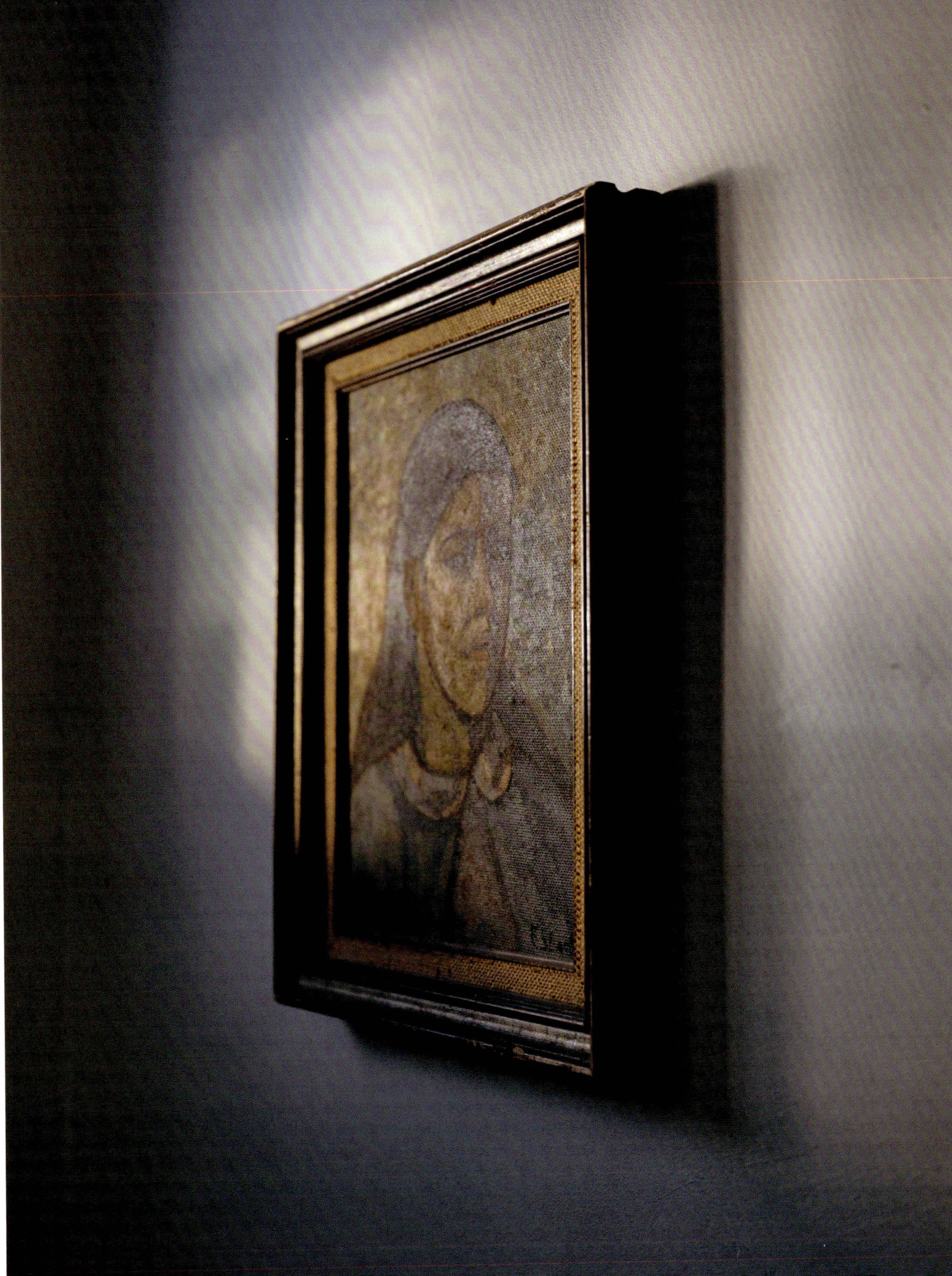

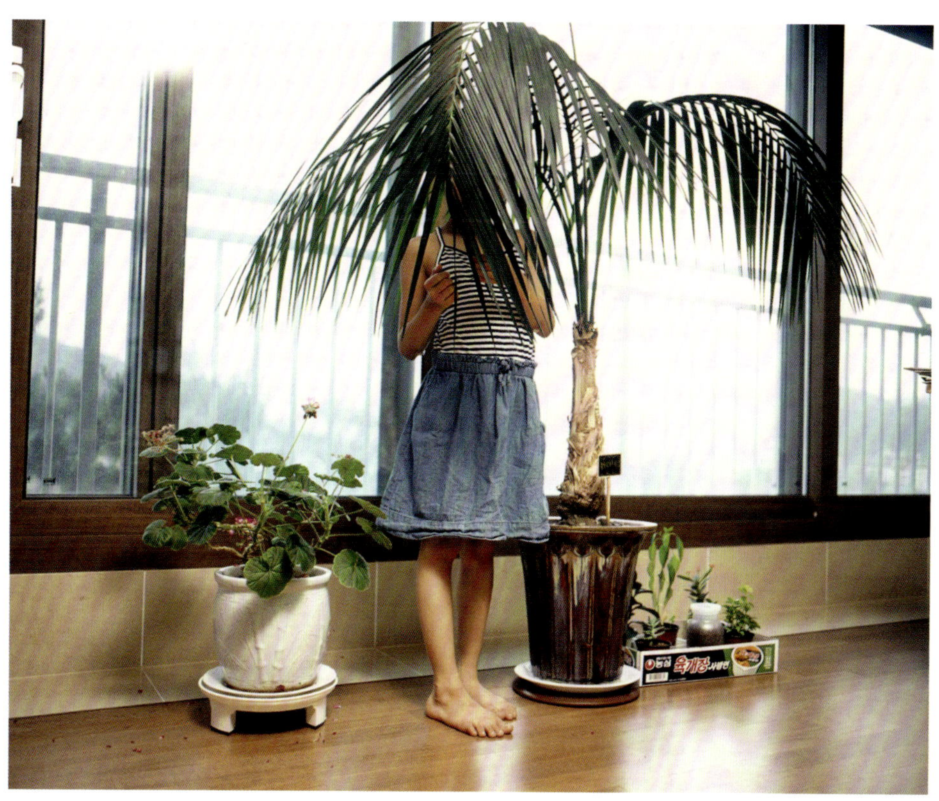

Facing, FIGURE 67. Kathya Maria Landeros. *Latina Girl, 2020*

Above, FIGURE 68. Hye-Ryoung Min. *Untitled* from the series *Yeonsoo*

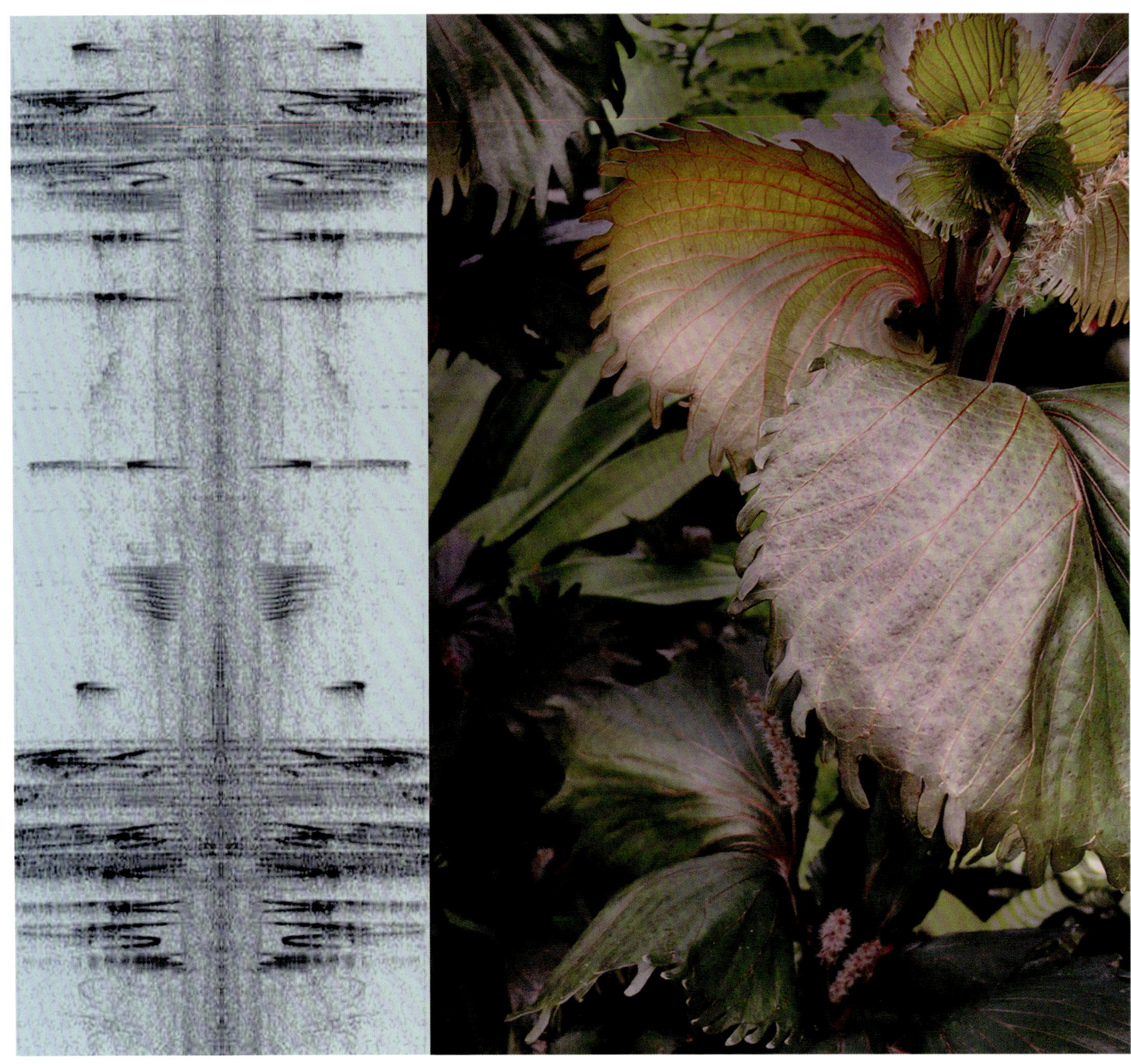

FIGURE 69. Alice Hargrave. *Suffragist Bird, River Tyrannulet (female calls)*

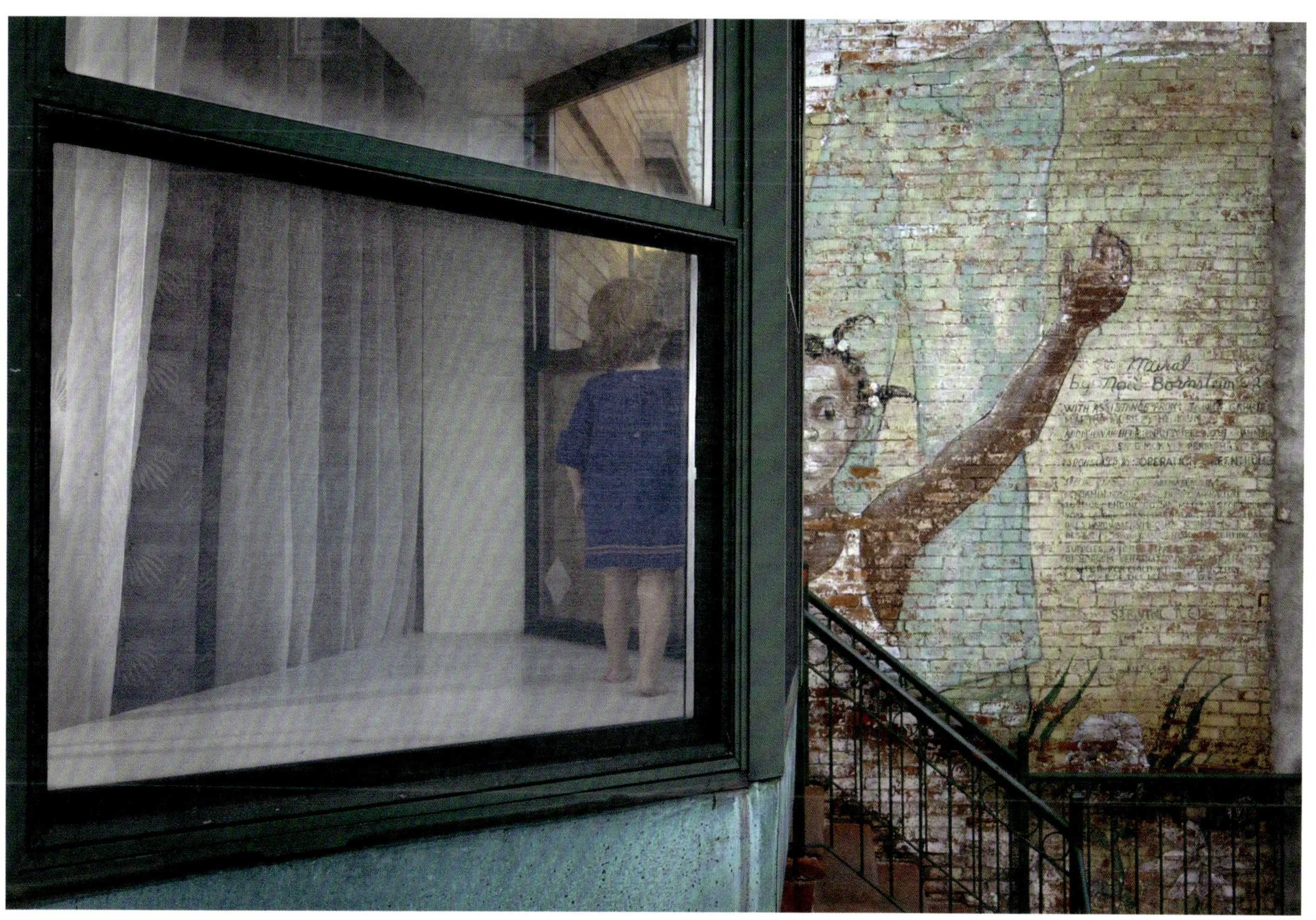

FIGURE 70. Jennifer McClure. *Untitled*

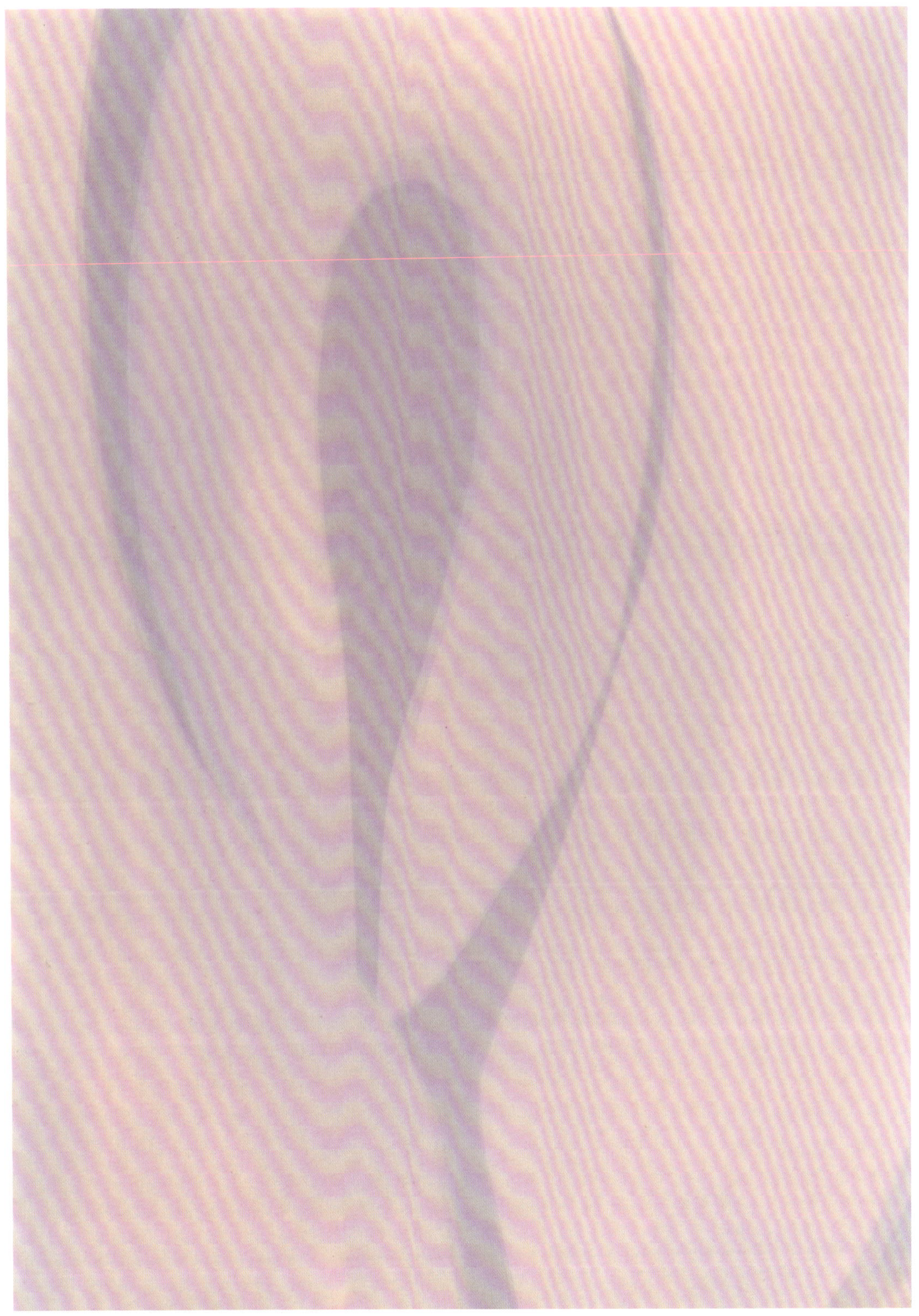

FIGURE 71. Alyssa Minahan. *Untitled*

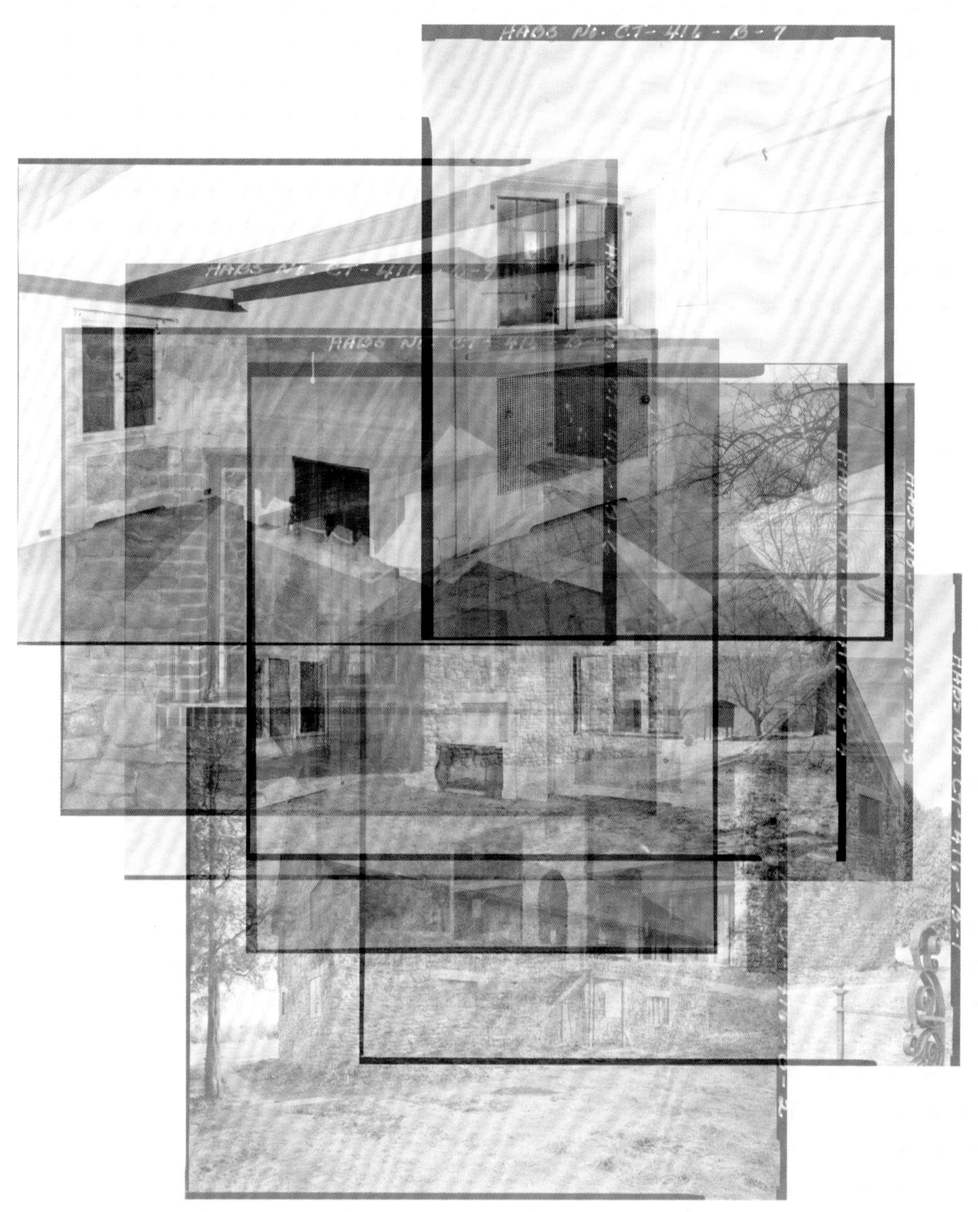

FIGURE 72. S. Billie Mandle. *Esther Lape's home at what is now the Stewart B. McKinney National Wildlife Refuge; Habitat for the endangered Rose of Plymouth*

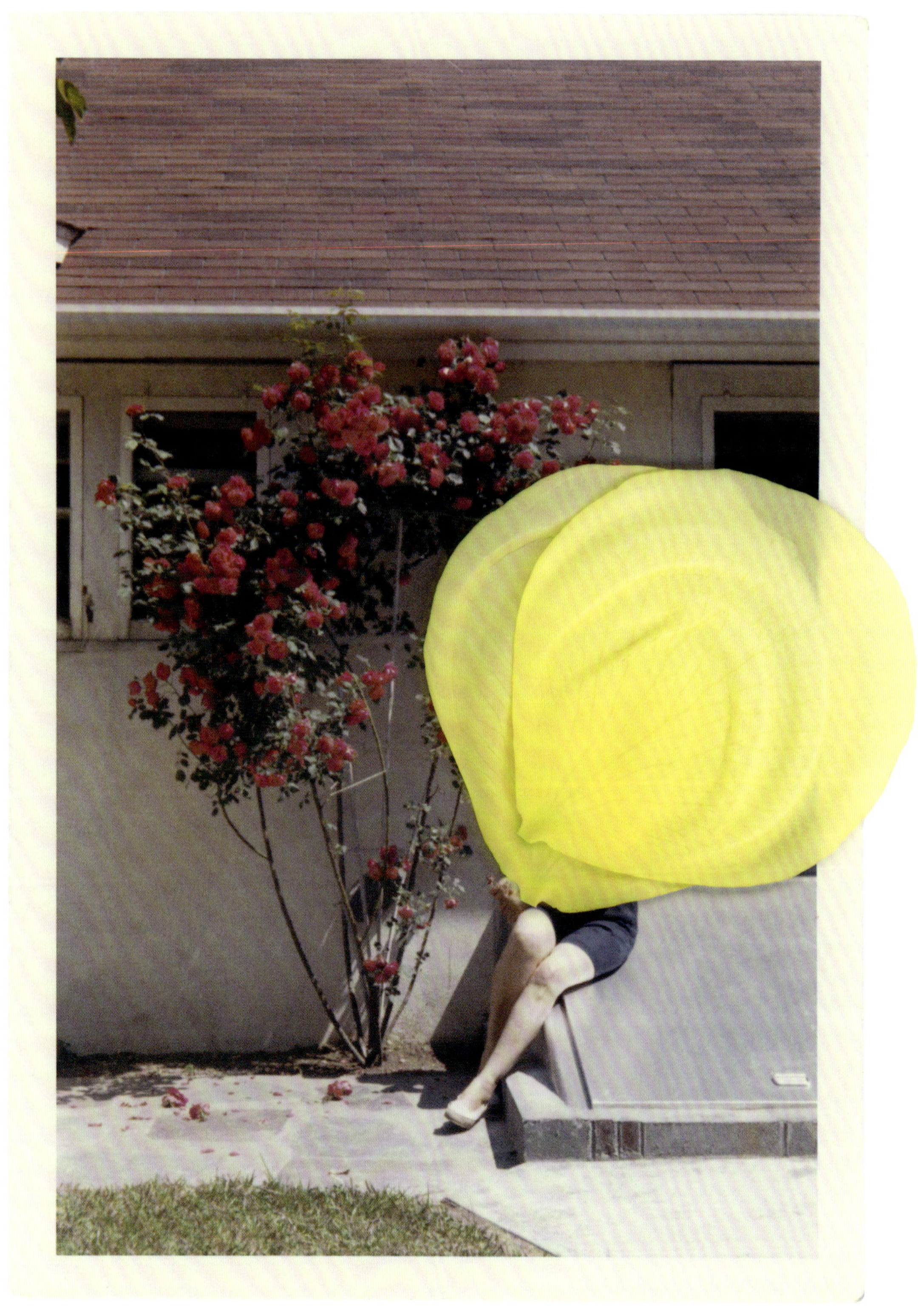

FIGURE 73. Odette England. *Untitled*

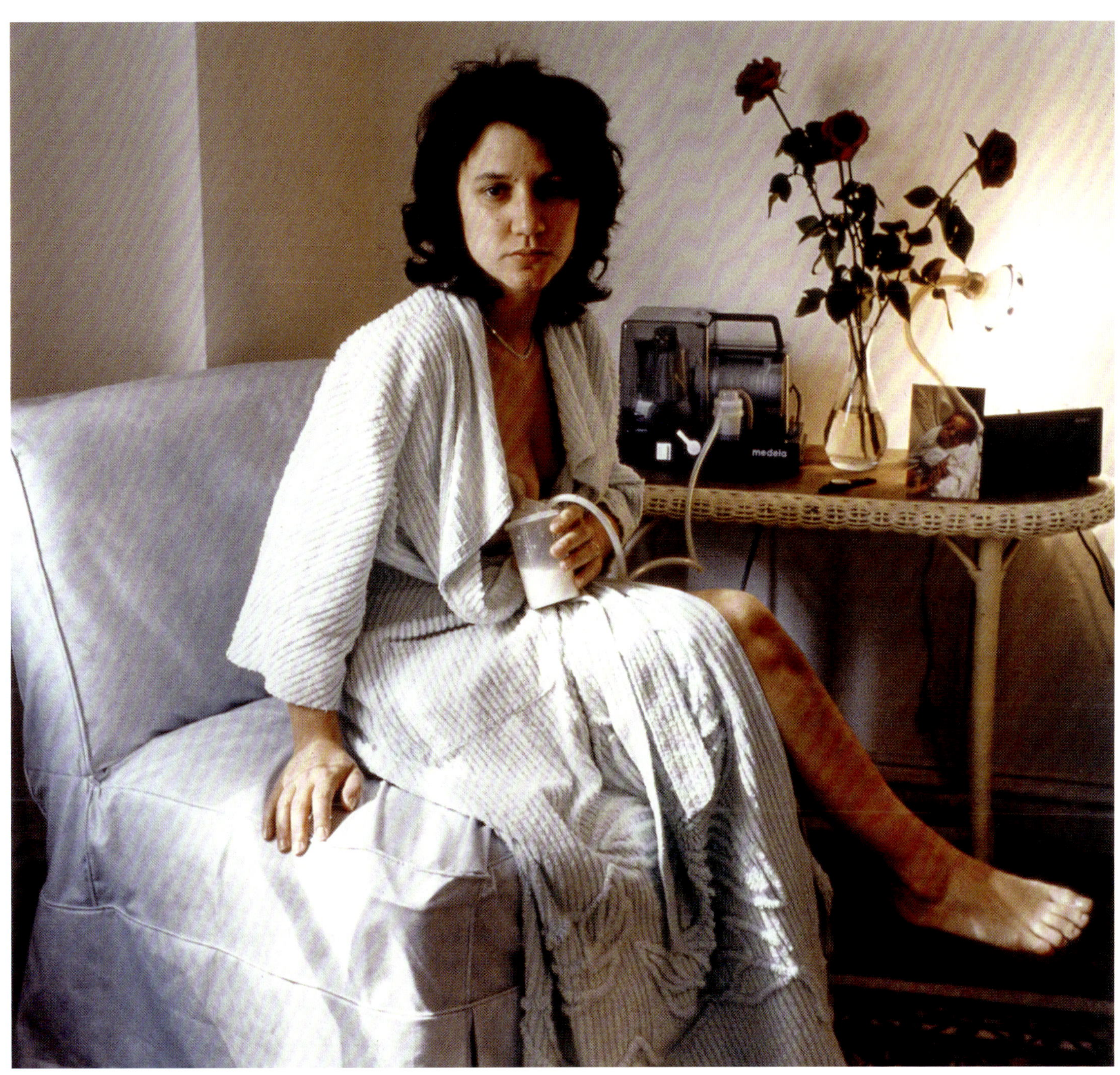

FIGURE 74. Joni Sternbach. *Premature*

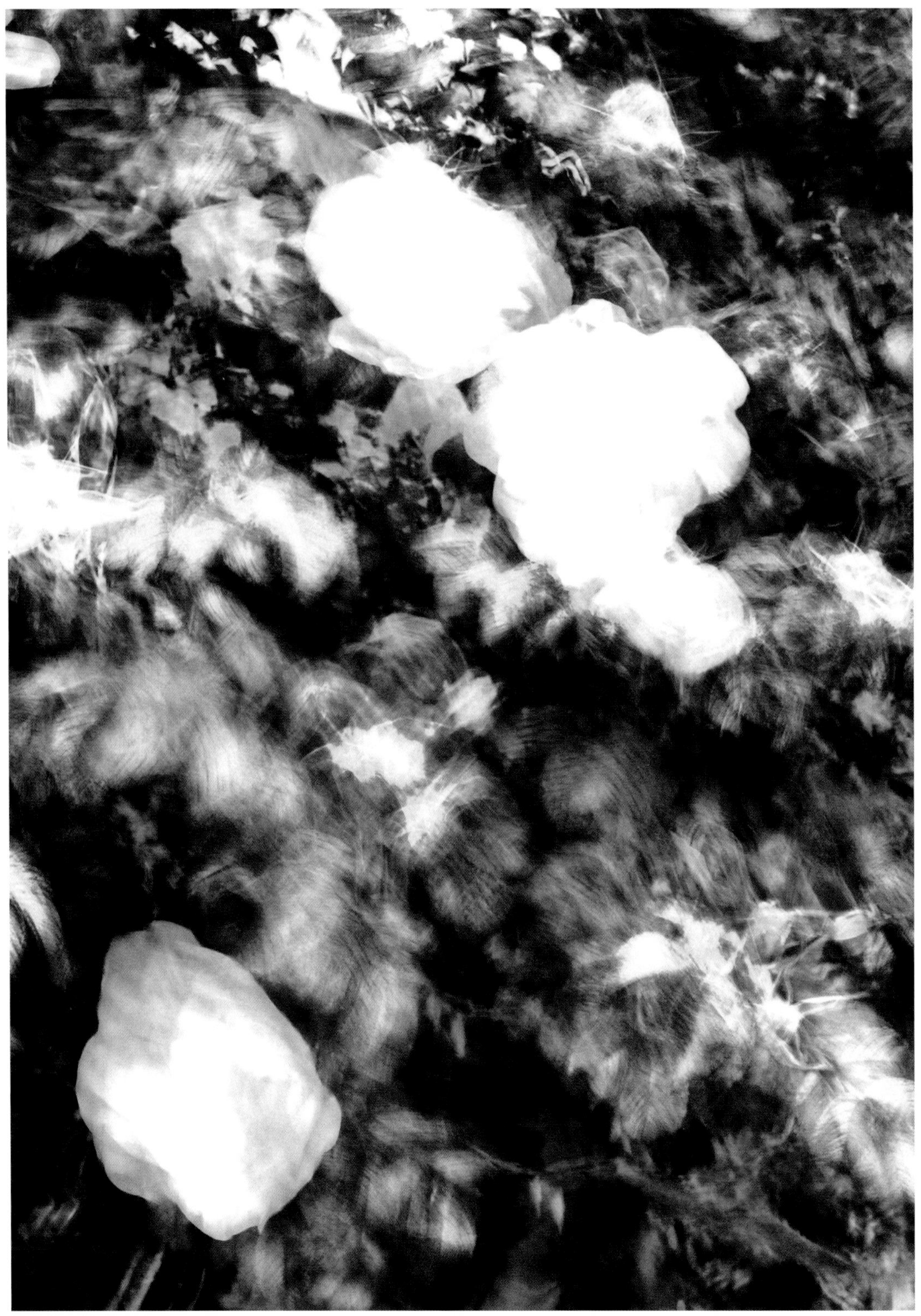

FIGURE 75. Thalassa Raasch. *Blooming roses with wind*

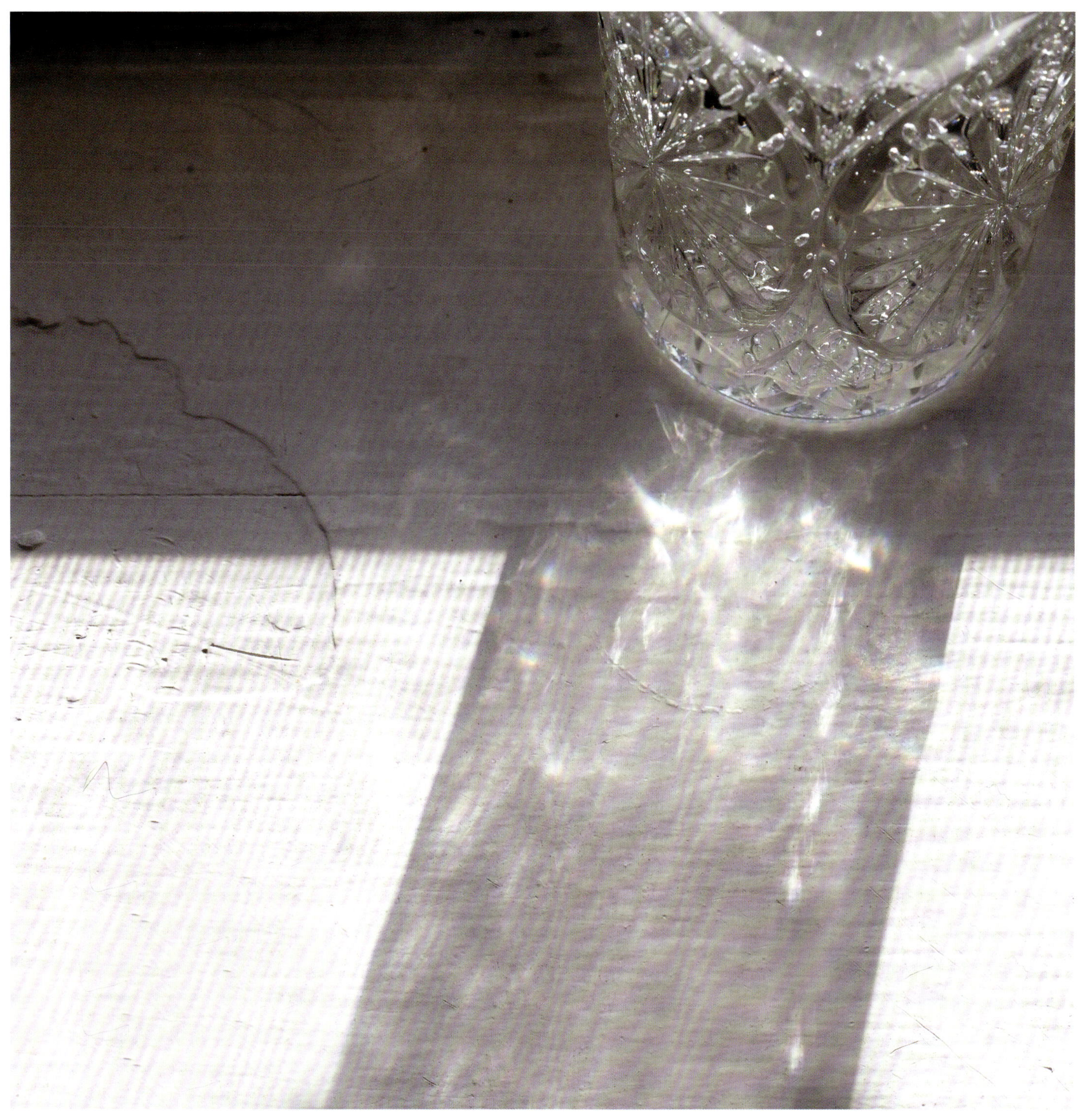

FIGURE 76. Deedra Baker. *Manifest*

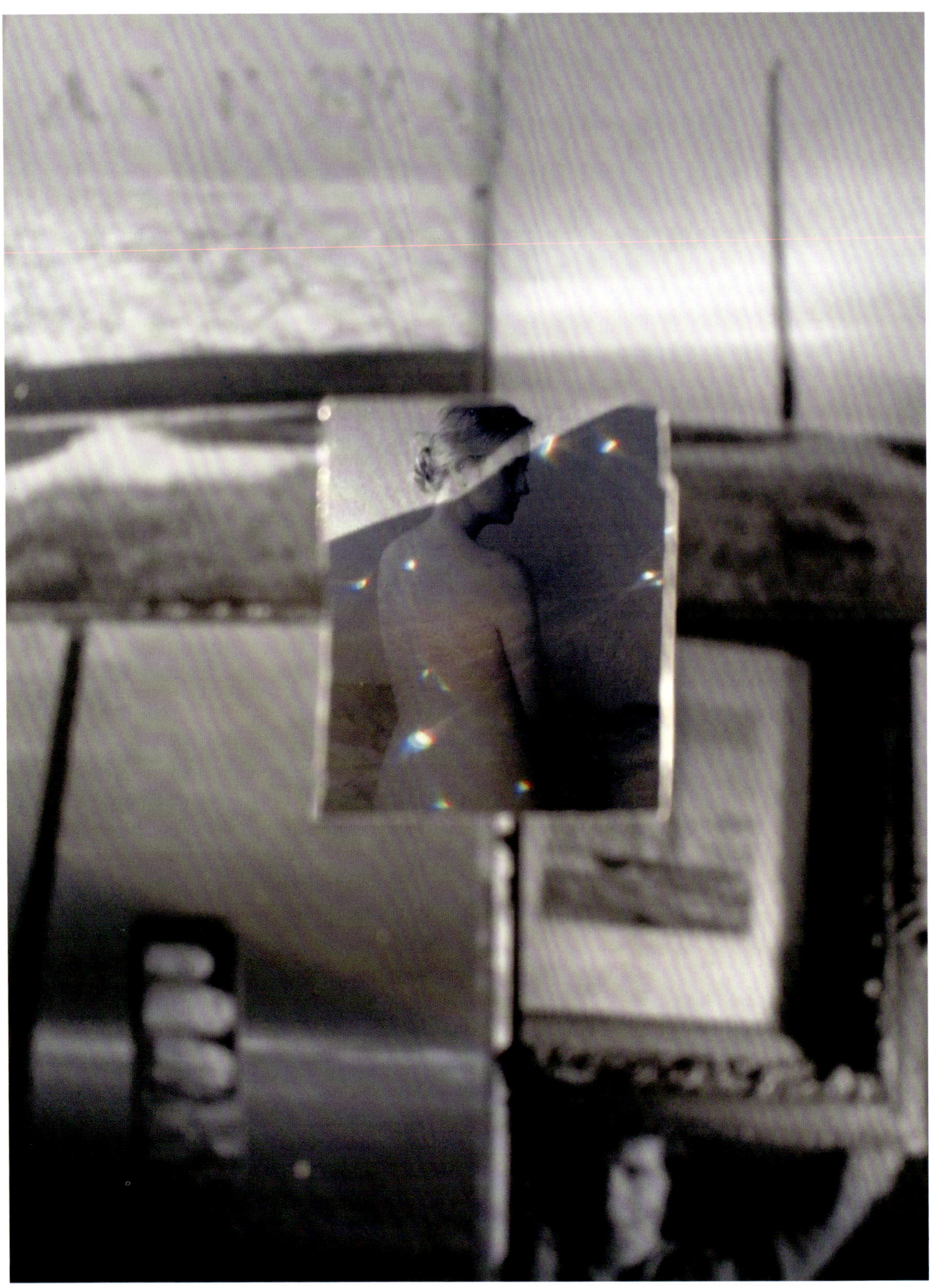

FIGURE 77. Jordanna Kalman. *Frank*

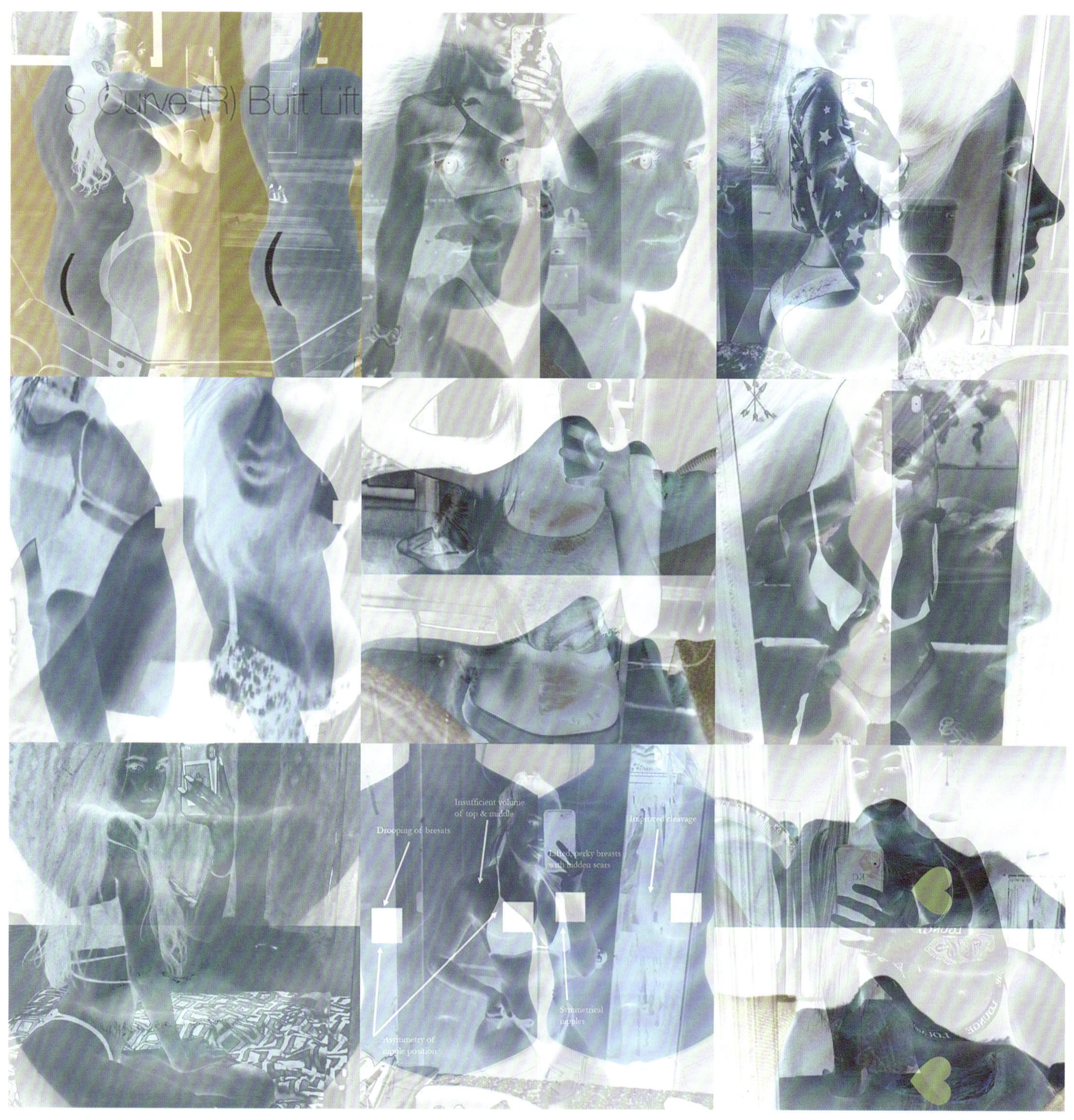

FIGURE 78. Cassandra Zampini. *Liked*

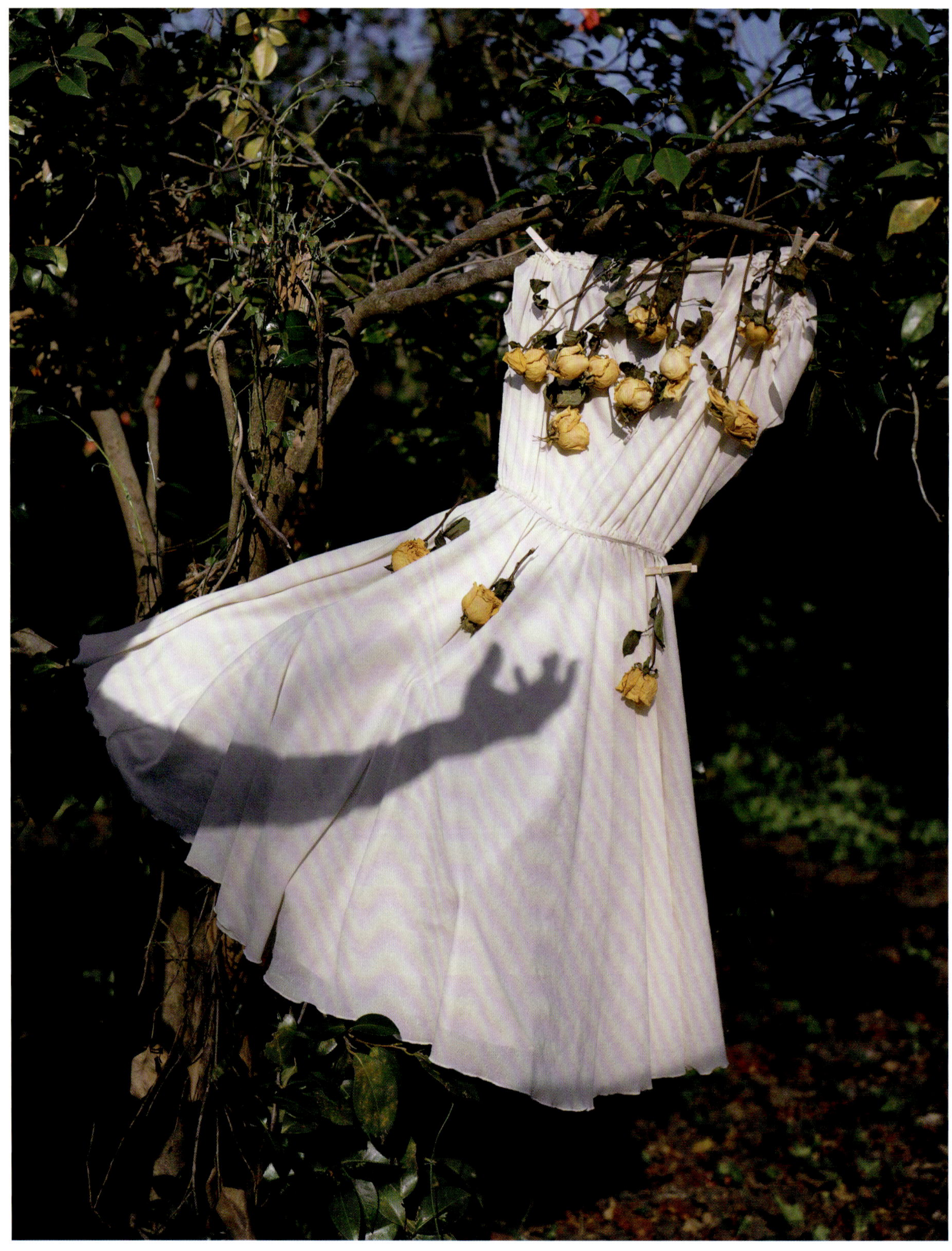

FIGURE 79. Ashley Kauschinger. *After The Vote (US Suffragists 1920)*

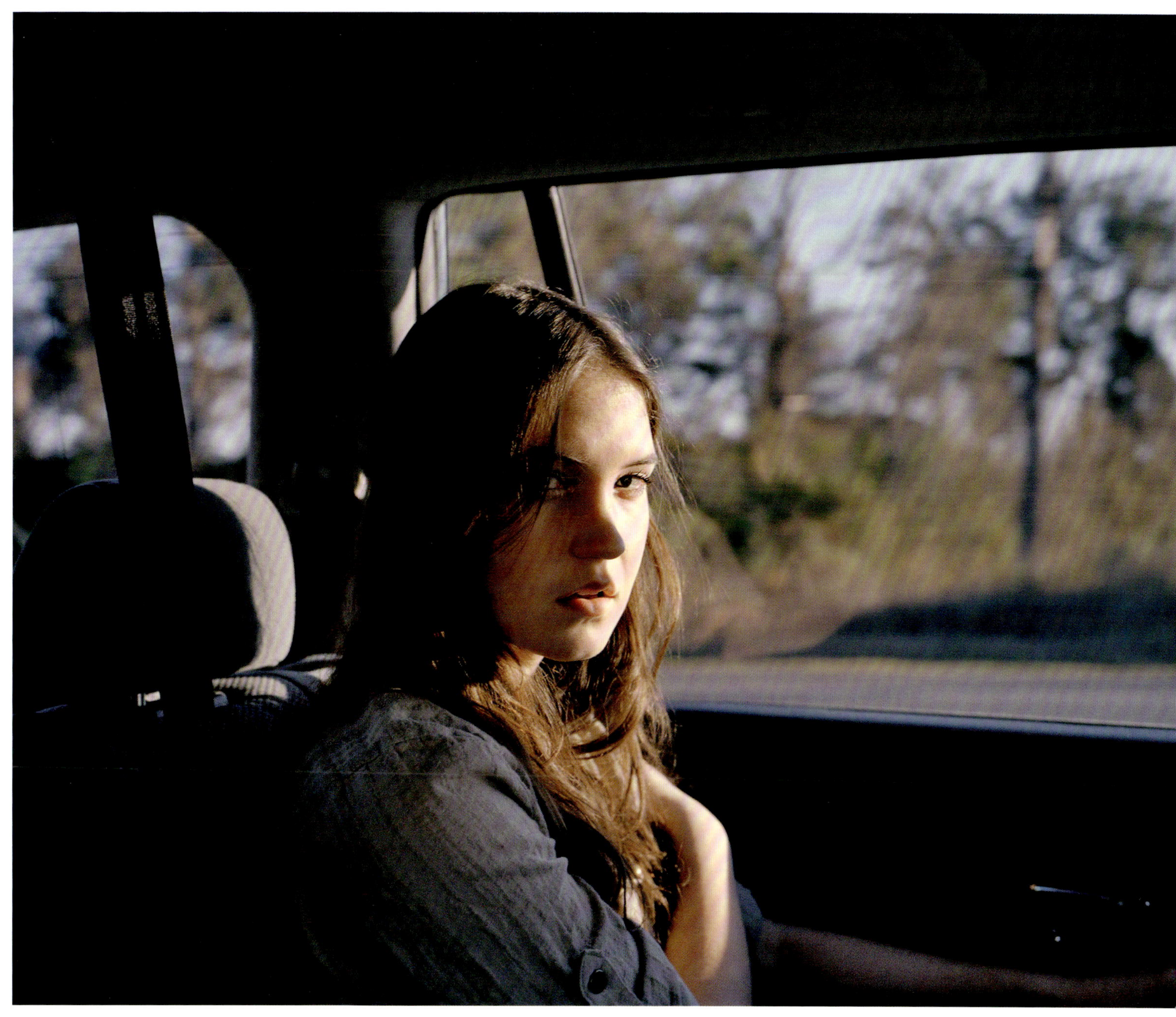

FIGURE 80. Sara Macel. *Dana at Fifteen*

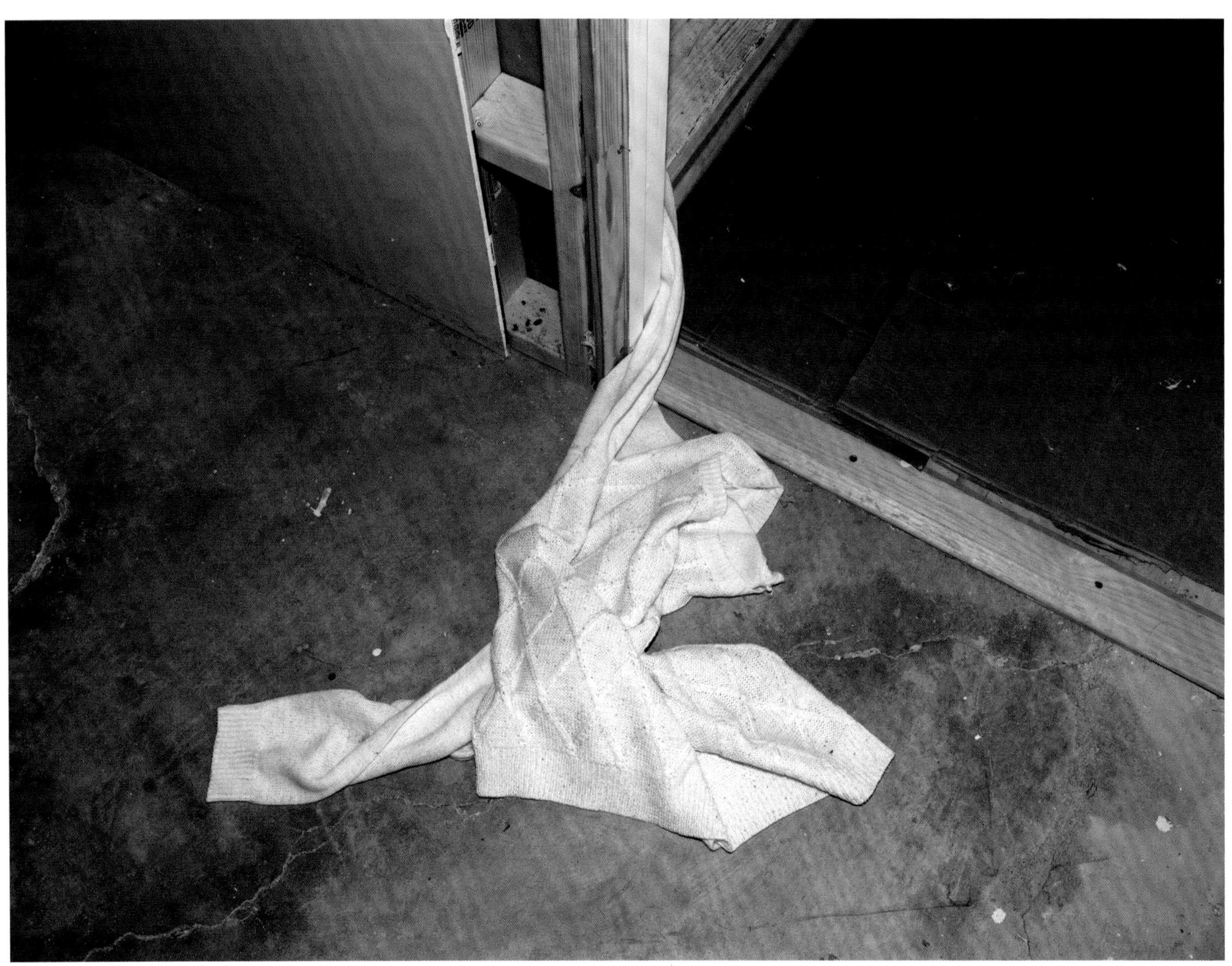

FIGURE 81. Elizabeth M. Claffey. *Untitled*

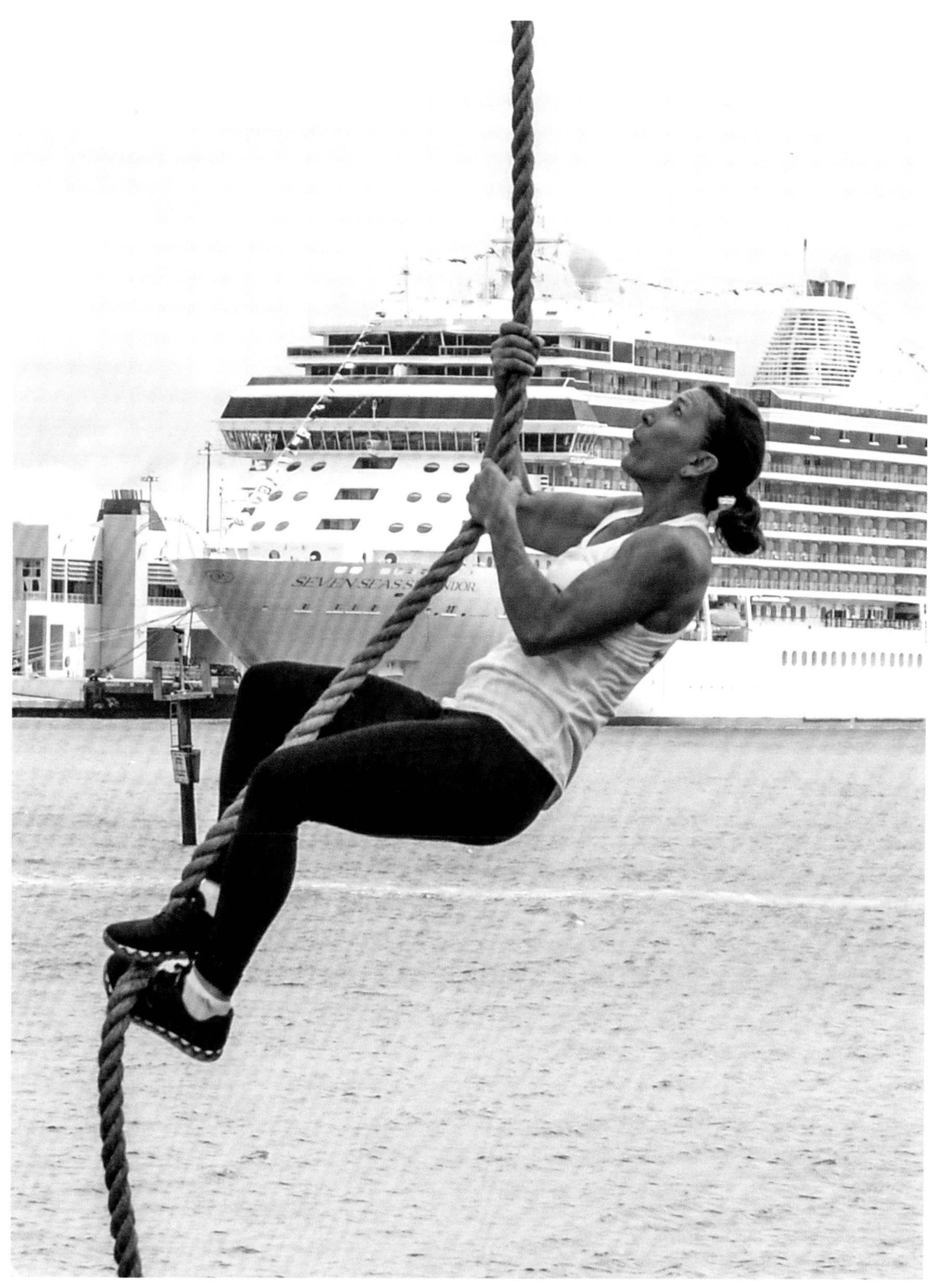

FIGURE 82. Marie Triller. *Portrait of an Athlete*

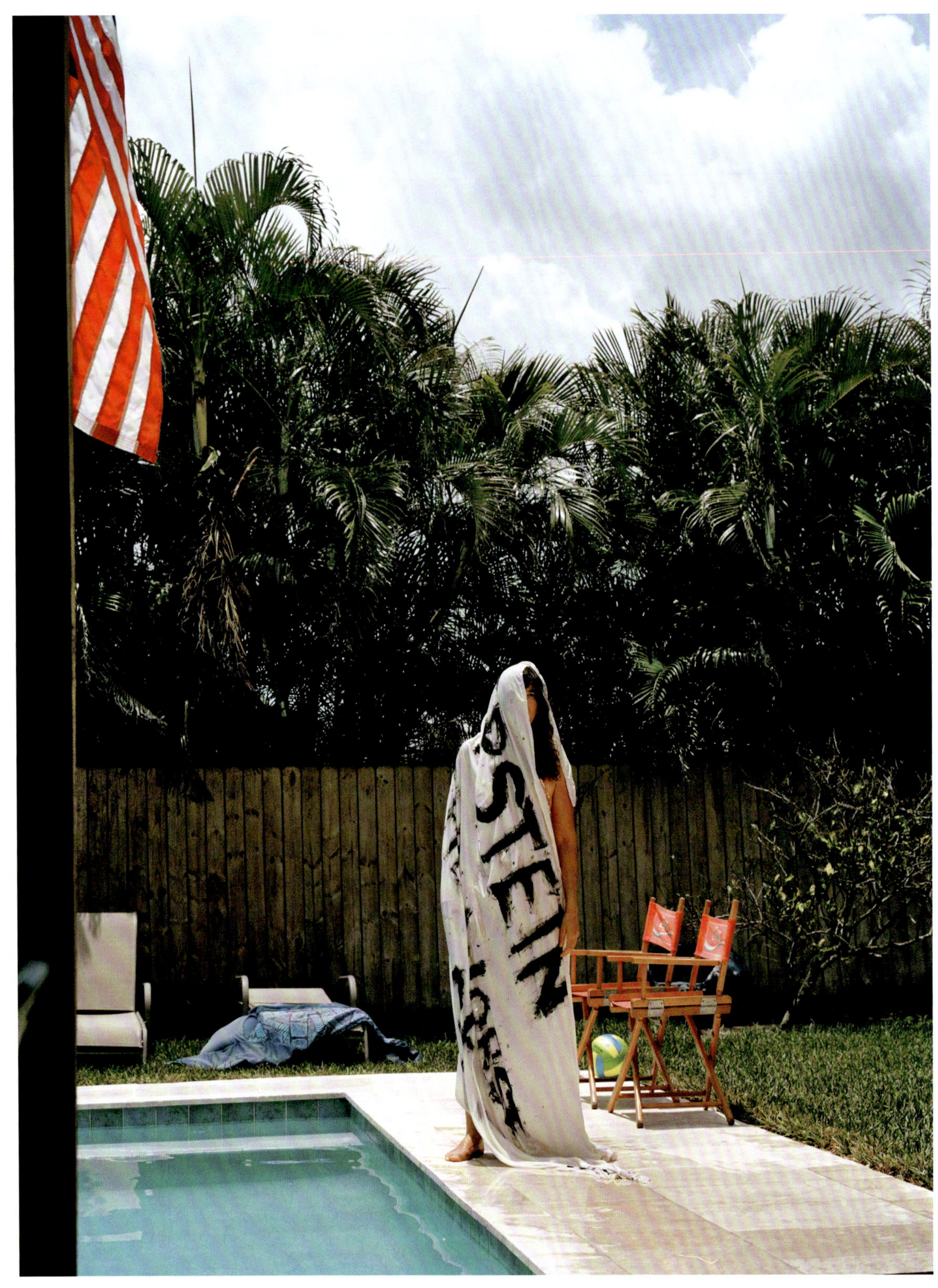

FIGURE 83. Katelyn Kopenhaver. *Covered in Filth (Epstein Is The Worst Kind of Virus) July 4th, 2020*

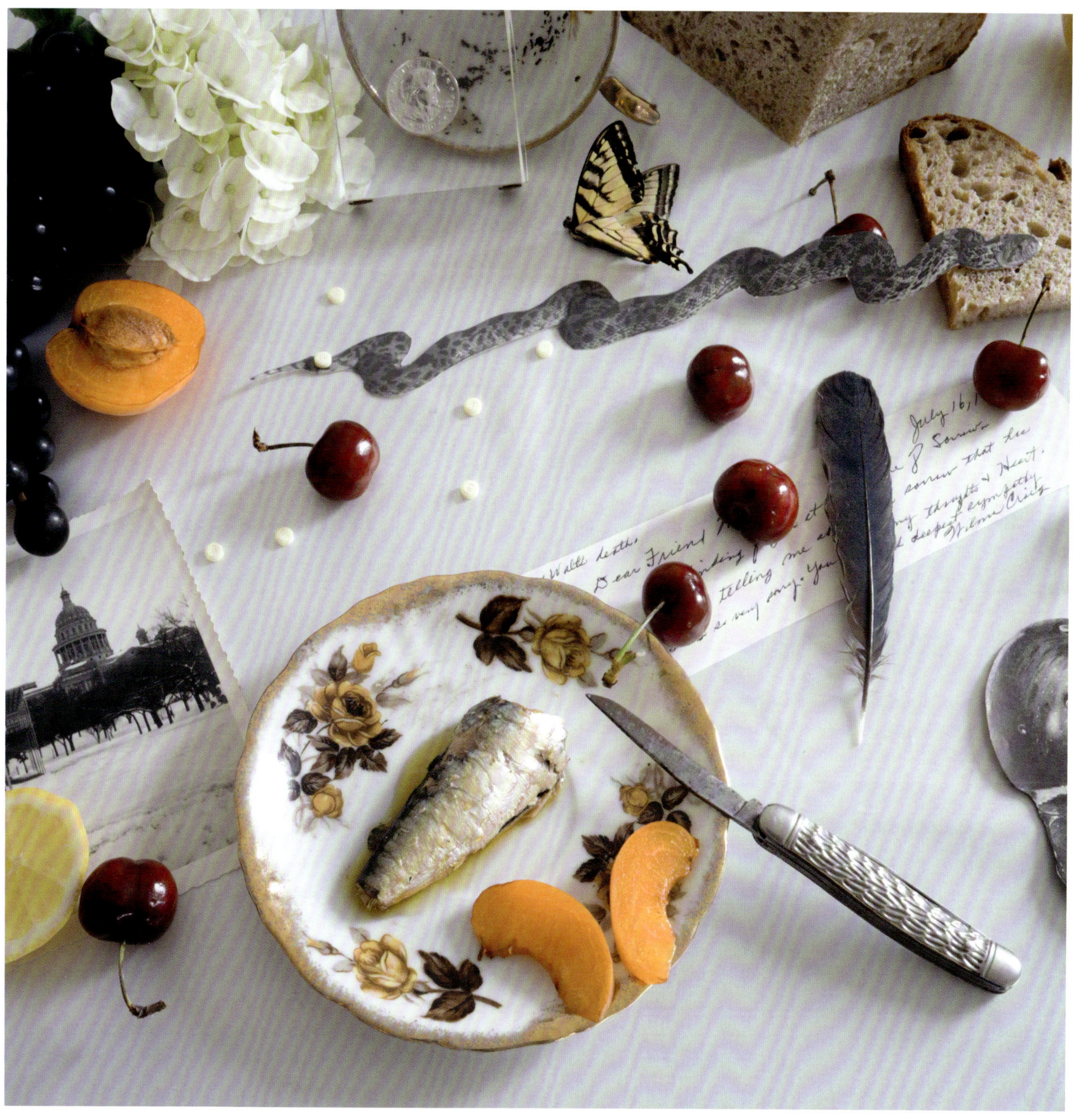

FIGURE 84. Meg Griffiths. *Subtle Fusion of Time*

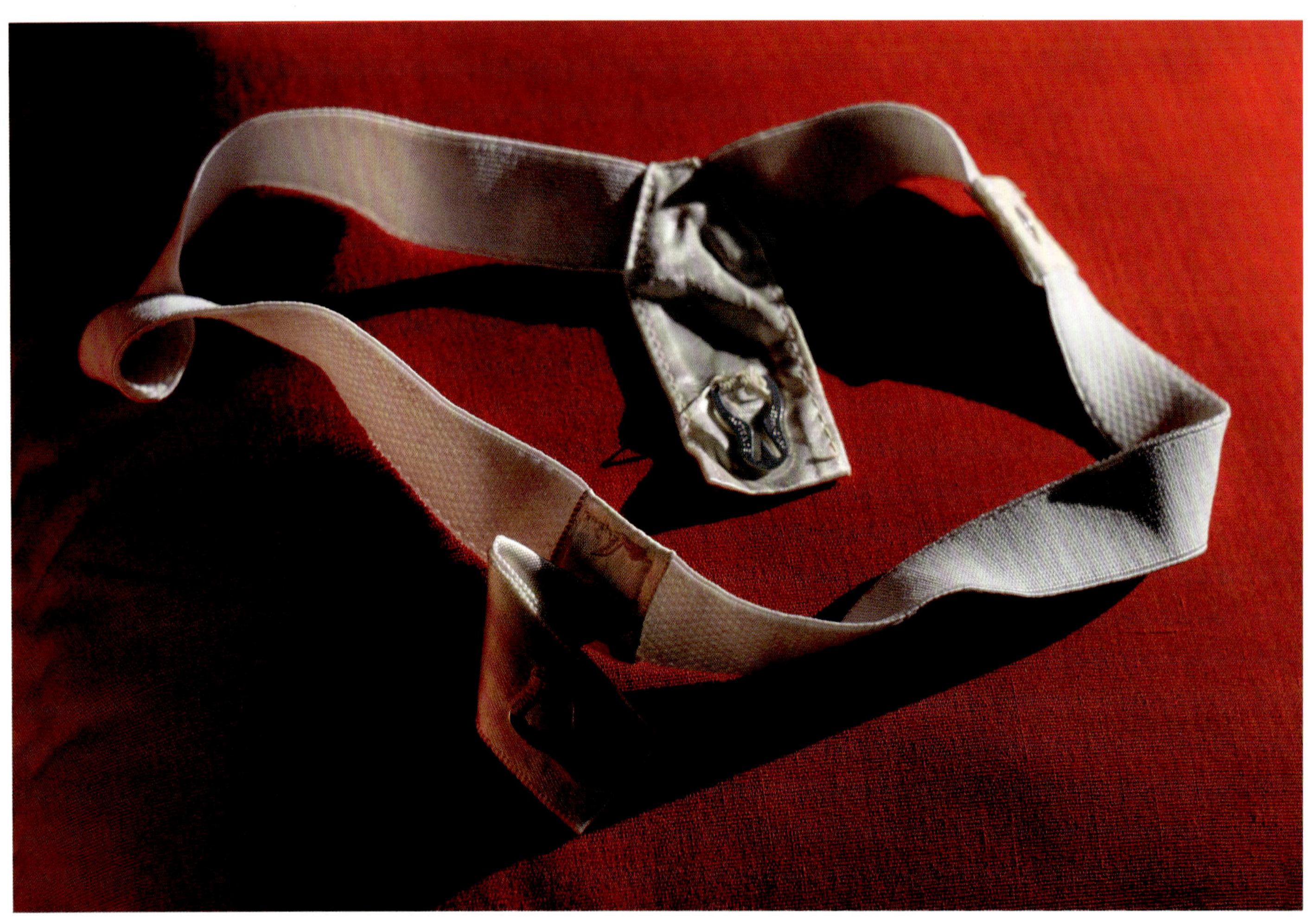

FIGURE 85. Yvette Meltzer. *Advances for Women Celebrating 100 Years*

FIGURE 86. Larissa Ramey. *Dirty Hands*

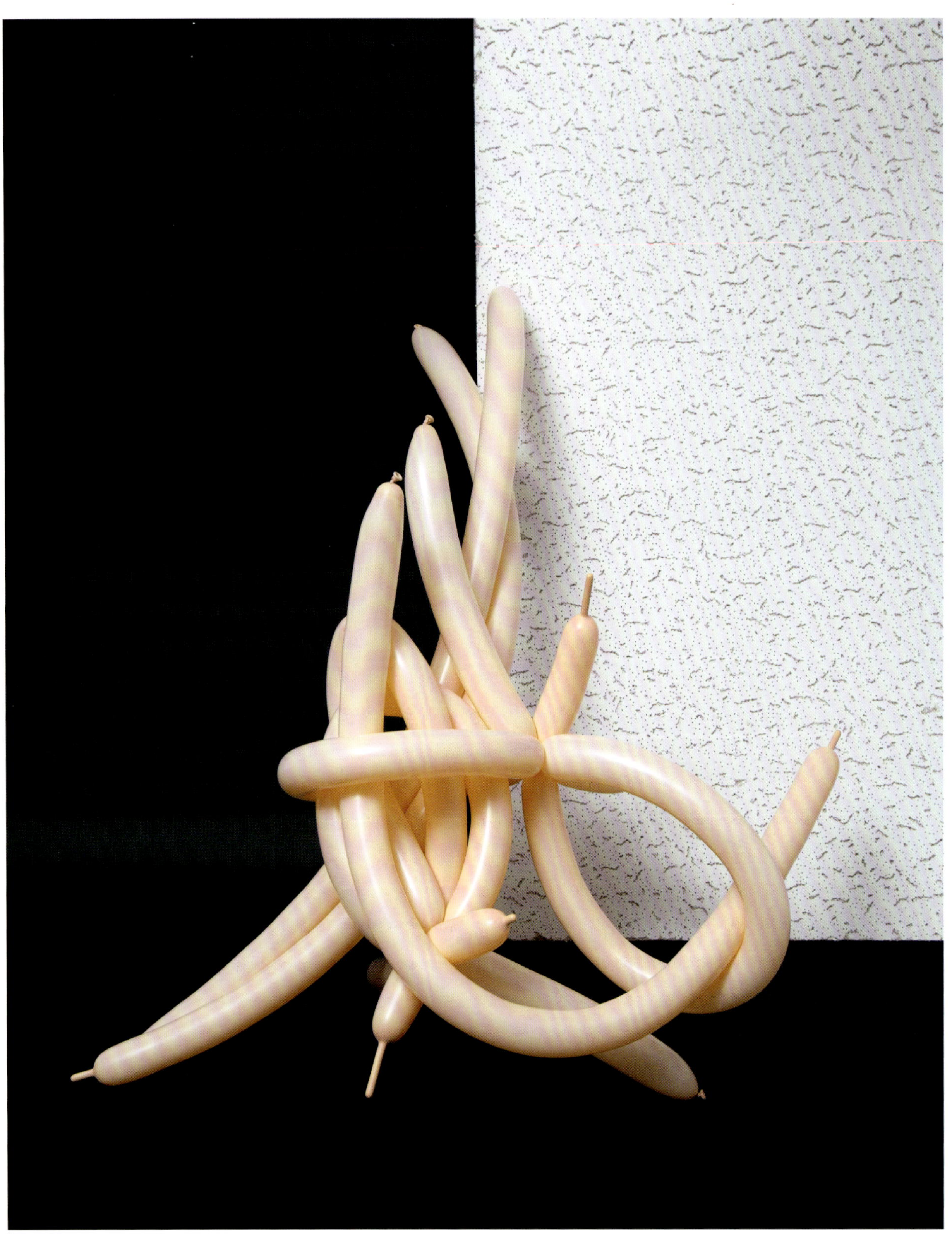

FIGURE 87. Rebecca Drolen. *Balloon Study No. 1*

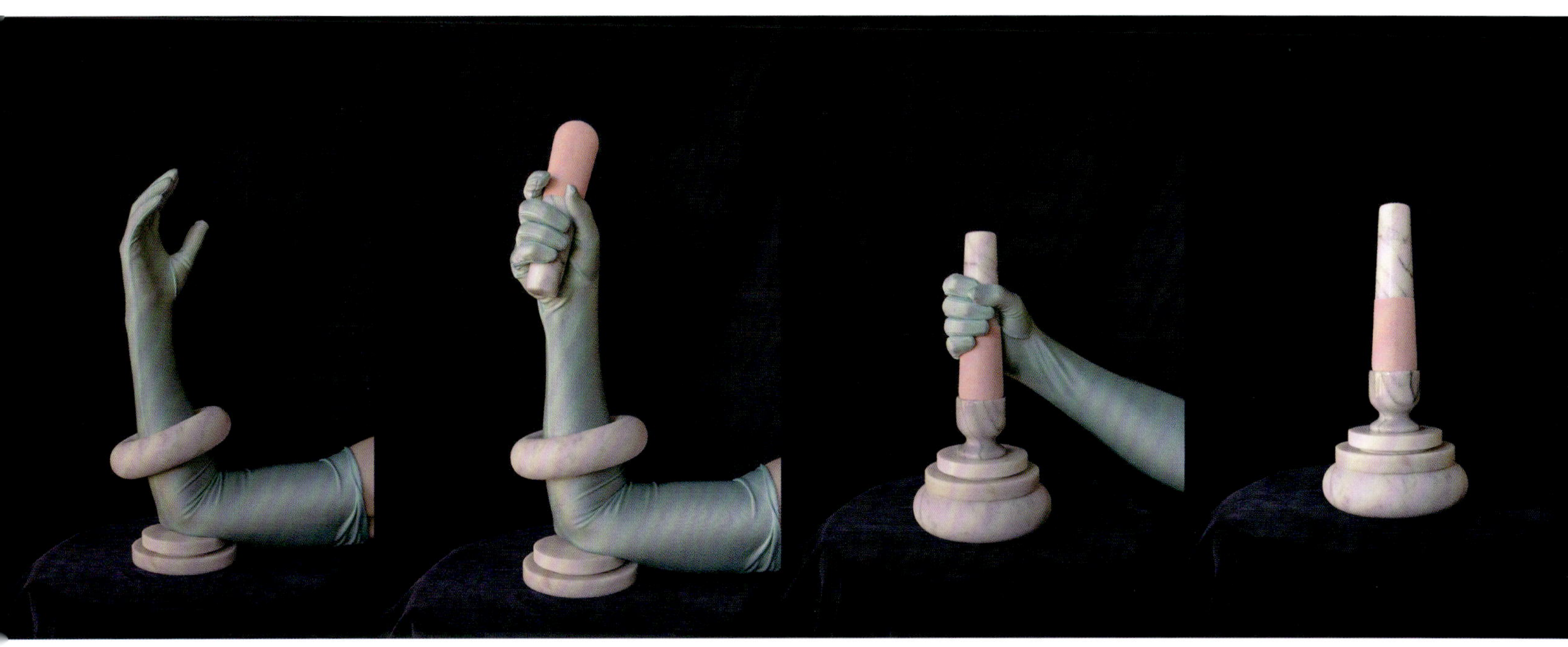

FIGURE 88. Emily Peacock. *Untitled*

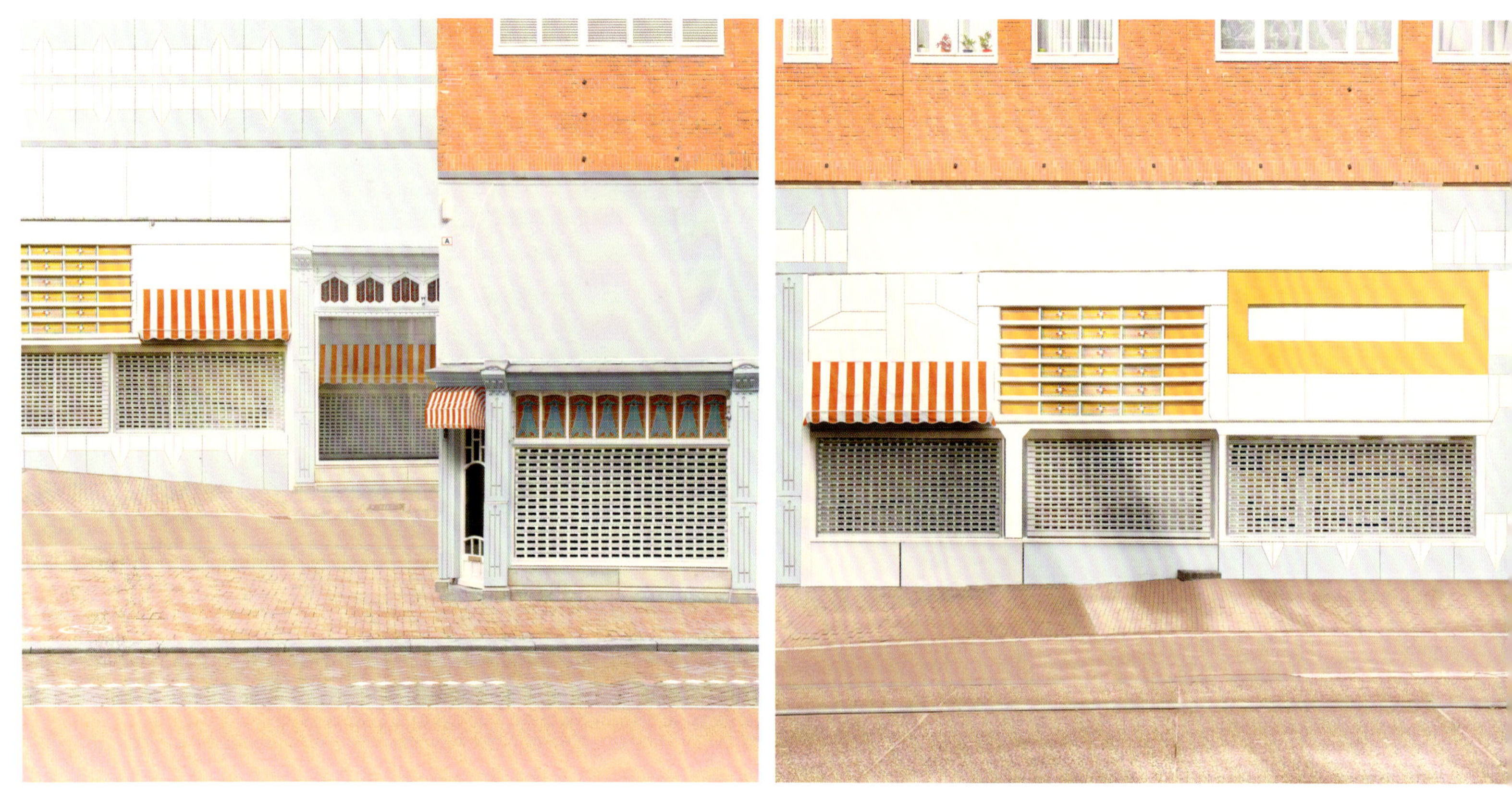

FIGURE 89. Leigh Merrill. *Untitled*

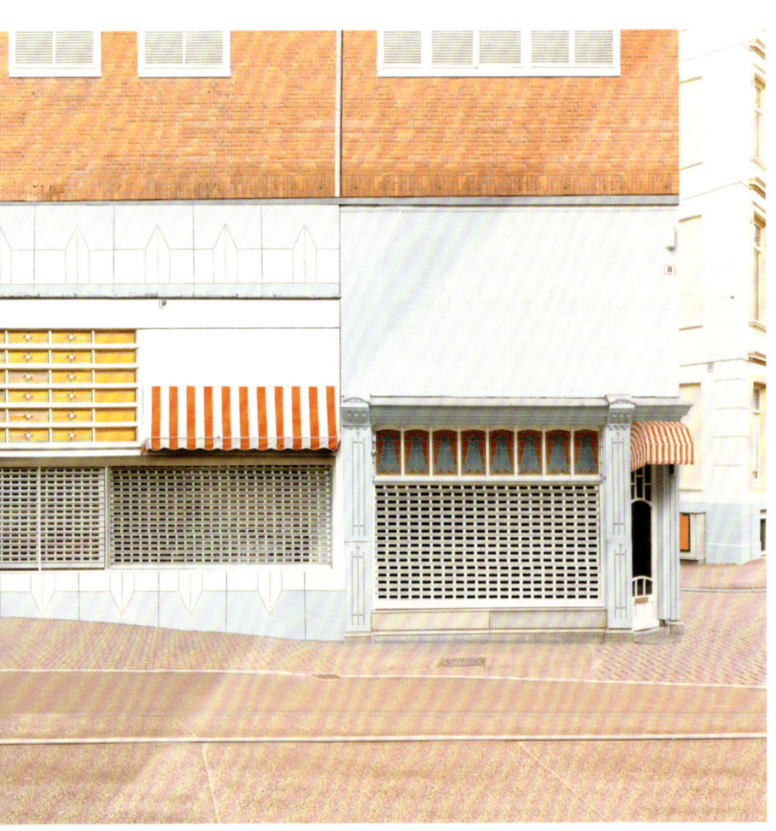

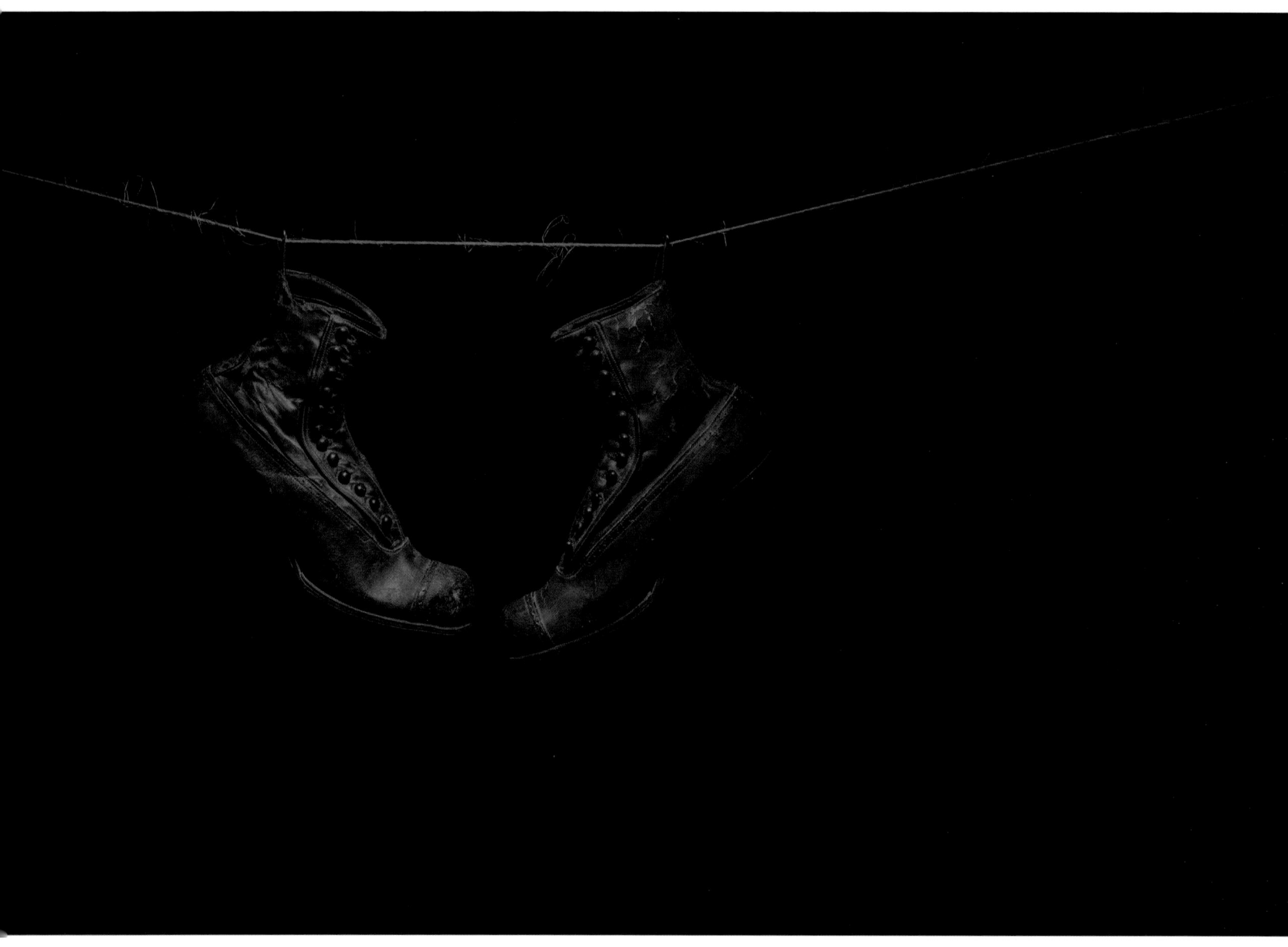

FIGURE 90. Tami Bahat. *Strung Along for Too Long*

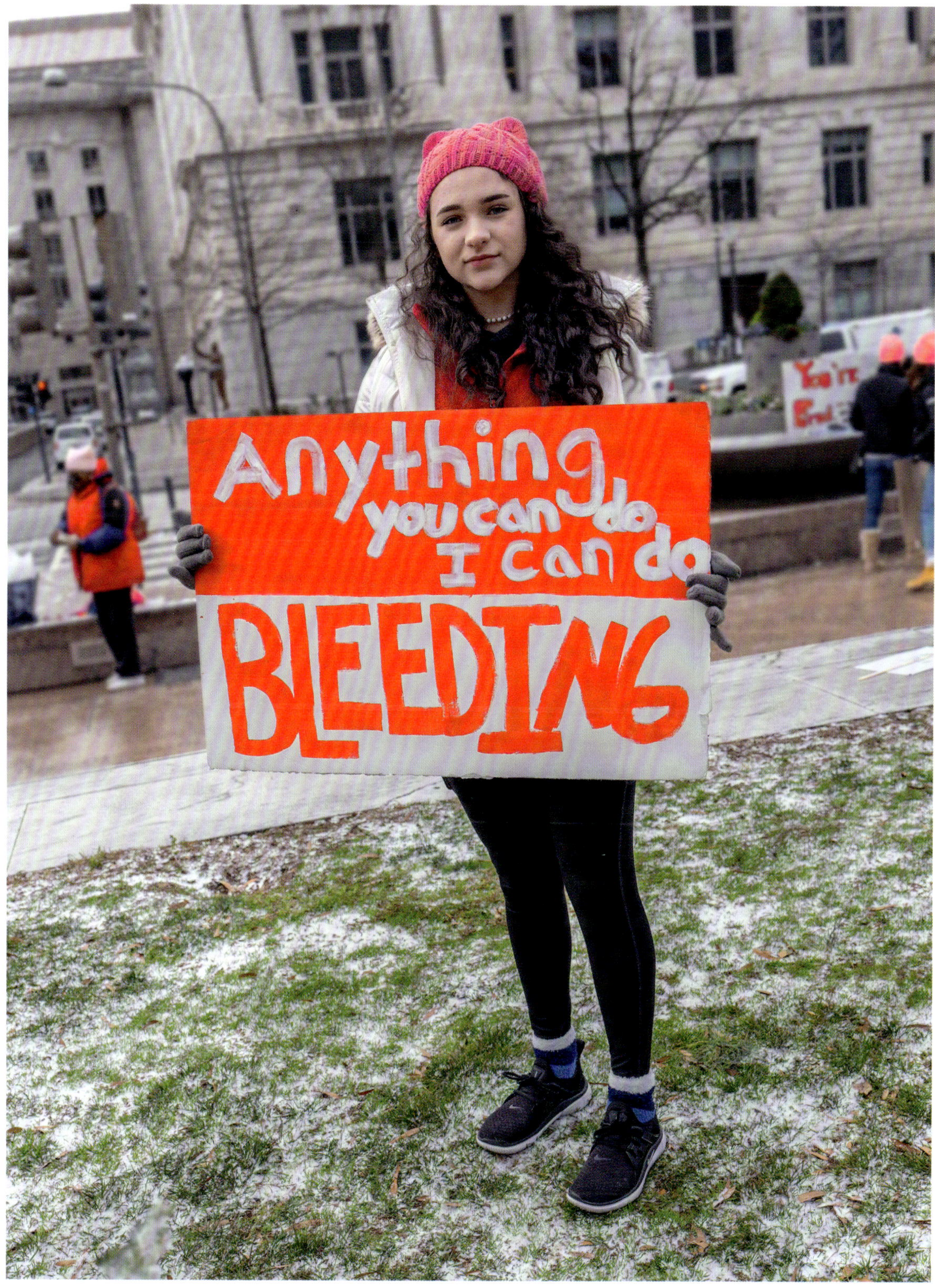

FIGURE 91. Greta Pratt. *Untitled*

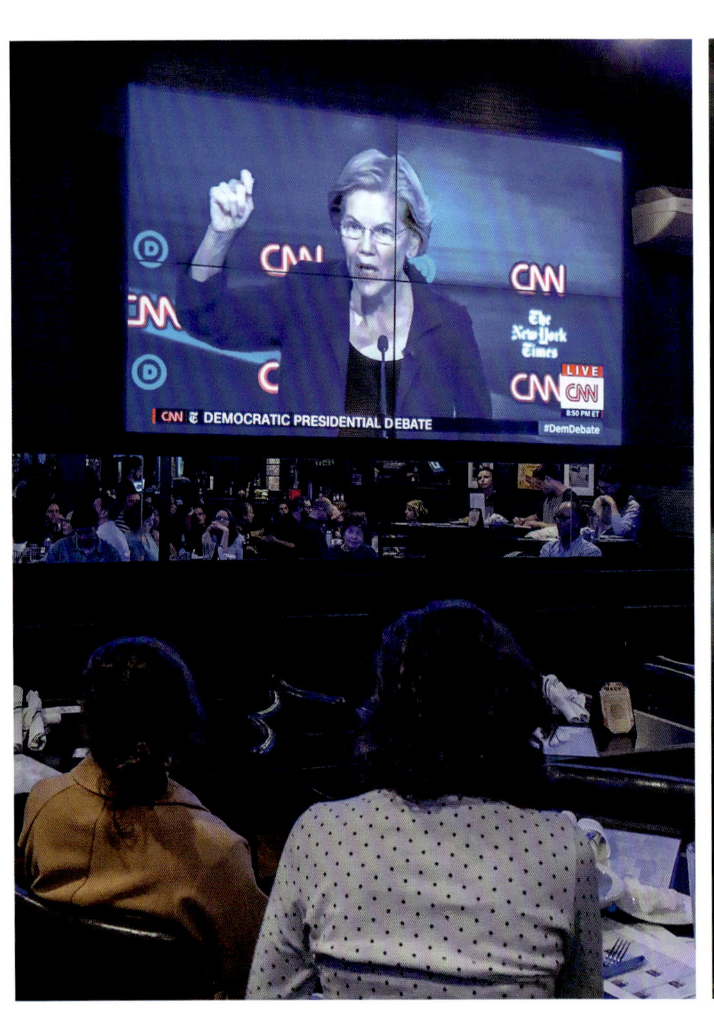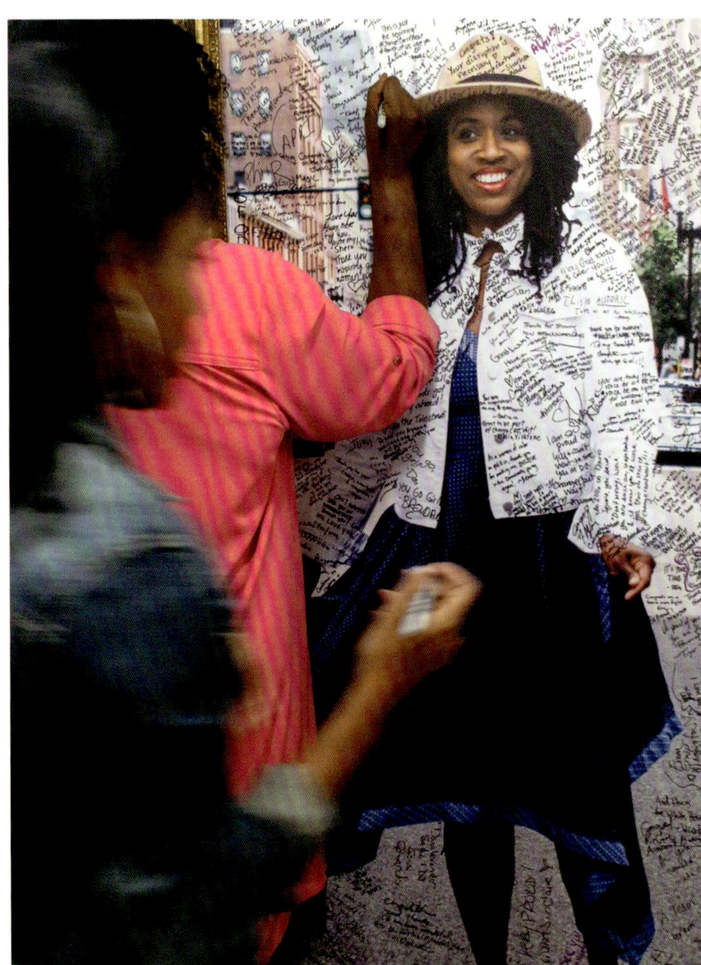

FIGURE 92. Ellen Feldman. *Suffragists Knew–Dare to Act!*

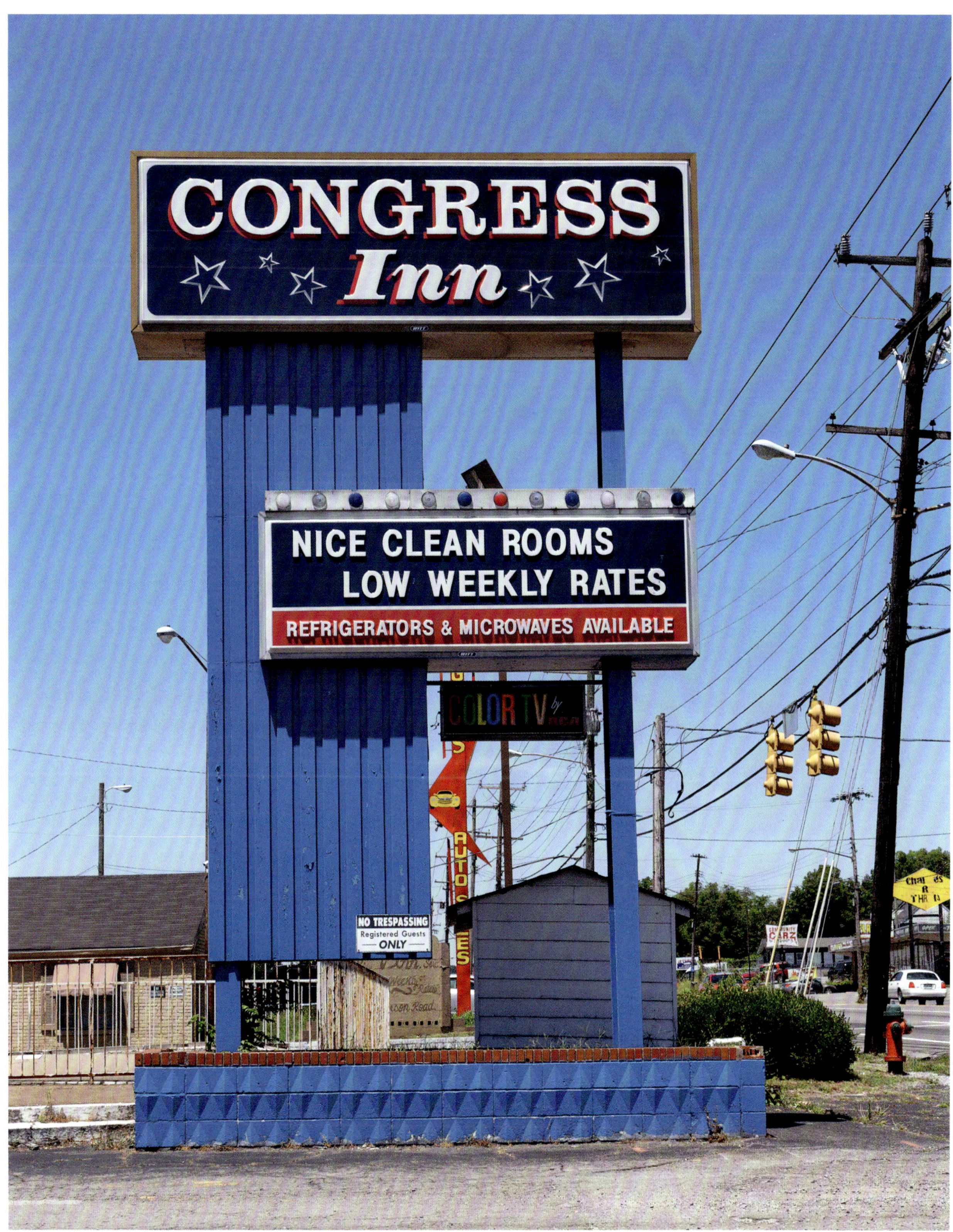

FIGURE 93. Tamara Reynolds. *Untitled*

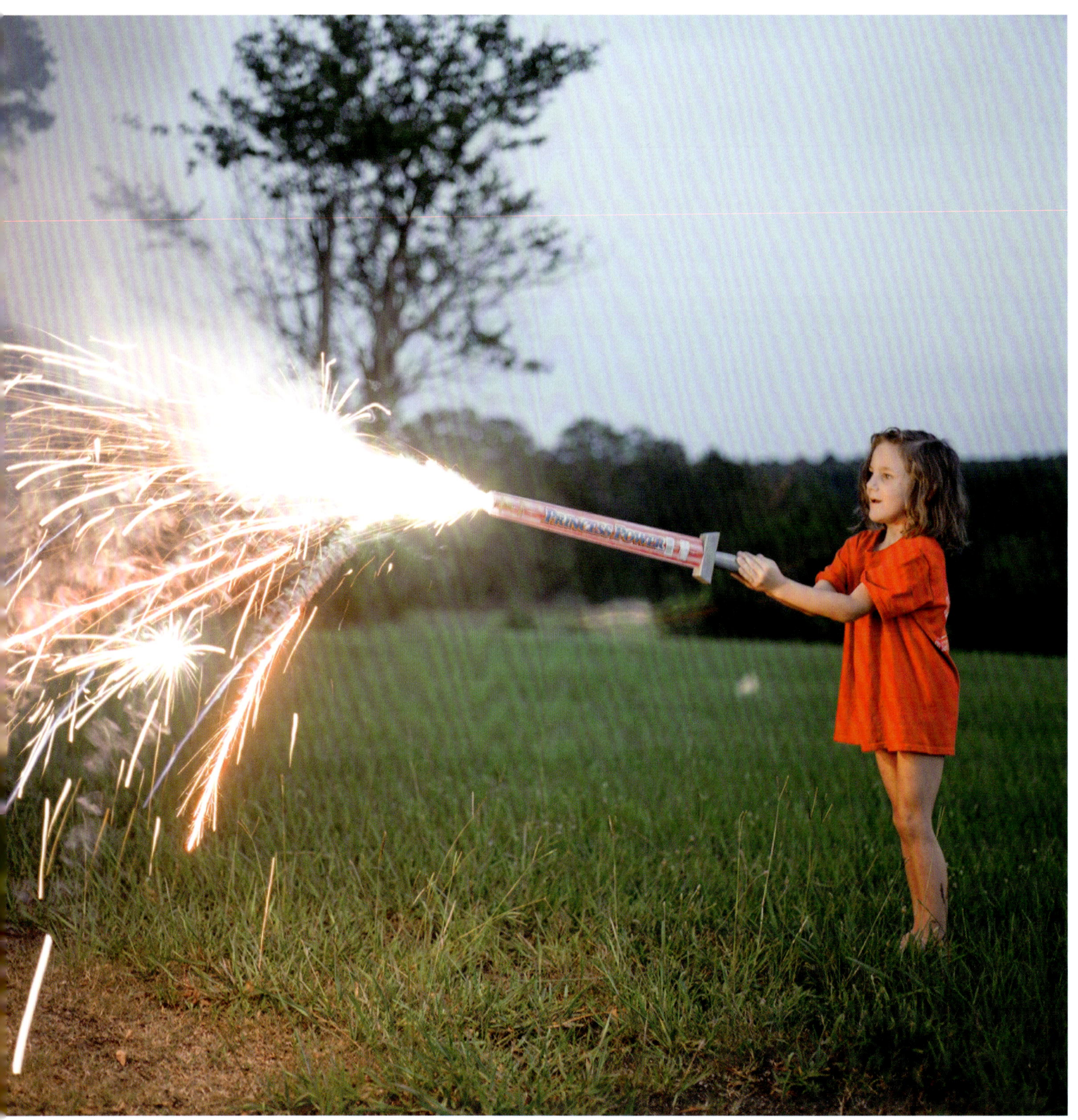

FIGURE 94. Ashleigh Coleman. *Power(ful)*

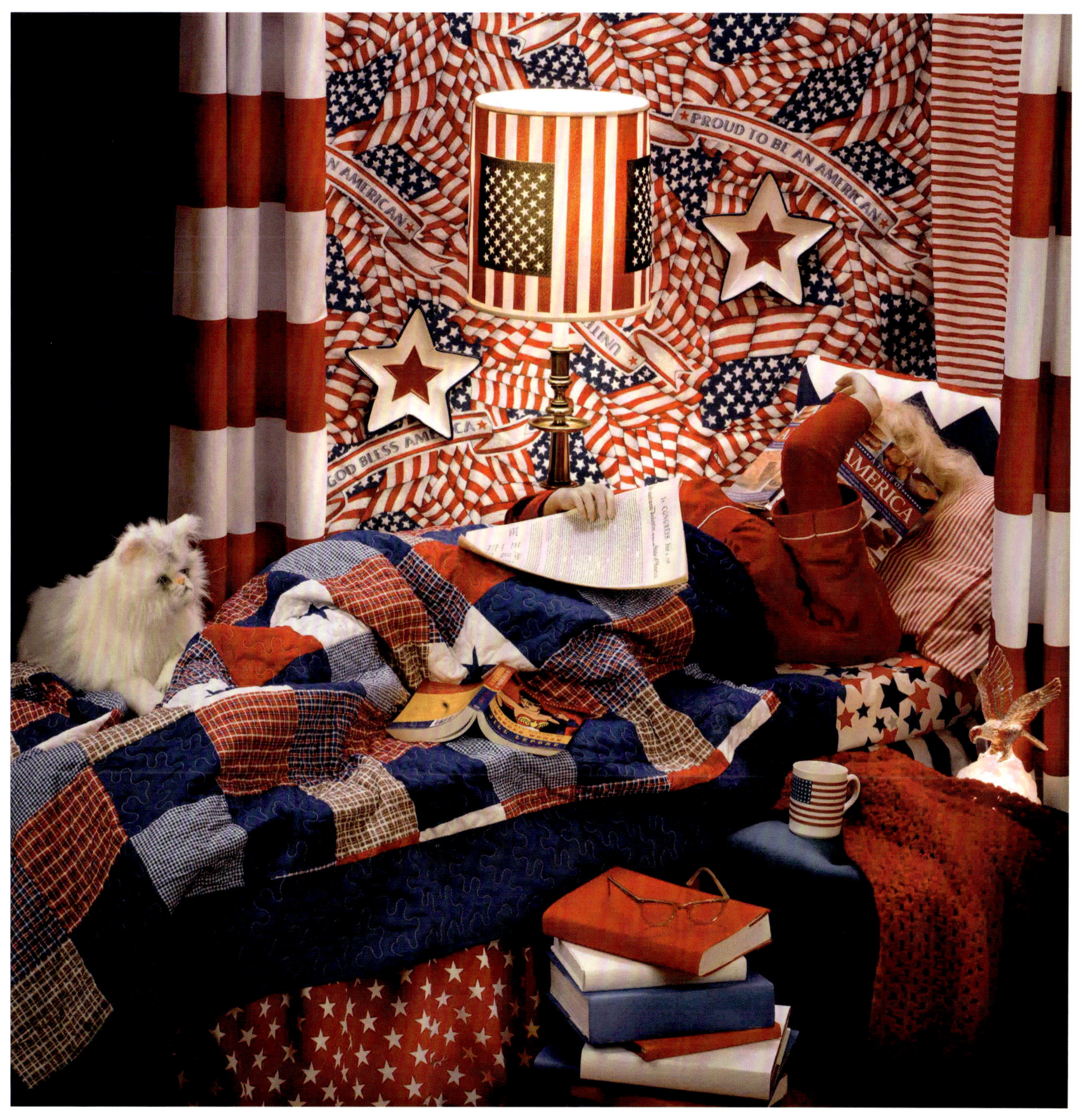

FIGURE 95. Patty Carroll. *Bedridden*

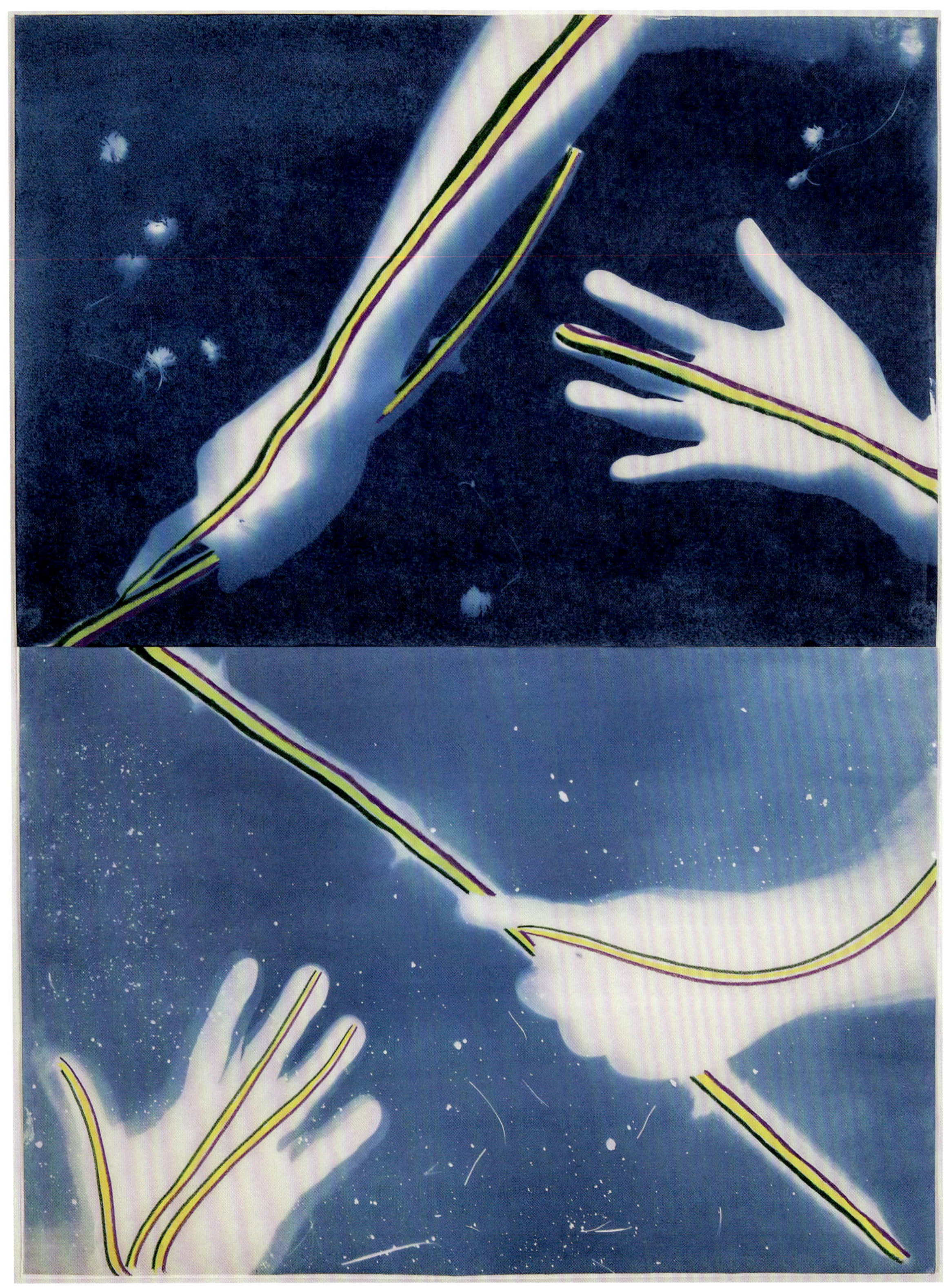

FIGURE 96. Edie Bresler. *Our Right*

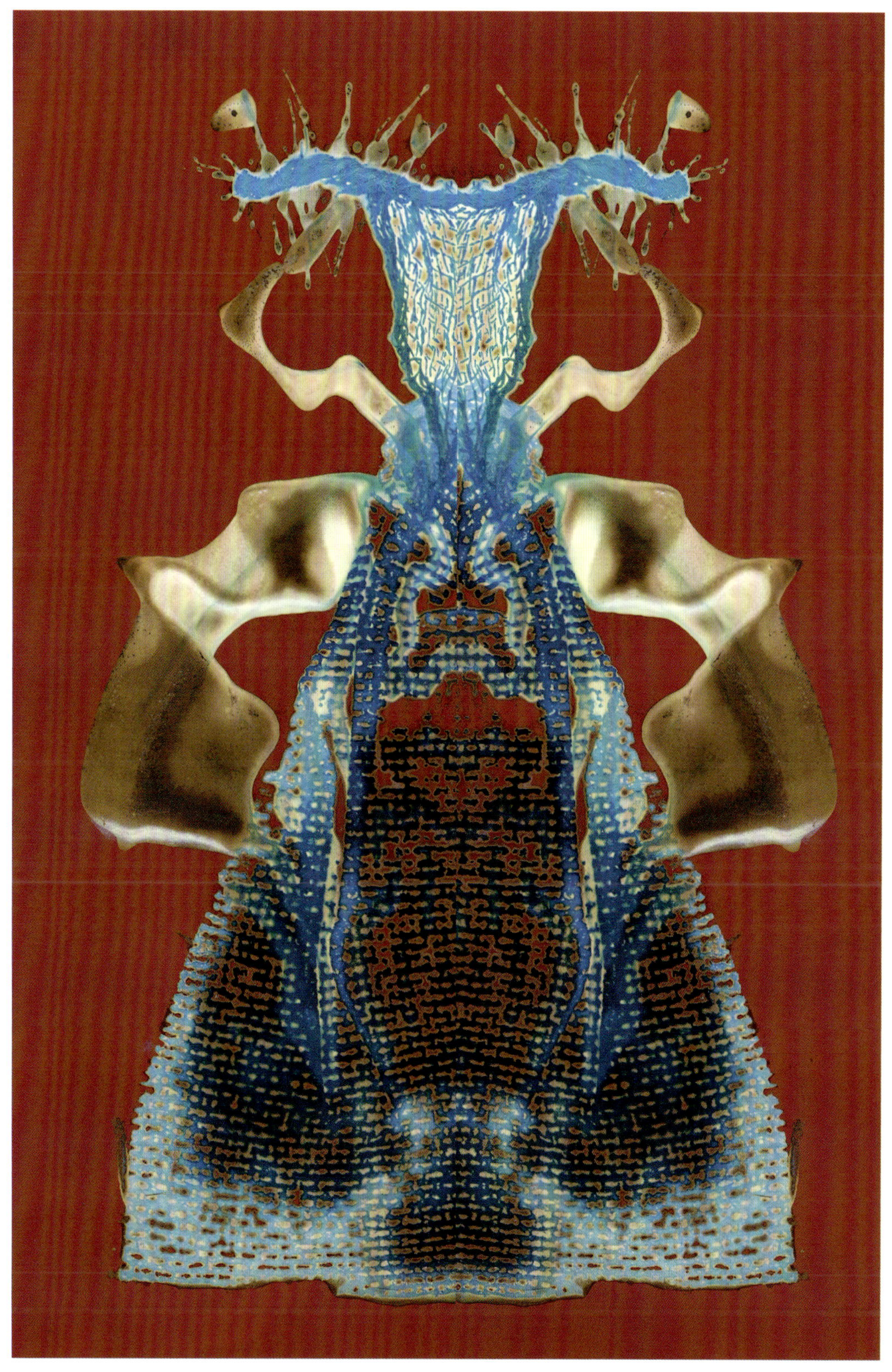

FIGURE 97. Marky Kauffmann. *Eloise in Blue Dress*

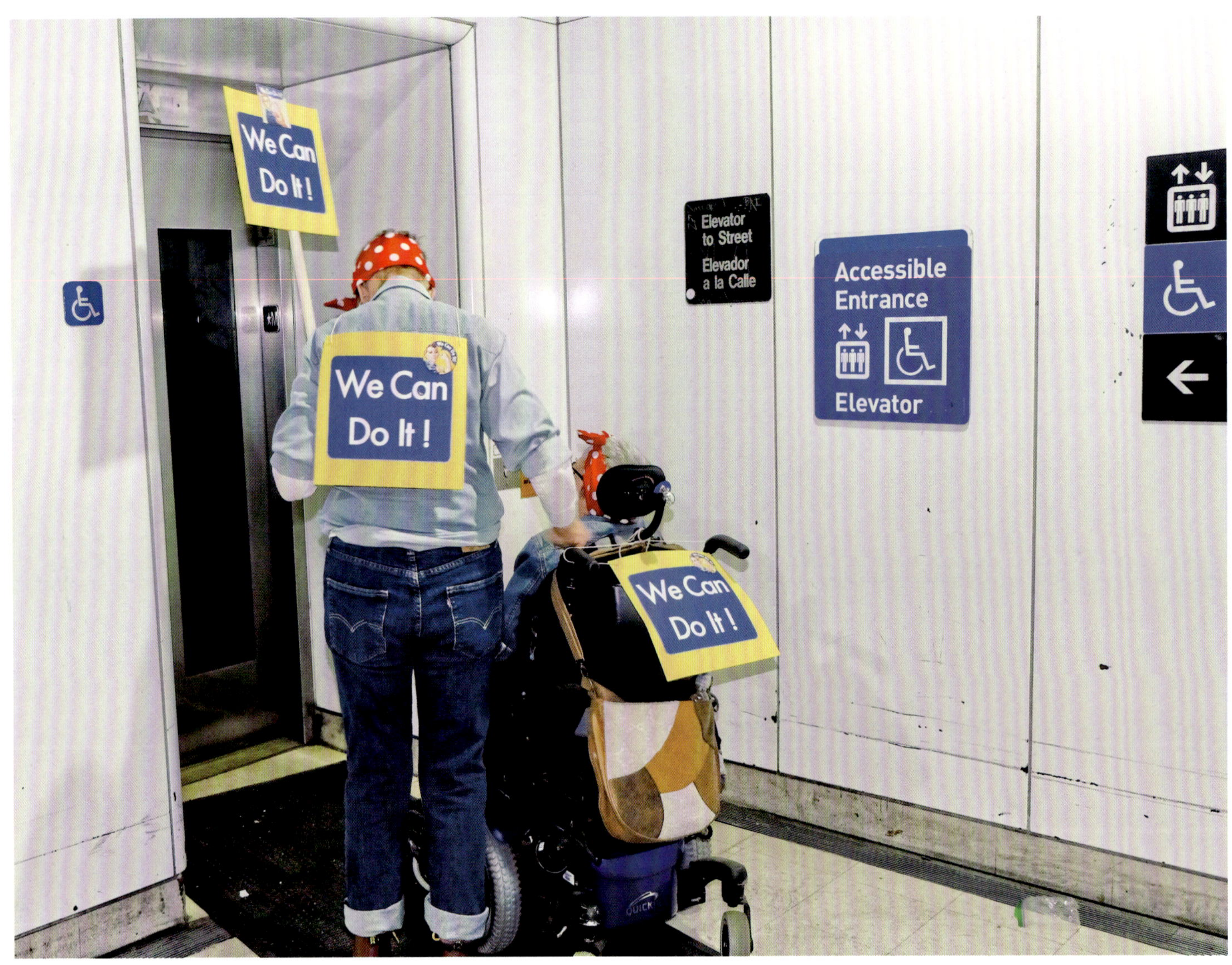

FIGURE 98. Nancy Baron. *To Be Heard*

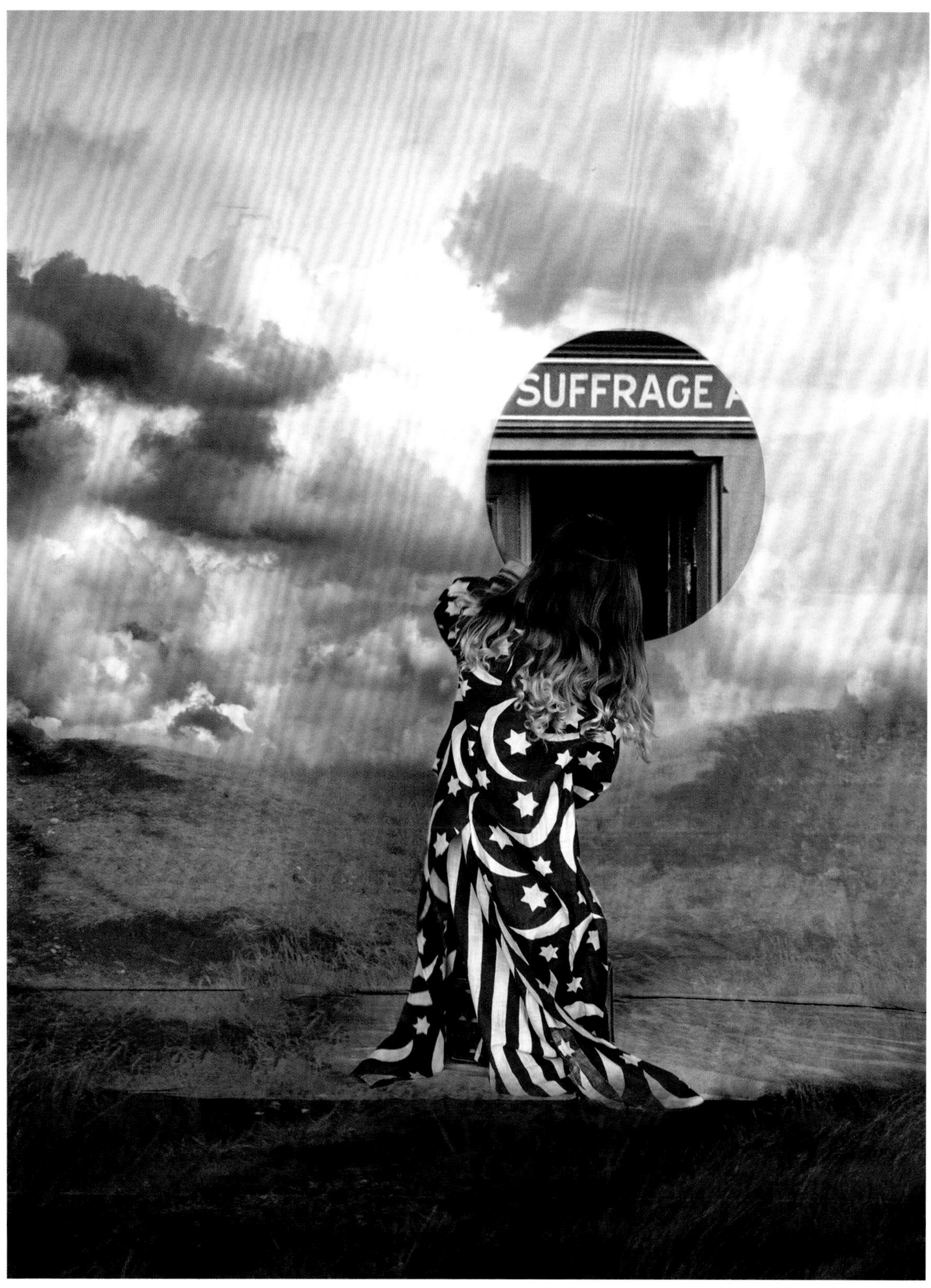

FIGURE 99. Ann Marye George. *Age and Antiquity*

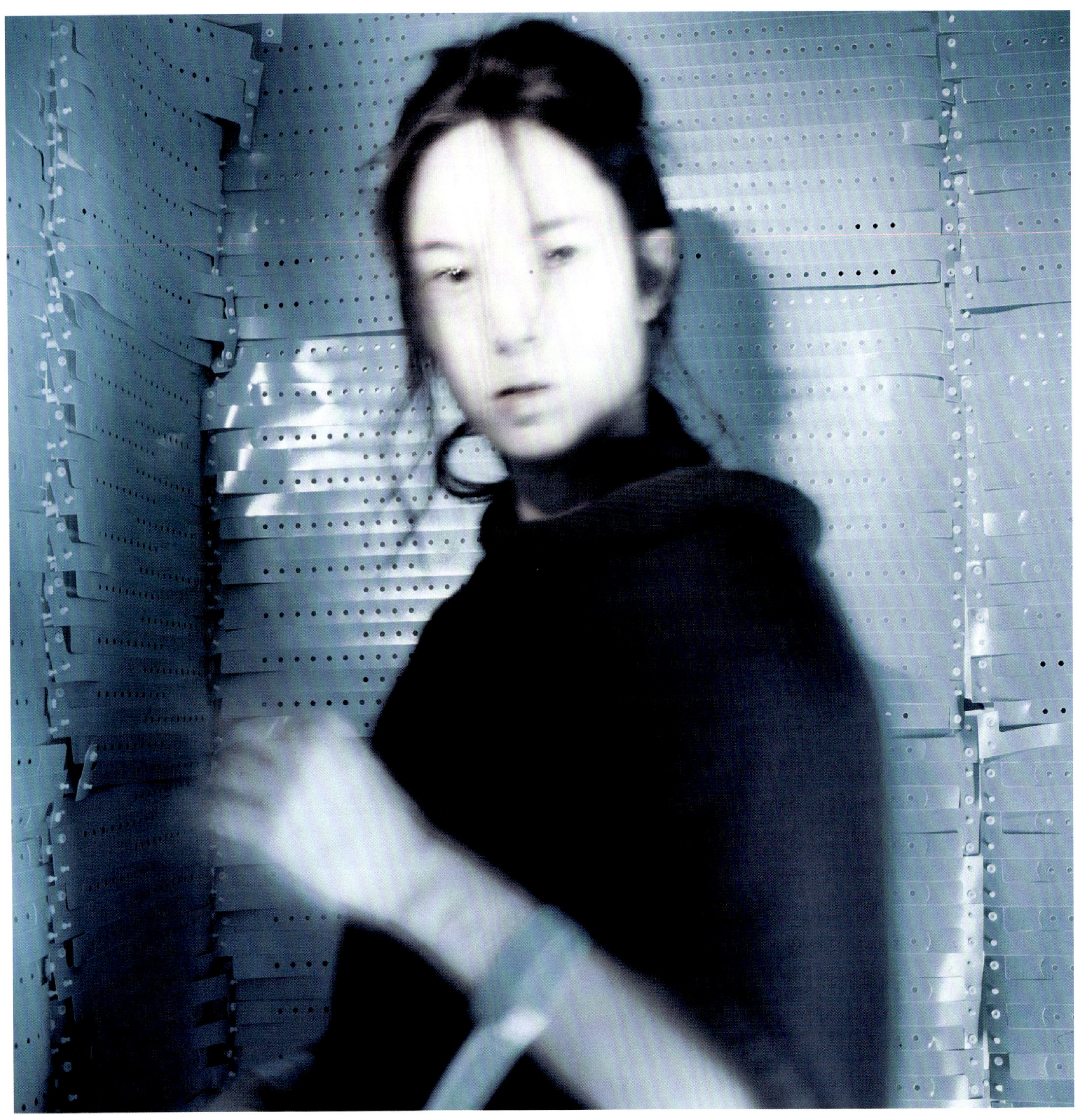

FIGURE 100. Tara Cronin. *Entry* from the project *Thens*

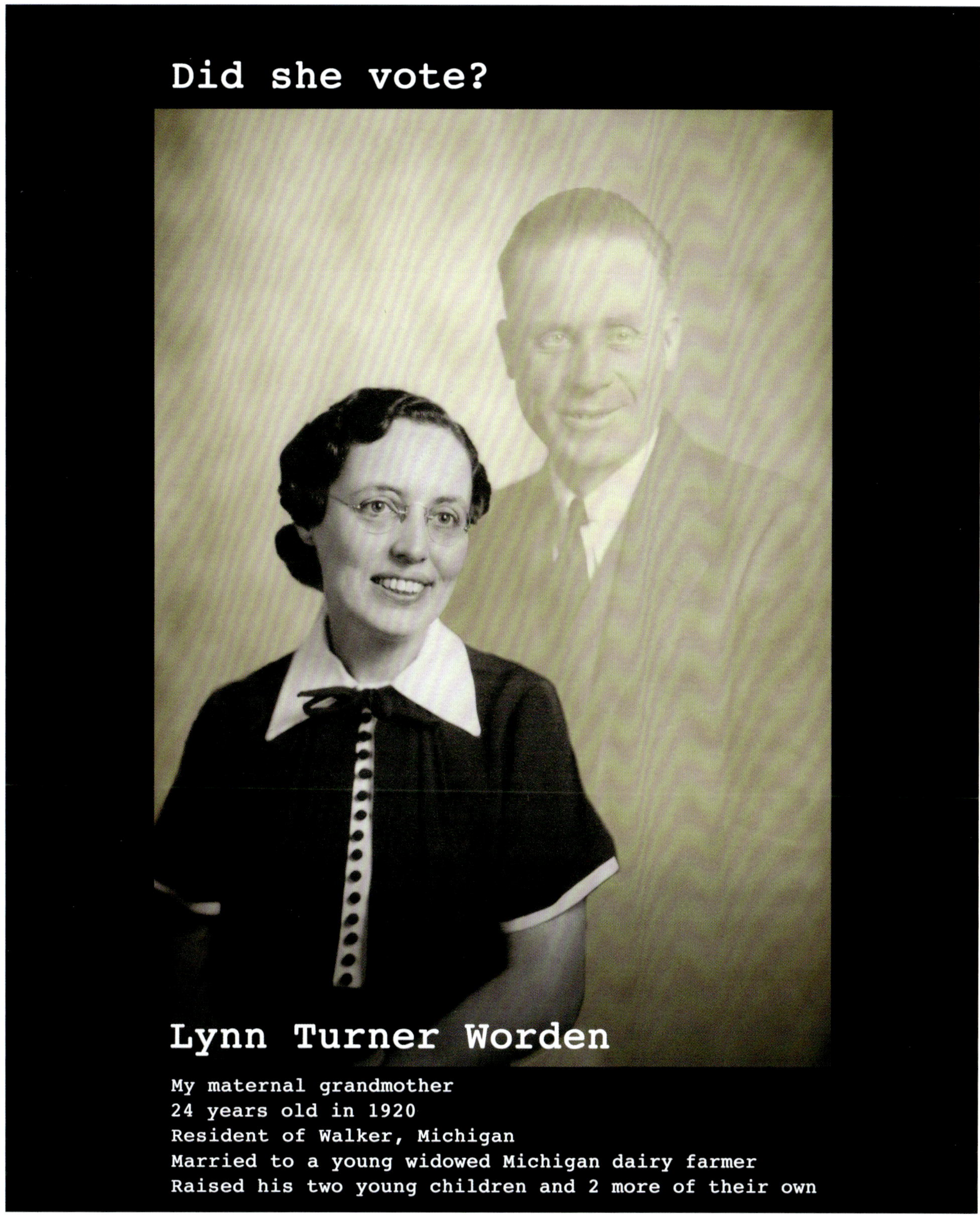

FIGURE 101. Carol Erb. *Did She Vote? Lynn Turner Worden*

FIGURE 102. Lindsey Beal. *Second Wave*. Original image courtesy of the Library of Congress: LC-DIG-ppmsca-55373.

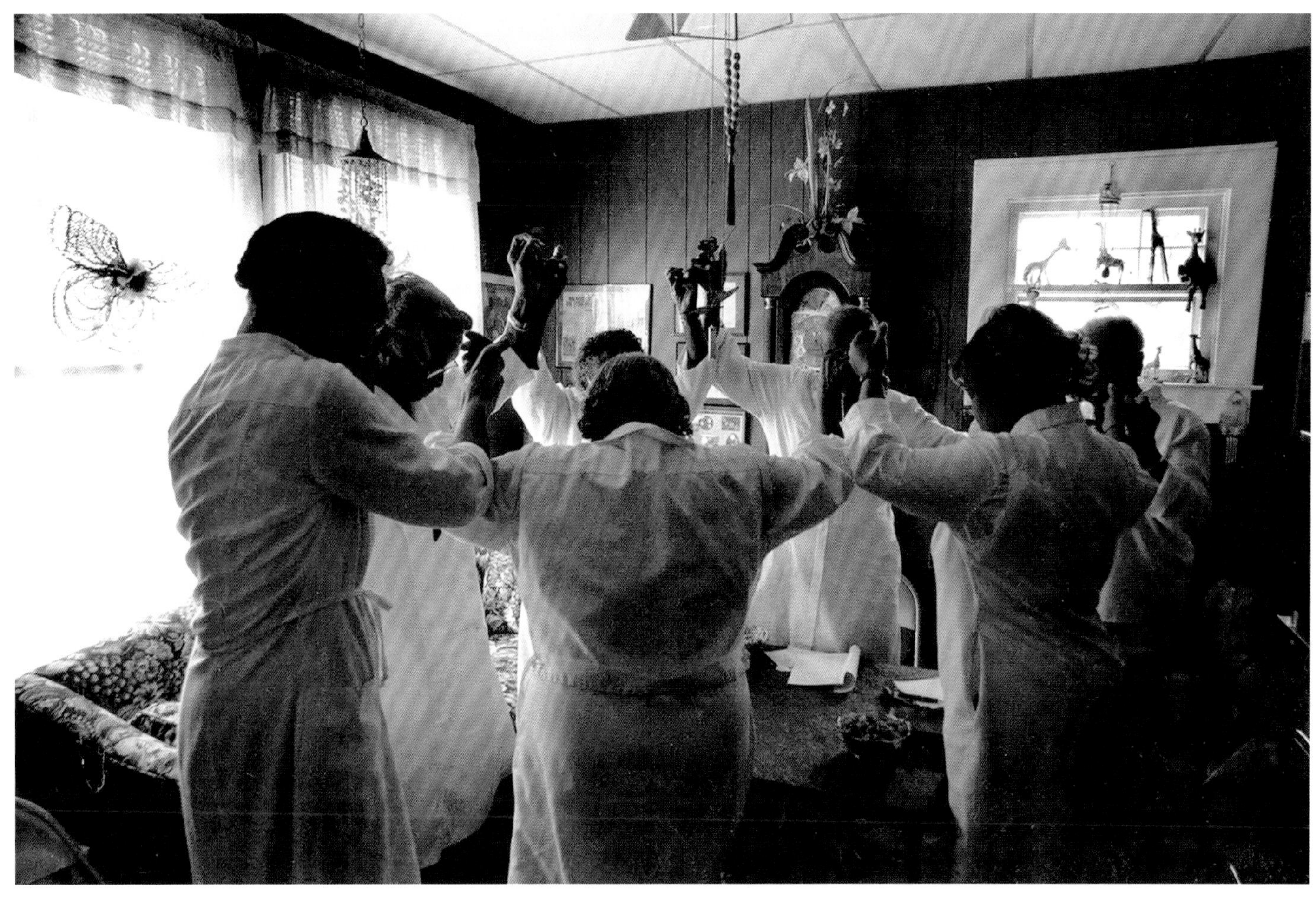

FIGURE 103. Sarah Hoskins. *The Benevolent Sisters, Their 99th Year*

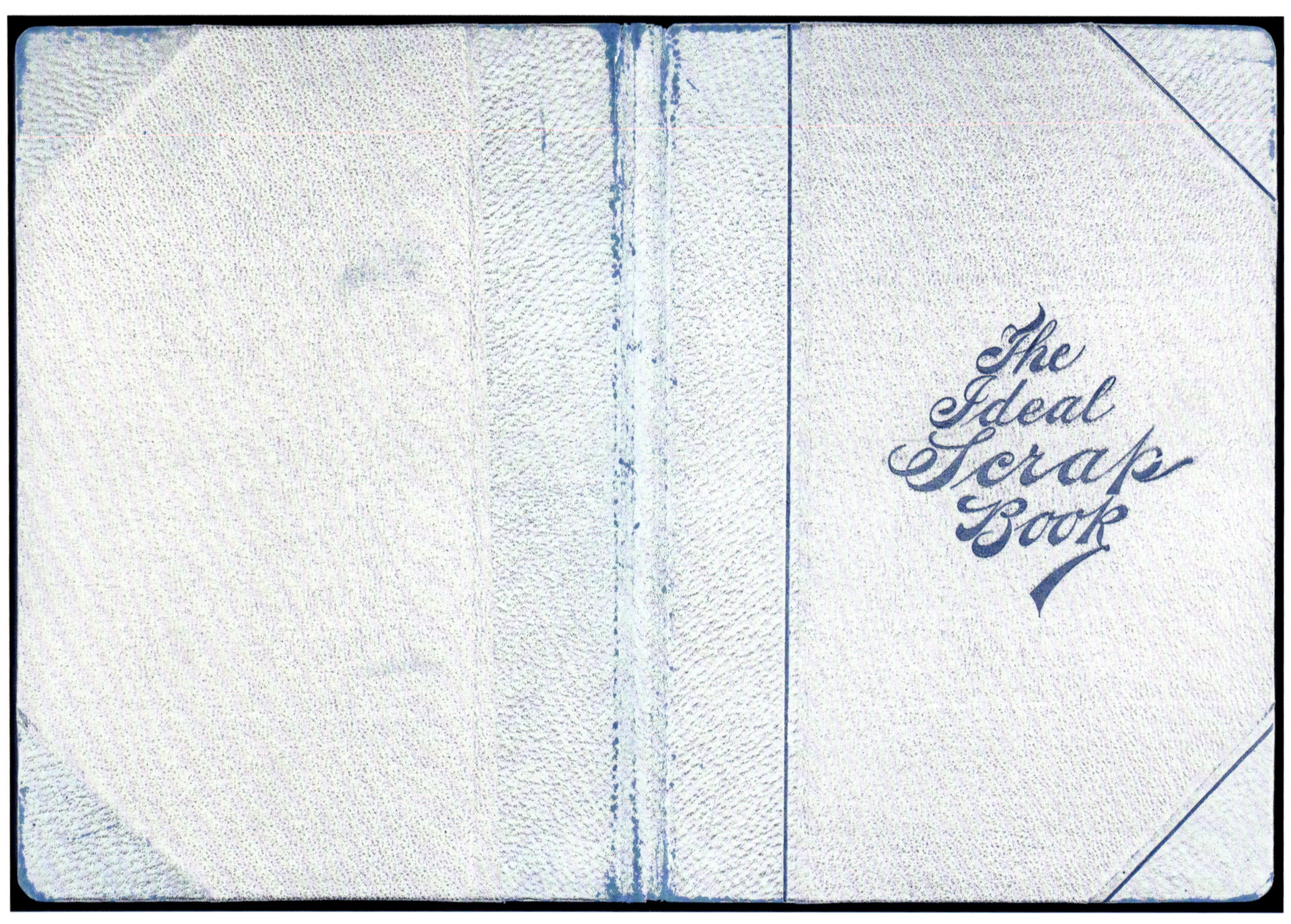

FIGURE 104. Emily Sheffer. *The Ideal Scrap Book, 1905–1906*

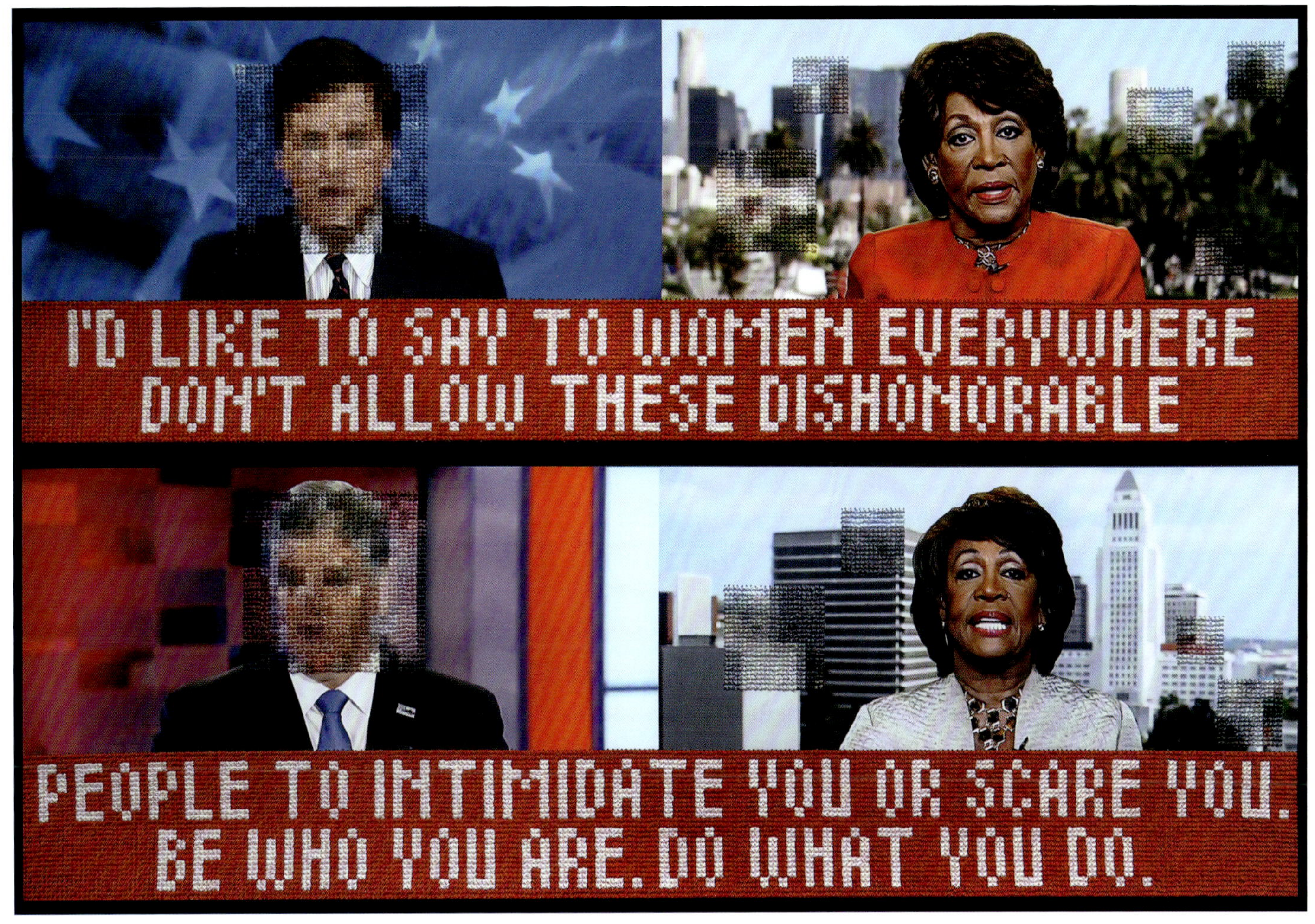

FIGURE 105. Diane Meyer. *Maxine*

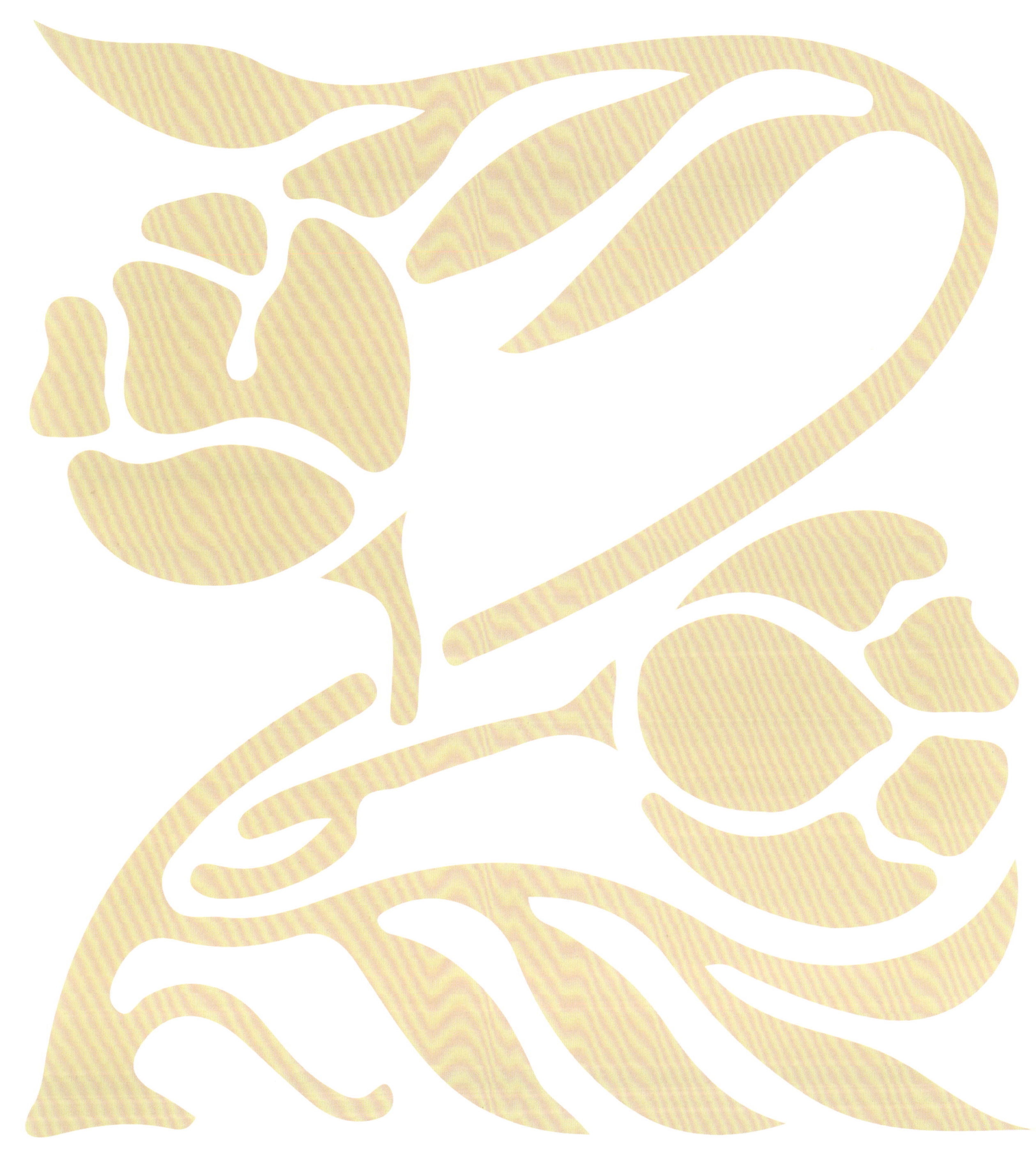

Artist Statements

1

MARINA FONT
Equality

Marina Font is a multidisciplinary artist working in photography, mixed media, installation, and video. Her studio practice explores ideas about identity, gender, territory, language, memory, and the forces of the unconscious. Strongly influenced by psychoanalysis, her works often explore womanhood and the domestic sphere.

For the *A Yellow Rose Project*, she photographed the female body in a pose that resembles an anatomy study that ultimately represents openness and vulnerability. She then manually manipulated the images with embroidery, threads, and fabrics. These materials helped her connect with a life-long association with women's traditions, as in telling a story that departs from the depths to the surface. Through this intimate performative ritual, the embodiment of the photograph becomes the common ground where the familiar and the foreign meet, as an individual attempts to blur the lines between the internal and external spaces of the body. The construction of these works evokes diverse psychological states and emotions with meanings that are in constant flux, never fixed, just like our identities. The body becomes a topographic surface intending to express thoughts on the mysteries and intricate secrets of the self, the life lived, the past, and the roads yet to transit. The works ultimately intend to express the intricate forces that have driven these women to fight not only for their right to vote, but for equality.

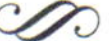

Marina Font was born in Argentina in 1970. She studied at the Martin Malharro School of Visual Arts, Argentina, and photography at the Spéos Paris–Ecole de la Photographie and earned an MFA in photography from Barry University, Miami, Florida, in 2009. She has exhibited extensively at galleries, museums, and institutions in the United States and abroad. Her work is in various public and private collections, such as the Museum of Art and Design at Miami Dade College, Boca Raton Museum of Art,

Patricia and Phillip Frost Art Museum at FIU, LOWE Art Museum at the University of Miami, and FoLA–Fototeca Latinoamericana, Argentina. She currently lives in Miami and represented by Dina Mitrani Gallery.

2

CINDY HWANG

Forgotten Suffragist No. 3 Tye Leung

The Forgotten Suffragist Series highlights four women activists of color, who made invaluable contributions to their communities yet have been largely overshadowed by their white contemporaries. One of them, Mabel Ping-Hua Lee, was barred from voting even after the passage of the Nineteenth Amendment due to the Chinese Exclusion Act of 1882, which denied Chinese immigrants like Lee eligibility for US citizenship and was not repealed until 1943. Another one, Tye Leung, became the first Chinese American woman to cast a ballot in 1912, thanks to California's suffrage laws, and the first Chinese American woman to hold a federal job as an interpreter for Angel Island Immigration Station. The series resurfaces newspaper clippings about the four women but obscures their portraits—a visual indication of our collective, racially inflected forgetting.

Cindy Hwang was born in 1993 in Phoenix, Arizona, and is a designer and artist based in Brooklyn, New York. In her personal practice, she explores the relationship between politics and aesthetics, using language and commonplace forms to complicate normative assumptions. As a professional designer, she has worked for the *New York Times* and Hillary Clinton's 2016 presidential campaign, and assist-

ed various advocacy groups. She received a BA from Yale College in 2015 and an MFA from the Yale School of Art in 2020.

3

KELIY ANDERSON-STALEY

Daniela

Daniela is one of five tintype portraits of women I contributed to A Yellow Rose Project. All five women, like Daniela, pose confidently, filling the frame and bringing a strong sense of who they are to the portrait. Their strength and independence, apparent in their expressions, is emblematic of the power of their voice and their vote.

Keliy Anderson-Staley lives and works in Houston, Texas. Her work has been exhibited or collected by the Akron Art Museum, Bronx Museum of the Arts, Library of Congress, Museum of Fine Arts Houston, National Portrait Gallery, Ogden Museum of Southern Art, Portland Art Museum, and Shelburne Museum. She was a light work resident and New York Foundation of the Arts (NYFA) fellow.

4

LISA MCCARTY

Votes for Women 1920/2020

According to a 2020 study by the Center for American Women and Politics at Rutgers University, only 63.3 percent of eligible women report exercising their right to vote. Additionally, although women make up a slight majority of registered voters, women hold just twenty-three percent of congressional seats and only twenty-five percent of state legislative seats. For my contribution to A Yellow Rose Project, I have recreated and distributed suffrage buttons from the nineteenth and twentieth centuries to encourage twenty-first century women to vote and all voters to support women candidates. There are still many barriers, both social and structural, that prevent women from exercising their right to vote or holding political office. These buttons can help to serve as a continued reminder of people's capacity to create change. Each suffrage button was printed on archival paper using the cyanotype process, a photographic printing process popularized by Anna Atkins, considered the first woman photographer. Every button was unique, handmade, and wearable. The button designs themselves came from a variety of public collections devoted to women's history, including the Smithsonian's National Museum of American History, Georgia State University Library, University of Iowa Libraries, and the Ann Lewis Women's Suffrage Collection.

Lisa McCarty is a photographer and writer based in Boston, Massachusetts, where she is associate teaching professor at Northeastern University. McCarty has participated in over eighty exhibitions and screenings, both nationally and internationally. Her books include *Transcendental Concord* (Radius Books), *A Time of Youth* (Duke University Press), and *William Gedney: Only the Lonely, 1955–1984* (University of Texas Press).

5
SHERI LYNN BEHR
Alexandria and Shirley

To honor the one-hundred-year anniversary of the Nineteenth Amendment to the US Constitution, I created double portraits of modern women from the world of politics paired with their historical predecessors.

My photo work is technology based, and my projects often start on television or computer screens. For the portraits I made for *A Yellow Rose Project,* I sampled images from videos of successful women in politics today and rephotographed their faces using in-camera effects. Next, I looked for public domain pictures of suffragists and the women from previous generations who had won elections. These were the women who paved the way for their spiritual descendants in politics today. I combined and processed both pictures in order to merge the past with the present as we now look toward the future.

I chose women like Representative Alexandria Ocasio-Cortez, who became the youngest woman to serve in the US Congress at age twenty-nine, and Representative Shirley Chisholm, the first Black woman elected to the US Congress. We celebrate these women and the Nineteenth Amendment. One hundred years ago, women finally won the right to vote. Today, they win elections.

Sheri Lynn Behr is a visual artist interested in the electronic screens through which we view the world. Her project, *BeSeeingYou,* was exhibited at the Griffin Museum of Photography in 2018, and her corresponding book was selected by Elizabeth Avedon as one of the Best Photography Books of 2018. She has exhibited work at the Amon Carter Museum of American Art, MIT Museum, Center for Creative Photography, Colorado Photographic Arts Center, the Medium Festival of Photography, and many other venues. Her photographs have been featured in publications worldwide, including

Harper's Magazine, People's Photography in China, *Orta Format* in Turkey, *Toy Camera* in Spain, and *The Boston Globe.* Behr has received a fellowship in photography from New Jersey State Council of the Arts (NJSCA) and a grant from the Puffin Foundation.

6

TRACY L. CHANDLER

Elize and Lenee

This series of portraits bear witness to individuals as they come of age. During this vulnerable time of transition, we are tasked with building our personal identity and future path. We come to understand ourselves through our reflection within others, a reciprocal knowing that in turn informs our view of the world. As we grow and take on roles, we participate in society, shaping and being shaped by this world we inherit. This awkward dance continues forever, individuals and society growing together, intertwined in beautiful emergence.

Tracy L Chandler is a photographic artist based in Los Angeles, California. Her work explores peripheral communities and her own personal story reflected through portraiture and narrative and has been exhibited in galleries and institutions in the United States and abroad. Tracy was included in the 2019 Critical Mass Top 50 and is currently an MFA candidate in the Hartford Art School's limited residency program.

7

FRANCES JAKUBEK

New Jersey Voter Registration Form

These images are meant to depict the many barriers that restrict voter registration. The obfuscating treatment of these registration forms symbolizes the confusion and frustration created under restrictive measures. Literacy tests nearly impossible to interpret were failed with one wrong answer and set up to doom the taker with inconsiderate time restrictions. Obstacles like redistricting, documentation requirements, administrative fees, and lack of access have created barriers in receiving recognized IDs, and lack of voter education and support has led to rejection of many mail-in forms. We must continue working to improve the accessibility and safety of voter registration for the entire country and future generations of voters.

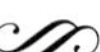

Frances Jakubek is an image-maker, independent curator, and consultant for artists. She is the co-founder of *A Yellow Rose Project,* former director of the Bruce Silverstein Gallery in New York City, and former associate curator of the Griffin Museum of Photography in Massachusetts. Recent curatorial appointments include *Potential Space: A Serious Look at Child's Play,* featuring works by Nancy Richards Farese; Critical Mass, Portland, Oregon; Filter Photo, Chicago; The Griffin Museum of Photography; *British Journal of Photography;* Les Rencontres d'Arles, France; SaveArtSpace, Los Angeles; and *Photo District News.*

8

CAROLYN MCINTYRE NORTON AND BETTY PRESS

Ellie Davis Dahmer

Vying for the attention of Ellie Davis Dahmer, reporters crowded in for interviews at the January 2020 dedication of a sculpture honoring her husband, Vernon, and his message, "If you don't vote, you don't count" (Wilson, 2 Sept. 2020). Her husband killed after their home was firebombed in 1966 for their family's tireless work defending voting rights in Mississippi.

Eight years after his murder, Mrs. Dahmer reflected, "Well the only way I can look at Vernon's death and not cry about it is when I walk in the bank, I see Black faces there. You see buses driving; you see Black faces on them. You see the police force; you see Black faces. Well, if his dying did all this—then, it's worth it and he would have done it again" (Wilson, 2 Sept. 2020).

Ellie Davis Dahmer was undeterred. Among her many contributions, she went on to serve as Forrest County Election Commissioner for twelve years and reopened her husband's case, which, in 1998, resulted in a murder conviction of a former Ku Klux Klan leader.

For some, the struggle for the right to vote did not end in 1920. Photographer Betty Press and I collaborated to photographically honor five Black women who worked during the 1960s to improve voting rights in Hattiesburg, Mississippi, an epicenter for voter registration activity. We found a common thread among them—these women never responded to hate with hate. With courage, faith, and an enduring expectation for progress, they worked to make real change against discriminatory practices with effective results for themselves and their community.

Carolyn McIntyre Norton spent her childhood observing natural areas around Chesapeake Bay and the mountains of North Carolina with a camera her father bought her from Sears and a box of watercolors. Today her projects include photographs, intaglio prints, and handmade books that investigate the defining qualities of landscapes and cultures. Norton's work has been shown in group and solo shows nationally and internationally in galleries, such as the Blank Wall Gallery in Greece, Davis Orton Gallery in New York, the Griffin Museum of Photography, Manifest Creative Research Gallery and Drawing Center in Ohio, the Mississippi Museum of Art, PhotoPlace Gallery in Vermont, and the Walter Anderson Museum of Art in Mississippi. She holds an MFA from Stephen F. Austin State University in Texas.

Betty Press grew up in Nebraska and has been an award-winning photographer for more than twenty-five years. She has contributed to many magazines and newspapers, taught photography, and photographed around the world. Her photographs have been widely exhibited and collected, as well as being selected for many juried competitions. She has lived and worked in Kenya for many years. In 2011, she published her award-winning photobook *I Am Because We Are: African Wisdom in Image and Proverb,* which captured a stunning, life-affirming portrait of the African people and culture.

9

SARA BENNETT
Linda

When I started photographing women with life sentences in New York state more than eight years ago, people with felony convictions were denied the right to vote until they were off parole, a process that could take years after being released from prison. Across the United States today, more than five-million people impacted by incarceration are denied that basic and treasured right. One-fourth of those disenfranchised are currently incarcerated.

Over the years, the women I've photographed have called to tell me they just registered to vote or just voted, almost always for the first time in their lives. They were sharing a huge milestone with me, a sign that they are finally free.

In May 2021, the governor of New York state signed legislation automatically restoring the right to vote the moment a person is released from prison. Still, Linda, shown in the photograph of the same name, reminds us that except in a handful of states, the right to vote is taken from women and men inside prison, denying them the fundamental right to have a voice in electing officials who determine the policies that inform their lives.

After spending eighteen years as a public defender, Sara Bennett turned her attention to photographing women with life sentences, both inside and outside prison. Her work has been widely exhibited in solo shows, including at the Blue Sky Gallery in Portland, Oregon, and Photoville in Brooklyn, New York, and in group shows, including MoMA PS1's *Marking Time: Art in the Age of Mass Incarceration.* Her work has been featured in publications such as *The New York Times, The New Yorker* Photo Booth, and *Variety* and *Rolling Stone*'s "American (In)Justice."

10
KRIS SANFORD
Women's March, Lansing, Michigan

My home state of Michigan became a real battleground during the Trump administration. I was initially shocked at the 2016 election results in our state and felt increasingly isolated in the small, Midwestern college town where I lived. It highlighted the importance of exercising the right to vote, as well as the right to assemble and make our voices heard. This work captures the crowd at the Women's March

on Lansing at the Michigan State Capitol in January 2017. This was a place I would return to both protest and photograph, as our state's divided politics played out in the public square.

Kris Sanford is an associate professor at Central Michigan University. She has exhibited work internationally, including exhibitions in Amsterdam, Boston, Chicago, Denver, Detroit, Houston, London, Miami, and New York City. Kris was a finalist for the 2018 Lange-Taylor Prize from the Center for Documentary Studies at Duke University. Her art explores intimate relationships and identity through appropriated images, video, and text.

11
KRISTINE THOMPSON
Suffrage in Washington, D.C. 1919–2017

This photograph situates an archival document related to the women's suffrage movement in the United States alongside a photo from the 2017 Women's March. Both documents, made nearly one-hundred years apart, depict women gathering in Washington, DC, to protest the political landscape and the actions of the president. By viewing historical records in the context of more recent events, we consider the progress made toward democracy and women's rights, some of the threats continually posed to those freedoms, and the work that remains.

Kristine Thompson is an associate professor at the School of Art at Louisiana State University. Her work considers how contemporary photographic imagery circulates and often addresses representations of loss, memorial practices, and mourning. She holds an MFA from the University of California, Irvine and a BS from Northwestern University. She is the recipient of several awards, including an Investing in Artists Grant from the Center for Cultural Innovation and a DAAD Artist-in-Berlin Program. Her work has been featured widely in exhibitions in the United States and Europe.

12
PRIYA KAMBLI
Devhara #1

Devhara—meaning house of idols in my native language of Marathi—is a photographic body of work that weaves together three generations of women: my mother, my daughter, and myself, while examining my identity as a migrant. As an artist whose work is bound in the personal and irrefutably placed in the context of a migrant narrative, the question is how does the personal, or private. intersect with the political, or public. Or simply in the face of rising white supremacy in the United States, how do I document this lived personal experience? I've been seeking an answer to this question by mining my quotidian inheritance, my mother's objects of worship, which are imbued with political realities and tangible memories and to me have become objects of mourning. I explore the resonance of these items from my mother's home altar as significant forms to create abstract images, meditations, and visual prayers.

With this series, I seek and offer solidarity. In a sense, the impact of this work lies in its simple existence; a body of work resulting from processes of abstraction and play—grounded in the concrete reality of the things I carry with me—but not obliged to provide a representation or portrait of those objects, nor of myself as their migrant creator. My contribution is simply my voice, and the attention it can bring to those of other migrants and women of color—as being rich, nuanced, and worthy of notice.

Priya Kambli received her BFA from the University of Louisiana in Lafayette and MFA from the University of Houston. She is currently professor of art at Truman State University in Kirksville, Missouri.

Kambli's work inadvertently examines the question asked by her son Kavi at age three: "Did she belong to two different worlds, since she spoke two different languages?" The essence of his question continues to be a driving force in her art making. In her work, Kambli strives to understand the formation and erasure of identity that is an inevitable part of the migrant experience, exploring the resulting fragmentation of family, identity, and culture.

13
INA JANG
Hada 2

Connecting the layers of the past and present, the work celebrates hopeful steps towards the future through its dreamlike colors and vibrant attitude.

Ina Jang is an artist based in Brooklyn, New York. Jang's works have been exhibited in internationally acclaimed galleries and festivals, including Daegu Photo Biennale, Paris Photo, Musée des Beaux-Arts Le Locle, and Foam Photography Museum. Over the years, she has been nominated for numerous awards. She was a Foam Talent and a finalist at the International Festival of Fashion, Photography and Fashion Accessories in Hyères. Her works have been published in *Time Magazine, British Journal of Photography, IMA Magazine, The New Yorker,* and *The New York Times Magazine.*

14

AMY THOMPSON AVISHAI
Voting Day, Easthampton, Massachusetts

As I make my way to the voting booth at the local middle school, I feel the weight of what is at stake. It's a rainy midterm election day in 2018. So much damage has been done in the past two years. Now a record number of women are running for office. I remember my mother, who only began voting late in her life. I think of my young daughters and all that they've taken in. Then, with a quiet fire in the belly, I vote.

Amy Thompson Avishai's photos have appeared in several publications including *The New York Times* and *The Women's Review of Books.* A Fulbright Fellow, Amy has taught at Massachusetts College of Art and Design and Griffin Museum of Photography. Featured in *National Geographic* and awarded Photolucida's Critical Mass Top 50, her photographs have been exhibited in group and solo shows from Boston to Berlin. Amy has lived in North Africa, the Middle East, Europe, and North America. In 2018, she moved to western Massachusetts and began teaching mindfulness photography.

15

LILY BROOKS
Henriette DeLille

The Venerable Henriette DeLille (1812–1862) was a New Orleans Creole and fourth-generation free woman of color. In 1836, she founded the Sisters of the Holy Family, an order of Black Roman Catholic nuns which still exists today. Her cause for canonization was opened by the Roman Catholic Church in 1988, and if completed, would make DeLille the first New Orleanian and first American-born Black person to reach the level of Sainthood.

Defying legal and societal barriers of antebellum Louisiana, Henriette DeLille and the Sisters of the Holy Family pursued a collective mission to educate enslaved and free Black children and care for the elderly, sick, homeless, and orphaned. She was also an outspoken critic of the plaçage system, a widespread practice which embodied the racial hierarchy of nineteenth-century New Orleans. Plaçage placed women of color in long-term sexual relationships with white men who had yet to establish enough wealth to marry American women of European descent. Despite this work, and like many free Creole people of color of her time, DeLille maintained ownership of an enslaved woman named Betsy, who she freed only in her final will. I am fascinated by DeLille's complicated, little-known history of both bravery and complicity. In her image, I find a reminder that the oppressive forces that shaped her world are still at work today. Her hands, eyes, and mouth become a mandate to remember my own responsibility and privilege. These cyanotypes were made by appropriating sections of the only known portrait of DeLille, a *carte de visite* made by A. Constant (date unknown).

Lily Brooks holds an MFA from the University of Texas at Austin and a BFA from the Massachusetts College of Art and Design. Her work has been exhibited nationally and internationally and featured in publications such as the *Los Angeles Times* and *Cabinet Magazine.* Brooks was the 2019 recipient of an archive documentation and preservation grant from the New Orleans Jazz and Heritage Foundation. Her editorial clients include *NPR's Weekend Edition* and the *Financial Times.* Brooks is a member of The Front, an artist-run gallery in New Orleans, and is an assistant professor of photography at Southeastern Louisiana University. She lives and works in Baton Rouge.

16

CHRISTA BOWDEN
I'll Never Know

Voting has always been important in my family, a sacred right, a civic duty. I am not sure when I came to understand that the right to vote was not/is not a given or foregone conclusion. But I always understood voting as something that must be done. Being taken by my grandmother to vote for Jimmy Carter when I was five years old was a thrilling moment. He was from Georgia like me. If he could be president, maybe so could I. Discussions about who to vote for were ones that my grandmother and I had frequently near election times, especially in her last few decades. This image explores my childhood memory of the 1980 election and conversations about presidential candidates with my grandmother in 2008 and 2016. While these conversations mostly centered around politics, they sometimes veered into an uncomfortable territory of race and gender. I adored my grandmother. It pained me deeply that these things might influence her decision of who to vote for, whether consciously or unconsciously. After many long phone calls in the fall of 2016 to talk about the election and try to convince her of the reasons she should vote for Hillary Clinton, she refused to tell me who she voted for. In the end, it is probably best that I'll never know.

Christa Bowden was born in Atlanta, Georgia, in 1975. She earned her MFA in photography from the University of Georgia and a BA in photography and film from Tulane University. She is a professor of art at Washington and Lee University, where she started the program in photography in 2006. Her work has been exhibited throughout the United States in both solo and group shows, and she has been the recip-

ient of a Virginia Museum of Fine Arts Fellowship, a Virginia Center for the Creative Arts fellow, and a nominee for the Santa Fe Prize for photography. She lives in Lexington, Virginia.

017

BOOTSY HOLLER
Tybee Island

Without Words chronicles intensely vivid episodes of depersonalization—a mental state that involves the surreal sense of observing oneself from outside the body. The spark for this series came from an illuminating moment in Savannah when I found myself alone in the humid night air. I walked to the railing of the deck and looked out to see my body face down in the pool below. I didn't know it then, but the feeling of detachment in that moment would follow me through the next few years.

Nature, in its complexity, sense of survival, and inherent beauty, helped me return back to my body. When I dug into the earth, felt the sea and the wind, and connected to the essence of self, I found a way back home.

Bootsy Holler is an intuitive artist creating art that examines the nature of identity, the reimagined family, and the deep secrets we all keep. Holler has been a working photographer for over twenty-five years in art, music, editorial, and advertising. Best known for her remarkably sensitive style of portraiture, she has been noticed and awarded by the SPJ Western Washington and Association of Alternative Newsmedia. After a career as a freelance art director, producer, and photographer in Seattle, she relocated to Los Angeles to focus on fine art.

18

KAT KIERNAN
The Voting Booth

States that had granted women partial voting rights used separate ballot boxes for men and women voters. These boxes were placed out in the open to prevent women from secretly casting ballots for offices for which they were restricted from voting. In my piece, The Voting Booth, I use an analog photobooth as a voting booth, equating the private spaces of each as a place to make oneself heard.

Kat Kiernan was raised on the coast of Maine. Now a city dweller, the influence of her rural upbringing can be seen in her autobiographical photographs rooted in the natural world. Often using herself as the subject, her work explores feelings of uncertainty. In 2012, she was named one of Artpil's 30 Under 30 Women Photographers to watch. She has exhibited throughout the United States and been featured in numerous publications. In 2015, she received the Griffin Museum's Rising Star Award for her contributions to the photographic community. Kat holds a BFA in photography from Lesley University College of Art and Design.

19

ANNE BERRY
1920 to 2020

The Garden of Endearment examines children as they explore imaginary lands and nature. Through play, children act out their fears and dreams. They still live in the Garden, close to nature, close to what's essential. As adults, we know that they can't stay. One gray night it will happen—a veil will fall, a gate will close, and the marvelous will cease to exist. They will realize that the adults have not taken care of their Garden. This work explores themes of brokenness, nostalgia for a green, fertile world, and a yearning to go back to the past to put things right. The elements in photographs, the settings, animals, and objects, are metaphors contributing to the narrative, which is a quest for the grail. This play is serious and edged with doubt, for this generation will have to find the grail, the cup which will heal the wounded king and thus the land. In my image for A Yellow Rose Project, a child, wearing her great-great grandfather's gown, holds an image of her ancestor, the first woman in the family granted the right to vote. In another image, she holds yellow roses. She is not yet thinking about struggles for equality, past or present, but the seriousness of her expressions indicates the will and strength to carry on.

Anne J Berry's photographs investigate the animal world, the domain of childhood, and the terrain of the southern wilderness. She also explores themes and metaphors from literature. In 2013 and 2014, Critical Mass included her work in their Top 50 portfolios. Her books include *Through Glass* (North Light Press, 2014), *Primates* (21st Editions, 2017), and *Behind Glass* (2021). Her work is in many permanent collections, including the National Gallery of Art. Anne lives in Newnan, Georgia. She is represented by the Catherine Couturier Gallery in Houston.

20

CLAUDIA RUIZ GUSTAFSON
Forward

This body of work, Votes for Women, is a tribute to suffragist and humanist Inez Milholland (1886–1916), who did more than speak and demonstrate for suffrage throughout her short life and her activism extended to trying to improve the lives of all disenfranchised Americans. After receiving her law degree from New York University, Milholland spoke fervently to various judges and public officials to advocate for the reform of law enforcement and the court system in the hope of keeping young people out of the workhouses. She also spoke out on labor reform, pushing for better wages and hours for the girls who worked in New York City's many department stores and for the city's many women factory workers. In her suffrage work, as well as her other advocacies, Inez engaged in a constant struggle with those in power to recognize the humanity of all classes and genders. At the time of her death, Milholland never got to see the passing of the Nineteenth Amendment granting all Americans, regardless of sex, the right to vote. Her last public words were, "President Wilson, how long must this go on? No Liberty" (Bernard, 7 Aug. 2020).

Claudia Ruiz Gustafson is a Peruvian visual artist based in Massachusetts, whose practice engages photography, assemblage, poetry, and artist bookmaking. Her work is mainly autobiographical and self-reflective; her cross-cultural experience and Peruvian heritage deeply inform her art making. Claudia's latest projects explore the stories of her Peruvian ancestors and aspects of her immigrant and liminal experiences. She is a 2021 Mass Cultural Artist fellow, 2020 Critical Mass 200 finalist, and 2020 Focus photo l.a. Top 20 finalist. Currently she is curator and participating artist of the traveling exhibition *Crossing Cultures: Family, Memory and Displacement,* a multimedia project made up of artwork created by multicultural artists reflecting on identity and diaspora. Claudia holds a BA in communications (comunicación para el desarrollo) from Universidad de Lima and a professional photography certificate from Kodak Interamericana de Perú.

21
KATIE BENJAMIN
Study 03

Examination in Pink: A Case Study

The moment a girl is born in the United States, society begins defining her gender role. She will inevitably be bombarded with things that are pink—pink garments, pink toys, sometimes a bedroom decorated entirely in pink. This one color establishes a subtle, but powerful, precedent that can spill over into adulthood. It is often the first of many visual cues that signify what is expected of girls and women.

Examination in Pink uses the color *pink* to evaluate gender equity. Each object in the study represents a male-dominated role, but each object has been completely coated in pastel pink. Through the use of this symbolic color, I confront these roles and ask why women are largely missing from them: she can lob a grenade, she can fly you across the country, she can run your company, and ultimately, why shouldn't she?

Katie Benjamin grew up on a rural route in northeast Mississippi. She is a photographer and award-winning art director, who has spent the last decade specializing in branding and advertising at agencies across the Mid-South. She is a founding member of Due South Co-op, a collective of Southern photographers. Images from *Examination in Pink: A Case Study,* her series that examines gender equity, were exhibited in a solo show at the Memphis College of Art, several group shows, and belongs in numerous private collections. Her work frequently explores the conflicting space that exists between the past and the present in her Southern landscape.

22
CLAIRE A. WARDEN
No. 15 Genetics

Mimesis is grounded in issues of identity, the other, and the psychology of knowledge and power. The creation of this series came at a time when the struggle to accept the unfamiliar was pervasive in our culture. When looking at these images, the urge to ask, "what is it?" echoes the question, "what are you?"—a question that has been directed toward me countless times as a person of color. In this series, I used a cameraless photographic process on negative film, which incorporates saliva and mark making. The negatives were scanned, and the final images produced as large-scale pigment prints. I find this process uniquely qualified to address the biologic and sociocultural forces that stimulate the emergence of an identity. This process produced a series of images that reveal certain truths in the abstract nature of identity, my personal experiences as an immigrant and a person of color, and the inadequacies of language to describe oneself. For No. 15 Genetics, I felt themes which already existed in my work could be recontextualized within A Yellow Rose Project. Among ideas of identity formation and perceptions, there is an acknowledgment of how this physical attribute—a fingerprint—unique to every person, has been used in personal identification and voting practices.

Claire's series *Mimesis* has been exhibited widely in the United States and abroad. She received an Artist Research and Development Grant from the Arizona Commission on the Arts, Contemporary Photography Exhibition award at the Philadelphia Photo Arts Center (PPAC), and the Ed Friedman Legacy Award from the Griffin Museum of Photography. Her work has been featured in publications including *Der Greif Magazine, Strange Fire Collective,* and *Lenscratch.* Claire was awarded artist residencies through the Center for Photography at Woodstock (CPW), LATITUDE Chicago, ACRE, and Light Work. Her work is in the collection of Archive 192 and the Bank of America permanent collection.

23
SUSAN KAE GRANT
Katharine (Mrs. Robert A.) Morton (1878–1956)

My portraits honor women from every class, race, ethnicity, and background who fought tirelessly to ratify the Nineteenth Amendment. For inspiration, I searched archives for photographs of and stories about suffragists. The image of Katharine (Mrs. Robert A.) Morton (1878–1956), chairman of the Wyoming Branch of National Woman's Party, portrays a suffragist in Cheyenne, Wyoming. She served as president of the Wyoming Federation of Women's Clubs (1913–17) and was elected Superintendent of Public Instruction of Wyoming (1919–35). In a 1914 conference address, she praised women working together, expressing, "No one woman is as wise as a group of women" (Rogers, 1976). Historian and author Adele Logan Alexander, granddaughter of suffragist Adella Hunt Logan, beautifully articulates who the suffragists were: "I would say it is not one person nor one event, but the scarcely recorded efforts of anonymous women of all races, educational and economic levels who, for decades, talked with neighbors, held meetings, challenged their fathers, sons, husbands and employers—often putting themselves in physical and economic jeopardy to do so. They are the unknown heroes of the movement" (Bennett and Chambers, 2020). I used the shadow as a metaphor to create each individual portrait while anonymously signifying all suffragists and the paths they blazed for the future. The shadow's lack of specificity enables us to see ourselves in them while imagining their activism, a perceived experience that takes on a sense of shared reality.

Susan kae Grant is a lens-based artist exploring dreams and memory to create portraits and fabricated narratives as editioned photographs and artist's books. Her studio practice and distinct personal vision represent a celebrated contribution to fabricated photography. She has lectured and exhibited her work throughout the United States and internationally from Spain to Japan. Her work is highlighted in numerous publications and collections including George Eastman Museum; the J. Paul Getty Museum; Smithsonian Institution Library, Special Collections; Minneapolis Institute of Art; the Tokyo Photographic Art Museum; Museum of Fine Arts, Houston; and Victoria and Albert Museum's National Art Library, London.

24
LETITIA HUCKABY
Sugar and Spice

My project Suffer/Rage focuses on the political ethos and gender issues in our world today. Suffrage is defined as the right to vote and a series of intercessory prayers or petitions. My piece Sugar and Spice includes an image of my then ten-year-old daughter holding a protest sign that says "Enough" in spray paint. Her pose is reminiscent of Norman Rockwell's painting The Problem We All Live With,

an iconic image of the civil rights movement. The image was printed on a six-foot vintage, cotton picking sack that references slavery, and the phrase "Enough" was taken from a speech by Dr. Martin Luther King Jr.'s nine-year-old granddaughter, Yolanda King, at the March for Our Lives rally in Washington, DC, where she spoke in front of a crowd of hundreds of thousands and said: "I have a dream that enough is enough, and that this should be a gun-free world, period" (Winsor, 2018).

Letitia Huckaby has a degree in journalism from the University of Oklahoma, a BFA from the Art Institute of Boston in photography, and her master's degree from the University of North Texas in Denton. Huckaby has exhibited at Phillips New York, the Tyler Museum of Art, the Camden Palace Hotel in Cork, Ireland, and Bridge Projects in Los Angeles. Her work is included in several prestigious collections, including the Library of Congress, the McNay Art Museum, and Crystal Bridges Museum of American Art. Huckaby was also an artist-in-residence at ArtPace in fall 2020.

25
GAIL SAMUELSON
Silk Blouse

My mother was born in New York City in 1928, the youngest and spunkiest of three girls. As a 1950's housewife, she felt pressure to conform, to be a good wife and mother, to care for others. My photograph for A Yellow Rose Project is of my mother's silk wedding blouse. As I gently withdrew it from my closet, the fabric began to fray and crumble in my hands. This worn but beautiful garment embodied the sweat and resilience needed to live in a society where women were not treated as equals.

With each generation comes change, my mother would have been happy and proud to see her granddaughters skillfully and gracefully balance work and family alongside supportive partners. But inequality remains a part of our culture, and many women continue to suffer from discrimination in the workplace, lack of access to quality healthcare and childcare, and inadequate legal protection from abuse. As we mark and celebrate the anniversary of the ratification of the Nineteenth Amendment, we also commit to ensuring that all women enjoy the same opportunities and choices as men.

Gail Samuelson lives and photographs in a small town southwest of Boston. Surrounded by protected forest and wetlands, she finds inspiration in the changing seasons of the New England landscape. Trained to make photographs through a microscope, she now uses a camera to examine the particulars and beauty found in everyday moments. Closing in tight on her subjects, she distills and intensifies their form and meaning.

Her landscapes, still lifes, and self-portraits have been exhibited at the Danforth Art Museum, Griffin Museum of Photography, the Cambridge Arts Association, Rhode Island Center for Photographic Arts, PhotoPlace Gallery, 555 Gallery, and the Davis Orton Gallery. Her work is in the permanent collection of the Danforth Museum. She currently serves on the board of directors at the Griffin Museum of Photography.

26

RANA YOUNG
Untitled (Probe 1)

Often serving as proxies for personal truths, photographs telescope our lives to unveil our most

vulnerable sentiments and circumstances, while critically shaping individual and collective memory. The opportunity to contribute to A Yellow Rose Project enabled me to approach image-making with renewed intention—an invitation to consider their framework in the context of my art practice. In my work, familial narratives aid me in rendering visual elegies to be investigated by a viewer, revealing the tension of uncertainty as I mine my mother's archive and matrilineal succession. As I retrace history, I'm thinking of how my considerations might molt into visual metaphors for circumstances and underscore the precarious bond between photographic record and the fragmented, abstract nature of memory. My contribution to this collection will forever stand as a reminder to never dim my light or hesitate in telling my truth. I offer the same reminder to all womxn.

Rana Young is a visiting assistant professor in the School of Art at the University of Arkansas. Rana holds an MFA in studio art from the University of Nebraska–Lincoln, where she was an Othmer Fellow, and a BFA in studio art from Portland State University. Her work has been exhibited nationally and internationally, as well as published online by *Hyperallergic, VICE, Huffington Post, The Wall Street Journal, British Journal of Photography,* and *The New York Times.* Kris Graves Projects published her first monograph, *The Rug's Topography,* in 2019.

27

SARAH HADLEY
On the Steps

As a child, I didn't understand the word feminist and thought I could do and become what I wanted. However, as I grew older, I saw discrimination in the world and experienced it as a female photographer and photojournalist. I also learned that my grandmother's generation didn't have the right to vote, to choose their vocation, or access to birth control—all things that I took for granted. In recent years as I saw women being badmouthed by politicians and the Me Too movement maligned, I felt compelled to raise my voice, as well as express myself through my art. Using old photographs, paper cutouts, color, symbol, and shadow, I have created images that explore memory and female identity and strength. The work is an homage to the courage of the suffragists and their selfless sacrifice, which changed the right to vote for generations to come. While America recently elected our first female vice president, there is still much work to be done, and we must continue the fight for equal pay, equal treatment, and equal access to voting. I hope to see more women in positions of leadership and power in the future. Though the battle is far from over, I am eternally grateful for all the women throughout history, who stood up for their rights and, especially to those women one hundred years ago, who fought for our right to vote.

Sarah Hadley is a Los Angeles based artist, whose narrative artwork centers around themes of memory, loss, and female identity. Hadley's photography and collages have been exhibited nationally and internationally in museums and galleries, as well as featured in numerous publications and blogs. Hadley studied art history at Georgetown University and photography at Corcoran College and received grants from the California Center for Cultural Innovation, the Illinois Arts Council, and the Ragdale Foundation. She founded the Filter Photo Festival in Chicago, and her first monograph, *Lost Venice,* was published in 2020. Hadley's artwork is held in private and public collections worldwide.

28 AND 29

YAEL EBAN & BREA SOUDERS
Untitled

This series was made in response to the one hundredth anniversary of legislation that granted women the right to vote in the United States. We collaboratively culled images of women's raised hands from anonymous vernacular photographs. We cropped the images in a way that would emphasize these strong gestures of assertion, serving broadly as a symbol of protest. By hand-coloring the black-and-white photographs, we further amplified their presence as a statement of solidarity, while bringing the images into a contemporary visual space. The images affirm the existence, participation, and power of women, while honoring those whose voices have been silenced and celebrating the ongoing fight for equal rights.

Yael Eban is an artist based in the Hudson Valley. She earned an MFA in photography at the School of Visual Arts in New York City. Her work has been exhibited at Stellar Projects in New York, FJORD in Pennsylvania, the Center for Creative Photography in Arizona, the Chrysler Museum of Art in Virginia, and the Houston Center for Photography. She has been featured in *Hyperallergic,* Artsy, *Lenscratch,* and *FADER* and has contributed writing to *Pan & The Dream* and *OSMOS* magazines. Eban has attended residencies at MASS MoCA, Wassaic Project, and Vermont Studio Center. She is currently co-director of Tiger Strikes Asteroid New York, a non-profit network of artist-run spaces.

Brea Souders is a visual artist working primarily with photography. Her work has been shown internationally, including solo exhibitions with Abrons Arts Center in New York, Baxter St. at City College

ofNew York, the Centre photographique Rouen Nor-
mandie in France, and the Peel Art Gallery, Museum
and Archives in Canada. She has received grants and
fellowships from the Pollock-Krasner Foundation,
Millay Arts, and the National Arts Club. A monograph
of her work spanning eleven years was published in
2021 by Saint Lucy Books.

30
ALINE SMITHSON
From 'Women I Don't Know'

Author David Eagleman has written that we all die
three deaths. The first when the body ceases to
function. The second when the body is consigned to
the grave. The third is that moment, sometime in the
future, when your name is spoken for the last time.
But the former editor of Life Magazine, David Shap-
iro, points out there is a fourth—the moment the last
remaining picture of you is seen for the final time.
I've had a lifelong obsession with collecting photographs of strangers. Some years ago, I produced
a project, People I Don't Know, where I rephotographed found portraits. I asked someone who was
the same age and gender as the person in the photograph to hold the image, allowing for a new con-
sideration of the subject and encouraging the viewer
to connect the portrait with the living and in doing
so, be fully seen one more time. As I considered
creating work for A Yellow Rose Project, I wanted the
women who blazed the trails for equality to have a
chance to be seen again. The most important gift we
can give someone is to be seen and acknowledged,
and so I collected found photographs of women
from the 1920s with a renewed curiosity. The wom-
en in these photographs may not have been rabble
rousers, but I'm hoping that they were. In Women I

Don't Know, I am creating one more opportunity to
see the sun on their faces and say thank you.

Aline Smithson is a visual artist, educator, and
editor based in Los Angeles, California. She has
exhibited widely, including over forty solo shows at
US and international institutions, including a commission by the Smithsonian National Air and Space
Museum. In 2018 and 2019, Smithson's work was
exhibited in the National Portrait Gallery in London
as a finalist in the Taylor Wessing Portrait Prize. Her
work has been featured in significant publications,
including *The New York Times, The New Yorker,* and
Photo District News (PDN). Her books include *Self &
Others: Portrait as Autobiography* (Magenta Foundation), *LOST II: Los Angeles* (Kris Graves Projects),
and *Fugue State* (Peanut Portfolio Press).

31
FRANCES F. DENNY
Anna (Red Hook Tavern), 2020

This image is from The Diners, a series of portraits
of women dining by themselves. Eating alone in a
restaurant is an act that, for many, requires furtive
oscillation between reflexive interiority and exteri-
or projection. It is also an act that is undoubtedly
connected to notions of belonging, freedom, and
privilege.

Frances F. Denny is an artist whose work investigates female identities. Her work is represented by
ClampArt in New York City. Frances's first monograph, *Let Virtue Be Your Guide,* was published in
2016 by Radius Books. Her second book, *Major Ar-
cana: Portraits of Witches in America,* was released
in 2020 by Andrews McMeel Publishing. Frances was

the recipient of a New York Foundation for the Arts 2016 fellowship in photography, and has won numerous awards, including the PDN 30. She received an MFA from Rhode Island School of Design. Frances lives in New York.

32
ILEANA DOBLE HERNANDEZ
Resistance

During the 2020 Women's March in Washington, DC, a group was protesting against the right to abortion. The confrontation between these protesters and the march's participants got heated as the protest group yelled insults backed up by their religious beliefs. The police, standing in between, prevented a violent clash. Suddenly, a woman walks in and starts dancing. No words, but her blue sign held up reading, "Keep Abortion Legal," and her body moving at the rhythm of whatever tune she was listening to or imagining. That action felt powerful. It reminded me of a Mexican saying that translates to: "to stubborn words, deaf ears." When thinking about A Yellow Rose Project, I wanted to create works that show the history of women's protests. I imagined many women before us on those same streets, fighting back inequality and patriarchal forms of oppression. I remembered this photo I took at the march when looking at photos of the suffrage movement at the Library of Congress, especially when I found this young woman with her sign, "Resistance to Tyranny is Obedience to God." Hers was a powerful statement too. One hundred years ago white women received the right to vote in the United States; it was later when women of color secured that same right. Today all of us keep fighting for the basic right of body ownership. We still have a long way ahead

of us, but those who have walked before us have certainly led the way. We just need to keep walking . . . and dancing!

Ileana Doble Hernandez is a Mexican visual artist; her socially conscious practice expands to photography, video, installation, and new media. Her artworks are part of public and private collections and have been published and exhibited in North America, Europe, and Asia. As an activist, Ileana believes art has the power to make people care; she works towards achieving stronger gun law reforms and the fair inclusion of immigrants within American society. Ileana is an alumna of the Massachusetts College of Art and Design and the Rochester Institute of Technology (RIT), where she received the 2019 RIT Outstanding Graduate Student Award.

33
MANJARI SHARMA
Uncertainty

As I created this piece, I thought about how we tend to gravitate toward a scaffolding that can stabilize us in times of uncertainty. In this piece, we see two women supporting each other. While their fingers interlocked, the image is also shrouded in folds of mystery. These hands belong to women from two different ethnicities: one is Irish, and one is Indian. I channeled the turbulence that women from all walks of life may have felt during the ratification of the Nineteenth Amendment. One hundred years ago, when women stood shoulder to shoulder awaiting the roll call of men that would decide their right to vote, all they had was their faith in each other. When unpredictability strikes, we look for anchors that can carry us through. My aim with this photograph was to memorialize and celebrate the historical significance of that moment in time. It highlights the bond of unity between us women, so we may continue the fight against oppression and brutality both then and now.

Manjari Sharma, born and raised in Mumbai, makes work rooted in portraiture addressing issues of identity, multiculturalism, and personal mythology. Manjari's work has been awarded, published, and exhibited internationally, and is recognized by *The New York Times, Vice,* CNN, *LA Times, The Huffington Post,* and NPR, to name a few. Manjari has taught at institutions like the School of the Museum of Fine Art at Tufts University, the Rubin Museum of Art, the Asia Society, and the School of Visual Arts in New York City, and her work is collected by the Metropolitan Museum of Art; Museum of Fine Arts, Houston; Carlos Museum; and Birmingham Museum of Art, amongst various private collections.

34
MELANIE WALKER
MisJudge

> mis·judge
> /ˌmisˈjəj/
> verb
> 1. form a wrong opinion or conclusion about. to make an incorrect estimation or assessment of.

MisJudge is part of a larger project entitled the MisNomer Pageant, which considers gender biases inherent in language. After reading the book, The Alphabet Versus the Goddess, I began thinking about the nature of words, and how they can influence thinking. Mis, as a prefix on a word, means "wrong or incorrect." As women, historically we have been referred to as Miss "Father's Name," so what are those

implications implied within language? MisJudge incorporates a self-portrait of the Dadaist political artist John Heartfield as a background image. I mirrored his self-portrait, making my own costume and props to convey the idea of MisJudge.

Melanie Walker has an exhibition history that spans more than fifty years. She received a BA from San Francisco State University and an MFA from Florida State University. She is a mixed media artist invested in ideas. Her approach to materials includes analog and digital photography, alternative processes, sculpture, installation, fiber art, printmaking, and public art. She has exhibited her work both nationally and internationally and has work in more than 200 permanent collections. She has received numerous grants and fellowships, including a National Endowment for the Arts (NEA) Fellowship, Colorado Council on the Arts Fellowship, Polaroid Materials grants, and an Aaron Siskind award.

35
CHEHALIS DEANE HEGNER
Mary Ann McClintock

After a Quaker meeting on July 9, 1848, five women gathered for an afternoon tea party in Waterloo, New York. Reflecting on the gathering, Elizabeth Stanton concluded, "I poured out, that day, the torrent of my long-accumulating discontent, with such vehemence and indignation that I stirred myself, as well as the rest of the party, to do and dare anything" (Women's Rights: Special History Study). I, too, felt my blood begin to boil as I dove deeper into the stories of our brave and brilliant suffragists. I created five portraits, one of each of the women at that groundbreaking, Waterloo tea party. I worked hungrily, striving for tenderness, gratitude, and the hope that I'd be able to achieve a small fraction of their formidable grit. Sometimes I allow my hands to create freely, as they often seem to have minds of their own. Such was the case when I responded to the prompt for A Yellow Rose Project. My re-photographed historical portrait of Mary Ann McClintock is torn and put back together one hundred years after the Nineteenth Amendment was finally brought into law. My drippy plastic overlay speaks of feminine reproductive organs and how layered the experience of being a woman still is.

Chehalis Deane Hegner was named in the 2018 and 2020 Julia Margaret Cameron Awards and is a recipient of the Gjon Mili Prize in 2010 in Kosovo. Solo and group exhibitions include the Griffin Museum of Photography in Massachusetts, the Photographic Resource Center (PRC) in Boston, the Art Institute of Boston, Maryland Art Place (MAP) in Baltimore, Saint-Gaudens National Historical Park in Cornish, New Hampshire, the Cultural Center in Varigotti, Italy, Perspective Gallery in Evanston, Illinois, Interlochen Arts Academy in Michigan, MIT Museum in Cambridge, Massachusetts, and the National Gallery of Kosovo. With an MFA in photography from Lesley University, Hegner serves on jury panels and workshops and is a co-founding director at Halo Hill Art Farm northwest of Chicago.

36
ELLEN CAREY
Crush & Pull

Light's immateriality challenges its makers today; analog versus digital doubles our challenges. The question, "What is a twenty-first century photograph?" finds my answer in partnering nineteenth century photograms with twentieth century Polaroid instant technology. Crush & Pull links my photographic experiments in color with process, minimalism and abstraction and light and its variations, often with zero exposure, uniting the "linked ring" of my twin practices—Struck by Light and Photography Degree Zero—for the first time. Without exposure—black—only using Polaroid color sees a monochrome palette that evidences the delicate craquelure of the Polaroid positive from the photogram-as-Polaroid negative, presenting a new photographic object for the twenty-first century.

Ellen Carey, born in the United States in 1952, is a Pictures Generation contemporary and member of Buffalo's avant-garde, which includes Cindy Sherman and Robert Longo, and upends the medium's collective histories in lens-based art, photography, and technology with abstract, minimal "picture" signs. *Photography Degree Zero* (1996–2021) in Polaroid 20 × 24 and *Struck by Light* (1988–2020) in photogram are her dual practices. Ellen Carey is an educator, independent scholar, guest curator, photographer, and lens-based artist. Her unique experimental work spans several decades and is highlighted in many one-person exhibits, plus several hundred group ones, and in her writing under *Pictus & Writ* from 2008–2021.

37
RACHEL PHILLIPS
Growing Pains

For the series called Growing Pains, I began with a few literal nods to the historical artifacts and symbols of the suffrage movement: A yellow rose was a prominent suffrage symbol. Also, Phoebe Burns used a (coincidentally?) yellow envelope when she wrote to her son Harry, the twenty-four-year-old representative to the Tennessee legislature who changed sides and cast the tie-breaking vote needed to ratify the Nineteenth Amendment. To these elements, I added photographs made by pioneering professional photographer Frances Benjamin Johnston around 1899 and now reside in the Library of Congress. I chose to work with scans of Johnston's photographs, including several antique cyanotype prints, for several reasons. First, I found them visually striking and, in their own way, representative of the strength, struggle, and aspiration of the women's movement. Also, I respected Benjamin Johnston as a champion of photography as a profession for women. Finally, by looking at work made by Johnston two decades before the Nineteenth Amendment passed, I realized how that particular moment sits in a historical continuum: women worked and fought to become self-realized and equal members of society long before suffrage, and ambiguity, imperfection, and struggle toward that ideal still exists today, a hundred years on.

Rachel Phillips began photography while completing her undergraduate degree at Skidmore College, graduating in 2005. In numerous group and solo exhibitions, she has presented a series of projects exploring the photograph as object, often resulting in unique works incorporating a specialized transfer printing technique, as well as other processes like encaustic wax, and materials ranging from old envelopes to nineteenth-century cabinet cards. A frequent theme in the work is a desire to *reanimate* the vernacular photographs and paper ephemera in her collection by reworking them in a variety of ways to create imagery that is resonant with the past yet has a new vitality and reflection of our own time and perspective. Her work has been exhibited and published widely, and her artist's books are held in numerous university special collections. Rachel is represented by Catherine Couturier Gallery in Houston and Dina Mitrani Gallery in Miami.

38
MARY BETH MEEHAN
Tell the Story

I Shall Wear a Crown is part of an ongoing collaboration by Mary Beth Meehan and Jonathan Pitts-Wiley, artist, educator, and grandson of Mrs. Annye Raye Pitts. Entitled Annye Raye Pitts: Witness, the project seeks to document, interpret, and share Mrs. Pitts's vast archive, which tells the story of a life lived assured of her own divine value even as she walked a path constricted by a racist America. By the time Annye Raye Pitts was born in 1933, American women had been granted the right to vote for over a decade. Yet as a Black woman in the South, Pitts would have to leave her birthplace of Montgomery, Alabama, and make a new home in Providence, Rhode Island, in order to seek full enfranchisement as an American citizen under the law. At the time of her passing, Mrs. Pitts's archive included more than a thousand newspaper clippings, writings, and other artifacts that recorded her thoughts, while also bearing witness to the magnificence of her Black sisters and brothers worldwide. She had also collected more than a hundred church hats, along with dress shoes, purses, and suits that she wore on her journey through this world. I Shall Wear a Crown seeks to echo the majestic hats worn by the twentieth-century suffragists, while reminding us of the Black women who were left out of that contract. The title refers to one of the many songs sung by Pitts in her lifetime as an accomplished gospel singer.

Mary Beth Meehan uses photography to transform public spaces and jolt people into considering one another anew. Combining image, text, and large-scale installation, Meehan's work challenges notions of representation, visibility, and equity and prompts people to connect with one another about what they see. Meehan's projects have been featured in *The New York Times* and *The Washington Post,* as well as publications in Europe and Asia. She has held artist residencies at Stanford University, the University of Missouri, and Brown University. Her first photography book, *Seeing Silicon Valley: Life Inside a Fraying America,* was published by the University of Chicago Press.

39
JULIA BENNETT
Five Wounds

When reflecting on the centennial of the Nineteenth Amendment's passage for this project, I was struck by the pang of melancholy I felt. Beneath the surface of pride and triumph for this hard-fought milestone was the hard truth that we remain still in the throes of a war on our bodies, choices, and voices. All women everywhere continue to bear the scars from this fight. Five Wounds pulls from the lore of the passionflower, with its five stamens representing the five wounds of Christ's crucifixion (his hands, feet, and heart). In this photographic rendition, the flower, along with other symbolic materials in the composition, recall the wounds of women who continue to rail against the systems that seek to silence them.

Julia Bennett is a marine scientist, fine art photographer, and book artist exploring the intersections between science, visual art, and the contemporary social landscape and focusing on how those intersections influence our understanding of a natural world in transition. Julia's photographs have been featured in solo and group exhibitions throughout the United States and abroad, including the Columbia Museum of Art in South Carolina, the Pence Gallery in California, and the Commonwealth Scientific and Industrial Research Organisation (CSIRO) in Australia. Julia's work has been published both in print and online, most notably through *WIRED, Feature Shoot,* and *PetaPixel.* Julia is currently residing and making work in Los Angeles, California.

40
ASTRID REISCHWITZ
Working Woman with "Votes for Women" Plate

A widely distributed Votes for Women china was commissioned by Newport socialite Alva Belmont (1853–1933), who was a major figure in the American women's suffrage movement. I encountered the china on a visit to Mrs. Belmont's Marble House Estate Museum in Rhode Island and incorporated it in this photography project as an anchor, a reminder that equal rights should be as much a part of daily life as everyday china. It is a salute to the willingness of the women of the suffrage movement to challenge convention.

Astrid Reischwitz is a Boston-based photographer, whose work explores storytelling from a personal perspective. Her projects include intimate views of private spaces and reflections on her own history and values. Using keepsakes from family life, old photographs, and storytelling strategies, she builds a visual world of memory, identity, place, and home. Her current focus is the exploration of personal and collective memory influenced by her upbringing in Germany.

41
NOELLE MCCLEAF
Altar for Marie Louise Bottineau Baldwin

Altars for Suffragists honors five women who marched, protested, or gave their lives to the fight for women's suffrage in the early twentieth century. An altar is a religious structure where offerings are given to gods or goddesses, dating back to countless historical faiths. The still life, similar to the altar, offers a collection of deliberately placed objects charged with meaning. Each photograph contains a combination of carefully composed artifacts specific to the suffragist's story, elevating the sacrifices, struggles, and triumphs they made for the good of all. Altar for Marie Louise Bottineau Baldwin was constructed to pay homage to Marie Louise Bottineau Baldwin for her contribution to the suffrage movement and her work advocating for the rights of Native American women. The still life contains two long braids in reference to a photograph that Bottineau Baldwin posed for while working for the Office of Indian Affairs (OIA). Bottineau Baldwin posed for her personnel file photo in Native dress with braided hair—a bold statement for a government employee at the time. Other items in the still life include found turtle shells to represent her tribe, horsehair, and a single lit candle. Marie Louise Bottineau Baldwin went on to march in the 1913 Woman Suffrage Procession organized by Alice Paul, spoke at the first meeting of the Society of American Indians, and continued to advocate for Native American women during her lifetime.

Noelle McCleaf is an artist exploring themes of memory, relationship, and identity in the landscape of South Florida. Born and raised in Virginia, Noelle received her BFA from the Ringling College of Art and Design and her MFA from the Minneapolis College of Art and Design, both with a concentration in photography. Her work has been exhibited and published throughout the United States and internationally. She currently lives and works in Venice, Florida, as an exhibiting artist and full time faculty in the Photography and Imaging program at the Ringling College of Art and Design.

42
PRESTON GANNAWAY
Untitled

Preston Gannaway, born in 1977, is an American documentary photographer and artist. For twenty years, she has focused on intimate stories about American families and marginalized communities, while addressing themes such as gender identity, class, and our relationship to the landscape. Gannaway is best known for her long-term projects like Remember Me, which was awarded the 2008 Pulitzer Prize for Feature Photography. Her photographs are held in both public and private collections and have been exhibited widely. Born and raised in North Carolina, she is now based in Sonoma County, California.

43
SANDRA KLEIN
The Banner

I am privileged to have been born with the right to vote, a right first granted to white women on August 18, 1920. A Yellow Rose Project offered me the chance to study the history of that right, and I delved into the story through the internet and with books by Kenneth Florey, which include photographs of contemporaneous postcards and memorabilia. I chose to honor the years-long history of the struggle. Being an artist that loves to composite, I began creating my art piece by layering images from postcards from Florey's books and added important documents, including a copy of the final amendment. Another layer included is of a request with signatures of "colored" citizens from the District of Columbia asking that Congress grant the right to vote to all women, which was denied. Layered on top of these images is a stitched photograph I took of a yellow rose, the symbol of the suffragists, taken in Los Angeles, my hometown. Although the right to vote wasn't mine to struggle for, the inequality experienced by women in the arts is something I know well. I attended college during a time when any perceived femininity in a student's work was ridiculed. Museums and galleries were filled with work almost exclusively by men. I chose as my final layer of this image a comment on the dismal history of inclusion of women in the art world. I look forward to a time when the art world is color and gender blind.

Sandra Klein is an artist whose images, whether captured with a camera or composited, portray a layered world which, though filled with anxiety and trauma, still is rich with joy. She received a BFA from Tyler School of Art and Architecture in Philadelphia and an MA in printmaking from San Diego State University. Her images have been shown throughout the United States and abroad. She has had one person shows at the Griffin Museum of Photography, the Lishui and Yixian Festivals in China, and A Smith

Gallery. She was the recipient of the Lorser Feitelson grant jointly with artist Betye Saar.

44

TONI PEPE
Mrs. Nixon

Mrs. Nixon is part of a larger body of work entitled Mothercraft, which is comprised of press photographs culled from flea markets and eBay, images that are also objects unto themselves marked by time. Typed and handwritten text along with date stamps, creased edges, and stains layer the surface of the photographs. These images are time capsules, showing us the event pictured, but also the frame through which they were received. They illustrate movement—both socially/politically—as records of women's liberation and voting rights on a global scale, but also durationally as physical images that were held, touched, and eventually abandoned. The dynamic push and pull between the personal and political is reflected in the fragmented captions, which often slip past their descriptive roles into more dogmatic territory. Offering information ranging from the objective, such as age and location, to the more partial and idiosyncratic details tied to tradition and duty, these images provide a glimpse into the shifting nature of truth and the complex relationship between image and word.

Toni Pepe is chair and assistant professor of photography at Boston University. She received her MFA from the Rochester Institute of Technology and an MLA in visual culture from Boston University. Her photographs and installation work explore the construction of identity, specifically the icon of the mother. Pepe was a finalist for the Massachusetts

Cultural Council fellowship, a Critical Mass Top 50, a Review Santa Fe 100, and was most recently awarded an Artist Trust grant for 2020. Her work is in the permanent collections at the Danforth Art Museum, the Magenta Foundation, and many private collections.

45

GREER MULDOWNEY
Be a Good Boy from the series *Rhetorical Image*

Small words have such seminal impacts, especially those forgotten by history or falsified to bolster it. When researching women's suffrage, I was immediately drawn to the quotes and catchphrases that became the rhetorical history of the era—or the myths that surround it. Quotations are often taken out of context or attributed to new meanings in every era, so it was no surprise to find the language quoted in the history books had in many accounts been altered, forgotten, or the legendary utterance had never occurred at all. The piece featured for this publication refers to the hinging point of the passage of the Nineteenth Amendment in the Tennessee State Legislature, a body who would pass ratification by one vote. Originally a "No" vote by representative Harry Burn and his emblazoned red rose, his mother wrote him a long letter that included only one sentence to implore her son, "don't forget to be a good boy and help Mrs. Catt put the RAT in ratification." It is said that this cajoling changed the history for the amendment and the course of our history. What a precarious weight to put on a casual letter. In the century that has passed, so many individual histories have been re-illuminated or forgotten that made the Nineteenth a reality. Rephotographing and distorting the documents where these prophetic words were first elicited felt fitting, allowing pho-

tography and its trustworthiness (or lack thereof) to also be a fitting parallel for such a complicated history.

Greer Muldowney is an artist, professor, and independent curator based in Boston, Massachusetts. Her work often tackles the relationship of policy making and its effects landscape, housing, and community. She received an undergraduate degree from Clark University and an MFA from the Savannah College of Art and Design. She has served on the board of directors for the Griffin Museum of Photography and is the founder and director of Undergraduate Photography Now, an arts organization bolstering the work and professional development of photography students. She has juried and curated exhibitions nationally, and currently is an assistant professor at Boston College.

46

SERRAH RUSSELL
I could finally let my smile drain away. We were mostly quiet. Digital collage using photograph by Annie Leibovitz from Vogue Magazine *archive (1993)*

When I inked the oval next to Hillary Clinton's name on the ballot, I believed I had voted for the first Madam President. And I am still aghast that despite over one hundred years since (some but not all) women gained the right to vote, a woman has not broken through that highest, hardest glass ceiling and served in the most powerful position of the United States.

The First Ladies Club: or How to Get a Woman in the Oval Office is a series of digital collages made using photographs of First Ladies sourced from the archive of *Vogue Magazine,* which has been featuring the wives of US Presidents for over one hundred years. Each title is also sourced from *Vogue,* using words either spoken by or spoken about the First Lady.

Here Hillary Clinton recalls the 2016 election. She expected to win and was devastated but determined to put on a strong face and give a gracious concession speech. It was only after all the work was done and she was driven away by Secret Service that she could "finally let [her] smile drain away."

Look as a woman's face burns, melts, dissolves, and disappears. Watch it happen once and then watch again, the same number of attempts this First Lady made to enter a new role in the White House. Here there are no forced smiles or determined eyes. Her mask has faded away, but even without it we cannot see her. She remains a First Lady.

Serrah Russell is a visual artist and independent curator living in Seattle. She holds a BFA in photography from the University of Washington. Her practice uses collage, photography, and sculpture to address the relationship and tension between one's internal emotions and their external surroundings. Often pulling from advertising and editorial images, Russell transforms what was intended to sell or influence into space for meditation, compassion, and protest. Russell's first artist monograph, *tears tears,* was published in 2019 by Yoffy Press and features collages created during, and in response to, the first one hundred days of the forty-fifth presidency.

47

SARAH POLLMAN
Dragonfly

Radical reformers in the nineteenth century emphasized individualism and autonomy of self in a fight for human rights that included abolition, gender equality, suffrage, and marriage and dress reform. Among these reformers were spiritualist mediums and public trance speakers, whose leadership commanded a new public respect in the Antebellum South. Turning toward their femininity instead of away from it, these speakers embraced and weaponized societal assumptions to push for radical change. Their presence on stage was a curious combination of intellectual power and feminine display joined together for the first time in the minds of many Americans.

These pictures, contact printed in a process recalling photography's earliest incarnations, marry baubles and jewels with printed book surfaces that promise knowledge. Can femininity and intellectual power coexist? Do assumptions of gender binaries inform what one is capable of? Like the reformers before me, I have a long fraught relationship with the expectations of being born female in Western society. It is from this place of questioning—and revisitation of the ideas of these reformers—that I utilize the visual language of femininity in my photographs. Saturated pink recalls both the blush of childhood and the fleshiness of being human. Object and illustration compete with one another and refuse to resolve, highlighting ever-present tensions between seeing and being seen and between speaking and being heard, extending these historic conversations outward toward the future.

Sarah Pollman is an interdisciplinary scholar, who works across art and art history. Her research examines networks of meaning making in material culture with particular emphasis on photographic history, theory, and production. Her book, *The Distances Between Us,* was published by Trema Förlag in 2016, and she has exhibited at the Museum of Fine Arts in Boston; the Danforth Art Museum; and the Rourke Art Gallery + Museum, among other venues. Sarah holds an MFA from Tufts University and a BFA from the School of the Museum of Fine Arts at Tufts University.

48

MAUDE SCHUYLER CLAY

Ishy's Haircut

This piece is called Ishy's Haircut from my Mississippi History project. Ishmael was a rather obstreperous fox terrier, who belonged to our son Schuyler. Here our friend Pablo, who also had wire-haired terriers, is giving Ishmael a haircut with our daughter Anna looking on. The light was so perfect on her face, and I loved the framing of the dog and the arms of Pablo and Capel holding up the dog in the foreground. This was taken around the 1990's.

Maude Schuyler Clay started her color portrait series *Mississippi History* in 1975, when she came upon her first Rolleiflex 2 1/4 camera. At the time, she was living and working in New York and paid frequent visits to her native Mississippi Delta, whose landscape and people continued to inspire her. Over the next twenty-five years, the project, which began as *The Mississippians,* evolved into an homage to Julia Margaret Cameron. A definitive pioneer of the art of photography, Cameron lived in Victorian-era England and began her photographic experiments in 1863, after receiving the gift of a camera. The expressive, allegorical portraits of her friends and family and Maude Schuyler Clay's artful approach to capturing the essence of light are the driving forces behind Clay's nostalgic recollection of carefree moments

of family life and play in Mississippi in the 1980s and 1990s.

Maude Schuyler Clay's photography is in the collections of the Museum of Modern Art; the Museum of Fine Arts, Houston; and the National Museum for Women in the Arts, among others. Maude Schuyler Clay continues to live in the Delta with her husband, photographer Langdon Clay, and their three children.

49

SASHA TIVETSKY

Shoes

These Are the Shoes They Wore

A thunderous roar
A wild cry

Joined in arms with voices shouting
through all the pain
and moments
that build a woman
into a solid rock.

It takes a lot of cracking to break the mold

They wiped the sweat from their brows
and the hair stuck to their faces

Together a
Squeaky wheel
made of iron and blood
And blisters and rock

Sasha Tivetsky is a photographer based in Los Angeles. They have been professionally photographing architecture and design since 2012. After graduating with a BFA in photojournalism from San Francisco State University, Sasha moved back to their native Los Angeles.

Aside from their commercial architecture and lifestyle work, Sasha spends the rest of their time on personal projects, currently the series *House Portraits* and their ongoing project *Grandma Luda.*

50

MOLLY LAMB
My Great-Grandmother's Yellow Rose

Among my family's belongings is a ceramic yellow rose pin. On one side of the jewelry box I keep it in, my great-aunt's cursive handwriting reads, "Yellow Rose." On the other side, my brother's manuscript handwriting reads, "Yellow Flower Pin." I've always loved this pin and the generations of family history infused in the box. I believe the yellow rose pin belonged to my great-grandmother Nora. She was born in 1886 and lived all her ninety-seven years in Arkansas, the twelfth state to ratify the Nineteenth Amendment. She would have been thirty-three years old in 1920, when the Nineteenth Amendment was passed, and she would have been able to vote for the next sixty-four years of her life. My brother and I grew up nearby in Tennessee. We visited our great-grandmother and great-aunt when we were very young, driving through the peach trees and cotton fields to spend the day with them. Was my great-grandmother one of the women who wore a yellow rose in support of women's suffrage? I wonder about her life even more now, and I cherish the few years that we had together.

Molly Lamb's work is a meditation on the resonance of loss and memory through the language of nature. She holds an MFA in photography from the Massachusetts College of Art and Design. Her work has been exhibited nationally and is included in public and private collections. Recent awards include being named a Massachusetts Cultural Council fellow in photography, a finalist for the New Orleans Photo Alliance–Clarence John Laughlin Award, a Critical Mass Top 50 recipient, and one of PDN 30 New and Emerging Photographers. Molly is represented by Rick Wester Fine Art in New York.

51

KAREN ZUSMAN
Dear Sojourner

I shot this image and wrote the accompanying poem in early March 2019; today it's even more relevant. After becoming involved with the Black Lives Matter protests in the summer and fall of 2020 in New York City and meeting and working with many young women of color activists, as well as older protesters, I witnessed firsthand the power that was unleashed with their collective voice. According to the Center for American Progress, women of color make up thirty percent of voting age women. Black women had the highest voter turnout in 2012 out of any demographic, and in 2020, ninety percent of them voted for Biden. It's often stated that he owed his win to them. While voter suppression—especially targeted at people of color—is a serious obstacle, Black, women-led groups are leading the charge to overcome it. Sojourner Truth, who was born into slavery yet went on to become one of the first abolitionists and women's rights activists, would be horrified at the recent developments around voter suppression—and yet she'd be incredibly proud to learn of the booming power of the women's vote, particularly of Black women and to learn that our first female vice president is also our first Black one. The year 2020 may go down in history as one of the most challenging years ever and it may also go down as the year when Black women, with the power of their voice—and their vote—finally made Black lives matter.

Karen Zusman came to photography while making an audio story about human trafficking in Malaysia. She received a Pulitzer Center for Crisis Reporting grant, and it was featured on PBS and NPR. After that, Zusman decided to learn photography. Her first images documented her free, education non-profit for child laborers in Myanmar. Next, Zusman spent extensive time creating intimate, visual stories throughout Cuba. While self-taught in photography, she earned an MFA in poetry. She received the Leica Women Foto Project Award for her *Super Power of Me* project, celebrating youth of color and young immigrants for a New York City public art exhibit in 2022.

52

K.K. DEPAUL
Silent No More

This piece is a reminder to young girls today that we must not take hard-won rights for granted. They can be taken away. The fight continues . . . even now.

K.K. DePaul is an explorer of secrets, combining and recombining bits and pieces of memory to make sense of her family stories.

> I have always been fascinated by multiple interpretations, double exposures, and the ambiguities that arise depending on which character is telling the story. My process begins with a collection of elements . . . images . . . writing. As I move the elements around, a visual narrative begins to take shape, signaling a new understanding of parallel stories. My use of collage indicates a story told in two voices, representing identities that have been torn apart, stripped, reflected upon, and ultimately reconstructed.

Her work has been published in Black & White Magazine, EYEMAZING, Diffusion, and Photoworld China. Most recently, she was the recipient of the 10th

Julia Margaret Cameron Award, with two exhibitions in Barcelona, and was part of the exhibition, Tribe, at the Fox Talbot Museum at Lacock in the United Kingdom.

53

LAURA MIGLIORINO
Courage

When I was first asked to participate in A Yellow Rose Project, I thought about how delicate and rebellious the act of self-governance is. Over the course of human history, periods of democracy are few, and participation by the masses is even less. Recently, the United States of America barely survived a slide toward autocracy, and we continue the fight to access the ballot box. Why is it such a radical notion to allow everyone the right to determine the laws and policies that govern their lives? I didn't have an easy answer but realized I live in Minnesota, the state with the highest voter participation in the United States—around seventy percent in presidential elections. What does this say about the state? What would America be if seventy percent of eligible voters cast ballots? Minnesota is far from perfect, struggling with racism, disparities, and division; the murder of George Floyd in Minneapolis is with us every day. I decided to focus on the suffrage movement in Minnesota, my adopted home, and the women who spearheaded the cause. This piece encompasses Clara Ueland, the prototypical educated white woman, and African American Nellie Griswold Francis, who founded the Everywoman Suffrage Club in 1914. The photographs are in the style of my series The Hidden Life of Books, a project capturing rare books, archival documents, and antique musical scores. I turned to the Minnesota History Center, offering an endless number of letters, posters, photographs, pamphlets, and ephemera. There was no lack of material to explore.

Migliorino was born in Cleveland, Ohio, and grew up in Chicago Heights, a Chicago suburb. Migliorino's BFA is from the School of the Art Institute of Chicago, and her MFA is from the University of Minnesota. She is a professor of art at Anoka-Ramsey Community College near Minneapolis. Migliorino has received numerous grants from the Jerome Foundation, several Minnesota State Arts Board grants, and various exhibition prizes. Migliorino was the Community College Humanities Affiliated fellow at the American Academy in Rome in 2017 and the 2018 James Weldon Johnson Foundation fellow. She is the recent recipient of a 2021 Fulbright Fellowship to the British Library in London, researching Rosamond Johnson and Pan-African composer Samuel Coleridge-Taylor. She is currently photographing the archives of the Tretter Collection of GLBT [LGBTIAQ+] history at the University of Minnesota. Her work is in the permanent collection of the Walker Art Center, Weisman Art Museum in Minneapolis, the Minnesota Center for Book Arts, and the Warehouse in Atlanta. She has exhibited internationally for over thirty years. Migliorino's work has been featured in *The Huffington Post, DOMUS Magazine, Pittsburgh Post-Gazette, The NewsHour with Jim Lehrer,* and *Dwell Magazine.*

54

HEIDI KIRKPATRICK
Let Our Voices Be Heard

My work is about voice, about family and things that have happened to me and my people, and about sharing stories and images to keep them alive. The work I made for this project is about strength in numbers, how our voices collectively make a difference, then and now. I have had the right to vote my whole life, my mother as well, but when my grandmother came of age, she did not. Because of collective voice, my grandmother was able to vote in her lifetime. Many advocated for the right to have a voice. I am grateful to those who stood up and fought for the right to vote.

Heidi Kirkpatrick is a fine art photographer and educator based in Portland, Oregon. Kirkpatrick combines film positives with found objects to create intimate photo-based objects that explore themes of family, history, love, and loss. During the Oregon summers, Heidi creates cyanotypes on vintage linens and clothing, using personal possessions and specimens from her garden that address similar issues. Kirkpatrick has displayed her photo objects and cyanotypes in over one hundred exhibitions in the last twenty years. Her work is held in numerous private and public collections. Kirkpatrick is represented by G. Gibson Projects in Seattle and Dina Mitrani Gallery in Miami.

55

FARAH JANJUA
Afghan Eyes

This photograph was taken in the fall of 2001 in one of the Afghan settlements along the border between Pakistan and Afghanistan. I was working on a story for Seventeen Magazine, covering the educational plight of Afghan girls and women during the rule of the Taliban and later living in the refugee camps. This young woman volunteered to have her picture taken and requested I show it to the world. She wanted to make a bold statement which defied the law prohibiting her to go to school. Several girls in the camps and settlements were vocal about wanting to pursue their dreams of getting educations and working in professional fields of their choice. The decades-long conflicts on Afghan soil, both by internal and external forces, have left millions dead, countless people homeless, and deprived many of a sustainable, hopeful future. The unfortunate impact of war has manifested itself through a destroyed infrastructure, which might take years to rebuild, meanwhile opening doors to an unstable political system, and poor governance leading to extremist elements that have caused immense damage to the most vulnerable in their society, including women and children. I like to believe these eyes staring back at us through the veil are the eyes of Afghanistan, specifically the Afghan women full of heartache but brimming with stories to share. Stories of resilience, defiance, and the will to survive.

For Farah, her art is a means to explore the infinite possibilities to highlight the faces of humanity, connect their diverse lives, and break their barriers divided by boundaries. Besides her extensive traveling, Farah has daringly stepped into Afghan and Kashmiri refugee camps in Pakistan and has rendered her services to humanitarian organizations. She has to her credit international publications and nine solo exhibitions in the United States. Farah recently published a photography book, *Jerusalem— Three Souls in One City,* a pictorial testimony of how humanizing one another is the first step toward achieving peaceful coexistence.

56

KYRA SCHMIDT
Chinese Girl Wants to Vote

This lumen print considers ideas of collaboration, community, subjectivity, and collective memory. It is a durational sun print made with outdated, black and white, darkroom paper. This image was created through a collaborative meditation between a group of dear girlfriends and me. A news article depicting Mabel Ping-Hua Lee was superimposed onto the final unfixed lumen via a Xerox printer. The economical process merged with the fragility of the paper suggests the ephemerality of our defining moments, while considering how the archive not only curates memory but buries it as well. Text borrowed from our conversation was embossed into the paper's surface by hand. The act of mark-making is symbolic of perseverance, recognizing the countless individuals that have and still fight for equality. The juxtaposition of the repetitive phrase "I'm sorry it isn't what you hoped for" against the news headline "Chinese girl wants to vote" calls attention to the unequal representation of women and minorities in news media. Merging past with present, their layering evokes obscured remnants of civil and political strife still relevant today. This series of images aims to prioritize universality and mindfulness within a pluralistic society, focusing not on gender or class, but individuality and personal connection.

Kyra Schmidt has exhibited nationally and internationally, including the SCAD Museum of Art in Savannah, the House of Lucie in Los Angeles, Candela Gallery in Richmond, Edition One Gallery in Santa Fe, 621 Gallery in Tallahassee, and the Lishui Photography Festival in Lishui, China. Her work has been published in *Aint—Bad Magazine, BETA developments*

in photography, and as a 2017 Top 50 photographer by Critical Mass. Kyra's first handmade monograph was published with Dust Collective in fall 2019. She received her bachelor's degree from the University of Southern Indiana and her MFA in photography from the Savannah College of Art and Design. Kyra currently works at the Eleanor D. Wilson Museum at Hollins University in Roanoke, Virginia.

57
RACHEL LOISCHILD
#180

In this selection, Loischild highlights the yellow rose, a symbol of the women's suffrage movement worn by suffrage leaders and supporters as a sign of solidarity. The use of flowers to support suffrage dates back to 1867, when Elizabeth Cady Stanton and Susan B. Anthony used sunflowers, the state flower of Kansas, to support a state-level suffrage referendum. The golden yellow color was then adopted for the movement—"Gold, the color of light and life, is as the torch that guides our purpose, pure and unswerving" (The Suffragist 1913). The rose was most prominently on display in 1920, when the Tennessee legislature became the final state to ratify the Nineteenth Amendment—during the historic and tense debate supporters of women's suffrage wore yellow roses, while the opposition wore red. The moths in the image represent the different roles women played in the suffrage movement.

Inspired by eighteenth-century artist Barbara Regina Dietzsch's botanical paintings, Loischild used her scanner to create these images. She layered glass from vintage frames, local plants, and insects composing diorama-like vignettes. The imagery combines a feminist reflection on the history of science, botanical drawing being the one place women were allowed to participate, with a sense of whimsy found in the micro-narratives created with her insects that directly reference children's literature and picture book art.

Rachel Loischild is a Boston-based artist, mother, professor, and Massachusetts Cultural Council fellow in photography. She holds her MFA in photography from Pratt Institute. Her work is shown nationally at galleries and museums, including the Danforth Museum of Art and the Newport Art Museum, and internationally at the Jeonju International Photo Festival in Korea. Her work is held in numerous collections, including the Beinecke Rare Book and Manuscript Library at Yale University and the Magenta Foundation. Loischild is a recipient of multiple City of Boston Arts Opportunity grants and is a Berkshire Taconic Community Foundation Artist's Resource Trust (A.R.T.) grant recipient.

58
MEGAN JACOBS
Equality Then & Now

The one hundredth anniversary of the hard-fought battle for women's suffrage has opened critical dialogues about the steps we have and have not made toward equality as a nation. The photographs in the series, Equality Then & Now, were created in collaboration with four honors students from the University of New Mexico: Hyunju Blemel, Sydney Nesbit, Sierra Venegas, and Tilcara Webb. The images aim to encourage dialogues about areas of continued inequality and the need to push for equal rights. Utilizing a poetic tone, the work seeks to make connections from 1920 to present day regarding power and independence. The right to cast a vote in a democracy and the right to make decisions about one's body are continued fights for independence in our society. The image in this book depicts the historic image of suffragist Julia Marlowe layered on top of Generation Z feminist Tilcara Web, Marlowe's uncanny, contemporary likeness. The visual similarities in appearance and the fight for equality are explored through this layering.

Megan Jacobs is an artist based in New Mexico and an associate professor at the University of New Mexico. Her work explores delicate relationships, our existence as material and concept, the interweaving between two partners in love, and the bond of parent and child. Jacobs's work has been featured in *Musée Magazine, Lenscratch, Feature Shoot,* and *Frankie Magazine.* Her *Hidden Mothers* series was selected for Photolucida's Critical Mass Top 50 and Review Santa Fe. Her work has been exhibited at Aperture Gallery, Saatchi Gallery, the Museum of New Art (MONA), Blue Sky Gallery, and the Photoville FENCE.

59
TSAR FEDORSKY
A Yellow Rose

When I was invited to participate in A Yellow Rose Project, I did not hesitate. I thought about the women and men who fought hard over the span of many years for the Nineteenth Amendment. I was reminded of the ongoing struggles for women to gain equal pay, secure personal safety, have their voices heard during the #MeToo movement, crash through the glass ceilings, and fight against voter suppression. We are still waiting for the first female president . . . an ongoing journey. In approaching this project, I knew that I needed to make it personal. One of my pieces includes a framed photograph

of my mother and her sister, who sang as a duo on local radio in the mid-1940s. They were the oldest of nine children, raised by a single mother during the Depression. Looking at the framed portrait, I am reminded of the hopes and dreams they carried as young women in mid-twentieth-century America, as well as the barriers they overcame. The coins on the dresser are a reminder of the financial challenges my mother faced as she raised two children on her own. While there is still much to do, I am aware of the opportunities in my life that were not available to my mother. We must not stop fighting for equal rights and justice.

Tsar Fedorsky is an American photographer. She received a Guggenheim Fellowship for Creative Arts in photography in 2018. She was a Critical Mass finalist in 2015 and 2017 and received an Artist Fellowship grant from the Massachusetts Cultural Council in 2015. Her photographs have been exhibited and published nationally and worldwide. Her work centers on personal, yet relatable, narratives. *The Light Under the Door* was published by Peperoni Books in 2017. She received an MFA in photography from the University of Hartford and a BA from Amherst College. Ms. Fedorsky resides in Gloucester, Massachusetts.

60
SUSAN ROSENBERG JONES
Emily and Anne

For my contribution to A Yellow Rose Project, I considered the efforts of the brave and determined women of the suffrage movement, who fought for all women the rights to have an equal voice in the democratic process. While it is inspiring to look back at those before us who bravely spearheaded the movement, our work is not done. I photographed Emily and Anne in their beautiful home. They met in 1989 at feminist author Kate Millett's Women's Art Colony Farm, where Anne was a founding member. At that time, Emily was a member of an activist group that staged women's peace camps in Battery Park, participated in civil disobedience at the Nevada missile test site, and many other actions. Married in 2014 and "domestic partners" since 1993 when Mayor Dinkins made it legal in New York City, they have a daughter in her twenties. As they related to me, Emily and Anne continue to listen, learn, and find ways to be useful. I'm proud to call them friends and motivated by their efforts and energy for creating change.

Susan Rosenberg Jones, based in New York City, is a portrait and documentary photographer focused on home, family, and community. Susan's body of work, *Second Time Around,* was exhibited at the Center for Fine Art Photography in 2016, received honorable mention in the 2017 Baxter Street at CCNY Annual Juried Competition, and was named a 2017 Critical Mass Top 50. *Widowed,* a 2019 Critical Mass finalist, was exhibited at the Griffin Museum in the fall of 2019. Susan's work has been exhibited internationally and featured in publications, such as *Strange Fire Collective, These Streets Magazine,* and *The American Scholar.*

61

CARLA JAY HARRIS
aTriptych

My mission is to document intellectual, emotional, and psychological environments. I trained as a photographer; however, in recent years, I've developed a multidisciplinary practice that includes photography, installation, collage, and drawing. This transformation was inspired by my desire to bring together my interests in image-making, space, and spectatorship. These themes continually inspire me and serve as a binding thread through all my works. I describe the end-style of my work as narrative with a hint of fantasy. Conceptually, I start each project with an aspect of my own personal experience that I want to explore; then evolve the work into a lasting statement on human nature. My work for A Yellow Rose Project is from a larger series of self-portraits that examines and recontextualizes the relationship between the Black female body and what it means to be an American.

Born in Indianapolis, Indiana, but raised traveling the globe as the child of a military officer, Carla Jay Harris's social and artistic development was impacted tremendously by the geopolitical and natural environments she encountered. She fervently believes that space, physical and physiological, has a fundamental, lasting impact on personal identity. While the environment around us is constantly evolving, photography has the power to capture humanity in a place, in a moment—transforming a flicker in time into a lasting, appreciable statement. Carla's work has been exhibited nationally and internationally in New York City, Los Angeles, Washington, DC, Paris, and Quebec. She completed undergraduate coursework at the School of Visual Arts in New York City, received her bachelor's degree with distinction from the University of Virginia and her MFA from UCLA in 2015. She currently lives and works in Los Angeles. Her works are included in the collections of USC Fisher Museum of Art in Los Angeles, California African American Museum in Los Angeles, Museum of Art and History in Lancaster,

California, the Sherbrooke Museum of Fine Arts in Quebec, General Mills Art Collection in Minneapolis, and numerous private collections. She is represented by Luis De Jesus Los Angeles.

62
JEANINE MICHNA-BALES
Ready for Battle, 2019

Ready for Battle is from the photographic essay Standing Together: Inez Milholland's Final Campaign for Women's Suffrage (2016–2020). In October 1916, suffragist Inez Milholland was appointed as a "special flying envoy" to make a 12,000-mile swing through the American West. She was part of a radical campaign by the National Woman's Party to send dozens of suffragists from the East out to twelve western states and territories, where women had the right to vote. With the election just a few weeks away, their message to the West was simple: Stand together with suffragists in the eastern states by casting a protest vote against President Wilson, the Democratic incumbent who had failed to make their cause a national priority. Inez embarked on a grueling campaign traversing eight states in twenty-one days. Her itinerary, brutal even by today's travel standards, consisted of street meetings, luncheons, railroad station rallies, press interviews, teas, auto parades, dinner receptions, and speeches in the West's grandest theaters. Arriving in Los Angeles on October 23, Inez delivered her last speech to about one thousand people at Blanchard Hall, where she collapsed on stage while speaking. Her final public words were, "President Wilson, how long must this go on, no liberty?" Although she tried to be "indefatigable," according to the Los Angeles Daily Times, Inez's rapidly deteriorating health forced her to stop campaigning. She died only one month later on November 25, 1916, at the age of thirty—a martyr of the American suffrage movement.

Jeanine Michna-Bales is a fine artist working in the medium of photography. Her work explores our fundamentally important relationships—to the land, to other people, and to oneself—and how they impact contemporary society. Her work lives at the intersection of curiosity and knowledge, documentary and fine art, past and present, anthropology and sociology, and environmental and activism. Her practice is based on in-depth research—taking into account different viewpoints, causes and effects, and political climates—and she often incorporates primary source material into her projects. Michna-Bales has released two monographs, *Through Darkness to Light* in 2017 and *Standing Together* in 2021. Her work has been exhibited extensively throughout the United States, is held in many permanent collections, and has been featured in numerous media outlets.

63
KALEE APPLETON
Untitled

Set on a backdrop of wallpaper covered in yellow roses, the print used by suffragists is on display. This relic reminds us of the endurance of women from the past, who sacrificed and fought for equality. Their determination is celebrated and on display as a badge of honor and respect through this image. The legacy of brave women who battled for their right for equality reminds us that this fight continues today, and it is our responsibility to continue their cause.

Kalee Appleton is a photography-based artist and assistant professor of photography at Texas Christian University in Fort Worth. Originally from Hobbs, New Mexico, Appleton attended Texas Tech University in Lubbock and received a BFA in photography in 2005. Shortly after graduation, she worked as a corporate and aviation photographer and later attended Texas Woman's University in Denton, where she received an MFA in art in 2014. Appleton has exhibited her work nationally, including Filter Photo in Chicago, Erin Cluley Gallery in Dallas, Ivester Contemporary in Austin, Fotofest in Houston, and Houston Center for Photography.

64
PAULA RIFF
Because of Sunflowers

Paula Riff is a Los Angeles based artist known for creating one of a kind cameraless photographic works on paper that embrace bold colors, form, and design. She combines the historical processes of cyanotype and gum bichromate, allowing her a physical and intimate relationship with the materials, which she uses to push the boundaries of the medium while considering themes of abstraction and the natural world.

Paula graduated from UC Berkeley with a degree in Japanese language and worked as an interpreter in Tokyo, Japan, for several years. Returning to Los Angeles, she switched careers after interning at the Los Angeles County Museum of Art in the photo department. Her work was selected as a Critical Mass Top 50 in 2019, the Critical Mass Top 50 in 2018, and was a 2018 finalist for the Julia Margaret Cameron Award for Women in the alternative process category. Paula also received the Museum Purchase Award at the Medium Photo Festival in 2019. Her work appears in numerous museums, galleries, publications, and exhibitions throughout the United States and internationally and is held in private collections.

65
RANIA MATAR
Kayla

My work addresses the states of Becoming—the fraught beauty and the vulnerability of growing up—in the context of the visceral relationships to our physical environment and universal humanity. It is about collaboration and empowerment. I am interested in exploring what it is like to be a girl and a woman today and how we make sense of a world that poses endless questions on girls and women of all backgrounds. For A Yellow Rose Project, I photographed young women, voting in the presidential election for the first time at this historic moment of our history, which happens to serendipitously coincide with the hundredth anniversary of the ratification of the Nineteenth Amendment. I gathered a quote from them on why it was important for them to vote this year.

> "Many years ago, my ancestors fought and died for my right to vote. Black men AND women sacrificed everything so that I could have the chance and choice to voice how I actually want to live my life. When it comes to voting, matters of feminine health pertaining to rape and abortion rights/laws affect women everyday—affect me every day. Not voting makes it one step closer for a white man I've never met, that particularly doesn't even care for my rights solely because I am black and also a woman, to then decide for me what I can and cannot do with my reproductive parts. Just to then later publicly and deliberately joke about grabbing me by 'em. I vote to have a word."—Kayla, Roxbury, Massachusetts

Matar's work has been widely exhibited in museums and galleries worldwide and is in the permanent collections of several museums. She had mid-career retrospectives at the Cleveland Museum of Art, Amon Carter Museum of American Art, and American University of Beirut Archaeological Museum. Matar received several grants and awards, including 2018 Guggenheim Fellowship, 2017 Mellon Foundation grant, 2011 Griffin Museum of Photography Legacy Award, and Massachusetts Cultural Council Artist Fellowship. In 2008, she was a finalist for the Foster Prize at the Institute of Contemporary Art/Boston. She has published four books: SHE in 2021, L'Enfant-Femme in 2016, A Girl and Her Room in 2012, and Ordinary Lives in 2009. She is an associate professor of photography at the Massachusetts College of Art and Design.

66

COLLEEN MULLINS
8:58 AM

The women's suffrage movement has such a complicated history. To celebrate the one hundredth birthday of the Nineteenth Amendment is to celebrate a milestone of privileged histories and barely veiled institutionalized white supremacy, and yet an amendment to the Constitution of the United States isn't anything about which to sneeze. But until 1965, African American women were omitted from this calculus we now celebrate. It is perhaps for this reason that my neighbor Frankie and her downsizing move to an assisted living community at age ninety-five became the focus of my gaze in this work. In 1976, when I was nine, Frankie moved into an apartment on the first floor of the twelve-unit building in which I grew up. The images of her office, now

dismantled, resonated in a new way with the lens of the pandemic. As we age and get around less, these nerve centers not only become the center of our memories and connections to history, but essential centers to keep an active voice in the community. This room allowed her to push her activism outward. And when she had me photograph her objects before discarding them, I realized that for me the power in any one law is that they are bricks in a foundation of power, and we are all, with our feet and votes, the mortar. Frankie is mortar.

Colleen Mullins is a photographer and book artist. Her work has been recognized with two McKnight Fellowships, four Minnesota State Arts Board grants, and she was a nominee for the Leica Oskar Barnack Award for her project *Expositions are the timekeepers of progress* in 2020. Her work is in the numerous US public collections, and she has authored articles for *Afterimage* and *PDNedu.* Her books include *Opening Day* (1998) and *Rolls & Tubes: A History of Photography* (2021), along with numerous periodicals including *Photo District News, The Oxford American* "Eyes on the South," and *The New York Times* "Lens."

67

KATHYA MARIA LANDEROS
Latina Girl, 2020

The photographs I made for A Yellow Rose Project reflect my experience as a woman, a mother, and a Latina. Just before I was invited to participate in this photographic project, I gave birth to my first and only child, a daughter named after her grandmothers. My daughter's maternal namesake carries the legacy of a generation of women in my family whose lives were shaped not only by their gender, but by socioeconomic and cultural considerations. A Yellow Rose Project offered me the opportunity to further consider what it means to be an American, the struggles and aspirations within the intersection of race, class, and gender. In this sense, the photographs I made are both a tribute and a reminder to my daughter of her ancestors, their struggle to gain citizenship, and the rights and responsibilities that come with it.

Kathya Maria Landeros is a Mexican American photographer and educator. Influenced by her bicultural upbringing, her work of over fifteen years focuses on Latinx communities and the exploration of history, migration, representation, and belonging. Her research has been supported through fellowships from the Guggenheim Foundation and the Fulbright and residencies at the Rayko Photo Center and the Center for Photography at Woodstock. Prior to joining the faculty at Wellesley College in Massachusetts, where she is currently the Knafel Assistant Professor of Humanities in the department of art, she taught at public institutions of higher education in northern California and Massachusetts.

68
HYE-RYOUNG MIN
Untitled from the series Yeonsoo

In Korea we have a saying: "naughty seven years old." We think a child of six or seven is at their most mischievous, which is when I started photographing my niece, Yeonsoo. Every kid is special, but she was simply the most impressionable and sensitive girl, and it made me want to look at her more closely.

This process of observation required much delicate care. It was a fragile journey to the life and heart of a most unpredictable and sensitive girl, into her relationship with those around her—her family and friends, although they remain unseen in the photographs—and to my own childhood. It came as a surprise for me to see how the little girl managed to express herself and react to the world. It took a while for me to understand that a kid has a character that hasn't settled down yet, so she can be the sweetest girl at one moment and yet bitter or outrageous in the next. Her experience of the world is very limited by her young age, so that my sister is at once Yeonsoo's best-loved companion and her biggest rival. And yet, a kid's imagination is unlimited; they can be anybody they want to be.

Beyond my interest in her, there is also a reciprocal relationship between us. Looking at her, I often felt as if I was looking at myself as a child. It allowed me to meditate about how I came to be the woman I am today, and indeed what sort of person I've become.

Hye-Ryoung Min is a South Korean photographer living and working in New York City. Among other shows, her work has been exhibited at the Center for Photography at Woodstock, Contemporary at Blue Star, the Bronx Documentary Center, Newspace Center for Photography, the Detroit Center for Contemporary Photography, the Center for Fine Art Photography, Griffin Museum of Photography, Photoville in the United States; Benaki Museum in Greece; Seoul Museum of Art, Sejong Art Center, Gallery Lux, Gallery Comma, and Datz Press in Seoul; and GoEun Museum of Photography in Busan. Her work has been exhibited at international photography festivals in Japan, Malaysia, Greece, France, Albania, and New York.

69

ALICE HARGRAVE
Suffragist Bird, River Tyrannulet (female calls)

The Suffragist Bird work began upon noticing the parallel between women gaining their voice through the ratification of the Nineteenth Amendment at approximately the same time as a certain female bird lost hers—Martha, the last surviving passenger pigeon, died leaving that species extinct. She is honored in this body of work with calls from a diverse group of avian species who struggle to thrive today.

Suffragist Bird, River Tyrannulet (female calls) uses its voice to send out resounding vocalizations, reminding us of the urgency for conservation, speaking out, and diversity of voice. The birds are our surrogates. It's all about voice equals power. The calls are photographed sound wave patterns of their vocalizations from sonograms. They are toned in the vibrant, and often surprising, colors of the birds themselves, contradicting the ubiquitous argument "why save that simple brown bird?" The calls are recontextualized alongside their fragile and likewise endangered habitat.

The calls of extinct or threatened bird species are housed in libraries due to the accelerating pace of climate change and habitat loss. Our ways of interacting and experiencing wildlife are now mediated through the use of technology. Hearing archival recordings of the last mating calls of now extinct male birds summoning nonexistent females is chilling. The incredible sense of loss and poignancy of a library containing this evidence of biodiversity past was deeply moving to me, inspired this project, and led me to collaborate with the Cornell Lab of Ornithology.

Alice Hargrave, a photography-based artist in Chicago, incorporates sound, video, and photographic imagery to address environmental insecurity, habitat loss, and species extinctions. Hargrave has exhibited and published internationally, received numerous awards, and *Paradise Wavering,* her monograph from Daylight Books and extensive solo exhibition, traveled to multiple venues across the United States. Hargrave is included in many permanent collections, such as the Museum of Contemporary Photography and the Art Institute of Chicago artist book collection. Her research has awarded her several artist residencies, including in the Florida Keys and Montana.

Hargrave previously taught full time at Columbia College Chicago and is currently pursuing commissions and conservation work.

70

JENNIFER MCCLURE
Untitled

We moved to Harlem in 2017. We were not the first gentrifiers in the neighborhood, but we felt the weight of our presence. The simple fact that we both made it home alive from the hospital was a result of our privilege. As much as we try to raise our daughter to know that we are all equal, we still encounter entire systems that do not reflect this. I am reminded every day when we walk outside our apartment that not all people were included when women were given the right to vote.

Jennifer McClure is a fine art photographer based in New York City. Her first book, *You Who Never*

Arrived, was published as one of nine Peanut Press Portfolios in 2020. She was a 2019 and 2017 Critical Mass Top 50 finalist and twice received the Arthur Griffin Legacy Award from the Griffin Museum of Photography's annual juried exhibitions. Her work has been featured in publications such as *NatGeo Travel, Vogue, GUP Magazine, The New Republic, Lenscratch, Feature Shoot, L'Œil de la photographie, The Photo Review, Dwell,* and *PDN.* She also founded the Women's Photo Alliance in 2015.

71

ALYSSA MINAHAN
Untitled

On the one hundredth anniversary of the ratification of the Nineteenth Amendment, women are still fighting for autonomy of their reproductive and sexual rights. This image, an unfixed abstract lumen print, is a meditation on the continued elusiveness females experience regarding legal control over their own bodies.

Alyssa Minahan utilizes photographic materials, including unfixed gelatin, silver paper and large format negatives, in nontraditional ways to express ideas integral to the medium of photography, specifically its complex relationship to time, space, and memory. In September 2019, Alyssa released *NOTES,* a handmade photo book published by Datz Press. *NOTES* is held in numerous public and private collections, including the New York Public Library, International Center for Photography Library, and Stanford University Library. In addition, Alyssa has exhibited her work at various galleries and museums, including the Datz Museum of Art, Center for

Creative Photography, and Pingyao International Photography Festival.

72

S. BILLIE MANDLE
Esther Lape's home at what is now the Stewart B. McKinney National Wildlife Refuge; Habitat for the endangered Rose of Plymouth.

Esther Lape (1881–1981) was an activist and educator who advocated for women's suffrage, health care reform, labor rights, and the anti-war movement. She was one of the founders of the League of Women Voters and a close friend to Eleanor Roosevelt. In 1927, she and her life-partner, lawyer Elizabeth Read, built their home at Salt Meadows in Connecticut. In 1972, Lape donated the 147-acre property to the US Department of the Interior as the first National Wildlife Refuge in Connecticut. In 1987, Salt Meadows was renamed for US Congressman Stewart B. McKinney.

This image was created with negatives archived in the Library of Congress, documenting the remnants of Esther Lape's home at Salt Meadows. The drab negatives on their own didn't do justice to her vibrancy or the impact of her work. By collaging them, I better saw fragments of her complex life and the traces she left on the world.

S. Billie Mandle is an artist whose longform projects focus on the intersections of history, politics, vulnerability, and place. Her exhibitions include the Addison Gallery of American Art, Garden in Los Angeles, Syo Gallery in Korea, and the Hyeres International Festival in France. Her work has been featured in publications such as *Aperture, Cabinet Magazine,*

and *Wired,* and her monograph, *Reconciliation,* was published in 2020. She has taught at Hampshire College, the International Center for Photography, and is currently an associate professor of photography at Massachusetts College of Art and Design (MassArt). She received a BA in biology and English from Williams College and an MFA from MassArt.

73
ODETTE ENGLAND
Untitled

I knew snapshots would be my starting point for representing the supporters of suffrage, wearing yellow roses in public. I love the complexities of collage and collage techniques long used by women and, in particular, feminist artists. The wearing of roses interests me because they can be decorative, symbolic, or ceremonial. Our bodies wear history. They are powerful vessels and surfaces for conveying information—for protesting, caring, and crusading. I searched for snapshots of females, ideally with roses in the background, including red ones worn by anti-suffragists. I then used home-grown, yellow rose petals to cover and shield them. To highlight a basic human right in need of protection—the right to vote—without which women's voices would be unheard.

Odette England is an artist and writer whose work about home, land, and gender has been shown in more than one hundred solo, two person, and group exhibitions worldwide. Her books include the critically acclaimed *Keeper of the Hearth, Past Paper // Present Marks* with Jennifer Garza-Cuen, and

Dairy Character for which she won the 2021 Light Work Photobook Award. England's work is held in collections including the George Eastman Museum, Museum of Contemporary Photography, New Mexico Museum of Art, and Fort Wayne Museum of Art, among others. She received her MFA from the Rhode Island School of Design.

74
JONI STERNBACH
Premature

In 1983, Joni Sternbach began working with a medium format camera documenting her experience as a new mother. Her baby was born two-months premature, which led to months of pumping breast milk and daily visits to the hospital. The photographs from this body of work, titled Something Between the Two Of Them, developed into a narrative, feminist-based initiative exploring both the personal and cultural identity concerning motherhood, marriage, and maternity.

Joni Sternbach is an American artist, photographer, and filmmaker. Over the course of a decades-long career, her portrait based work explores a variety of themes, including domesticity and the family and sexuality and the body. Issues of gender, identity, and feminism were the most critical themes in her early work from the 1980–90s, where the female figure—including her own—was a central motif. In her current work, Sternbach experiments with a variety of historic photographic processes and is best known for her wet plate collodion, tintype portraits of surfers and surfboards made around the globe.

075

THALASSA RAASCH
Blooming roses with wind

The one about the suffragist holding her ground.

The one about the wolf girl who grows up to be a wolf woman.

The one about the delicate flower resisting insurmountable odds.

The one about the girl who kept her calm but studied for the earthquake.

The one about the yellow rose.

In dialogue with artist Kiki Smith's Wolf Girl (1999) and artist Nyeema Morgan's project THE FLOWER (2020), this photograph, Blooming roses with wind, is part of a series that lives in the tangled, contradictory undergrowth of American legends about women, both historical and contemporary. Woman's great power and potential has long attracted both awe and fear. Women's right to vote is no different. The one hundredth anniversary of the Nineteenth Amendment is cause for celebration, especially now that most women have the ability to vote—not just affluent, cis white women. Still, the reductionist, neutralizing treatment of women persists: the one about the outspoken congresswoman called a "fucking bitch" by her colleague. Women are cast into types, into stories, into rumors. But here, the one about the yellow rose. A century gone by, and this bright flower, this bright collaboration, resists the conflicting sexual, cultural, and political pressures that seek to categorize, identify, and oppress women. Here, the yellow rose is in full bloom, in all her windblown complexity and strength.

Thalassa Raasch is a French American artist, educator, and beekeeper based in Iowa and Maine. Their practice explores perceptual boundaries, translation, and loss. Their research has included blind photography, traditional grave digging, and closed-eye hallucinations. Their work has been exhibited and published nationally and internationally. Raasch earned a BA in visual and environmental studies from Harvard University in 2010 and a masters in photography from Rhode Island School of Design (RISD) in 2016. They are an assistant professor of photography and experimental media at the University of Iowa.

76
DEEDRA BAKER
Manifest

To manifest is to make evident to the eye or the understanding; to show plainly; to prove; to put beyond doubt or question. It was the strong woman's hour of the twentieth century that manifested a woman's right to vote on August 18, 1920, with the ratification of the Nineteenth Amendment. The decades-long women's suffrage movement pushed back against the Cult of True Womanhood and lit the way for women in the decades to come to have the right to voice their opinion in the form of a vote in the United States of America.

While the Nineteenth Amendment delivered political autonomy for women: "We hold these truths to be self-evident that all men and women are created equal," as proclaimed in the "Declaration of Sentiments," the triumph was only for white women

(Stanton, 1848). Not all women or men could vote even after the Nineteenth Amendment—concealed freedom due to the color of their skin.

Manifest visually explores the Nineteenth Amendment's false promise for women's freedom. The color photograph illustrates the duality of the manifestation women witnessed in 1920 with light and shadow coupled with familiar domestic objects and settings. While the Nineteenth Amendment did give a voice to white women in the United States, it continued to place women of color in the shadows—proving there was a long journey ahead for true equality. The patriarchy and white supremacy continue to loom over the citizens of the not-so United States of America.

Deedra Baker was born in El Dorado, Kansas, in 1989. She received her bachelor of fine arts in 2011 from Washburn University in Topeka and her master of fine arts from Texas Woman's University in 2016. Her creative work explores themes of femininity, gender roles, personal and psychological spaces, and self-identity. Throughout her oeuvre, Deedra has explored various media, such as photography, video, printing processes, bookmaking, and works on paper. Currently, her research investigates the lineage of the feminine and explores the nexus of her family through three generations of females. Deedra currently lives in Fort Worth, Texas.

77
JORDANNA KALMAN
Frank

In my formal education in photography, 99.9 percent of the work I was introduced to and studied was made by men. When we're taught by example that this is the important and correct work to emulate—a male point of view—where does that leave me? If I'm ever able to unlearn the rules of male photography, truly express myself as a woman—and I don't mean the female gaze, a condescending term—would that work be rejected? In this series, my photographs are seen through a window cut into photographs made by some of my favorite (male) master photographers. I wonder if my work will always be constrained by a male dominated photo history and forever be considered less than because it wasn't made with an 8×10, an American poet's (male, of course) prose as inspiration, or of new topographics or it was uninteresting because the nudity isn't sexual and therefore useless to a male viewer or irrelevant because I'm over thirty-five and have children.

Jordanna Kalman lives and works in New York. Her work explores loneliness, anxiety, womanhood, and individuality. Jordanna has had her work shown nationally, internationally, and online. She works on many different things, very slowly, and all at once. Her recent work includes a monograph of her series *Little Romances* with Daylight Books, and she is currently working on a series about the male dominated history of photography and its influence on her practice.

78
CASSANDRA ZAMPINI
Liked

Liked is a double composite portrait containing hundreds of inverted images in golden and blue hues. Each of these portraits are UV printed on separate acrylic panels sandwiched together—one cannot be seen independently of the other. The bottom panel is a grid of inverted mirror selfies with each woman using their phone to snap a seductive pose.

These images, however, were not pulled from their Instagram accounts, instead, they were culled from websites designed for male audiences, where the selfies are reposted, monetized, and their agency stripped away. The top panel includes hundreds of inverted, side-by-side, "before and after" images scraped from the millions of cosmetic surgery posts on Instagram.

To encourage the billions of likes and comments on social media, women arrange themselves in a bewildering number of carefully posed, curated, and heavily-edited selfies. The more sexualized the pose, the more likes and comments—and sometimes profits—she receives. Creating an endless cycle, it refuels her desire for acceptance, coaxing her to adopt other unrealistic cultural standards of beauty. These images also work to recruit other women, especially younger generations, to aspire to this standard of beauty. While women's bodies have been objectified for centuries, today's social media creates content at an unprecedented scale and magnitude. *Liked* explores the darker side of how women portray themselves on social media and encourages the viewer to ponder the consequences.

Cassandra Zampini is a New York-based photographer turned digital artist. She creates mined-image collages from social media and other internet sources that aim to stimulate introspection of both self-identity, through selfies and gestures, and cultural identity, using memes and videos, through the lenses of politics and consumerism. Her work has been featured in solo and group exhibitions throughout the country, including the Museum of Fine Arts in Houston and the Center for Creative Photography in Tucson. Additionally, her artwork is collected by private, public, and corporate collections, including the Museum of Fine Arts in Houston.

79

ASHLEY KAUSCHINGER
After The Vote (US Suffragists 1920)

After The Vote (US Suffragists 1920) was created after the 2016 election. The white suffragist-inspired dress is what I wore to vote. The yellow roses, dead and dried by the time I took the photograph, were given to me by my husband to celebrate voting for a woman. A performative shadow looms over the center of the dress—I can't bring myself to write the former president's words of what it is doing. This photograph is also the first in a series about women's history, Cycles, is still ongoing.

Ashley Kauschinger is an artist that explores identity, social structures, and women's voices. She received her BFA from Savannah College of Art and Design and her MFA from Texas Woman's University. Her photographs have been exhibited and published internationally. Her work is in the collections of Vanderbilt University and the Sir Elton John Collection. She currently lives and works in Atlanta, Georgia.

80

SARA MACEL
Dana at Fifteen

As an artist, a feminist, and an educator, I feel compelled to use my voice to fight against inequality in both the art world and world at large. While the centennial anniversary of the Nineteenth Amendment is important and worth celebrating, voter suppression remains an ongoing issue. According to the ACLU's website: "Since 2008, states across the country have passed measures to make it harder for Americans—particularly black people, the elderly, students, and people with disabilities—to exercise their fundamental right to cast a ballot. These measures include cuts to early voting, voter ID laws, and purges of voter rolls" (ACLU Vermont). To vote is to hope. For A Yellow Rose Project, I photographed the young women who inspire me through their activism to continue the fight for voting rights for all.

Sara Macel is a photographic artist living in Queens, New York. She received her MFA in photography, video and related media from the School of Visual Arts and BFA in photography and imaging from NYU. Her work has been internationally exhibited and collected. She was awarded the Aaron Siskind Fellowship, Light Work artist-in-residency, and PDN 30. Her photo books include *May the Road Rise to Meet You* (Daylight Books) and *What Did the Deep Sea Say* (Kehrer Verlag). Sara is a full-time professor and photography program coordinator at SUNY Rockland Community College.

81
ELIZABETH M. CLAFFEY
Untitled

Invisible Crime uses the vernacular of crime scene photography to visualize the crime(s) resulting from the 2016 United States presidential election. Through fabricated depictions of aftermath, clothing becomes a metaphor for resistance and evidence of invisible, as well as visible, abuse.

Clothing represents complex power issues and cultural significance. White clothing has been adopted by many women in the United States as a symbol of empowerment and autonomy. During the 1920s, white clothing became a symbol of the women's suf-

frage movement. In 1968, on the night she became the first Black woman elected to congress, Shirley Chisholm wore white. In 2016, when Hillary Clinton became the first female Democratic nominee for president, she wore white, as did many women who cast their votes. On January 4, 2019, Alexandria Ocasio-Cortez was sworn in to the US Congress wearing a white suit, stating, "I wore all white today to honor the women who paved the path before me, and for all the women yet to come" (Sullivan and Killough, 2019).

While many people are clear that the election of our forty-fifth president led to a wide range of injustices, the full impact has yet to be realized. The consequences unfold slowly, over time, and well beyond a four-year term, in a manner that can seem politically abstract or intangible. In these images, clothing remains as evidence of a body, a gesture, or a physical event—a surviving symbol of struggle that indicates with its mere presence the continuation of whatever fight left it mangled or discarded.

Elizabeth M. Claffey is an assistant professor of photography at Indiana University in Bloomington and a 2019–20 research fellow at the Kinsey Institute for Research in Sex, Gender, and Reproduction. She has an MFA in studio art from Texas Woman's University, where she also earned a graduate certificate in women's studies. In 2012, she was awarded a Fulbright Fellowship. Elizabeth's work focuses on identity, kinship, isolation, issues of the body, family history, and cultural/institutional practices. Among others, her work has been recognized by *PDN Magazine,* Center Santa Fe, the Eddie Adams Workshop, and *Don't Take Pictures Magazine.*

82

MARIE TRILLER
Portrait of an Athlete

It was women gaining the right to vote that created a whole new emphasis on women's freedoms in many other areas of life—including the realms of sports and fitness. The great advances women have made in the past one hundred years allow today's women to compete in areas once accessible only to men. I photographed my sister Maureen Triller to exemplify today's female athlete. Captured here competing in an international three-day fitness competition in Miami in February 2020, she states, "Through fitness, I can prove to myself that I am stronger and more powerful than I ever thought I could be. This translates into every aspect of my life." This image, On the Ropes, is from the series Portrait of an Athlete. It captures Maureen in one of seven events designed to test the athletes across the spectrum of fitness. Through the lens of my camera, I witnessed Maureen's strength, stamina and endurance, confidence, and determination. I saw my sister in a way I never had before.

Photographer and educator Marie Triller resides in Miami. Her book, *Ten Years: Remembering 9/11,* chronicles a decade of September 11 observances at Ground Zero. Her photographs are in the permanent collections of George Eastman Museum and the National 9/11 Memorial Museum. Triller received her MFA in photography from the State University of New York at New Paltz. She has taught photography and exhibited her work for over thirty-five years. Her images have been featured online at Your Daily Photograph, *Pro Photo Daily,* and *Eye of Photography.* Triller is a member of Women's Photo Alliance NYC and a submissions reviewer for *LensCulture.*

83

KATELYN KOPENHAVER
Covered in Filth (Epstein Is The Worst Kind of Virus)
July 4th, 2020

Women's liberation and power have undeniably grown and flourished since the ratification of the Nineteenth Amendment. I am thankful for those women, their supporters, and their courage in granting women the right to speak. However, there is still a dark reality waiting to be exposed about the nature of predators and their penchant for purchasing children and women. Jeffrey Epstein and Ghislaine Maxwell, both having prominent connections to the world's most powerful people, have come to symbolize sex trafficking and child trafficking in the modern age.

Their social circle was full of high profile individuals in political, art, media, medical, educational, and Hollywood spheres, including Prince Andrew, Leslie Wexner, Alan Dershowitz, Donald Trump, Ivana Trump, Donald Barr, Rupert Murdoch, Bill Clinton, Bill Cosby, Bill Gates, Kevin Spacey, Andrew Cuomo, Alexander Acosta, Ehud Barak, Frédéric Fekkai, Jean-Luc Brunel, Glenn and Eva Dubin, Leon Black, Lynn Forester de Rothschild, Harvey Weinstein, and Woody Allen to name some notable individuals connected to the pair. The well-connected British socialite Ghislaine Maxwell worked as Epstein's primary female recruiter to bring in vulnerable underage girls for him and others to have sex with. Maxwell was charged in 2020 and found guilty in 2021 of "conspiracy to transport minors with intent to engage in criminal sexual activity, transportation of a minor with intent to engage in criminal sexual activity, and sex trafficking of a minor." Maxwell, sixty-two as of 2024, was sentenced in 2022 to twenty years in prison and fined $750,000. She attempted to appeal her case in 2024, but the Manhattan-based 2nd US Circuit Court of Appeals shut her down. She remains in a Florida prison serving her twenty-year sentence for her role in procuring, manipulating, and abusing teen girls for Epstein and others between 1994 and 2004. Epstein was likely murdered to conceal the network of wealthy businesspeople and politicians he regularly met with and obtained blackmail on.

The predator banner is a site-specific photography performance where I walk in the footsteps of two of the most evil, repugnant individuals known in twenty-first-century America, while simultaneously, uncovering the institutional corruption that procures and protects such atrocities and psychopathic personalities. The Associated Press picked up the banner in 2020 after seeing me with it outside a New York City courthouse during Ghislaine's arraignment hearing. It has since appeared in numerous documentaries on TV and publications worldwide.

Let's not forget, elite co-conspirators continue to walk free– dictating some of the world's most significant decisions, hiding behind their ostensible, manufactured disguises. If we take anything away, the Epstein/Maxwell cases give us a prime example and confirmation that you can indeed be above the law if rich, powerful, and well-connected enough, and unfortunately Jeffrey Epstein and Ghislaine Maxwell are just the tip of a *very* ominous iceberg.

Kateyn Kopenhaver's conceptual works and performances interrogate atrocities society has been conditioned to accept or has come to ignore. From Doylestown, Pennsylvania, Kopenhaver received her BFA in photography from the School of Visual Arts in 2016. She has been published and exhibited nationally and internationally, including *New York Magazine,* Netflix, ABC News, and *The Brooklyn Rail.* She was awarded the 2021 NYSCA/NYFA Artist Fellowship in interdisciplinary work for her harrowing body of work, *Predators and Prey,* and is a 2024 Miami Individual Artists grant recipient. Watchful of advertising, media, and the place where truth and lies circulate, she utilizes print-based media and her body to deliver commentary that raises questions and challenges our perception of reality and of ourselves.

84

MEG GRIFFITHS
Subtle Fusion of Time

Making pictures is my way of processing the intimacy of my lived experience, while simultaneously trying to understand more about the world we have been given as women. Drawing upon photographic archives, written suffrage accounts, and my own personal history, this still life image, Subtle Fusion of Time, was constructed to process and connect me to the past from the present moment. Everyday household objects were arranged to create layers of meaning. I chose familiar domestic relics plucked from particular time periods to reference symbols or people in the movement, as well as multiple generations of women in my own family.

Meg Griffiths is an artist, educator, and the co-founder of *A Yellow Rose Project.* The wide arc of her work grapples with the various modes of domestic, cultural, and political engagement that structure the female experience in the United States. Her inquiries are driven by a desire to capture, develop, and share a closer understanding of self-identifying female subjects. Each project she creates, whether individual or collaborative, focused on the personal or the collective, are at heart about the intrinsic connection between self and other, between interiority and positionality, as much as kinship and community.

Her work has traveled nationally and internationally and placed in collections such as Center for Creative Photography, Capital One, and the Museum of Fine Arts, Houston. Her book projects, both monographs and collaborative projects, have been acquired by various institutions around the country, such as the Metropolitan Museum of Art, Yale University Library, Duke University Libraries, Museum of Modern Art, and the Getty Research Institute, to name a few. She currently lives in Denton, Texas, where she is an associate professor of photography in the visual arts division at Texas Woman's University.

85
YVETTE MELTZER
Advances for Women Celebrating 100 Years

I included the photo of the sanitary belt—my own actually—because not only was 2020 the one hundredth anniversary of the Nineteenth Amendment granting women the legal right to vote, but also the one hundredth anniversary of the invention of the sanitary belt. The parallels of these historic events run deeper than their shared dates. While both milestones offered women the freedom to participate in a fuller life, they had each initially discriminated against women of color. Not until 1965 were women of color allowed to exercise their right to vote with the passage of the 1965 Voting Rights Act. The sanitary belt was initially crafted by Mary Davidson Kenner in 1920. This revolutionary invention offered females the freedom to leave their homes without fear of blood staining their clothing on the days they were on their period. Ms. Kenner continued to improve her early invention that kept a pad secured in a waterproof pocket. In 1957, she ultimately secured a patent on the belt, and major companies showed interest in marketing her invention. When they learned that she was African American, they withdrew their offer, and Ms. Kenner never received any formal recognition for her valuable inventions. My hope is this image stimulates us to remember the discriminations of our past and guides our actions to a just and inclusive future for all.

While advancing in her career as a children's advocate, Yvette Meltzer always kept a camera tucked close by. Captured by the magic and mystery of photography, she ultimately traded in her briefcase for a camera bag. Through her lens, she enjoys the convergence of color, light, and form. Yvette's fine art and social documentary photography reflects her interest in people, the narratives of their lives, and the environments that shape them. Based in Chicago, Illinois, her award-winning photography has been exhibited in galleries and publications both nationwide and internationally and is held in numerous private collections.

86
LARISSA RAMEY
Dirty Hands

My goal is to collect works of different womxn on how they express their passions about the ratification of this amendment through imagery. I have collected visual imagery of different mediums decided by the subject. Following the theme of A Yellow Rose Project, my works reflect, react, or respond to the ratification of the Nineteenth Amendment and were curated to share a diverse storyline.

Larissa Ramey is a multimedia artist, who primarily works with photography. Her works display themes about race, identity, body image, and ecology concerns. She graduated with a bachelor of fine arts degree with a concentration in photography from the Pennsylvania College of Art and Design in 2019. Currently, Ramey is based out of Leesburg, Virginia.

Larissa is making work that challenges her to explore the relationships, environments, and roles of her identity as a biracial woman and artist. The act of documenting her environments and interpreting levels of her identity through portraiture has given her the ability to pass through experiences and expand upon her own self-worth—allowing her to acknowledge her heritage, ancestry, and the present landscapes that have forged a connection toward the meaning of place in her practice. Portraiture is a way for Ramey to capture the intimate and subtle ways in which she has carved out her place of identity and perspective of what being black means to her as an individual. While capturing landscapes gives a way to understand the attachment to land as an individual and through a community.

87
REBECCA DROLEN
Balloon Study No. 1

Within a series of performative gestures which resulted in a suite of photographs, I blew up one hundred balloons to celebrate and struggle through each year that has passed since the Nineteenth Amendment was ratified. This meditative action allowed me to consider each year individually, letting it take up space and use my physical body to give it form. I sought to understand the complexity and

history these one hundred years represent. I created a delicate, figural mass and then let it deflate. I twisted different years together and sometimes they broke. I added things up and then tore them down. The resulting photographs represent an homage to the efforts and struggles of many women working together, who have preceded my time. It is also a reminder of my own accountability to question the past and pursue the work that has been left undone.

Rebecca Drolen, born in 1983, is an artist, educator, and independent curator working in Arkansas. Her photographs are concerned with how individuals visually assemble their identity. Her work balances built spaces, assemblage, and performance, but the end result is persistently photographic. Drolen's work has been internationally published and exhibited in group and solo exhibitions. She has photographs held in public and private collections throughout the United States. Drolen received her MFA in photography in 2009 from Indiana University. She is an assistant professor and co-area head of photography at the University of Arkansas.

88
EMILY PEACOCK
Untitled

I visited Washington, DC, on an eighth-grade trip in 1998. I remember climbing on all the statues and being incredibly inappropriate with their frozen male bodies. Monuments of men by men for men everywhere, made of marble and stone, the slick, beautiful surfaces. It was supposed to be so important and sacred, but I was just too young and full of confusing hormones to fucking care. But I also believe it was a visceral reaction to the lack of representation in the visual history of DC. For A Yellow Rose Project, I composed a series of four photographs depicting a strange ritual with four small pieces of marble and my sister's delicate satin-gloved hand and arm. In the final image, a phallic monument stands as a result of the stacked marble pieces. I stand with my fellow women of all kinds and celebrate one hundred years of voting history. I even have a yellow rose tattoo on my elbow.

Emily Peacock is a Houston-based artist, whose work explores her familial and personal experiences. She received her MFA in photography and digital media from the University of Houston and is an associate professor of art at Sam Houston State University. Peacock was a 2013–14 Lawndale Artist Studio Program participant. In 2016, she received the Houston Arts Alliance Individual Artist grant and the New Faculty Research grant in 2019. She has exhibited her work throughout the United States and in Vienna, Austria, and the United Kingdom. Peacock's work is in the collections of the Art Museum of Southeast Texas and the Museum of Fine Arts, Houston.

89
LEIGH MERRILL
Untitled

Working primarily with photography, I create digitally collaged images that explore the impact of desire, simulation, and perception on our contemporary landscapes. Culling through thousands of individual photographs and videos I make of architecture and landscaping, I digitally assemble these sources to create my work. Some of the images have veracity, but more often, they suggest a visual hyperbole—an embellished scene circulating around a small object or detail. I am continually fascinated with photography's ability to be both evidence of existence—creating an image with seeming reliability—and simultaneously a system to mediate and construct reality. I use photography as a tool to observe and then digitally combine my photographs to construct spaces that do not exist, allowing the creation of images that through metaphor and illusion reveal both the desire and simulacrum present around us and within photography itself. Through the abstraction and articulation of source photographs, this multi-panel piece created for A Yellow Rose Project becomes a metaphor for movement through place and the collective residue found in the spaces we inhabit and travel. The street is a partial mirror of itself with architectural elements repeating throughout the photograph. This repetition speaks to movement, possibility, choice, and change over time. The urban space depicted is bathed in warm yellow light as a nod to the yellow rose worn by the suffragists.

Leigh Merrill is an American artist born in 1978. She grew up in the American Southwest and received her BFA from the University of New Mexico in Albuquerque and her MFA from Mills College in Oakland, California. Merrill's work has been a part of exhibitions throughout the United States and abroad in venues such as the Phoenix Art Museum, the diRosa Art Preserve, FotoFest International, the Fries Museum in the Netherlands, and the Museum of Texas Tech University. Leigh Merrill lives and works in Dallas, Texas, where she is a professor of art at Texas A&M University–Commerce.

90

TAMI BAHAT
Strung Along for Too Long

Tami Bahat, born in 1979, is a fine art photographer from Tel Aviv, Israel. Raised by a former dancer and a graphic artist, Bahat's family resettled in Los Angeles when she was young. Championed by parents who encouraged her artistic expression, she acquired a stronger knowledge of herself and others through experimentation in various media. Taking the unconventional route, she left school at the age of fifteen and was given guidance by her father, who had taught at Bezalel Academy of Arts and Design in Jerusalem. He encouraged her independent study through workshops and seminars of art history, photography, sculpture, and design, further enhancing her creative vision. A series of family trips around the world exposed Bahat to humanity as a whole and the myriad ways that people live, providing her with a keen awareness of the beauty and loss an earthly existence brings—an undertone in much of her work. Most recently her work has been exhibited at prominent photography events internationally, including Fotofever Paris, Scope NY, the Photography Show presented by AIPAD, and the LA Art Show. Tami lives and works in Los Angeles, CA.

91
GRETA PRATT
Untitled

This photograph was made during the 2020 Women's March in Washington, DC. I attended the first Women's March on Washington in 2017 and was moved by the massive turnout and the comradery that enveloped me. In 2020, the anniversary of the Nineteenth Amendment, I decided to go back to make photographs of individual women sharing their truths via their bodies, voices, and handmade, personal signage. The experience of being in the company of strong women, both young and old, continues to empower me today.

Greta Pratt is an artist, educator, and author, whose work explores ideas surrounding American myth and identity. Pratt's four monographs include *In Search of the Corn Queen, Using History, The Wavers,* and *Nineteen Lincolns.* Her work has been exhibited internationally and nationally. Pratt's work is in the collections of Smithsonian American Art Museum, the Museum of Contemporary Photography, Museum of Fine Arts, Houston, the Chrysler Museum, and Minneapolis Institute of Art, among others. Pratt was nominated for a Pulitzer Prize, and her photographs have been featured in *The New York Times Magazine, The New Yorker,* and *Harper's Magazine,* along with numerous books and catalogs.

92
ELLEN FELDMAN
Suffragists Knew—Dare to Act!

Dare to Act! is one image in a visual manifesto, Suffragists Knew, about how to create a movement—as necessary now as it was one hundred years ago. Dare to Act! is specifically about the need for women to throw their hat in the ring and run for elected office. Consider Susan B. Anthony, Elizabeth Cady Stanton, Sojourner Truth, Lucretia Mott, and Matilda Joslyn Gage, none of these leading suffragists lived to see the passage of the Nineteenth Amendment, let alone women serving in elected positions. Their fight for the vote took decades—1848 to 1920. Could they have imagined Elizabeth Warren and Ayanna Pressley winning positions in the Massachusetts delegation to the US Senate and House of Representatives? Imagine perhaps, but foresee? Perhaps not. The other image titles in Suffragists Knew remind us that women's power has always been uniquely hard-fought and hard-won: Build Coalitions! Combat Misinformation! Channel Your Rage! Get Stuff Done! Consider this image as a call to act. No action is too small . . . or too ambitious. While full equality—legal, social, and economic—remains stubbornly beyond our grasp and may yet take decades to achieve (read: the unratified ERA, introduced in 1923), it is our collective work that will get us there. Susan B. Anthony had her own manifesto: "Organize, agitate, educate, must be our war cry" (Women on 20s). We can follow her lead and continue the struggle with purpose, courage, and persistence.

Ellen Feldman is a fine art photographer and book artist, photography editor of *The Women's Review of Books* at Wellesley College, and activist since the 1960s. Her book, *We Who March: Photographs and Reflections on the Women's March, January 21, 2017,* includes photos by thirty photographers. Feldman co-curated with Marky Kauffmann *Moved to Act! Demonstrations, Marches, Political Actions,* an exhibit of photographs from the Women's March, Black Lives Matter, and March for Our Lives, among others. It premiered at the Davis Orton Gallery in Hudson, New York. Feldman's photography appears in solo and juried group shows. She holds a PhD in cinema studies from New York University.

93
TAMARA REYNOLDS
Untitled

The image of the Congress Inn was photographed while working on the project, The Drake. The inn is in an area of Nashville near The Drake Motel and is also a relic of the past. It represents my sentiments about Congress and how women still must fight the old battles for equality.

Tamara Reynolds is a documentary photographer, whose unflinching eye considers what it means to be human in today's society. In particular, her work focuses on the lives of those who are usually unseen. Reynolds' photobook, *The Drake,* published by Dewi Lewis in 2022. The work—portraits, still lifes, and streetscapes that document the lives of people existing just above survival on one square block around a motel in Nashville, Tennessee—has received numerous honors, including the prestigious Santa Fe Center 2018 Project Launch Grant, the 2019 Tennessee Arts Commission Individual Artist Grant, a 2020 Puffin Grant, the 2021 BarTur Photo Award: Faces of Humanity, and the Guggenheim Fellowship grant for 2021. Reynolds was born in Nashville, Tennessee, and has lived there all her life.

> Tamara Reynolds "weave[s] into [her] compelling images a sense of urgency, so that what might have begun as a private inquiry could assume broader significance in our current moment. This is an exceedingly difficult thing to do, and I am in awe whenever I encounter a body of work that seems to open up new paths towards understanding the world around us."—Sarah Hermanson Meister, former curator, department of photography, The Museum of Modern Art.

94
ASHLEIGH COLEMAN
Power(ful)

As I talk with my children about voting rights, my mind turns to metamorphosis—change that is sometimes slow, sometimes hidden, oftentimes painful, then blazing into the foreground, striking everyone with awe and terror and wonder.

Ashleigh Coleman lives in rural Mississippi. Through her work, she is exploring dichotomies within domesticity, the marginalized, and a history of place. Her photographs have been shown in solo and group exhibitions at the Fischer Galleries, the University of Mississippi's Center of Southern Culture, the Claire Elizabeth Gallery, the Ogden Museum of Art, the Mississippi Museum of Art, the University of West Virginia, the University of Southern Mississippi, Barrister's Gallery, the Griffin Museum of Photography, the Meadows Museum, Looking for Appalachia, the Soho Gallery, and the Bo Bartlett Center. She is the 2020 South Arts State fellow for Mississippi.

95
PATTY CARROLL
Bedridden

Anonymous Women: Domestic Demise

My work is about entangling women and home, leading to the word *housewife.* All of the narrative still-life photographs are imagined interior spaces of rooms filled with décor and objects, engulfing a lone figure of a woman, camouflaged, often with only bits of her visible. She is both a victim of her obsessions, activities, and circumstances, as well as the invisible creator of such; both satisfying and problematic, pathetic and humorous. I create imaginary, humorous worlds in the studio on a full size stage set that critique and satirize claustrophobic expectations of domestic perfection—an unending but frustrating endeavor. My photographs are metaphors for the interior lives of women; how we substitute every-day objects and artifice and turn them into obsessions. As we all were confined to our homes during the Covid pandemic, the meaning and overwhelming experience of being *at home* has become humorous, yet sadly dreadful. During the lockdown, my anonymous woman became particularly overwhelmed by political discord and disinformation, which led to a deeper and darker demise in her soul. Trying to escape the outer world into her own beloved domain proved impossible.

Patty Carroll has been known for her use of highly intense, saturated color photographs since the 1970s. After teaching photography for many years, she has returned to the studio creating her most recent project, *Anonymous Women,* which consists of a three-part series of studio installations made for the camera, addressing women and their complicated relationships with domesticity. The photographs are exhibited in large scale and were published as a monograph in January 2017 and again in 2020 as a monograph of the later work named *Anonymous Women: Domestic Demise.* The *Anonymous Women* series has been exhibited internationally, featured online in many blogs, and has won multiple awards.

96
EDIE BRESLER
Our Right 2

While reading and researching the suffrage movement, I became enamored with the colored banners carried by marchers. Like a visual manifesto, each color stood for a foundational belief: purple for loyalty, white for clarity of vision, and gold for the light illuminating a way forward. Real change requires a multitude of people joining together, sometimes working for decades against enormous odds. Even today political rallies are transformative, communal expressions against injustices. Let us remember that although women won the right to vote in 1920, many more decades passed before this same right was extended to all Native Americans, Asian Americans, and African Americans. Collaboration and chance are at the heart of my artistic process.

For this diptych, I use cyanotype, a nineteenth-century photographic emulsion that is exposed in bright sunlight. Walking through my city, I carry the pre-coated papers inside a light-tight bag. I approach random passersby to see if they are willing to join me and sit for the required twelve-minute exposure. The hand silhouettes playing tug of war with string and sticks in these two prints belong to four different participants. After developing the prints in water, I added ribbons of color to echo the suffragist banners. Purple, yellow, and instead of white I chose green. For me green represents the hope for a genuinely inclusive, and more equitable, future. I am honored to be part of this commemorative curatorial vision developed and nurtured by Meg Griffiths and Frances Jakubek.

Edie Bresler creates artworks focusing on collaboration and chance. Her grants include a Mass Cultural Council fellowship, numerous Somerville Arts Council fellowships, a Berkshire Taconic Artist's Resource Trust grant, and a New York Foundation for the Arts grant. Represented by Gallery Kayafas in Boston, Bresler's work is in the permanent collections of the Museum of Fine Arts, Houston, the Danforth Art Museum, and private collections. Her projects have been featured on Good Morning America and PBS Greater Boston and in *Photograph Magazine, Esquire, Lenscratch, Slate,* and others. Bresler lives in Somerville, Massachusetts, and directs the photography program at Simmons University in Boston.

97

MARKY KAUFFMANN
Eloise in Blue Dress

The passage of the Nineteenth Amendment, granting American women the right to vote, was a struggle that lasted for more than eighty years. Why? Why did men deny women the right to vote for years after the ratification of the US Constitution, which gave them that very same right? In considering the struggle to ratify the Nineteenth Amendment, I wanted to examine, through my image, the idea of gender. What does it mean to be female? How do you identify a female? In Michelle Tolini Finamore's essay, "A Curator's Perspective," for the exhibit Gender Bending Fashion at the Museum of Fine Arts in Boston, she states that clothing "serves as a primary means of non-verbal communication signifying identity" and that the "traditional division between menswear and womenswear reflects a history in which institutions across society—not only fashion, but education, religion, medicine, the legal system and beyond—have sought to describe gender as a strict binary, established on notions of biological difference." Traditionally, donning the dress identified us as female, certainly in the years between 1840, the beginning of the suffrage movement, and 1920. When men gazed upon us wearing dresses on the streets, in places of worship, or at home, they had a certain notion of who we were, i.e., members of the weaker sex. I want to take back the dress in the same way that women took back the color pink by donning pussy hats during the 2017 Women's Marches. My dress, Eloise in Blue Dress, is a symbol for all that I love about identifying as female. It is wild, creative, and bold! With this dress, I celebrate the power and possibilities of the franchise. Voting is the first step toward self-determination, creating a world in which women can do, be, and wear whatever we want!

Marky Kauffmann is a graduate of Boston University and the New England School of Photography. She is the recipient of numerous awards, including a 2017 Mass Cultural Council Artist Fellowship in photography. Kauffmann is a passionate educator, who has taught photography at numerous secondary schools. She also spent twenty years teaching photography to adults at the New England School of Photography's evening workshop program. Kauffmann has curated several exhibitions, including *Outspoken: Seven Women Photographers* and *Moved To Act! Demonstrations, Marches, Political Actions.* Kauffmann utilizes traditional darkroom techniques, alternative processes, and digital technologies to create her unique images.

98

NANCY BARON
To Be Heard

The 1913 Woman Suffrage Procession, held one day before Woodrow Wilson's inauguration, was the first suffragist parade in Washington, DC. It was also the first large, organized march on Washington for political purposes. Although the police looked the other way when the marchers were attacked verbally and physically (over one hundred required hospitalization), the women finished the parade that led to major news coverage and congressional hearings. For Women's History Month in 2016, President Barack Obama proclaimed, "In the face of discrimination and undue hardship, [women] have never given up on the promise of America: that with hard work and determination, nothing is out of reach" (Cohen, 2016)

I can only imagine the energy the act of protest in the 1913 Woman Suffrage Procession gave to the fighters for women's right to vote. At a time when women were expected to be wives and mothers, whose only purpose was seen to be caring for home and family, participating in this show of strength and sisterhood was life-changing for participants and observers alike. Participating in contemporary protests, particularly against the previous, democracy-threatening regime in America, I am indebted to my suffragist sisters for their example of strength and courage and for never giving up on democracy. I'm grateful to *A Yellow Rose Project* for memorializing these women and their mission. I'm honored to be included.

Visual artist, Nancy Baron, is based in Los Angeles and Palm Springs, California. In her fine art documentary photography, she uses portraits, landscapes, and architectural photographs to record the world with a hopeful bias. Her background in filmmaking, including the documentary form, has inspired her to honor the still image, while giving it a cinematic tone. Baron's prints have been shown in group and solo exhibitions internationally and are held in public and private collections. Her three monographs are in the collections of museums and universities, and her work has been published in notable magazines and newspapers worldwide.

99

ANN MARYE GEORGE
Age and Antiquity

In examining the word suffrage as a starting point to present an image that reflects the movement and victory for women to have the right to vote, I was intrigued by the source of the word. Suffrage has been used since the fourteenth century to mean "prayer, " especially a prayer requesting divine help or intercession. The more I examined the plight of the women of the suffrage movement both before and after the ratification of the Nineteenth Amendment, it became clear that equality for all humans, regardless of race, creed or religion, is a prayer, even today. It is my prayer. We arm ourselves with the knowledge that change takes time. Change is a process and not an event. In this image, we recognize that while one hundred years have passed since women received the right to vote, we are still young as voters. In our youthful quest for other transformations of equality for women, we must reflect on the patience, diligence, and sacrifice required to secure these changes using the suffrage movement as our teacher and hope. We peer through history to gain insight from and pay homage to these women. They embroidered themselves into the governance of our country with the vote and presented voting as a primary right of citizenship, paving the way for demands for gender equality in all aspects of society by proposing the Equal Rights Amendment (ERA) in 1921. A representation of answered prayer. God bless these women, and God bless America!

Ann George grew up in a small Louisiana town with people and places that grounded her roots deep into the Southern soil and her heart into its fertile personality. She uses photography to celebrate her native Louisiana and the people, places, and stories that move her. Her critics say her photographic approach is mysterious and poetic and continues a pictorial tradition important in the history of photography. Ann has won numerous awards both nationally and internationally. Her work has been published in multiple periodicals and books and has been acquired in many private collections. She has exhibited in the United States and abroad, including Argentina, Australia, and Europe. Through her presentations, lectures, and workshops, she readily shares her inspiration and recipes for image making. Ann creates images that call to her vintage eye, propelling her to seek different approaches and techniques with the camera, computer, printing, and paint.

100

TARA CRONIN
Entry from the project *Thens*

For nearly a century, within psychiatric and medical establishments, members of marginalized communities, including those of queer identity and the disabled, were characterized within the psychiatric diagnostic manual, the DSM, as mentally ill and treated as such by the community at large.

This project highlights the history of mischaracterizing marginalized community members as psychotic, unstable, unhinged, and crazy so that society can remember what these communities had to struggle through to reach their current status of equality. It underlines how psychiatry and other institutional ideas have unfortunately been used to oppress and suppress members of *other* groups and continues to be used in that way. This speaks to the larger idea of how institutions can be wielded both for good and harm.

This project also takes the viewer through my own struggles navigating the murky waters of the US psychiatric hospital systems and the sense of being overwhelmed by what it takes to truly embark on the journey to overcome the struggle of learning to find balance and control in one's own psyche. The mentally ill are often viewed as the *other,* but the truth is everyone has had difficulty at one time with mental stress and stability. There is an extremely fine line between when it is an illness and when it is a daily mild anxiousness or other ailment. The black-and-white perception we put on this line is part of the reason the issue tends to persist.

Tara Cronin is an artist and writer focusing on photography, installation, and works on paper. She received a BA in writing from The New School, an MFA from International Center of Photography. Having exhibited throughout New York City, North America, and internationally, Tara won the Director's Choice Award in 2019 with the CENTER in Santa Fe and was a winner for Klompching Gallery's *Fresh 2020* exhibition. Tara and her partner, Ed Chen, took on a coffee farm in 2015 to apply their agricultural technology. She has taught with ICP and Donkey Mill Art Center, and is based in Kona, Hawaii.

101
CAROL ERB
Did She Vote? Lynn Turner Worden

When asked to make work for A Yellow Rose Project, I immediately thought of the women in my own family tree. Did they exercise their newly won right to vote in 1920? I could only speculate based on what I had been told about their life circumstances and personal character. From a collection of family photographs, I selected portraits of five women. The work in this book is of my grandmother, Lynn Turner Worden. Lynn grew up in Wrangell, Alaska, during the gold rush. Local townsfolk, prospectors looking to strike it rich, and Indigenous Tlingit tribe members populated the small town. It was an exciting and diverse environment for a child, despite being so far away from civilization. After graduating from high school, Lynn moved to Michigan to live with relatives. There she met Robert, a recently widowed dairy farmer, who had two young children in dire need of a mother. They married, and the couple had two more children of their own. In 1920, Lynn was a twenty-four-year-old mother and farmer's wife. For her, and I imagine most other women of her class, life must have been an exhausting cycle of daily chores. Was the opportunity to exercise her newly won right to vote an important event?

Carol Erb was born and raised in the Midwest. She attended the School of the Art Institute of Chicago and received a BA from DePaul University. Erb's images have been exhibited at the Center for Fine Art Photography, the Phoenix Art Museum, the Houston Center for Photography, and several other institutions in the United States, Japan, China, France, and the Netherlands. Carol's work was selected for the 2017 Critical Mass Top 50. Her photography has been featured in several publications including *Black & White, Fraction,* and *Adore Noir.* Carol currently resides in Los Angeles, California.

102

LINDSEY BEAL

Second Wave

Using open-source imagery from the Library of Congress, I printed select images from each wave of the feminist movement using the anthotype process with beets as an emulsion. Each movement is printed in the same, bright pink—the suffragists marching for the right to vote, the second wave marching for the passage of the equal rights amendment, the inaugural Women's March, and finally a blank coated sheet of paper, waiting for the next movement to be documented and printed on its surface. The prints are framed and housed in a black box, both protecting the fugitive prints from the light while also referencing the ballot box.

Lindsey Beal is a photo-based artist in Providence, Rhode Island, where she teaches at Rhode Island School of Design and Massachusetts College of Art and Design. She is currently a Mellon Faculty Fellow at the Rhode Island School of Design Museum. Lindsey's work was featured on *New York Times Lens, Slate France,* BBC Mundo, and *New Scientist,* and published in various textbooks and periodicals. She has shown at national museums, galleries, and universities, including a recent solo show at the Vermont Center for Photography. She was a finalist for Photolucida's Critical Mass Top 200 in 2016 and 2018 and recently received a RISD faculty development grant for her new work.

Inspired by how contemporary, American society views women, she investigates how women lived in the past, drawing parallels and contrasts between women's lives then and now. Both through presentation and subject matter, she connects the viewer to the past and how it reflects today's political and social culture. She connects her imagery to photographic history and how it was practiced, developed, and presented by early photographers.

103

SARAH HOSKINS

The Benevolent Sisters, Their 99th Year

For the past twenty years I have been photographing historic, African American hamlets in Kentucky's Inner Bluegrass region, including this image. These hamlets, like so much African American history, have been overlooked and neglected, especially women and women-led groups and organizations like this one, the Sisters Benevolent, founded in 1905.

One important, shared story of theirs was how they maintained a bathroom in a hair salon, so they had somewhere to go while walking home after work. As we focus on this historic anniversary of women getting the right to vote, let us not forget women who worked harder for much less.

Sarah Hoskins's photographs have been included in over one hundred exhibitions and are in the permanent collections of the Archive of Documentary Arts at Duke University, the Smithsonian Institution, the Museum of Fine Arts, Houston, the University of Kentucky Art Museum, and the City of Chicago. NPR's *Picture Show* and NPR's *Weekend Edition* did features on her and her *Homeplace* project. She has been the recipient of numerous grants and fellowship, including an Illinois Arts Council fellowship in photography. Sarah was a graduate student in the

SAIC New Arts Journalism program and received her BA from Columbia College Chicago.

104

EMILY SHEFFER
The Ideal Scrap Book, 1905–1906

The act of scrapbooking was subversively adopted by Elizabeth and Anne Miller to exhibit their vast archive of documents from the women's suffrage movement. Within the pages of these seemingly innocuous books were hundreds of artifacts tracing a countercultural movement that challenged archaic and oppressive gender norms. This scrapbook was made in 1905 and is one of six. The conversion of the cover to a negative encourages the viewer to look beyond what is expected and into a movement that ultimately elevated and advanced the legal rights of womanhood.

Image courtesy the Library of Congress, Rare Book and Special Collections Division, National American Woman Suffrage Association Collection.

Emily Sheffer is a fine art photographer and book artist. In 2017, she founded Dust Collective, a hand-made photography book collective, and has since published over a dozen titles. She earned her BFA in photography with departmental honors from the Massachusetts College of Art and Design in 2015. After graduation, Emily was listed as a 2015 Lens-Culture Top 50 emerging photographer. In 2019, Maine Media Workshops invited Emily to be their book artist-in-residence. She currently works as a studio director in New England. Emily is currently enrolled in the University of Hartford photography MFA program, where she was awarded a merit scholarship.

105

DIANE MEYER
Maxine

This is a hand embroidered photograph based on Maxine Waters, my congresswoman in Los Angeles. I feel very fortunate to live in Maxine Water's congressional district, California's forty-third congressional district. She has dedicated her life to public service for as long as I have been alive—she entered the California State Assembly in 1976, the year I was born. While I have always found her to be inspirational in her resolve to fiercely advocate for important, progressive social justice issues, I found her continued and passionate determination to speak truth to power to be a consistent source of hope in the dark days following the 2016 election. She has shown that she is unafraid to speak her mind and will not be silenced. I feel that Maxine Waters has become a symbol for the rising tide of female voices that have powerfully emerged since 2016. I wanted to create a piece that referenced her recent media appearances, especially as her voice has become inspirational for a growing younger generation. My piece centers around a quote from Maxine Waters from an interview with Chris Hayes of MSNBC: "I'd like to say to women out there everywhere, don't allow these . . . dishonorable people to intimidate you or scare you. Be who you are. Do what you do" (2017).

Diane Meyer received a BFA in photography from NYU Tisch School of the Arts in 1999 and an MFA in visual arts from the University of California San Diego in 2002. She has been living in Los Angeles since 2005. Her work has been included in numerous exhibitions in the United States and abroad and is in the permanent collections of the George Eastman Museum, the Clarinda Carnegie Art Museum, the Hood Museum, the Museum of Contemporary Photography in Chicago, and the. University of Maryland. She is represented by Klompching Gallery.

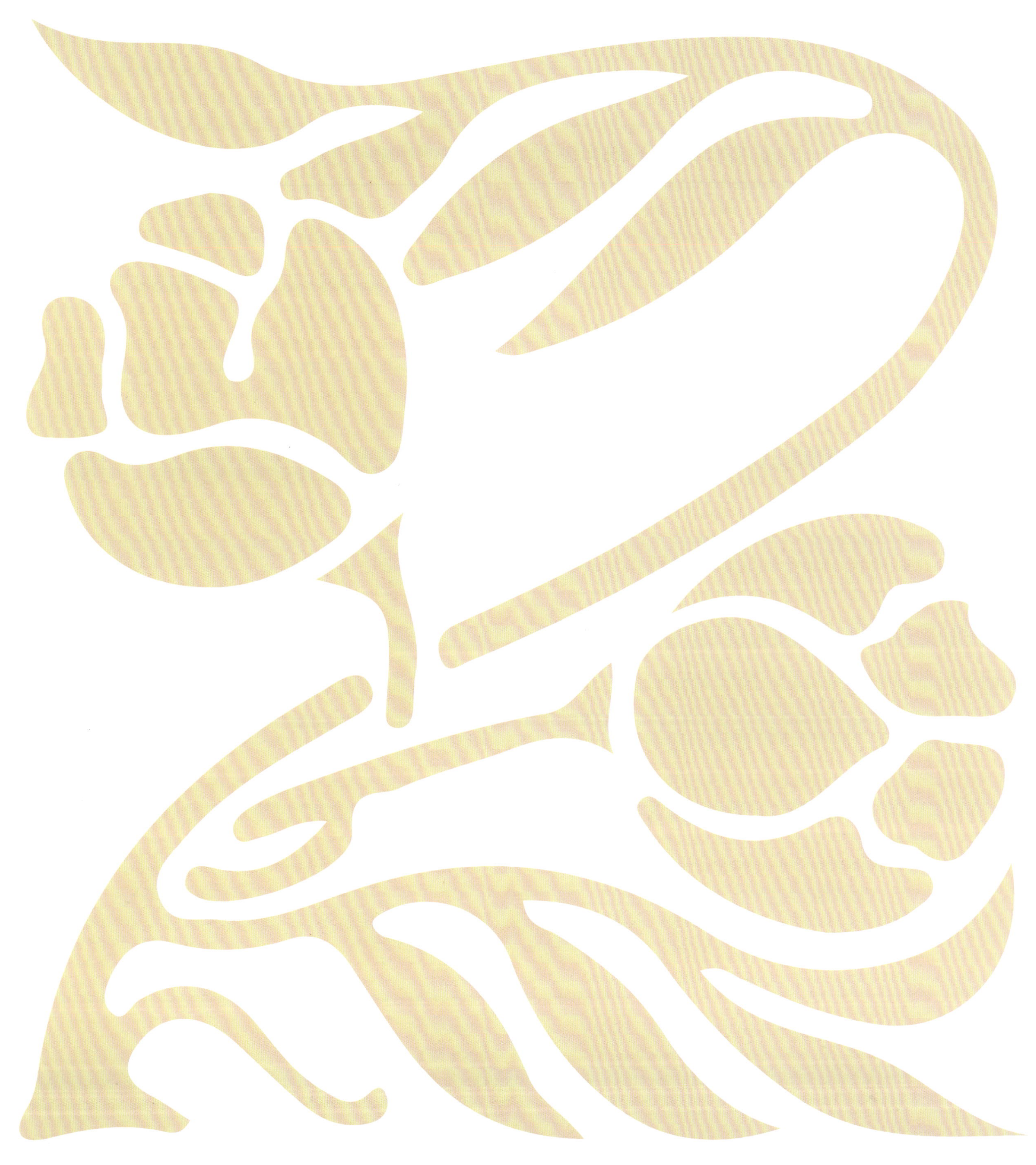

Bibliography

ACLU Vermont. "Voting Rights." Accessed September 26, 2024. https://www.acluvt.org/en/issues/voting-rights.

Alice Paul Institute. "The History of the Equal Rights Amendment (ERA)." Accessed September 26, 2024. https://www.alicepaul.org/equal-rights-amendment-2/.

Alter, Charlotte. "A Year Ago, They Marched. Now a Record Number of Women Are Running for Office." *Time*. January 18, 2018. https://time.com/5107499/record-number-of-women-are-running-for-office/.

Bejarano, Christina E., and Wendy G. Smooth. "Women of Color Mobilizing: Sistahs are Doing It for Themselves from GOTV to Running Candidates for Political Office." *Journal of Women, Politics & Policy* 43 (2022): 8–24.

Bennett, Jessica, and Veronica Chambers. "Suffrage Isn't 'Boring History.' It's a Story of Political Geniuses." *New York Times*. July 10, 2020.

Bernard, Diane. "She was the glamorous face of suffrage. Then she became its martyr." *Washington Post*. August 7, 2020. https://www.washington-post.com/graphics/2020/local/history/inez-milholland-suffrage-parade-womens-rights/.

Brown, Brene. "Read-Along Resources." Accessed September 26, 2024. https://brenebrown.com/read-along-resources/.

Broz, Matic. "How Many Pictures Are There in 2024?" Last modified September 12, 2024. https://photutorial.com/photos-statistics/.

Burn, Febb E. "Febb E. Burn in Niota, Tennessee to Harry T. Burn in Nashville, Tennessee." Volunteer Voices Collection. University of Tennessee, Knoxville Libraries, Knoxville, TN. https://digital.lib.utk.edu/collections/islandora/object/volvoices%3A5523#page/1/mode/2up.

Cahill, Cathleen D. *Recasting the Vote: How Women of Color Transformed the Suffrage Movement*. Chapel Hill: The University of North Carolina Press, 2020.

Carey, Bill. "The Other Meaning of the Phrase 'Perfect 36.'" *Hendersonville Standard,* June 8, 2022. https://www.mainstreet-nashville.com/life

/history/the-other-meaning-of-the-phrase
-perfect-36/article_ebefaf5e-d2e1–11ec-8252
-db0e2844e422.html.

Center for American Women and Politics (CAWP). "Gender Differences in Voter Turnout." Accessed September 27, 2024. https://cawp.rutgers.edu /facts/voters/gender-differences-voter-turnout.

Cohen, Danielle. "This Day in History: The 1913 Women's Suffrage Parade." Obama White House Blog Archives, March 3, 2016. https://obamawhite-house.archives.gov/blog/2016/03/03/this-day -history-1913-womens-suffrage-parade.

Dautrich, Kenneth, David A. Yalof, and Christina Bejarano. *The Enduring Democracy*. 6th ed. Washington, DC: CQ Press, 2020.

Dolan, Julie, Melissa Deckman, and Michele L. Swers, eds. *Women and Politics: Paths to Power and Political Influence*. 4th ed. New York: Rowman & Littlefield Publishers. 2019/

Gender Bending Fashion. Curated by Michelle Tolini Finamore, The Museum of Fine Arts in Boston, 2019.

Harris, Maya. "Women of Color: A Growing Force in the American Electorate." Center for American Progress. October 30, 2014. https://www.ameri-canprogress.org/article/women-of-color/.

Jones, Martha S. "The Politics of Black Womanhood, 1848–2008." In *Votes for Women: A Portrait of Persistence*, edited by Kate Clark Lemay, 29–47. Princeton, NJ: Princeton University Press, 2019.

———. *Vanguard: How Black Women Broke Barriers, Won the Vote, and Insisted on Equality for All*. Basic Books: New York, 2020.

Lange, Allison K. *Picturing Political Power: Images in the Women's Suffrage Movement*. Chicago: The University of Chicago Press, 2020.

Lee, Kristen, Ihaab Syed, and Leila Rafei. "100 Years and Counting: The Fight for Women's Suffrage Continues." ACLU. August 28, 2020. https://www .aclu.org/news/voting-rights/100-years-and-counting-the-fight-for-womens-suffrage-continues.

Lewis, John. *Across That Bridge: Life Lessons and a Vision for Change*. New York: Hachette Book, 2012.

Montoya, Celeste. "Intersectionality and Voting Rights." *PS: Political Science & Politics* 53, no. 3 (2020): 484–89. https://doi.org/10.1017 /S104909652000030X.

Power-Drutis, Tamara. "It's Time to Restore and Strengthen the Voting Rights Act." *Yes! Magazine*. August 10, 2017. https://www.yesmagazine.org /democracy/2017/08/10/its-time-to-restore-and-strengthen-the-voting-rights-act.

Rogers, Mary Read, ed. *Our Heritage: The Wyoming Federation of Women's Clubs*. Cheyenne, Wyoming: Pioneer Printing and Stationery Company Publisher, 1976.

Sullivan, Kate, and Ashley Killough. "Women invited to wear white to Trump's State of the Union address." CNN. Updated January 29, 2019. https:// www.cnn.com/2019/01/29/politics/democratic-women-group-state-of-the-union-wear-white /index.html.

Tetrault, Lisa. *The Myth of Seneca Falls: Memory and the Women's Suffrage Movement, 1848–1898*. Chapel Hill: The University of North Carolina Press, 2014.

The Suffragist 1 no. 4 (December 6, 1913).

Waters, Maxine. Interview. By Chris Hayes. *All In with Chris Hayes*, MSNBC. March 28, 2017.

Welter, Barbara. "The Cult of True Womanhood: 1820–1860." *American Quarterly* 18, no. 2 (1966): 151–74. https://doi.org/10.2307/2711179.

Wilson, Joshua. "Courage Photographed: Hattiesburg Photographers Contribute to National Women's Suffrage History Project." *The Pine Belt News*. September 2, 2020. https://www.hubcity-spokes.com/yellowroseprojectarticle.

Winsor, Morgan. "Martin Luther King Jr.'s granddaughter tells March for Our Lives crowd: 'I have a dream that enough is enough.'" ABC News. March 24, 2018. https://abcnews.go.com/US/martin-luther-king-jrs-granddaughter-tells-march-lives/story?id=53986952.

Women on 20s. "Susan B. Anthony." Accessed on September 28, 2024. https://www.womenon20s.org/susan_b_anthony.

Women's Rights: Special History Study. "The McClintocks." Last modified December 10, 2005. https://npshistory.com/publications/wori/shs/chap6.htm.